The Chinese Opium Wars

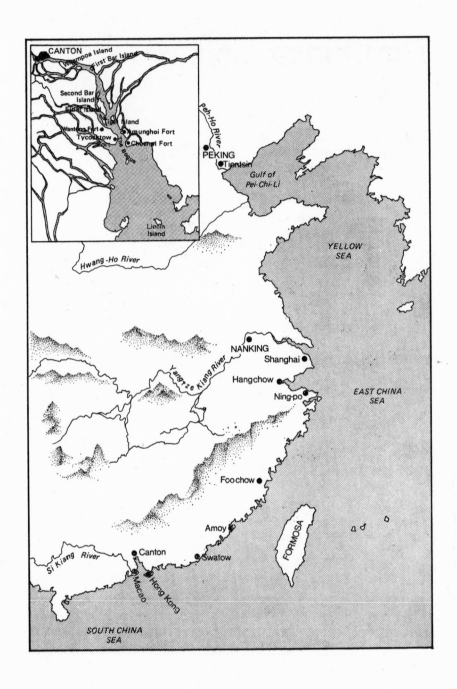

CANTON
Whampoa Island
First Bar Island
Second Bar
Island
First Island
Tiger Island
Wanteng Fort
Tycocktow
Amunghoi Fort
Chuenpi Fort
Bogue

Peh-Ho River

PEKING
Tientsin
Gulf of
Pei-Chi-Li

Lintin
Island

Hwang -Ho River

YELLOW
SEA

NANKING
Shanghai

Hangchow
Ning-po

EAST CHINA
SEA

Yangtze Kiang River

Foochow

Amoy

FORMOSA

Si Kiang River
Canton
Swatow

Macao
Hong Kong

SOUTH CHINA
SEA

Jack Beeching

The Chinese
Opium Wars

Harcourt Brace Jovanovich

New York and London

Library of Congress Cataloging in Publication Data

Beeching, Jack.
    The Chinese Opium Wars. *New York, Harcourt Brace Jovanovich, 1975.*
    Bibliography: p.
    Includes index.
    1.   China—History—War of 1840–1842.   2.   China—
History—Foreign intervention, 1857–1861.
    3.   Opium trade—China—History.   I.   Title.
DS757.5.B35   951'.03   75-16414
ISBN 0-15-117650-7

First American edition 1976

B C D E

352 p.
24 cm.

DS
757.5
B35

To Dr Helene Zahler

A nation that oppresses another cannot itself be free

Contents

The course of events   11

1 The Red Barbarians   15

2 Napier's Fizzle   40

3 Commissioner Lin   63

4 Playing at War   94

5 Soothe the Barbarian   132

6 Pirates and Rebels   164

7 The City Question   206

8 Taku Back and Forth   258

9 The Burning of the Summer Palace   295

A note on methods and sources   332

A guide to sources and further reading   335

Index   339

Illustrations

Between pages 192 and 193

1 Emperor Ch'ien Lung arrives in state for his meeting with Lord Macartney at Jehol (*British Museum*)
2 Western gate of Peking (*Radio Times Hulton Picture Library*)
3 Frigates *Andromache* and *Imogene* forcing the Bogue (*National Maritime Museum*)
4 Macao (*The Mansell Collection*)
5 Commissioner Lin supervises the burning of opium (*British Museum*)
6 The Emperor Ch'ien Lung (*Hong Kong City Museum*)
7 His Excellency the Earl of Macartney (*Hong Kong City Museum*)
8 Commissioner Lin (*F. Lewis, Publishers*)
9 Admiral Sir Charles Napier (*Radio Times Hulton Picture Library*)
10 The Bridge of Nanking (*Radio Times Hulton Picture Library*)
11 The city of Nanking (*Radio Times Hulton Picture Library*)
12 Opium clippers off Lintin Island (*National Maritime Museum*)
13 The European Factories at Canton (*Radio Times Hulton Picture Library*)
14 The Royal Navy attack the fort at Chuenpi 7th January 1841 (*National Army Museum*)
15 William Jardine (*National Portrait Gallery London*)
16 James Matheson (*National Portrait Gallery London*)
17 The Rev. Dr Karl Gutzlaff (*The Mansell Collection*)
18 Howqua (*The Tate Gallery*)
19 Whampoa from Dane's Island (*Radio Times Hulton Picture Library*)
20 HMS *Columbine* attacking Chinese pirates (*National Maritime Museum*)
21 North Taku Forts immediately after capture 21st August 1860 (*Radio Times Hulton Picture Library*)
22 Taku Fort (*Radio Times Hulton Picture Library*)

23 The bombardment of Canton (*Radio Times Hulton Picture Library*)

24 Baron Gros (*The Mansell Collection*)

25 Sir John Bowring (*Hong Kong City Museum*)

26 Sir Henry Pottinger (*The Oriental Club*)

27 Ch'i-ying (*Courtesy Museum of Fine Arts Boston*)

28 The state entry of Lord Elgin into Peking 1860 (*Hong Kong City Museum*)

29 The signing of the Treaty of Tientsin (*The Illustrated London News*)

30 The Summer Palace Peking (*The Mansell Collection*)

31 The Eighth Earl of Elgin (*National Galleries of Scotland*)

32 A self-portrait of George Chinnery (*National Portrait Gallery London*)

33 Prince Kung (*National Army Museum*)

34 Lord Palmerston (*National Portrait Gallery London*)

35 Rear Admiral James Hope (*National Maritime Museum*)

36 General de Montauban (*Radio Times Hulton Picture Library*)

37 General Sir James Hope Grant (*National Army Museum*)

The course of events

1516 Portuguese first arrive in China.
1604 Dutch ship first arrives at Canton.
1637 Captain Weddell bombards Bogue Forts.
1662 Chinese expel Dutch from Formosa.
1689 China–Russia Treaty of Nerchinsk.
     English begin to trade at Canton.
1715 East India Company Factory established at Canton.
1724 Roman Catholic priests expelled from China.
1729 First Edict against opium.
1757 Foreign trade limited to Canton.
1784 First American ship arrives.
1793 Lord Macartney in Peking.
1796 Edict prohibits opium-smoking.
1801–1820 Opium imports at about 5000 chests per annum.
1806 Russian ship forbidden to trade at Canton.
1807 First Protestant missionary arrives.
1814 Publication begins of first English/Chinese dictionary.
1816 Lord Amherst in Peking.
1820 East India Company cuts opium price, increases production.
1821 Tea trade stopped in an attempt to enforce opium ban.
1828 Jardine Matheson partnership formed.
1831 Opium imports at about 19 000 chests per annum.
1832 French hoist their flag in Canton.
     Triads put up Golden Dragon King as pretender to throne.
1834 East India Company trading monopoly ends; Napier's
     Fizzle.
1836 Captain Charles Elliot, RN, becomes Chief Superintendent
     of Trade.
     Opium imports go over 30 000 chests.
1839 Commissioner Lin destroys opium at Canton.
     Naval action at Chuenpi begins war.
1840 Peel's vote of censure motion on the war in China lost by
     nine votes.
     Tin-hai on Chou-shan Island taken.

11

1841 Elliot and Ch'i Shan negotiate ineffectually.
Canton ransomed.
Sir Henry Pottinger arrives as plenipotentiary.
Tin-hai re-taken.
Chinhai and Ningpo taken and occupied.

1842 Shanghai occupied.
Chinkiang captured.
Treaty of Nanking signed.

1843 Treaty of Nanking ratified.
Cession of Hong Kong proclaimed.

1844 American Treaty of Wanghia signed.
French Treaty of Whampoa signed.
Emperor grants toleration to Christianity.

1847 First coolies shipped from Amoy.

1849 Royal Navy destroys eighty-one pirate junks.

1851 Taiping march north from Kwangsi.

1853 Taiping army enters Nanking.
Rebels capture Amoy.
Hwangho River changes its course.
Triads capture Shanghai and are attacked by French.

1854 Rebels capture towns close to Canton.

1855 Taiping attack on Peking fails.
Yeh in Canton beheads 70 000 rebels.

1856 Père Chapdelaine executed in Kwangsi.
The *Arrow* incident.
Admiral Seymour attacks Canton.
Americans bombard Barrier Forts.
Chinese burn down Canton Factories.

1857 Parliamentary debate on *Arrow* incident brings down
British government.
Lord Elgin reaches Canton.
Anglo-French force captures Canton.

1858 Yeh sent prisoner to Calcutta.
Foreign envoys arrive at Taku, occupy forts.
Russian, American, French and British Treaties signed.

1859 Russian Treaty ratified at Peking.
Anglo-French attempt to force a passage past Taku Forts
fails.
American envoy reaches Peking overland.
American Treaty ratified at Peh-tang.

1860 Taiping counter-attack, take Hangchow, Soochow, threaten
Shanghai.
Foreign troops defend Shanghai.

Elgin, Gros and Anglo-French army land at Peh-tang.

Taku Forts captured, Tientsin occupied.

Parkes and others taken prisoner by Chinese at Chang-chia-wan.

Prince Seng defeated at Pa-li-chi'ao, Prince Kung negotiates.

Summer Palace looted.

Peking surrenders.

Elgin orders destruction of Summer Palace.

British and French conventions of Peking signed, and 1858 treaties ratified.

Russian convention of Peking signed.

1 The Red Barbarians

'In view of the inordinate lengths to which the corruption of morals have advanced, I almost think it necessary that Chinese missionaries should be sent us to teach the aim and practice of natural theology.'
Leibnitz

In the hot August of 1793 a fleet of Chinese junks and sampans, carrying an important passenger and all his retinue, made way upstream to Peking against the sluggish current of the Peh-ho River. A boring landscape: mud river-banks, a flat alluvial plain covered interminably with ripening corn, villages of mud huts faced with chopped straw, and, occasionally, Chinese tombs.

Any literate Chinese who happened to be standing on the river-bank could have observed, nailed to the mast of the Ambassador's houseboat, a large sign which announced in black characters: *Tribute from the Red Barbarians.*

The usual people to send tribute to the Emperor in Peking were those near the Chinese border, the Mongols, the Annamese, or Koreans. But that sign had been fixed to the mast of the boat carrying the British Ambassador. The boats that trailed behind bore a cargo of gifts. They had cost £13 124, and had been carefully chosen to represent the best that Great Britain then had to offer ancient China. The cargo of samples included telescopes, brass howitzers, globes, clocks, musical instruments, a pair of wheeled carriages. There was even a hot-air balloon, together with a man willing to fly in it.

On 6 August, the British Ambassador, Lord Macartney, had gone ashore for an interview with the Viceroy of Pechili. The Viceroy informed Lord Macartney that the great Manchu Emperor Ch'ien Lung, now 83, who had reigned over China for fifty-seven years, had left Peking, to stay in his hunting lodge at Jehol. He would grant an audience there. Meanwhile, the bulkier presents were to be put on display, not in Peking, with its three million inhabitants, but some miles away, in the vast ornamental park –

15

60 000 acres of buildings and gardens, lakes and willow-pattern-plate bridges – known as the Summer Palace.

Thanks to his knack of combining Irish charm with a lawyer's sagacity, Lord Macartney had done surprisingly well in his career. The son of an impoverished Irish gentleman, sent to London to study law, he had made his mark when very young. At 27 he had been given a knighthood and sent as Envoy Extraordinary to the court of Catherine the Great. Macartney promptly succeeded in winning the heart of that ample and amorous Empress, which perhaps had been the object of his mission.

Back in London three years later with the jewelled snuff-box which the Empress gave him as a valuable memento of their long discussions, Macartney entered the urbane intellectual circle that included Burke, Reynolds and Dr Johnson. In 1774 he had been raised to the Irish peerage, and in 1780 sent to govern Madras. But the diplomatic mission in which his lordship was now engaged, at the age of 55, was one to tax all his self-possession. There had never before been a British embassy to China.

Jehol was a beauty spot made romantic by its crags and waterfalls. On 14 September 1793, at dawn, Lord Macartney presented himself there to the Chinese Emperor, wearing the mantle of a Knight of the Bath over a suit of spotted mulberry velvet, and accompanied by Sir George Staunton, baronet, who had decided the correct impression would be made by wearing his scarlet gown as an Oxford Doctor of Civil Laws. Sir George Staunton's 12-year-old son-and-heir, also called George, was their page.

The astute old Emperor, to make it clear that this conference was not with equals but with barbarians, had decided to confront Lord Macartney not within the four walls of a palace but in a yurt – one of the large horse-hair tents used by the wild horsemen who lived beyond the frontier of China proper.

One ceremony to which other barbarian envoys customarily were made to submit was this time left out – the kowtow. As a sign of respect on being brought into the Emperor of China's presence, an outsider was expected to prostrate himself three times, knocking his head humbly on the floor three times at each prostration. This was altogether too much for Lord Macartney, who had made it clear he was willing to go as far in the way of bowing and kneeling as was customary in European courts, but not any further.

16

Though not much was known of the Chinese Empire in the eighteenth century, its administration was often, if rather fancifully, put forward by literary men in Europe as a model of rational enlightenment. Observing the Emperor that early morning – the benign and acknowledged ruler of an enormous population – the thought passed through Lord Macartney's mind, and was later made a note of, that here before his very eyes was perhaps the supreme instance of human felicity.

The aged Emperor was graciously pleased to accept personally the letter from King George III which Lord Macartney bore to his presence inside a gold box studded with diamonds. Hearing that the little page, young George Staunton – brought up by his father to be an infant prodigy – had somehow learned to speak and write Chinese on the voyage out, the Emperor asked him a couple of questions, expressed himself delighted by the halting Chinese answers, and presented little George with a yellow silk purse.

To get on terms with the Chinese, Lord Macartney was free to make concessions. One paragraph in his instructions went so far as to concede that the East India Company would if necessary prohibit the export of Indian opium to China – since, strictly speaking, the traffic in opium was illegal there. But the question was never discussed. An exchange of compliments apart, the embassy got nowhere. The presents on show in the Summer Palace were looked upon by the mandarins who examined them as so much trash, though Josiah Wedgwood's pottery caught their interest. They were quite willing to express astonishment when Lord Macartney tried later to impress them by igniting sulphur matches. They never even got to see the hot-air balloon – not that even a hot-air balloon (a French invention) would have tilted the balance of Chinese opinion in Britain's favour. The reason was simple.

As Ch'ien Lung observed in his formal reply to George III, 'Our ways have no resemblance to yours, and even were your envoy competent to acquire some rudiments of them, he could not transplant them to your barbarous land... Strange and costly objects do not interest me. As your Ambassador can see for himself, we possess all things. I set no value on strange objects and ingenious, and have no use for your country's manufactures.'

Several generations later, when China's possibilities and limitations as a vast new market were beginning to be better understood, an Englishman who had spent his life there put the truth bluntly. 'The Chinese have the best food in the world, rice, the best drink, tea, the best clothing, cotton, silk and furs. They do not need to buy a penny's worth elsewhere.'

The old potentate who sat under the black horse-hair tent that August dawn in Jehol, chatting with young Master Staunton, was the last great Manchu Emperor. Shortly after Lord Macartney's embassy was dismissed, he decided to retire. His descendants somehow lost the knack of governing China. The new problems were intractable, and government institutions were manned by officials who had been taught only the old answers.

Through all Chinese history the real danger was seen as coming not so much from internal disturbance – popular rebellion was part of the national tradition – as from barbarians who managed to penetrate the Imperial frontiers. Against wild horsemen from central Asia the Great Wall had been built; and Chinese foreign policy amounted to no more than a set of manoeuvres for 'soothing' such barbarians when they came too close for comfort. To Chinese eyes, Lord Macartney merely represented a new breed, who during the past century or so had been arriving not at the Great Wall on horseback but on the Chinese coast in sailing ships. Their conduct had at first been piratical, but by now they were successfully soothed into being peaceable traders.

The first Portuguese ship arrived off China in 1514, the first English ship appeared in 1626. Both behaved violently. The Chinese had never forgotten their first brush with the English. In 1637 Captain Weddell, a merchant venturer on a voyage in which King Charles I had a £10 000 share, imposed his will on officials at Canton by bombarding, in time of peace, the Bogue Forts on the Pearl River estuary. These foreigners continued to drop anchor and look for opportunities to buy cheap and sell dear, so the Emperor by 1685 had designated Canton as a port where they might legally trade.

Limiting trade to Canton kept them at arm's length – the city was a three-month journey overland from Peking, in a southern province separated by mountains from the heartland of China. Control on the Chinese side was vested there in the Viceroy of Kwangtung and Kwangsi, a political magnate administering a territory larger than Britain on the Emperor's behalf, but he almost never dealt with the foreign community at Canton face to face. A mandarin called by the British the Hoppo – he was always a Manchu – put up a handsome price in Peking for his appointment

18

as Director of Customs at Canton, the price he paid being one easy way of diverting the profits of this foreign trade into the coffers of the court. A group of Chinese merchants, sometimes under compulsion, formed a syndicate called the Cohong, and were granted a monopoly of foreign trade, but were systematically squeezed – a second way for the court to tap the profits of trade. Sometimes, when the pressure was not nicely judged, the Hong merchants would be squeezed all the way into bankruptcy – in China considered a social crime – and often punished with exile to the cold north. At a time when merchants in Britain and America were pillars of respectability, in China they still came fourth in the traditional order of social esteem, after scholars, farmers and craftsmen.

The system had worked not unhappily for many years because like was dealing with like. A syndicate of Chinese merchants under governmental remote-control – the Cohong – did most of their business with a similar syndicate of foreign merchants, the Honourable East India Company. Not only had the East India Company organized the conquest of India for Great Britain, but since the Company enjoyed a legal monopoly of trade between Britain and the East it could easily outweigh all competitors in the Chinese market. Though China had nothing she wanted to buy abroad, she offered for export a commodity which in those days could be procured nowhere else – tea. By 1785, the East India Company was buying and selling fifteen million pounds' weight of China tea per year.

But what would China take in exchange? This was a question that might have been usefully explored, if Lord Macartney's mission had got beyond polite formalities. The British woollens that the East India Company were obliged by law to include in cargoes to China were almost unsaleable there, and were handled by the Cohong only as a favour, the Chinese preferring their own silks and cottons. Britain had, to begin with, paid for her tea with treasure, sending to the East between 1710 and 1759 a sum of £26 833 614 in silver and gold, and only £9 248 306 in goods. The British needed to find some article the Chinese would crave to buy, and so restore the balance of trade. But the Chinese were self-sufficient.

Yankee traders who arrived in Canton after sailing 12 000 miles round the Horn and across the Pacific were unhampered by official monopolies and more enterprising, but so far had found only short-term answers. Some tried importing ginseng – a forked root with a far-fetched resemblance to a human being, and with

19

a reputation, particularly among Manchus, as an aphrodisiac – but there were limits to the market in ginseng. A Connecticut man, John Ledyard, who sailed on Captain Cook's last voyage, had seen skins bought in Oregon for ten cents and sold in Canton for a hundred dollars. When Cook reported the immense colonies of seals in the Falkland and Aleutian Islands his motive had been scientific, but New Englanders hungry for profit were quick to draw a commercial conclusion.

The crew of a small ship could make a big pile. Killing the seals at their breeding-grounds and dressing the pelts on board, the Yankees arrived at Canton with something the Chinese were glad to pay cash for. The little *Pilgrim* (62 tons), leaving Boston in September 1803, dropped anchor at Canton with a cargo of over 12 000 sealskins. The *Betsy* (93 tons), on an outlay of under $8000, brought back net proceeds of over $120 000. It was a bonanza; but within a generation the seals had become almost extinct. The import of skins into China dropped from the enormous total of 1 730 000 in 1812 to a mere 6000 in 1830, as American hunters, by over-killing the seals, wiped out their breeding grounds.

The Chinese also liked pretty chiming clocks, but not in such quantity as to account for all that tonnage of tea.

To the Chinese, their vast, unchanging Empire was the only place on earth that mattered. Their population was then perhaps twenty times that of Great Britain, and the outer border of China enclosed an area twice that of the continental United States. Like the Romans in their day, the Chinese felt profoundly that whatever lay beyond the frontier must be dark, blank and hostile.

In telling Lord Macartney so bluntly, 'Our ways have no resemblance to yours', the old Emperor had been right. The Chinese scale of values was an entire contrast to what Britons or Americans take for granted. Britain had spread her flag all the way across the world by trade and war; the Chinese despised a merchant only a little less than a soldier. The British were the first in the world to produce saleable objects cheaply, by steam power, and the Americans were soon to outstrip them. All important work in China, from the huge canal systems to the Great Wall itself, had been done by hand with pick and shovel. The typical Chinese invention was not the steam engine but the wheelbarrow.

The notion of individual personal liberty under law – the right of a man to do what he liked with his own – had never been arrived

at in China. The system there was based instead on moral obligation. The Chinese social sense originated in the family, and extended outwards, on a basis of mutual responsibility, through
village and province, to society at large – with the Emperor as
moral figure-head, as well as ruler. The Chinese Emperor was not
so much a man exercising political power, like a King or a President,
as a figure of spiritual authority, who from time to time might by
his position be obliged to immerse himself in worldly affairs,
rather like the Pope.

In theory, all the land in China was owned by the Emperor, as
a kind of supreme trustee, giving him a moral right to the land
tax and rice tax which made up state revenue. Scholars who had
passed the Imperial examinations kept the administration going.
Though in real life they might steal taxes, lend money at high
interest and lay their hands on all the landed property they could
grab, in theory they were superior people, since they had been
rigorously trained to govern in harmony with the moral precepts
of Confucius. The decline of a dynasty was always marked by an
increase in the fortunes amassed by mandarins unworthy of their
trust, at the expense of the farmers, craftsmen and merchants
it was their duty to protect.

China's self-adjusting mechanism was popular rebellion.
Mandarins who pressed unreasonably hard on the common people
could expect to provoke at first banditry or piracy, then local
insurrection, and if abuses were not put right, perhaps in the end
a tidal wave of popular revolt so widespread as to sweep away a
decadent dynasty, and bring in a new one, likely at the start
to govern better. This had been the essential pattern of Chinese
history for many hundreds of years.

When Lord Macartney had gone away, the mandarins reporting
on his mission in Peking were obliged to decide what must be
done about his refusal to kowtow. Rather than establish a bad
precedent, they decided to falsify the archives. Officially, Lord
Macartney had kowtowed, thus acknowledging that Great Britain
was a far-off country subordinate to China. Chinese officialdom
under the Manchus was approaching that danger point of decadence – not unknown in present-day Europe – where so long as the
records are kept straight, actual reality no longer matters.

By the time another British Ambassador presented himself in
Peking – Lord Amherst, in 1816 – the old Emperor had made

way for his son. The new Emperor who reigned under the name of Chia Ch'ing was a man too timid, obstinate and set in his ways to change traditional procedures. Sensing weakness in Peking, the people of China had been quick to react. In 1795 the White Lily Society led a rising against the dynasty. By 1807, off the south China coast, a pirate fleet under Ching Yih could muster 500 sail – Chinese piracy was sea-banditry with political overtones. In 1813 a rising by the Society of Divine Justice was put down at a cost of 20 000 executions. The twenty-five-year reign of Chia Ch'ing indicated the decline of the Manchu dynasty. But which power would take its place?

On his embassy Lord Amherst was advised by the Chairman of the East India Company's Select Committee in Canton, an experienced businessman and competent Chinese scholar called Staunton – in his boyhood, the page to whom the old Emperor had given a yellow silk purse. Though some members of the embassy were inclined to waver, Sir George Staunton knew from long experience in China that if the Ambassador submitted to the kowtow he would spoil any chance whatever of entering into real discussion in Peking, now or later. China had so far never officially acknowledged that barbarian powers might be equals. The kowtow was the symbol of a tribute-bearing embassy, and traditionally, in such an embassy, there was no place for negotiations.

Britain had just emerged from the Napoleonic Wars not only dominating trade at Canton but possessing, in her Royal Navy, the most mobile and powerful weapon of war at that time existing on earth. The Chinese had virtually no national navy whatever. Though the British Ambassador wanted merely to discuss re-organizing the Cohong system – even though it might mean upsetting some secret vested interest in Peking – the Chinese authorities acted as if quite unaware of realities. Lord Amherst might represent victorious Britain, the mistress of India and of the high seas; his embassy resolved itself into a sequence of farcical charades, and ended in fiasco.

When asked to show his goodwill by kowtowing, in relative privacy, to the Emperor's empty chair, Lord Amherst was advised to make it clear that he would happily give nine courtly bows, even on bended knee, but no more. The mandarins therefore tried to wear him down. They had falsified the record of the last British embassy; now they must somehow make what was written in their archives come true.

They cleverly arranged for the British Ambassador to be separated from his baggage and most of his suite. He was hurried wearisomely through the night, to arrive at the Summer Palace. If at dawn he could be brought into the Imperial presence exhausted, a well-placed shove by a nearby mandarin might convert the semi-kneeling posture his lordship had already agreed to adopt into some kind of accidental sprawl which might in the Emperor's eyes pass for the kowtow of an ignorant barbarian doing his best.

With Sir George Staunton at his elbow, Lord Amherst managed to dodge the undignified scuffle. He refused to kowtow, and that was as much as his embassy achieved. On this level of childish trickery the official diplomatic relations between Peking and London were to remain for several decades. The focus of conflict became centred, meanwhile, at Canton, and the trouble was opium.

The linkage that comes at once to mind between the word *Chinese* and the word *opium* might make one suppose that the Chinese had been drugging themselves with the stuff for thousands of years. In fact the Chinese took to opium a long while after Europeans first started drinking coffee or smoking tobacco. The opium poppy travelled from Asia Minor along Arab trade routes into Persia, reaching India only with the Moghuls, and China even later.

When, in the mid-eighteenth century, they conquered Bengal, the soldier-merchant-administrators of Britain's Honourable East India Company inherited, along with much else worth having, the Moghul Emperor's monopoly of selling Patna opium, which came in 1773 under the direct control of the Bengal government. Into their hands had accidentally fallen abundant supplies of a product which any keen merchant might be forgiven for regarding as the answer to his dream – an article which sold itself, since any purchaser who has acquired a taste for opium always comes back anxiously for more, cash in hand.

The French and Dutch had traded in Patna opium long before the British established their monopoly. Holland's *Vereenigde Oost-Indische Compagnie* began exporting opium in 1659 from Bengal, and by 1759 was shipping a hundred tons of the drug every year to Batavia alone. The Dutch had used the drug in Java and elsewhere not simply as an article of commerce – trading it for pepper – but as a useful means for breaking the moral resistance of Indonesians who opposed the introduction of their semi-servile but immensely profitable plantation system. They deliberately spread the drug habit from the ports, where Arab traders used opium, to the countryside, and were, to begin with, hotly opposed. 'Now sales begin to diminish, because the princes object to it, and the common people follow their chiefs', an official wrote warningly, in 1756. The back of this opposition was cleverly broken: the Dutch paid an agreed subvention to the rajahs, partly in cash, and partly in opium. To get their hands on the full amount the native rulers were obliged to debauch their own people.

The British at first went more slowly than the Dutch. In 1771 the East India Company's Select Committee at Canton had asked the Presidents of Madras and Bombay to prevent opium exports from India to China, since they were technically illegal, and so put difficulties in the way of normal trade. Warren Hastings, Governor of Bengal, decided there was no need to follow the Dutch example with the conquered Bengalese. He wrote of opium as 'not a necessary of life but a pernicious article of luxury, which ought not to be permitted, but for the purposes of foreign commerce only, and which the wisdom of the government should carefully restrain from internal consumption'. His administration, however, with its expensive corps of European soldiers and administrators, was always hungry for revenue. Up to now tea had always been paid for in Spanish silver – the foreign coinage in which the Chinese had most confidence. But with Spain an ally of the infant United States during its War of Independence, the British had no market in which they could buy Spanish silver. In 1781 no silver remittances had reached India for two years, and the opium production of two years remained unsold. The situation was critical; the solution obvious.

As well as being a pain-killer, opium is a specific against dysentery, and the word then current in China for opium, *a-fu-jung*, derived from Arabic, and signified *foreign medicine*. In 1678 the Chinese had put a duty on the small quantity of opium they imported for medical needs, and for the next seventy-seven years the annual import of the drug was fairly steady, never rising above 200 chests a year. As a medicine opium was swallowed raw.

Meanwhile, the remotest western provinces of inland China were becoming familiar with opium as a drug of addiction, the poppy having reached them by overland trade routes through Tibet and Burma. The ban on opium-smoking was apparently not complete. By 1767 the Chinese were importing 1000 chests of opium a year.

24

Opium-smoking was, however, strongly condemned in China, since according to Confucian morality the smoker's body was not his own, to demolish exactly as he chose, but had been entrusted to him by his ancestors as their link with his descendants. Since using the drug habitually led to this gross offence against filial piety, the Imperial decree against opium smoking was supported by public opinion, as Warren Hastings' opium venture of 1781 was to show.

He despatched 3450 chests of the drug, in two ships. The armed sloop *Betsy* was captured by a French privateer called *St Thérèse*. The other ship, *Nonsuch*, with 1601 chests of opium on board, managed by proceeding under false colours, French and Spanish, and by taking a roundabout course, to dodge the privateers, reaching Macao safely in July of 1782.

At first there were no buyers, the official Hong merchants looking askance at the opium they were offered, as a contraband venture. At last a newly appointed Hong merchant called Sinqua made a derisory offer of $210 a chest – stipulating payment in 'head dollars', which were at a discount, and asking for long credit. The captain of *Nonsuch* had bargained on a price of about $500 a chest, but in fact the best he could do was to dispose of some of his cargo in Malacca at a price of $340. Warren Hastings' experiment in unloading opium on the Chinese market made a total loss for him of about a quarter of a million dollars, but at least it furnishes a proof that, as late as 1782, very few Cantonese – the most accessible Chinese purchasers – can have become opium addicts.

In 1799 a new and more thoroughgoing Imperial decree condemned a growing traffic in opium. Observing that opium-smoking was now beginning to spread inland from the coastal provinces of Kwangtung and Fukien, the Emperor's Edict prohibited both the smoking of the drug and its importation. Opium alone was to be exempted from the 'free interchange of commodities' permitted with foreign nations at Canton. 'Foreigners obviously derive the most solid profits and advantages', said the decree of the opium trade, '...but that our countrymen should pursue this destructive and ensnaring vice...is indeed odious and deplorable.'

This Imperial Edict set the East India Company a problem. To the Company its immense trade in tea was all-important, and the tax on tea provided the British government with a large revenue. Tea must come first. But opium was proving to be one foreign commodity that the Chinese would pay cash for; and the market for the drug was expanding. In the year of the Imperial ban, 4000 chests, or twenty times the medical need, had successfully been imported.

The sailing orders of the Company's Indiamen were rewritten to prohibit strictly their carrying opium, but this was a piece of comedy, since unofficially the Company quite well knew what happened to the opium sold at its auctions in Bengal. It was bought and shipped by local British or Parsee merchants, known as 'country traders'. They trafficked between India, China and the East Indian islands, shipping their merchandise outwards for Canton with the south-west monsoon, and returning with the north-east, making one round trip a year in their 'country wallahs' – solid, picturesque replicas, in teak, of seventeenth-century galleons.

Country traders were free to buy East India Company opium at auction. (Indeed, after 1816, a country trader shipping opium bought anywhere else lost his licence.) This opium was landed near Canton as contraband, from 1780 to 1793 at Lark's Bay near Macao, which was safe from Chinese or Portuguese surveillance. Meanwhile, in its local dealings with the Chinese authorities, the Honourable East India Company was able to wash its hands of all formal responsibility for the illegal drug trade. At this time the policy of the East India Company was to limit the quantity of opium produced by its monopoly but to gain therefrom the largest possible revenue. Chests of Patna opium, each containing forty balls of crude opium, a juice like thick treacle, enclosed in a shell of dried poppy petals – about the size of an apple dumpling – were sold by auction in Calcutta at prices about four times the cost of production. This revenue rose from £39 837 in 1773–4 to £78 300 in 1783–4, and in 1793 reached a quarter of a million sterling which went some way to balance the silver sent to China to pay for silk and tea.

During ten days of its annual life-cycle, the seed-box of the white poppy exudes a milky juice of extraordinary chemical complexity, not yet fully understood, and from this is derived a bitter, brown, granular powder: commercial opium.

The white poppy had been grown as a crop in antiquity in Egyptian Thebes. Later, opium and poppyseed were carried in the caravans of Arab traders all through Asia. Some time before 1750 the white poppy was being grown as a crop in Szechwan, a remote Chinese province on the borders of Tibet, but the opium habit remained local there. What encouraged the spread of the drug on the seacoast of China was the new technique of opium-smoking.

The taste of raw opium in the mouth was somewhat repugnant and its absorption into the body slow; smoking overcame both these disadvantages. The smoker dipped a needle into his prepared extract, dried it over a flame, and put the bead of flame-dried opium into a tiny pipe-bowl of tobacco. The smoke reached the bloodstream through the lungs, giving a quick narcotic effect. At the time of the Emperor's Edict against opium in 1799 there would appear to have been about the same receptiveness to opium-smoking in China as existed in Europe in the 1950s, when drugs had an unfamiliar glamour, before the present wave of addiction. It is hard now to credit that in 1958 there were in Great Britain only sixty-two known heroin addicts (heroin being an opium derivative). By 1966 the number had increased tenfold, by 1971 over twenty-five times, to 1580 – although heroin in Britain is handled not by gangsters but under the rational control of medical authority. A drug culture can spread fast, and not least in such times of social unease as no doubt existed when the Manchu emperors were beginning to fail at their job.

Sensing that their ancient culture – which had surrounded them comfortingly from cradle to grave – might be entering the agony of breakdown, some Chinese must have sought a similar consolation to that found by the opium-eating romantic writers of Europe in their escape from the early horrors of urban industrialism. The use of opium in China was not simply a question of economics, though supplies may have been pumped in under an urgent economic pressure.

A few grains of opium give the novice a feeling of euphoria. His first pipe is the future addict's honeymoon; but afterwards comes a wearisome listlessness. To face life once more he must decide either to leave opium alone, or to go on repeating and, usually, increasing his dose. The Chinese formed from experience the view that one pipe smoked daily for a week or ten days would leave a man in the grip of addiction thereafter.

He would soon work up to three pipes a day, and at this point one day without opium would bring on acute withdrawal symptoms: giddiness, watering of the eyes, prostration, torpor. A three-pipe addict, denied his drug for longer than one day, might expect to go through hell: a chill over the whole body, an ache in all his limbs to the very bone, diarrhoea, and agonizing psychic misery. To break the habit by an act of will was somewhat rare.

A smoker well able to afford his daily dose, if by some lucky chance of body chemistry he was under no compulsion to increase it, might hope to reach equilibrium – as with the present-day heroin 'user', so-called. This was the lucky man the professional apologists for the opium trade were later fond of pointing to – the addict who lived to be 80. A prosperous Chinese official might well manage his life like this, but the money income of an ordinary Chinese who began smoking opium was liable to be so small that he could afford his drug only by neglecting his family, which would eventually exile him from Chinese society, and make of him a social pariah.

Intelligent Chinese saw opium in extreme terms – as a social poison introduced by foreign enemies. To their country's two armed conflicts between 1838 and 1860 with Britain (later allied with France) – periods of open warfare linked by a turbulent armed truce – they have, reasonably enough, given the name, the Opium Wars.

The East India Company supplied not only China but Great Britain with opium. The first British addicts seem to have been those given opium, or its tincture, laudanum, as a palliative on medical advice. The medical profession did not have the nature of opium addiction clearly defined for them until the end of the eighteenth century, and for a long time after that doctors who were a little out of date went on prescribing opium as if it were aspirin. Indeed the fashionable Brunonian school of medicine used opium almost recklessly. Dr John Brown of Edinburgh (1735–88) had taught that disease arose from a deficiency or an excess of excitement, and that laudanum was one of the best means of regaining the proper measure of excitability. Dr Thomas Beddoes of Clifton, a Brunonian, was medical adviser to Coleridge, De Quincey, and many of their circle. Beddoes lent Coleridge Dr Brown's *Elements of Medicine* to study; a couple of years after he had finished writing *The Ancient Mariner* Coleridge was consuming over half a gallon of laudanum a week.

William Wilberforce, the anti-slavery philanthropist, memorable also for having founded a society to stamp out drunkenness among the working classes, was himself an opium addict for forty-five years, having first been given the drug to ease his gout. The poet Crabbe, another lifelong addict, was a physician before he became a clergyman; even physicians in those days could not be sure what they were doing, when they took opium.

The opium habit did not take long in nineteenth-century Britain to spread from a literate minority to the mass of the people. Those living under atrocious conditions and working appalling hours in the industrial north found opium cheaper than beer or gin and gave it the nickname of *Elevation*. The local chemist in one Lancashire parish alone admitted that he could sell nearly two hundredweight of opium per annum, in small packets over the counter. Nor did the children escape. In one Lancashire town with an exceptionally high infantile mortality 1600 householders were found to be using Godfrey's Cordial, which, like Mother Bailey's Quieting Syrop, contained opium. Babies were being addicted to laudanum, and accustomed slowly to lethal doses.

After the Imperial ban on opium-smoking was imposed, in 1799, the East India Company and their Chinese counterparts managed for the next twenty years to keep upon businesslike terms. There were points of dispute. The Company, for instance, never ceased to resent the arbitrary nature of Chinese Customs charges. The Hoppo, on the other hand, having paid for his job in Peking, was anxious to recoup himself by making the traffic pay all it would bear. But since the Company had no competitors at home, the price to the British grocer could often be adjusted to pay squeeze in Canton. By 1830, before Indian tea began to be grown commercially in Assam, the Company was selling thirty million pounds' weight of China tea annually, at a net profit of £1 000 000 and at one time the tea tax provided a tenth of the British government's entire revenue.

All the East India Company's tea business – indeed, all China's foreign trade except for a Russian caravan across the Gobi Desert – was transacted outside the city of Canton, in a stone block of offices and warehouses between the city walls and the river frontage. Since this had originally been the place where the factors did their work, it was known as the Factory. Here the foreign merchants – mainly British, American and Parsee – lived under strict Chinese control, some in Factories of their own. The Dutch, British, American and Spanish flags were hoisted daily; the French, who did no trade to speak of, did not show their flag until 1832. The Dutch East India Company, once powerful, was represented now by a couple of officials and two or three clerks. The Americans were the opportunists of the China trade, seeking a profit wherever it could be found. The East India Company dominated. Its mark on a bale was such a recognized guarantee of quality that inspection was unnecessary. (One Yankee trader had the wicked idea of imitating the mark as closely as possible for his own bales.)

The presence of these 'foreign devils' under the walls of Canton was tolerated only during the months when the tea crop came in and was bargained for. Chests of tea were then loaded in melon-shaped Chinese barges, and towed ten miles downstream to deep water at Whampoa, conspicuous by its nine-storey pagoda, where ocean-going ships could wait at anchor for their cargo. Mandarin oranges – the 'China orange' – were also grown around Whampoa.

Though under official protection, and given every help in their trade, foreign merchants living in the Factory were not allowed to enter the city itself. Canton, with its million inhabitants, was encircled by a massive defensive wall, twenty-five feet high, twenty wide, and six miles around, which the Chinese regarded as impregnable. Foreigners were not allowed to carry weapons, nor were women allowed. Wives must wait in patience until the season was over, eighty miles downstream, in the old Portuguese settlement of Macao. (The mere sight of a European woman, with her uncommonly large feet, wearing a dress which probably disclosed her bosom, and perhaps even shaking hands with a man not her husband, was morally repugnant to the Chinese.)

Despite such petty restrictions as these, and a rush of work in the tea season, the East India Company's staff at Canton had a not disagreeable life, sweetened by the chance of making a small fortune. Memoirs of the time agree on the splendour of their dinners, when thirty or so sat nightly around the mahogany table under a huge chandelier, indulging in English meals of beef and mutton and boiled vegetables. (How, wondered the perplexed Chinese, could men feed so greasily and grossly?)

When a European ship's-boat crew arrived in Canton their behaviour also ran true to form. Bouts of fisticuffs involving drunken sailors were a common source of trouble, Jack ashore was catered for behind the warehouses, in Hog Lane, where honest

Chinese gin-shop owners with nicknames like Old Jemmy Apoo and Ben Bobstay served him with a concocted drink – *first chop rum number one curio* – which was lethal.

Exercise at Canton was a problem. The digestive stroll after dinner was limited to the Factory courtyard – known as Jackass Point – and was taken under the gaze of dozens of inquisitive Chinese. Regulations allowed a foreigner to be rowed, three times a month, across the 500-yard-wide Pearl River, to stretch his legs in the gardens on Hai-nan Island, but not in a group numbering more than ten, and only on the understanding that all concerned came home sober, and before dark.

The British 'country traders' who managed the contraband trade in opium, as well as their legitimate trade in rice, raw cotton and chiming clocks, had no legal right to dwell under the walls of Canton, but several had managed to take root there on one pretext or other. Though the trade done in China by Prussia or Sardinia might be of microscopic dimensions, the Prussian and Sardinian consuls were country traders of British origin. One enterprising Scot called W. Davidson actually turned up in 1811 with documents to prove he was a naturalized Portuguese and stayed doing business for the next eleven years. Over men like this, the Company had no jurisdiction, and it was thanks to their smuggling trade in opium that the haemorrhage of silver from Europe to China had by 1804 been stopped. Treasure was beginning, indeed, to flow in the other direction. Between 1806 and 1809 silver to the amount of seven million Spanish dollars was transferred from China to India.

Between 1801 and 1820 opium shipments found their level, rising only a couple of times over 5000 chests per annum. Opium addiction in China, during these twenty easy-going years, was in effect being kept within limits by the Company's policy of controlling production, and selling at a high price. Opium was bought only by those who could afford it, usually minor officials in the mandarinate, or idle members of Chinese garrisons. Though the drug was slowly moving up China's internal trade routes and into the cognizance of China's common people, opium was still a luxury they might have heard of, but knew they could not afford.

This relatively small sale at a high price had been nicely judged by the Company to restore the balance of trade in their favour, yet keep on such terms with the Chinese as would not put at risk the valuable trade in tea. 'Were it possible to prevent the use of the drug altogether,' the Company's directors stated, rather smugly, 'except strictly for medicine, we would gladly do it, in compassion for mankind.' The calm before the storm.

Once the tea crop had been shipped downriver, the foreign devils at Canton were free to return to their picturesque villas and Chinese mistresses at the Portuguese settlement of Macao. The journey took three days in hired boats, through the anchorage at Whampoa, past the Bogue Forts, which stood forty miles downstream guarding the mouth of the Pearl River, then another forty miles along the western shore of Canton Bay.

The young clerks, after having been cooped up for months in bachelor quarters, would pass the gilded flower-boats – floating brothels, where a row of painted faces twittered greetings from each window. Their invitations were not to be taken seriously. A foreigner who went into a Chinese brothel would soon be found floating face downward in the river. Chinese laundry girls at Whampoa were another matter, generous, but also renowned for their honesty. The story went that a seaman who left a dirty shirt behind when the tea-fleet sailed for home found it waiting for him, pressed and laundered, as his ship dropped anchor in Whampoa a year later.

Once Macao's skyline came into sight, punctuated with the towers and spires of its twelve churches and monasteries, the young clerks could relax. On the seaward side, a crescent of white baroque houses fringed Macao's bay: the Praya Grande, a seaside promenade where sea breezes cooled the humidity of the Cantonese summer.

The neck of the little peninsula was separated from mainland China by a wall pierced by a gateway – the Barrier. Portugal's greatest poet, Camoens, had composed his epic, the *Lusiad*, in a grotto nearby, when serving in Macao as a soldier. On the offshore island of Shang chu-au, at one time a Portuguese trading base, the great Jesuit missionary St Francis Xavier had died, on a December night in 1552, while waiting in vain for permission to enter China. Macao lived in the past. The Portuguese fort was armed with antique bronze cannon, ornate with moulded figurines and fit only for ceremonial salutes. To the thrusting Anglo-Saxon mercantile community Macao was a pleasant but effete resort – a place for musical parties, horse-racing, amateur theatricals, a good place to pass the summer.

About 1820, this not too disagreeable annual routine came under various kinds of stress.

Three years earlier, by Act of Parliament, the East India Company had lost its monopoly of trade to India – though still keeping full control of trade between Britain and China. By applying steam power to textile manufacture, and filling their mills with little children who worked until they dropped, Lancashire manufacturers had managed in recent years to produce cotton cloth so cheap and yet so good that a native craftsman depending on his spinning wheel and hand loom could hardly hope to compete. Aided by a grossly favourable tariff, British textiles poured into India. The 30 000 looms that had woven the famous Cashmere shawls were slowly reduced to 6000 and the weavers made destitute.

The opium-growing cultivators of Bengal, paid cash by the government for their crop, were precisely the kind of thriving market Lancashire was looking for. The more opium grown, the more cotton cloth sold. Moreover, if steam-manufactured cottons could be forced so profitably on India, what price China? As the industrial north of England in the next few decades grew in wealth and political effectiveness, the pressure on the British government to 'open up' China became difficult to resist.

By washing its hands of responsibility for the trade in opium, the East India Company had, of course, lost any possible chance of controlling it. The Americans and the Portuguese soon moved into the business, and the Company's policy of high prices and good intentions came under threat, since opium could be procured in other parts of the world more cheaply than in monopolistic Bengal.

The first American opium speculation was in 1811 when the fast Philadelphia brig *Sylph* (Captain Dobell) dropped anchor in Macao on 22 July with a cargo of opium from Smyrna in Turkey.

In 1817 the Americans (whose share of the opium trade at Canton was normally about a tenth) made a huge purchase of half a million dollars' worth of Turkish opium, which they shipped into Macao. But since Turkish opium was an inferior article, and not to local taste, the speculation had only a mixed success. There happened, however – until the Mahrattas were defeated in 1817–18 by the Marquis of Hastings – to be an independent source of opium in India. Although Malwa opium so-called – grown in Rajputana – had to be transported some distance across country to the coast, the drug could be sold there at a price which usually undercut Patna opium as sold at Company auctions in Bengal. In 1818, after four years of increasing competition, cheaper

Malwa opium to the amount of 2000 chests a year was being imported into Macao.

The chain of vested interests in the drug traffic had grown too weighty to be broken by mere good intentions. With a tenth of its revenue coming from a tax on China tea, the British government had a strong motive for making sure tea arrived from Canton without interruption. But the purchase of tea was financed by silver procured by the sale of opium. And opium-growers in India bought Lancashire cottons. And the opium was put on the market by a company which owed its very existence to a British Parliament where all these other vested interests could exert a contrary pressure, if the Company yielded to competition, and let itself be forced out of the opium business.

Reacting as any other trader would, the East India Company decided to undercut the competition from Malwa by increasing its own opium production and bringing down the price. After 1819, the Company's declared policy was 'to endeavour to secure the command of the Market by furnishing a Supply on so enlarged a scale and on such reasonable terms as shall prevent competition'. A chest of opium had sold for $2075 in 1820; by 1821 the price was down to $1552. Once Mahratta territory had come under British rule, the output of Malwa opium was channelled by means of a transit duty through the nearby port of Bombay, and the Portuguese were cut off from their source of supply. The available supply of Malwa opium had risen from 600 chests in 1815–16 to 4000 in 1822–3. The Company, though defeating the competition, was landed with vastly increased stocks of opium, which somehow had to be sold.

In other words: so that the British public could go on drinking their millions of gallons of tea each year, twice as many Chinese opium addicts (and, for that matter, British opium addicts) had somehow to be created.

This urgent need to flood China with cheaper opium happened to coincide with the first serious Chinese campaign against opium since the Emperor's Edict of 1799.

The earliest Manchu Emperors, though foreigners from Tartary, had at first made life easier for the ordinary Chinese. Certain forms of serfdom were extinguished and in 1712 the Emperor fixed land and poll taxes and decreed that they were not to be increased while the dynasty lasted. Since no dynasty had ever managed to rule China without the cooperation of its scholarly civil service – the mandarinate – the Manchus were careful to respect Confucian institutions, but stiffened them with a parallel Tartar military government. Every provincial governor now had looking over his shoulder a Tartar General, equal in rank, who commanded the local garrison.

The one outward sign in China of Manchu domination was the shaven forehead and plaited pigtail, which, combined with wide sleeves to cover the hands, were supposed to give their subjects a resemblance to the sacred Manchu ˉanimal, the horse. Though there were secret societies, particularly in south China, who had sworn opposition to the Manchus, yet provided these foreign overlords from Tartary ruled with average efficiency and justice, and so long as ordinary Chinese stood in awe of Manchu military prowess, the dynasty was safe.

But the military reputation of the Manchus had been based on their skill with the bow and arrow – the musket had only recently come into use – and the last of the great Manchu administrators had been the old Emperor who conferred with Lord Macartney.

The old Emperor's mediocre successor was succeeded in 1820 by an Emperor who took for the title of his reign Tao Kuang – Glorious Rectitude. The new man was forty years old, parsimonious, unimaginative, but with a strong sense of duty. He tried at the outset to reform his court – to get a grip on the mandarins and eunuchs who were enriching themselves at public expense – though his zeal soon waned.

The illegal import into Canton of opium caused silver to flow out of China but it had begun also to corrupt the government. In 1813 court eunuchs and members of the Imperial Guard were found to be addicts. New penalties were imposed on the army: an officer caught smoking was flogged and cashiered.

The import of opium was contrary to Chinese law and should be stopped. But official interference with opium sales in Canton was bound, now, to have economic and political repercussions all over the world. China's huge tea export connected her inescapably with the new, aggressive trading society which had developed in Europe and America in the past century, but the Chinese had not yet grasped what that meant. The world had become one market, complex, interconnected – and China, whatever the Chinese might think, was no longer a place apart.

Little more than lip-service had been paid at Canton during the last reign to the Imperial prohibition of opium. In 1809 the Governor of Canton had obliged the Hong merchants, under bond, to guarantee that foreign ships discharging at Whampoa contained no opium. In 1815 all the vessels in Macao – then the centre for traffic in Malwa opium – had been searched for the drug. But an Imperial Edict, like a papal bull, depended for its effectiveness on public opinion rather than on police measures. And two groups of Chinese were already deeply involved in helping the foreigners smuggle opium; those in whose pockets the trade put money, either as profits or bribes, and the growing tribe of addicts who needed a steady supply and would gladly break the law to get it.

The Chinese authorities now tried using force.

In 1821 all trade in tea was stopped for two months. Chinese opium dealers were fined, imprisoned, and sent into exile in the frozen wastes of Central Asia. Three British ships at Whampoa were seized, after a flagrant case of bribery. Half their cargo was confiscated and they were forbidden even to trade in tea. Since, with Chinese connivance, the game had gone on for so long, the smugglers were highly indignant at being caught. 'These foreigners', primly reported the mandarin responsible for soothing the barbarians, 'feel no gratitude, nor wish to render a recompense, but smuggle in opium, which poisons the Empire.'

Chinese harassment continued for two years; in Macao, when opium chests had to be moved from one building to another, they had first to be disguised as packages containing innocuous goods. The easy-going days were over; but Chinese addicts were unable to stop their craving for the drug. The trade became more furtive but it increased enormously; by 1835 the number of Chinese opium addicts was estimated at two million.

There were powerful national interests behind the drug trade, and not all of them British. Although to their honour a few American merchants declined on principle to handle opium – J. P. Cushing withdrew from the trade in 1821, Olyphant & Co. never touched it – American traders as a body were badly in need of some article the Chinese would buy, since the seal breeding-grounds by now were almost wiped out. If Chinese had not bought opium from Americans, then United States imports of silk, porcelain and tea would have had to be paid for in silver coin. But there was not enough silver available in the United States. As the House of Representatives Committee on Currency had gloomily reported in 1819, 'the whole amount of our current coin is probably not more than double that which has been imported in a single year to India, including China in the common term'. Opium smuggling had turned out to be good for the dollar.

Imperial China had no navy in the European sense. Governors of coastal provinces had at their disposal a local force of junks, armed with cannon, for use against unruly fishermen, who were apt in bad times to turn pirate. Often the cannon in these junks were fixtures, which fired without taking aim, and the gunpowder supplied was more suitable for fireworks than for broadsides. Any sizable armed Western merchant ship had nothing to fear from a Chinese war junk, and to a ship of war they were sitting ducks.

The Chinese authorities could still exert their will on shore, but at sea they were powerless, therefore the obvious way to evade Chinese control was to find a convenient opium depot well out in Canton Bay.

The opium smugglers chose as their depot the small, mountainous island of Lintin in Canton Bay, twenty miles north-east of Macao, where they would be safe under their own guns. The clumsy teak country wallahs, arriving from India, would pause and discharge their chests of opium into hulks moored in the roadstead at Lintin, before proceeding upriver with any legitimate cargo they might be carrying – raw cotton, if it had been a bad year for the Tientsin cotton crop, rice, if there happened to be a local shortage. The hulks at Lintin – *Merope*, owned by Matheson, *Samarang*, shared by Dent and Magniac, joined later by *Eugenia* and *Jamesina* – were usually commanded by British officers, who domesticated these floating warehouses with verandahs and potted plants, and might even have their wives and children aboard. *Jamesina* was a former British warship – the 18-gun sloop HMS *Curlew* (382 tons) – which the Admiralty had disposed of at auction in 1823. The Spaniards based on Manila had their own hulk at Lintin, called *General Quiroga*. From 1821 onwards one receiving ship there always flew the Stars and Stripes (or the Flowery Flag, as the Chinese called it).

An American called Forbes who owned the receiving ship *Lintin* between 1830 and 1832 was reputed to have made his fortune in three years and asked to be buried in a coffin made from her mast.

Crews aboard the hulks were usually lascars – or, as the Chinese called them, 'black barbarians'. Opium was by and large a cash business, deals being made either on board, or through a Chinese broker on shore. The receiving ship worked on a commission basis, five dollars being paid for each chest accepted aboard, with two dollars demurrage if an order were not presented within seven days. There was little to fear from Chinese war junks, but the hulk was insured against damage from typhoons.

The drug was re-packed on board into mat bags for ease of handling, and, at a time agreed, out from one of the innumerable creek villages fringing Canton Bay would row a fifty-oared, two-masted galley, specially built for the trade, and so heavily armed that any mandarin junk on coastal patrol would think twice before closing with her. The bags of opium were landed ashore with the connivance of local officials – not a difficult matter when so many minor bureaucrats were avid opium-smokers. The network of bribery grew, corrupting the administration until at one time even the Governor of Canton was said to be involved.

In the season of 1820–1, 4244 chests of opium were shipped from India to China. By the end of the decade, in 1830–1, the total had increased over fourfold, to 18 956 chests – one firm alone, Jardine, Matheson & Co., disposing of more opium in 1831 than the entire Chinese import of 1821. Trade by private firms through Lintin was, by 1831, two and a half times greater – despite the enormous dimensions of the tea trade – than legitimate business going through Canton.

For traffic on this scale, the old sluggish 500-ton country wallahs were no longer up to the job. The opium dealers began to buy or build the fastest ships procurable.

Money for building *Red Rover*, the first opium clipper, built in 1829, was advanced by Lord William Bentinck, Governor-General of India, on the shipbuilder's promise that she would be able to bear up against the north-west monsoon, and so make three trips to China annually in opium, instead of one. When the builder, Captain William Clifton, made good his promise, he was given £10 000 from public funds.

The drug-smugglers scoured the world for fast ships which could be armed and put into their service – as clippers, to fetch opium from India, or, later, as coasters, fast vessels of shallow draught for dangerous inshore work along the China coast. Several opium clippers were former slavers, captured off the coast of Africa and auctioned as prizes. *Sylph* was designed for the trade on private contract by Sir Robert Seppings, Surveyor of the Navy, and *Falcon*, later the flagship of Jardine, Matheson & Co.'s fleet, had been Lord Yarborough's private yacht. She too was built to the model of a man-of-war, and had been flagship of the Royal Yacht Squadron. These clippers usually had a broadside of four or five guns port and starboard, and a long-tom – a heavy gun, often a 68-pounder – amidships. Considered as a naval force, the opium clippers alone were much more powerful than any fleet the Emperor of China could bring against them.

Well aware that action of some kind against opium-smuggling was still expected of them by the Imperial Court, the authorities in Canton were reduced, at last, to making helpless symbolic gestures. When clippers which had unloaded their cargo at Lintin put about and made for the open sea, for another run to India, forty or so war junks would come in sight. Once the clippers were safely out of range, the junks would open fire. Though every single Chinese cannon-ball did nothing more than make a big splash in the sea, the furious bombardment could provide subject-matter later for a despatch to Peking, describing eloquently how a squadron of armed smugglers, when fired on by the Chinese, had sheered off, and sailed away over the horizon.

In 1782 there had been no sale for the cargo of Bengal opium that Warren Hastings had sent hopefully to Canton. By 1830, the opium trade there was probably the largest commerce of its time in any single commodity, anywhere in the world.

2 Napier's Fizzle

'Trade with China is our only object; conquest would be as dangerous as defeat, and commerce never prospers where force is used to sustain us. No glory is to be gained in a victory over the Chinese...Our grand object is to keep peace, and by the mildest means, by a plastic adaptation of our manners to theirs, to extend our influence in China, with a view to extending our commercial relations.'

Sir James Graham, First Lord of the Admiralty, to Lord William Bentinck, Governor-General of India, 1832

One picturesque character frequenting Macao and Canton was George Chinnery, the woman-hating Irish painter, who had arrived there in 1825, aged 51, on the run from his wife. He described her as 'the ugliest woman I ever saw in my life'. Whenever she threatened to leave Calcutta and join him, Chinnery would go up the river to Canton, because, as everyone knew, European women were not allowed there.

George Chinnery lived on at Macao until his death in 1852, painting portraits of local celebrities, both Chinese and European, and marine studies full of glowing light and dipping masts, which touch with romanticism the arrival of Western shipping in the Orient. He enjoyed amateur theatricals and was immensely popular as Mrs Malaprop. His Chinese students learned Western perspective from him and oil-painting technique and for years went on producing imitation Chinnerys.

Thanks to his shrewd if respectful portraits of William Jardine and James Matheson we can to some extent gauge these eminent opium smugglers as human beings. Chinnery's likeness of Jardine shows a strong-willed face, not lacking intelligence and used to command – but not a personality one would want for an enemy. Matheson looks sprightlier than Jardine, a little more arrogant, perhaps a little more opportunist. They were evidently a formidable team.

Both had been country traders. They founded their partnership in 1828, when Jardine, the older man, was 44, and Matheson 32. Jardine had first seen China in 1802, as an 18-year-old assistant-surgeon on board HMS *Brunswick*. The surgeon of an Indiaman had then the privilege of seven tons' cargo space for himself, and country traders in Canton were usually glad to buy it off him at from £20–£40 a ton – or he could dabble in trade on his own account. By 1816, Jardine had managed to scratch together enough capital to set up on his own.

In 1820 he went into partnership with a Parsee merchant called Framjee Cowasjee, and became his Canton agent for Malwa opium in 1822, joining forces with Matheson six years later. Jardine's Chinese nickname was Iron-Headed Old Rat – from the unflinching way he had once stood his ground and borne blows showered at his head when trying to deliver, at the city gate, a petition which the Chinese had no wish to accept. Though never varying his tone of contempt for the Chinese, Jardine had a well-developed political sense. He strongly advocated, for example, making the large island of Formosa an offshore base for the Western powers. When news came in 1832 of an insurrection there against the Chinese Emperor he wrote: 'What an opportunity for us to lend them a little hand, and gain a footing on the island.'

The Scottish *r* in Jardine's voice may still be audible in this ironic evidence given verbatim to a House of Commons committee when asked if he were ever troubled personally by doubts about the morality of the opium trade. 'When the East India Company were growing it,' said William Jardine, 'and selling it, and there was a declaration of the House of Lords and Commons with all the bench of bishops at their back that it was inexpedient to do it away, I think our moral scruples need not have been so very great.'

James Matheson, Jardine's partner, was a Highlander from Sutherland, and had left Edinburgh University at 19 to enter the Calcutta firm of Mackintosh, run by his uncle. At 22 he was supercargo on the opium ship *Marquis of Hastings*. By 23 Matheson was in Canton, and became there a partner in a Spanish firm, adroitly eluding East India Company control by getting for himself an appointment as Danish Consul. He brought a capital of £20 000 with him to Jardine in 1828, and the legal protection of the Danish flag. For house flag, Jardine and Matheson – for one moment sentimental – chose a white St Andrew's cross on a blue ground.

When opium became plentiful, Matheson had been the first to see the potential of the 'coast trade' – that is of running opium a long way up the China coast to open up provinces not yet addicted to the drug. This trade – on an uncharted coast and against official opposition – was tough and risky, but with reasonably good fortune the rate of profit was very high. Local mandarins often gave trouble but at certain places they could be bought or intimidated, and a regular trading station established. By a single lucky voyage to Amoy in his firm's brig *San Sebastian*, James Matheson had in 1823 fetched back silver worth $123 000.

A legitimate trade along the China coast was a non-starter, as the East India Company found in 1832 when they sent their *Lord Amherst* north with a cargo of 200 sample bales of textiles, and made a loss of £5647 on the venture. In the same year, Jardine, Matheson's *Jamesina* came back with $330 000 in silver under hatches from the sale of opium in Amoy, Foochow and Ch'uan-chou Bay, her supercargo writing in his journal that 'the only chance of pushing English manufactures on this coast is by having them as a small item in an opium cargo'.

In 1833 a reforming British Parliament abolished the East India Company's monopoly, which for long had been the target of industrialists with a doctrine of free trade. After 1833 it became 'lawful for any of His Majesty's subjects to carry on trade with any countries beyond the Cape of Good Hope to the Straits of Magellan'.

In 1834, the first year of free trade, 40 per cent more tea was shipped to Britain than the year before, and of course the price slipped sideways; but drug sales continued to soar. Between 1830 and 1836 the chests of opium shipped from India to China increased in number from 18 956 to 30 302. Traders hoping to share in this prosperity began arriving at Macao like bees to a honeypot. There had in 1832 been twenty-six Britons trading at Canton, apart from Company men. By 1834 there were sixty-six, and by 1837, 156. Trade became hectic. Matheson, fervent free-trader though he was, wrote, ironically, to an American correspondent: 'We are sighing almost for a return of the Company's monopoly, in preference to the trouble and endless turmoil of free trade.'

These new men had never known the old and ceremonious way of dealing with the Chinese, when deals involving huge sums often were done on the nod, or with an initial scribbled on a scrap of paper. The Hong merchants, who for years had worked amicably with the East India Company and taken advantage of Company authority to keep order in Canton, were at a loss.

Peking, too, was uneasy. The Court and the Imperial Treasury, thanks to what they squeezed out of Hoppo and Cohong, had always profited handsomely from the tea trade. Too many ordinary Chinese livelihoods were by now dependent on tea for the business ever to be brought to an abrupt and final end. Nevertheless, as opium-smuggling spread up the coast, Peking began to favour reverting to a traditional Chinese policy of keeping the barbarian traders fully at arm's length, and limiting them strictly to Canton. Lacking as yet an economic theory which would explain for them accurately the new world market brought into being by industrial capitalism, the Chinese at first defined the threat from outside in simplified terms. Foreign dirt, as they called opium, was quite clearly corroding their traditional values, and ruining human lives. Opium addiction was bad, and the loss of silver exported to pay for the drug might be worse, but suppose in the end these outsiders sought to rival the authority of the Emperor?

India was China's neighbour – and already by 1816 the British, the masters in India, had imposed their influence on Nepal, traditionally a Chinese dependency; by 1826 they were established in Assam. As for the vast leakage of silver from China, the Imperial Treasury had customs figures, and knew the alarming reality. Between 1829 and 1840 a sum of just over seven million silver dollars had entered China, but the much larger sum of fifty-six million silver dollars had been sucked out. Chinese peasants were in the habit of collecting copper cash, all the year round, to change when the time came into silver, for the tax-collector. This devaluation of the currency meant simply that more copper cash had to be collected for the same weight of silver. Taxation thus became a heavier burden on the peasant's back but with no advantage whatever to the Imperial Treasury – and discontented peasants would in the long run represent yet another serious threat to the dynasty.

Foreigners cared nothing for the problems thus created, on the contrary; as the *Chinese Courier* pointed out with a certain vindictiveness in 1833, 'perhaps nothing could contribute more readily to the final reduction of the Chinese to reasonable terms with foreigners than this steady, non-ceasing impoverishment of the country by the abstraction of the circulating medium'.

An aggressive policy against China had its advocates, too. Writing under the pseudonym of 'A British Merchant' in the *China Repository* – a magazine edited in Macao by missionaries – a voice that was almost certainly William Jardine's put in words the unspoken thoughts of the free-traders who, with the East India Company pushed aside, were arriving at Canton in such numbers: 'Obtain us but a sale for our goods, and we will supply any quantity...Nor indeed should our valuable commerce and revenue both in India and Great Britain be permitted to remain subject to a caprice which a few gunboats laid alongside this city would overrule by the discharge of a few mortars...The results of a war with China could not be doubted.'

To replace the East India Company's old Select Committee in Canton, the British Cabinet in 1834 appointed Lord Napier of Meristoun as Chief Superintendent of Trade. Lord Napier had no experience as a businessman, but was a retired naval officer of middling rank. He was sent out to China with instructions which suggest that the British government thought of him not as a spokesman on practical matters for the merchant community but as a representative of the Crown, who might somehow get in Canton by the back door the recognition that the Emperor had refused to successive British Ambassadors in Peking.

Lord Napier was 48. As a midshipman in HMS *Defence*, he had seen service at the Battle of Trafalgar and in 1815, when the Napoleonic Wars were over, he got married and retired with the rank of Captain to Selkirkshire, where he devoted himself to improving the breed of sheep. In 1823 he succeeded to his title, and in 1824 – a year when a few well-connected half-pay officers were lucky enough to receive employment off the coast of South America – his lordship was given command of HMS *Diamond*.

As a representative Scottish peer until 1833, Lord Napier had identified himself with the more advanced thinkers in the House of Lords – voting for Catholic Emancipation and the Reform Bill, advocating the abolition of slavery and even offering to serve in the unhealthy West Indies as a commissioner. Those free-traders who had resented the East India Company's monopoly would regard Lord Napier as their man.

On the face of it, Lord Napier – the only available peer who had seen service afloat – was in other respects not a bad choice for a tricky job like this, in China. His peerage might impress the Chinese, and, if trouble broke out, his naval experience, such as it was, would certainly come in useful. Unfortunately this conscientious peer and fervent Presbyterian was not blessed with either imagination or tact; he might have bullied the Chinese, but he was not the man to outwit them.

Lord Napier was descended from the inventor of logarithms.

Apart from the breeding of mountain sheep, his prime interests were mathematics and the scrutiny of Holy Writ. It was just one more stroke of bad luck that his lordship's personal appearance – tall, raw-boned, carrot-headed – happened exactly to coincide with the Chinese mental stereotype of a typical Red Barbarian. To the Chinese he was a figure of fun.

Lord Palmerston, then British Foreign Secretary, had decided to send out a man who, by temperament, was sure to fulfil all his instructions to the letter. But the instructions given to Lord Napier in London were bound to get him into trouble in Canton.

Lord Napier was, to begin with, warned to obey Chinese regulations – and then told to reside in Canton itself. But well-known rules laid down long ago by the Emperor, which local officials were powerless to change, made residence at Canton impossible, since the Factories there were provided for the use of merchants, and were occupied by them as a rule only while tea was being shipped. Lord Napier was not a merchant, but an official, and he happened to arrive at midsummer, when the tea season was over.

His next instruction ordered Lord Napier to communicate direct with the Chinese authorities. At one time the Chinese had permitted this, in emergencies. But Chinese policy was now to keep foreigners at arm's length, so all contact between foreign merchants and local authorities occurred through the Cohong. Only a threat of force was likely to bring about a change in such long-established procedure – but Lord Napier, while being pushed into action which might lead to hostilities, had also been warned that he must 'cautiously abstain from making any appeal for the protection of our military and naval forces'.

Finally, though his lordship's nominal duty was to superintend trade – and, to the Chinese, the contraband trade in opium was a thorn in their side, about which they might perhaps have been glad to negotiate unofficially – Napier had expressly been told not to interfere with the developing coast trade in opium: 'It is not desirable that you should encourage such adventures, but you must never lose sight of the fact that you have no authority to interfere with them or prevent them.' Napier was also instructed to survey the China coastline (with the help, there could hardly be the slightest doubt, of the coast traders themselves, since they were the only British seamen who knew it) and to choose out places where British naval vessels might operate safely in case of war.

The literal carrying-out of instructions like these was certain to make mischief as Lord Palmerston, a Foreign Secretary of immense ability but combative temperament, must have known. The only reasonable assumption is that mischief in Canton happened just then to suit his policy.

Lord Napier arrived off Macao aboard the frigate *Andromache* (28 guns, Captain H. D. Chads) in fetid summer heat on 15 July 1834. He had brought along his wife and two unmarried daughters – who were marked down by the local bachelors as 'rather good than otherwise'. Lord Napier's first official task was to announce his arrival by letter to Lu K'un, the Viceroy at Canton, who governed on the Emperor's behalf the two provinces of Kwangsi and Kwangtung. Not that the Viceroy could possibly take official cognizance of Lord Napier's announcement without getting into hot water in Peking. The British at Canton had always used a committee of local merchants to represent them. Why were they trying to force on the Chinese an officer – a 'Barbarian Eye'?

On 21 July the Viceroy issued an Edict to meet the case: 'the ... Barbarian Eye, if he wishes to come to Canton, must inform the Hong merchants, so that they may petition me...' Disregarding this reminder of Chinese procedure, but in literal obedience to his instructions, Lord Napier went in *Andromache* to the mouth of the Pearl River – foreign ships of war were not allowed into the river itself – setting off in fact for Canton at the very moment when the Hong merchants, hoping to avoid trouble, were on their way to Macao to deter him.

Not every British merchant was happy about an aggressive policy in Canton. Those deep in the legitimate tea trade were much more interested in avoiding trouble than opium dealers who made their money in a business that of its nature could do without official Chinese goodwill. Even some of those who privately hoped that one day China might be forced into trading more freely, having seen Lord Napier's style, were at the moment standing well back expecting him to blunder.

Under the guns of the Chinese forts at the Bogue, Lord Napier transferred from *Andromache* to the frigate's cutter, and was rowed by blue-jackets forty miles upstream to the English Factory under the city wall. He there kept company with his fellow Scot, William Jardine, whose guest he had been and whose advice he took.

The Chinese Customs had disrespectfully broken open Lord Napier's trunks and Chinese boatmen were already being withdrawn – two storm signals indicating that pressure on the foreign merchant community was likely to begin. At this time of year no tea was being shipped, so a British trade embargo would do no harm to the Chinese. The Viceroy, on the other hand, was by now in a strong tactical position – because Lord Napier, in coming to the Factory, which depended on the Chinese for every necessity had let himself be taken hostage.

As a civil administrator Lu K'un, the Viceroy, had a high reputation, but twice during his career he had also held important military posts. Already he was strengthening the garrison of Canton and encouraging the Governor, Ch'i Lung, in his plans to block the river.

Lord Napier had been instructed to get in direct touch with the Viceroy and though no formal procedure existed he was determined to do his best. At the perimeter of the foreign settlement was a gate into the city, where petitions for the Chinese authorities could be handed over: this would have to serve its turn.

Mr J. H. Astell, Lord Napier's secretary, was sent to the gate with a letter for the Viceroy, written in Chinese by Robert Morrison the missionary. A group of British merchants went along, to give Astell backing. However, at the Petition Gate only documents headed with the Chinese character *pin*, to signify 'petition', could be officially accepted from foreigners. Since Mr Astell was trying to hand over what clearly was not a petition but a letter, the mandarin on duty declined to take it. But a mandarin of higher rank was said to be on his way.

An hour passed. The Chinese crowd, on being told what was happening, began to rag the foreign devils. When the mandarin of higher rank did arrive he too refused to accept Astell's letter. At last, some of the Hong merchants turned up at the Petition Gate, smiling and bowing ingratiatingly. Please might they have the document? It was customary.

But Astell knew his orders better than to pass Lord Napier's letter into their obliging hands. Under the eyes of the delighted crowd, the comedy went on. Two mandarins of even higher rank arrived; both declined. And so it went on. The British had allowed themselves to be tricked into playing a game according to rules imposed upon them by Lu K'un. After three hours of standing about uselessly in the damp heat amid a jeering crowd, Astell called it off, and went back to the Factory.

Lu K'un, reporting with satisfaction to the Emperor in Peking about this British loss of face, observed, 'it is plain, on the least reflection, that in order to distinguish the Chinese from outsiders it is of the utmost importance to maintain dignity and sovereignty'.

He had Lord Napier off balance, and knew it. In a war of subtle bureaucratic manoeuvring, the Chinese could always win.

Lord Napier, in coming up with such alacrity to Canton, had neglected to provide himself with the usual red permit, the Chinese passport issued to all foreigners visiting the Factories. An Edict to the Hong merchants – in which the Viceroy had his little joke by transposing Lord Napier's name phonetically into two Chinese characters which could signify Laboriously Vile – made it clear that when the particular piece of business which brought Lord Napier to Canton had been transacted he must return to Macao, and wait there for his red permit. 'Should the said Laboriously Vile oppose and disobey, it will be because the Hong merchants have mismanaged the affair. In that case I shall be obliged to report against them.' A further Edict from Lu K'un on 30 July withdrew the concession to Lord Napier of letting him stay until the business in hand was finished. Napier was being gently squeezed out.

The Chinese were simply following their age-old policy of soothing and civilizing the barbarians by combining severity with leniency – gently teaching them the rules – a method which in the old days might have worked wonders on East India Company men, who wanted nothing better than to get their tea packed and away. But the balance of forces was no longer what the Chinese were used to. Britain's position in the world depended on the skill with which her seamen could employ a very particular form of power, then unrivalled – the mercilessly destructive effect of a naval broadside. The Chinese of this generation were simply unable to judge what could be done with a broadside as a form of ruthless argument. They were soon to find out.

William Jardine, when Lu K'un told Lord Napier to leave Canton, advised resistance. Jardine seems to have believed, shrewdly enough, that an open affront to the Crown's representative was likely to inflame public opinion in Britain, and this would help to bring about sooner what he had set his heart on – armed British intervention. Under Jardine's influence, Lord Napier wrote to Lord Palmerston on 14 August: 'Three or four frigates and brigs, with a few steady British troops, not sepoys, would settle the thing.' The former midshipman from Trafalgar sniffed powder; he had been three weeks in China, and was already being tempted to ignore that portion of his sign manual which discouraged him from calling in the Navy. 'The exploit', he urged Palmerston, 'is to be performed with a facility unknown even in the capture of a paltry West Indian island.'

Those were the days before the telegraph, when Lord Napier's despatch and the British government's reply would have to go round the Cape of Good Hope by sailing ship. Hence his lordship was unaware that the Cabinet which appointed him had fallen at just about the time he arrived in Canton. The Tories were in power, and the new Foreign Secretary was the Duke of Wellington, who detested Palmerston as a trouble-maker. As for the radical businessmen who were pushing their way into Parliament and itching to open up China, Wellington had already invented his own nickname for them: 'bad hats'. In a despatch written on 2 February 1835 which, as it happened, Napier never lived to read, Wellington rapped the Superintendent of Trade's knuckles, and defined the new government's policy towards China. 'It is not by force and violence that His Majesty intends to establish a commercial intercourse between his subjects and China, but by other conciliatory measures so strongly inculcated in the instructions you have received.'

On 16 August, Lu K'un imposed a partial stoppage of trade.

Andromache had been cruising near the Ladrone islands, over the horizon but within call. She returned on 17 August in company with the frigate *Imogene* (18 guns, Captain P. Blackwood), come to relieve her, since *Andromache* was due home with despatches. Lord Napier took this opportunity to develop his views about the Chinese government, pointing out in a despatch to Lord Grey that they were, 'in the extreme degree of mental imbecility and moral degradation, dreaming themselves to be the only people on earth, and being entirely ignorant of the theory and practice of international law'.

Napier urged the British government to answer the partial stoppage of trade by getting military and naval forces ready for September of the year following, 1835, to 'assert our ancient rights of commerce'. As for the present embargo, he pointed out that if the Viceroy did not lift his ban on trade 'the smugglers will do it for him'. Napier was here betraying the bias of Jardine's influence: smugglers might keep a trade in opium going, they had for years, but without Chinese partnership, no tea could leave Canton. 'What', Lord Napier went on to ask rhetorically, 'can an army of bows and arrows and pikes and shields do against a handful of British veterans?' When the troops he was asking for arrived, Peking should be obliged under threat of force to make a commercial treaty.

Though hair-raisingly warlike from a Superintendent of Trade, this despatch was not all bluster. Lord Napier had stated the military realities distinctly enough, and with acumen. Though the Chinese might go on haughtily treating the British as they always had done – as barbarians – they were, in the long run, the losing side. But at this very moment, Lord Napier, however emotionally belligerent he might feel, had at his beck and call only a couple of frigates. He was like a rich man after banking hours, with a huge credit balance behind locked doors and only a shilling in his pocket.

The partial Chinese embargo had been imposed because the Viceroy guessed, correctly, that by hitting some merchants harder than others it might open the split he knew to exist in the foreign community. Lord Napier's answer was to flypost a placard in Chinese, appealing over the Viceroy's head to the Cantonese, whose livelihood depended on trade. Deploring Lu K'un's 'ignorance and obstinacy' the poster wept crocodile tears over the 'thousands of industrious Chinese who must suffer ruin and discomfort through the perversity of their government'. But at a war of words the Chinese had every advantage. The Viceroy's answer laid it on hard.

'A lawless foreign slave', he began, 'has issued a notice. We do not know how such a barbarian dog can have the audacity to call himself an Eye' (that is to say, an official). The Viceroy continues: '... though a savage from beyond the pale, his sense of propriety would have restrained him from such an outrage. It is a capital offence to incite the people against their rulers, and we would be justified in obtaining a mandate for his decapitation.' On 2 September an Edict was issued which stopped trade altogether. 'The Barbarian Eye', it said, '...is indeed stupid, blinded, ignorant ... there can be no quiet while he remains here. I therefore formally close the trade until he goes.'

Other nations might continue peaceably trading – American merchants on the spot did very well indeed – but the British were all told to leave Canton and go to Whampoa or Macao. Their servants would be withdrawn, their supplies cut off, and their Factories surrounded by a cordon of soldiers.

The Chinese were giving the screw a couple of turns.

On the evening of 3 September, Lord Napier was sitting down to dinner in the English Factory with Sir George Robinson, his Third Superintendent of Trade, when outside arrived twenty Chinese soldiers, sent to hang up this new Edict on the gate. The gentlemen upstairs, whose main dish had been salt pork procured from the frigates, had just got to work on their plum duff when a Chinese servant, fearing the worst, ran in screaming. Lord Napier went down to see what was the matter. He ripped down with his own hand the thin board on which the Edict was posted and told the soldiers to go away.

Undeflected by the Chinese soldiers' angry gestures, he came back to finish his pudding. This was nothing to the battle of Trafalgar. Then, at the mahogany table, under the chandelier, as the decanter passed from hand to hand and a rubicund portrait of King George IV gazed down at them, the problem was discussed.

Lord Napier eventually decided – not wisely, as it turned out – to send Sir George Robinson to Captain Blackwood of HMS *Imogene,* at present lying becalmed, in company with HMS *Andromache,* in the Bay of Canton. His letter to Captain Blackwood ordered the two frigates up the river to Whampoa. If the Bogue Forts protecting the estuary fired on *Imogene* – as they must – they were to be silenced. Captain Blackwood was to anchor at Whampoa – as high up the Pearl River as a frigate could go – and send on his cutter, commanded by a lieutenant, with a dozen marines under a sergeant. This force would protect life and property at the Factories.

Lord Napier, whose nervous excitement was by now becoming apparent, had over-reacted. Accustomed all his professional life to applying force – preferably naval force – he was out of his element at Canton. When Chinese and foreigners were at odds there, a stoppage of trade was the recognized gambit. There had often been embargoes. They put neither life nor property at risk, since both sides had always a strong motive to renew commercial relations. This time, as the Chinese were making clear, the single obstacle to normal trading at Canton was the physical presence there of Lord Napier.

On 7 September a light breeze blew up, and the two becalmed frigates were able to enter the Bogue in obedience to Lord Napier's orders, the cutter *Louisa* following. The Bogue was where the Pearl River, varying between one and three miles in width, flowed between high sandstone hills to the sea. The river entrance was defended by five forts – two at the mouth, to right and left, three others placed upstream – to dominate the river as it defiled between these hills: the same ancient forts which, two centuries before, Captain Weddell had bombarded into silence. The Bogue Forts were, in fact, no more than a mimic threat. Some of their cannon had been in place ever since Weddell's time. Not mounted on gun-carriages but fixed in masonry to fire through loopholes, those guns could not be traversed or depressed to hit a moving target. They were more like fireworks than pieces of ordnance.

Imogene and *Andromache* carried forty-six guns between them, of which the largest were 32-pounders. As the varying wind shifted north, obliging the frigates to tack, the Chinese in Fort Wantong on the west bank and Fort Amunghoi on the east, opened up with blank shots, as a warning. When the frigates took no notice of their blanks, the Chinese fired shot: the forts mounted about sixty guns. Lord Napier's orders had been for the Chinese fire to be returned. From 1.16 p.m. to 2.05 p.m. expert gun-crews in the frigates hammered the two forts until they were knocked out, and then sailed on upriver.

The cutter *Louisa* also came under Chinese fire, but Captain Charles Elliot, Lord Napier's 33-year-old Captain Attendant, gave a memorable example of British phlegm by sitting under a large umbrella in the stern, very conspicuous, and taking no notice whatever. Elliot, a grandson of Lord Minto, had previously encountered the crash of cannon and the smell of powder during boyhood. Elliot served as a 15-year-old midshipman in the 74-gun ship-of-the-line *Minden*, at the time of Lord Exmouth's notorious peacetime bombardment of Algiers in 1816, when an Anglo-Dutch battlefleet discouraged the Algerians from piracy by dropping 49 815 rounds of shot on a Moslem city crammed with civilians – Elliot's own ship firing 4710 rounds. There had been nothing like those minatory broadsides in all history. By comparison, this brief peppering of Chinese forts must have been a jaunt for Captain Elliot.

At 2.20 p.m. a fort higher up the river, on Tiger Island, opened fire at 200 yards, but was silenced by a close-range answering fire from the frigates so accurate that many cannon-balls actually entered the embrasures and knocked over the Chinese gun-crews. In the Battle of the Bogue, as this unequal encounter was called, two British seamen were killed, and five wounded. *Imogene* and *Andromache*, again delayed by calms, reached Whampoa at 7.15 p.m. of 11 September.

Meanwhile, blockaded though they were by the Chinese authorities, the hardships in the English Factory were not in fact very great. Left without servants, the merchants and their clerks were managing to picnic on eggs and vegetables, fowls and bread, sold by amiable Chinese shopkeepers who, for excessively high prices, would defy the official ban. The Chinese pressure was sagaciously moderate – little more than inconvenience – but it was having its effect.

September in Canton is hot as well as humid – averaging 83°F at noon and 76°F at night. Feverishly – perhaps in real fever –

Lord Napier, when he heard the Bogue Forts had dared to open fire on his ships, again raised his voice against Viceroy Lu K'un. 'It is a very serious offence to fire on or otherwise insult the British flag ... they have opened the preliminaries of war ... there are two frigates now in the river, bearing very heavy guns, for the express purpose of protecting the British trade.' But was this the real position?

Though Lord Napier had claimed to act as he did with the motive of protecting 'the treasure of the East India Company' – a mass of silver, still in the Canton Factory, waiting for accounts to be closed – the Company's officials reported later, to London, that the treasure was never in any danger, and that if their opinion of bringing up the frigates had been asked, they would have advised against.

And what does he want to protect British traders from? mildly inquired Lu K'un. Have they not always lived in security? 'If the said Barbarian Eye will speedily ... withdraw his ships of war and remain obedient to the old rules', promised Lu, who was ready to call Lord Napier's bluff, 'I will yet give some slight indulgence.'

Meanwhile the merchant community was becoming disenchanted with its Superintendent of Trade. Why, for that matter, should a free trade need superintending? Even among the opium dealers there was discontent, Lancelot Dent of Dent & Co., who were Jardine, Matheson's bitterest rivals, taking his place at the head of the opposition.

And now Lu K'un had two more hostages within the palm of his hand, though unusual ones – the frigates *Imogene* and *Andromache*, moored down at Whampoa. Ch'i Lung, Governor of Canton, had blocked the channel between their anchorage and the city with a dozen stone barges, as well as drawing a cable across from bank to bank and staking the fairway. These obstacles were guarded by a fleet of war junks. Even to send up a boat with an armed landing-party would now be hazardous. Meanwhile, at Whampoa, in clear view of the British ships, a hundred fire-rafts loaded with firewood, straw, saltpetre and sulphur had been got ready. *Imogene* and *Andromache* were wooden ships filled with gunpowder. Ostentatious preparations were also being made to block the river above its bar with stones – thus boxing up the two frigates in a twenty mile stretch of the Pearl River.

To everyone's relief, Dr T. R. Colledge, who was treating Lord Napier for an intermittent fever, took the view that his lordship's health would benefit by a return to Macao. There was still one last chance of saving Lord Napier's face – suppose he went back to Macao in a British frigate? But the Viceroy wanted the Barbarian Eye's departure from Canton to be humiliating and exemplary. After elaborate negotiations between Dr Colledge, William Jardine and the Hong merchants, a bargain was struck, and the Viceroy had much the best of it.

If Lord Napier would order his frigates to proceed to the opium smugglers' base at Lintin – thus implying that the Royal Navy had arrived to defend the drug traffic – his lordship might be allowed to apply for a red permit to go down to Macao. But in a Chinese boat, and under Chinese escort. There was no alternative.

So, to the exultant clash of gongs and the bang of firecrackers, the sick peer was slowly taken down to Macao under military guard – precisely in the manner used by Chinese to convey criminals. The eighty-eight-mile journey took five days. In Macao, on his sickbed, the noise of church bells got on Lord Napier's nerves. During the night of 11 October, when the Portuguese had obligingly stopped ringing their bells on his account, he died.

After the dust had settled, William Jardine collected eighty-four signatures for a petition to King William IV from merchants who had given their support to an aggressive policy. The petition claimed simply that Lord Napier had not been backed by enough force. Next time, a plenipotentiary should be sent in a ship-of-the-line, with two frigates, and some sloops. An expedition like this, if the need arose, could put troops ashore, and make a direct threat to Peking.

The Chinese authorities for their part asked for a commercial man to be appointed next. 'This is an affair', they said, 'of buying and selling; it is not what officers can attend to.' Lord Napier was replaced by John Francis Davis, an old East India Company hand and a proficient Chinese scholar, who had been in Peking with Lord Amherst. Davis disliked the aggressive free-traders quite as much as they despised him; he believed in attending to business, and keeping quiet. But the quiet days were over, and Davis soon went home, being replaced early in 1835, by Sir George Robinson, who shared his views.

The Duke of Wellington had dismissed Napier's Fizzle, as it was soon nicknamed, in these measured words: '. . . the attempt to force upon the Chinese authorities at Canton an unaccustomed mode of communication with an authority of whose powers and of whose nature they had no knowledge had failed . . . as it is obvious that . . . such an attempt must invariably fail, and lead again to national disgrace.'

A conflict over British policy had now been stated, the Duke of Wellington representing an old-fashioned view that opium-smuggling might disturb other British interests and that the main job of the Superintendent of Trade should be to keep the smugglers well under control. Sir George Robinson set up his office, aboard the cutter *Louisa*, actually at the smuggling depot of Lintin. But his powers were undefined, and gave him no scope for effective action against the drug traffickers.

Lord Palmerston, the spokesman for a vigorous policy which might open up the Chinese market to British trade, was out of office from November 1834 to April 1835. When he did get back to the Foreign Office, Sir George Robinson applied for orders authorizing him to prevent British vessels from engaging in the opium trade, but of course they never arrived.

In February 1836 Robinson went so far as to suggest that 'a more certain method would be to prohibit the growth of the poppy and manufacture of opium in British India'. In a despatch of June 1836, Sir George got his reward – he was sacked, and replaced by Captain Charles Elliot RN, who had all this time been keeping Lord Palmerston privately informed about matters in Canton through a personal friend of his at the Foreign Office called Lennox Conyngham.

Napier's Fizzle also misled the Chinese, making it seem as if their traditional methods were sure to triumph, now as in the past. Fire-rafts, for example, had been a tactic used as long ago as A.D. 208 in a famous battle on the Yangtse. They were expounded in a standard Chinese military textbook, *The Essentials of Fire Raft Attack* dating back to 1412. Against wooden ships in a closed anchorage they had this time been an effective threat, but on the high seas the frigates would have had nothing whatever to fear.

Despite the clever way Lord Napier had been cornered, Chinese weakness was real. Against a seaborne attack such as Jardine recommended, China had no real military answer. If the free-traders could turn public opinion in their favour so that a majority in Parliament would accept without demur a suitable pretext for war on China, then the war Jardine advocated might be brought about.

James Matheson made his way back to Britain in the ship that carried the widowed Lady Napier and her daughters, with the plan of erecting a statue to the late Lord Napier – his lordship might not have been wholly satisfactory as hero and martyr, but he was better than none. Matheson also wanted to test what support might be drummed up in political circles for an extreme policy of aggression in China. The Napier fiasco, however, was too recent a memory.

Confidentially, James Matheson reported to his partner in Canton that the Duke of Wellington was 'a cold-blooded fellow ... a strenuous advocate of submissiveness and servility'. Even Lord Palmerston was not enough of a fire-eater for Matheson's liking. 'The fact is, Jardine', James Matheson wrote sadly, '...so long as domestic affairs, including markets, go right, they cannot really be brought to think of us as outlanders. Lord Palmerston means to do nothing.'

In London, Matheson published a tract, *The Present Position and Future Prospects of the China Trade*, which became a guiding light to all those merchants who were confident that China, when opened to trade, would be another huge market for cotton goods. Matheson, in his pamphlet, gives us a glimpse of his inner state of mind when he attributes Chinese dislike of free trade to their 'marvellous degree of imbecility and avarice, conceit and obstinacy'. By January 1839, James Matheson was once more back again in China, face to face with these oriental shortcomings.

William Jardine had carried on the drug business at Canton in Matheson's absence – as well as taking office as Vice-President of the Medical Missionary Society. Jardine decided to return to Britain and develop the political support Matheson had tried to arouse. John Abel Smith, the radical banker – another man whose subsequent political renown rests chiefly on his desire to stamp out drunkenness among the working classes – had for some years done Jardine, Matheson & Co.'s banking business in London, at Magniac Smith & Co., 3 Lombard Street. Abel Smith was MP for Chichester, and a crony of Palmerston's. Jardine bought a partnership in his banking house, and in due time a seat in Parliament was found for him without much difficulty, as member for Ashburton. Disraeli's novel *Sybil* gives a brief glimpse of the impression this radical drug-trafficker's rapid political rise made on his Tory critics:

'You had a formidable opponent, Lord Marney told me,' said Sir Vavasour, 'who was he?'
'Oh, a dreadful man! A scotchman, richer than Croesus, one Mr Druggy, fresh from Canton, with a million in opium in each pocket, denouncing corruption and bellowing free-trade.'

The offices at Canton of D. W. C. Olyphant – the one American merchant who always refused to handle opium – were known as Zion's Corner. Olyphant was well known for his readiness to give American missionaries free passages to China. Others might cruise

the China coast in armed opium clippers, to bully or bribe mandarins into complicity. In 1835 Olyphant decided to send his brig
Huron north to Shantung, with a cargo of religious literature. On
board was W. H. Medhurst, of the London Missionary Society, who
spoke the Shantung dialect. The Chinese there turned out, however,
to be in no mood for making fine distinctions. Red barbarians were
red barbarians. Off Shanghai, *Huron* was harassed by war junks,
sent after her by local mandarins exactly as if she had been an
opium smuggler.

The East India Company, being more concerned with shipping
tea than with saving souls, had in their heyday made things
awkward for missionaries. Robert Morrison, a Presbyterian from
Northumberland, had the honour of being the first Protestant
missionary to arrive in China. Though British, Morrison had
been forced to cross the Atlantic to New York, and take a passage
to China in a Yankee clipper; he reached Canton in 1807. Because
of Company hostility Morrison felt obliged at first to pass himself
off as an American. In 1809 he got a more secure footing by
becoming official translator to the East India Company; his salary
rose to £1000 a year.

A Chinese who taught his language to a foreigner was liable to
the penalty of death, so a competent linguist was a valuable man.
Everyday business was done in pidgin English – a curious and
comic lingo, wherein a vocabulary of English, Portuguese and
Indian words was put together as if forming a dialect of Chinese.
But pidgin English served its turn so well that Americans had been
buying and selling in China for all of forty-five years before the
first among them managed to master Chinese.

Rev. Robert Morrison spent more of his time as a scholar than
as a pastor – he compiled a Chinese dictionary, which was printed
at Company expense, and translated the Bible. Even so, by 1832,
a Protestant mission had been working in China for twenty-five
years, yet altogether had managed to baptize only sixteen Chinese.

Americans were more numerous than Britons as Protestant
missionaries, though their slice of the trade was much less. The
French, whose trade was negligible, got a toe in the door soon after
by asserting a right to protect the Roman Catholic community in
China, then about 200 000 strong.

Roman Catholicism had been the one version of Christianity to
strike native roots in China, though for more than a century
Roman Catholics had lived there under an official ban, and been
given little help from outside. Between 1784 and 1820, only
twenty-eight Catholic priests arrived in China, half of them re-

maining at Macao. Chinese priests had stepped into the breach: there were eighty of them at work by 1810.

Jesuit missionaries first reached Peking in 1601. The Jesuits rapidly gained acceptance for themselves in high official circles, and in a most extraordinary way.

For ritual reasons – to maintain harmony between society and nature – the people of China needed a calendar which would tell them the lucky dates for important events in their lives, such as marriage, or planting a new crop. Because the best calendar the Manchus knew how to produce was full of mistakes, public confidence in the dynasty was failing. Something had to be done to improve the calendar – but how?

The Mongols in their day had reformed the Chinese calendar with the help of classical Ptolemaic astronomy, which they learned from the Arabs. Under the Ming dynasty a number of necessary instruments – astrolabes, a gnomon, an armillary sphere, all specially constructed for the site where they were to be used – had been shifted bodily from the Mongol college at P'ing-yang, in Shansi, about 36°N, and taken to Nanking about 32°N, where of course the difference in latitude made them useless. The necessary knowledge was forgotten.

Father Mateo Ricci, the first Jesuit to make his mark in China, was like many of his Order a good mathematician and a competent master of the new Copernican astronomy. He recognized for what they were the ancient instruments which had stood useless in Nanking for two centuries. He was invited to reform the Chinese calendar. From then on, the specialized help that European mathematics could give the court of Peking was a political necessity.

Father Ricci also drew for the Chinese a world map (which, tactfully, showed China at the very centre) and the Jesuits carried out the first accurate Chinese land-surveys. Father Ferdinand Verbiest, SJ, after serving as director of the Astronomical Bureau, was created Master of the Ordnance. He cast European cannon to be used against rebels, naming them after Christian saints, and blessing them with holy water. The Jesuits designed a gorgeous baroque villa for the grounds of the Emperor's Summer Palace outside Peking. They anticipated Chinnery in bringing the techniques and discoveries of European painting to China. Jesuit success at court was for some years phenomenal. They made themselves indispensable in all these practical matters, and, meanwhile, conversions and missionary work were tactfully persisted in. At the high point of Jesuit influence, the Emperor

K'an Si went so far as to suggest that he might as well take one of the Pope's nieces as a concubine.

It was too good to last. By the early eighteenth century, complaints were reaching Rome that a number of the compromises with Chinese tradition the Jesuits made for tactical reasons were going too far. There were also theological objections to the Jesuit habit of financing their mission by money-lending at 24 per cent (though it must be noted that the current Chinese rate for ready money was 30 per cent). And the Manchus themselves were becoming dubious of these talented foreigners. In the face of the modern world, the dynasty was already becoming conservative. Might not any innovation – and Christianity was a radical innovation – turn out to be dangerous?

It had been an astounding century in China – but Jesuit influence at court after 1711 was not enough to protect the thousands of Chinese who had adopted Christianity, and in 1724 the Christian religion was officially suppressed by the Board of Rites. But police power in old China was never wholly effective. Dressed as merchants and living in great danger, the foreign priests continued to travel vast distances across China, and to serve their flocks. In conditions of illegality, they organized schools and seminaries. Though declining in numbers, and perhaps in clarity of faith, these scattered Roman Catholic communities had managed to survive, almost cut off from Christendom, until Anglo-Saxon traders came thundering, gun in hand, at China's door. The Chinese Roman Catholics then found themselves becoming a serviceable pretext for foreign intervention. The last European priest to serve the Emperor's Board of Astronomy, Father Pires, died in Peking as late as 1838, just before the opening shots were fired in the first Opium War.

As a young Christian who had made up his mind to reach China, Robert Morrison began studying Chinese in the British Museum in 1804, from a passage of Scripture the Jesuits had translated. The Jesuit Fathers acquired a masterly understanding of both Chinese literature and Chinese psychology, but later Protestant translations of Holy Writ – and they were many – must greatly have confused the mind of any benevolently inquiring Chinese. There was, first and foremost, the vexatious problem of how to name God – an idea not easy to grasp in its Christian formulation in China. The Jesuits had been in the habit of using an expression they found acceptable in the north: T'ien Chu – T'ien signifying Heaven. British translators, based on Canton, rejected T'ien Chu for the term Shang Ti, signifying Emperor Above.

A number of American Protestants decided, for good reasons of their own, to employ yet a third expression for the name of God, Shen. Other terms plumped for by different Protestant sects were apparently T'ien, Shang Chu, Chu, and Shen Ming. One Anglican bishop in south China multiplied the confusion by deciding that, after all, the old Jesuit expression was the best. (He also wanted to replace bread and wine in the Sacrament by rice and tea.)

A similar awkwardness arose about finding an expression in Chinese for the Holy Ghost which might stand a reasonable chance of being understood. Eventually, a compromise was reached. After an enormous sum of money had been subscribed by hopeful Protestants for a Chinese New Testament in a cheap edition of a million copies, blanks were left where the Greek original said $\Theta\epsilon\acute{o}s$ or $\Pi\nu\epsilon\hat{v}\mu\alpha$ so that missionaries of the various denominations could write in the missing words, as they saw fit.

Though to begin with each depended in certain obvious ways on the other, Protestant missionaries and the Anglo-Saxon merchant community parted company over two questions of moral conduct. Missionaries, understandably enough, objected to a habit that had become general among the traders of keeping a Chinese girl as a mistress. (A one-time partner of Jardine's, Daniel Magniac, was retired from his firm on a small pension in the 1820s, not, indeed, for living with an Asiatic mistress – who had in point of fact given him two children – but for going so far amiss as to marry her.) Missionary education of Chinese girls became a waste of time, for no sooner had a bright girl acquired enough English in school to make herself understood than a merchant would come along, and snap her up as his mistress.

And most missionaries, to their eternal credit, came out in the end against opium. Though Protestant converts long continued to be embarrassingly few, in proportion to the money and effort applied, a high proportion of them were former opium addicts, who had accepted Christian conversion as an escape route. Medical missionaries also worked hard to find a therapy for opium addiction.

In earlier days however, it was not ruled out for missionary and opium smuggler to work hand in hand.

In 1827 the Netherlands Missionary Society sent a young Prussian called Karl Gutzlaff, a former corset-maker, to Siam.

From Chinese settlers there he managed to learn the Fukien dialect, and in 1829 at Malacca he married an English heiress. She died shortly afterwards, so that when his missionary society declined to send him on to China, Gutzlaff was able to hire a junk, and proceed there at his own expense.

The Rev. Dr Gutzlaff established himself in Macao in a large rambling house, where his second wife, Mary Wanstell, a teacher, ran a home for blind Chinese children. Her husband made bold excursions up the coast and some distance inland, distributing tracts, ointment, Cockle's Pills, and his own rather ham-fisted version of the Bible. He is described as a short, squat man, wearing shapeless clothes, his big face usually covered by a large straw hat, and his eyes swivelling rather than looking directly at an interrogator. His teutonic claims to omniscience appear to have irritated everyone, and his medical skill was described by a qualified surgeon as being 'of the most moderate character'. But though Gutzlaff was evidently not the scholar he would have liked to be, he was certainly fluent in several dialects of Chinese, and was therefore, in Canton, a rare bird.

In 1832 William Jardine wrote to invite Karl Gutzlaff up the coast in his clipper *Sylph*. Jardine was frank. 'Our principle reliance', he admitted, 'is on opium...by many considered an immoral traffic, yet such traffic is so absolutely necessary to give any vessel a reasonable chance of defraying her expenses that we trust you may have no objection to interpret on every occasion when your services may be required ... The more profitable the expedition, the better we shall be able to place at your disposal a sum that may be hereafter employed in furthering your mission.' Jardine then offered to guarantee, for six months, the printing of Gutzlaff's magazine, in Chinese.

'After much consultation with others, and a conflict in my own mind', admitted Gutzlaff, with an almost audible gulp, 'I embarked on the *Sylph*.'

The Jardine, Matheson clipper on this venture took opium 1600 miles up the coast, right into the Gulf of Pechili, almost at the northern borders of China, and as close as any seaborne trader could get to the gates of Peking. Opium-smokers had once again been discovered among the men of the Imperial Guard: the vice had become established in the administrative heart of the Empire.

Four months later – and, let us hope, only after another wrestle with his conscience – Gutzlaff was out again, this time in *John Biggar*, expostulating in fluent Chinese with local mandarins who were bringing out war junks to stop the opium trade in

Chinchow Bay (Ch'uan-chou), north of Amoy and 400 miles distant from Macao.

Captain William McKay, arriving back from the cruise with silver worth £53 000 under *John Biggar*'s hatches, reported, 'I have received much assistance from Dr Gutzlaff ... The trade in Ch'uan-chou may now be considered to be placed on a firm footing, although the mandarins may occasionally make difficulties.' Jardine, Matheson & Co., in a syndicate with Dent & Co., were soon offering to pay the authorities at Ch'uan-chou a bribe of $20 000 a year, in exchange for the sole right to sell opium there.

In the autumn of 1835 the Cantonese spoke with awed curiosity of 'a cartwheel ship, that put axles in motion by means of fire'. This steamer, *Jardine* (58 tons), had been built in Aberdeen, and was intended for carrying mails between Macao and Canton.

She arrived at Macao on 25 September under sail, but after an engine had been installed her trials proved successful, and on 1 January 1836 she steamed into the mouth of the Pearl River for her first trip up to Canton. The forts at Chuenpi fired blank shots at *Jardine*, and the unnerving little vessel with her draught of only six feet hove to. The Chinese admiral came off with an escort of 100 men to inspect the 'cartwheel ship'. He got *Jardine* to tow his junk back and forth, was delighted with her performance and said that personally he was willing to let her proceed upriver. But his instructions from the Viceroy were strict. Sir George Robinson gave orders forbidding the use of the steamer on the Pearl River (this earned him a stinging rebuke from Lord Palmerston). The machinery was taken out of her, but *Jardine* was a portent.

Mount a gun in a small steamer, and for the first time in history you had a ship-of-war independent of wind and tide, able to beat against the monsoon, and to operate effectively up rivers and in shallow coastal waters. Against this technically advanced weapon of war the Chinese in coming years would have no possible means of defence. The age of gunboat diplomacy was soon to begin.

3 Commissioner Lin

'They had seen it asserted, over and over again, that the Government was advocating the cause of the contraband trade, in order to force an opium war on the public; but he thought it impossible to be conceived that a thought so absurd and atrocious should have entered the minds of the British Ministry.'

Thomas Babington Macaulay, Secretary for War, in the Parliamentary Debate of 7 April 1840

Captain Charles Elliot, RN, who in December 1836 stepped into Sir George Robinson's shoes as Superintendent of Trade at £6000 a year, was by ancestry another Scot – but one more sensitive and conscience-stricken than the hardbitten Calvinists who ran the opium trade in Canton. Captain Elliot liked to spend his spare time painting water-colours. Hot-headed, and given in a crisis to boyish displays of personal courage, Elliot never hid his distaste for the drug traffic. The smugglers disliked him too, though, in obedience to the policy laid down by Lord Palmerston, Elliot did his duty by them.

As a boy of 14, Elliot had volunteered for the Royal Navy. The Napoleonic Wars were nearly over, but family connections – his uncle, Lord Minto, became a Governor-General of India – helped him along in a peacetime naval career when many veterans were on the beach. Great Britain had taken upon herself the unpopular role of the world's policeman, using the Royal Navy for the job. After helping to bombard Algiers in 1816, and free the Christian prisoners there, young Elliot found himself putting down piracy in the Persian Gulf, and harassing slavers on the West African coast and the Bahama Cays before his retirement in 1828 with the rank of Captain.

Lord Howick, the Under-Secretary for the Colonies, was Captain Elliot's intimate friend, and not long after found him a post in British Guiana, as a member of the government, with the title of Protector of Slaves.

There was still slavery in British colonies – though trading in slaves had been forbidden since 1807. The job of officials like Charles Elliot was to make sure that slaves were accorded their legal due by the plantation owners. Elliot did his new job fearlessly, though he worried at times about the consequences. ('I am desperately unpopular', he wrote home, '... this colony is in a state of rebellion.') In 1833 a reforming government ordered him back to London, where he helped prepare the British legislation which finally emancipated the slaves. Then Lord Palmerston sent Captain Elliot out to Canton, keeping him there quietly in a subordinate position until the time was right to use this young, brave, conscientious and obedient naval officer as an instrument of policy.

Elliot's official title – Superintendent of Trade – now meant little, since he had been provided with almost no authority over the turbulent free-traders in and near Canton. His prime responsibility was to make sure the tea crop was safely shipped out – while keeping in mind that tea was paid for by opium. He might not like the buccaneering way opium was brought into China, but to interfere was not his business.

The Chinese had good reasons of their own – traditional, but also tactical – for not allowing Elliot to do business directly with high officials at Canton, though this was what Lord Palmerston particularly wanted. Elliot was obliged, therefore, slowly and patiently to improve his position in the eyes of the Chinese, accepting snubs with good grace, and sending messages to high Chinese officials in the form of 'petitions' superscribed with the character *pin*. (This, though it stuck in Lord Palmerston's throat, was little more than a conventional form of respect, indicating that Elliot, a man who had not passed the Imperial examinations, was addressing someone who had.)

Soon the high officials were able to report of Captain Elliot that 'the phrasing and subject-matter of the Barbarian's addresses are reverential and submissive'. To Lennox Conyngham, his useful friend ensconced in the Foreign Office, Elliot pointed out that he had 'had a quarterdeck education, and knew how to duck his head in a storm'. The storm was certainly building up.

The year 1836 had been one of persistent rumours that the Imperial government were shortly to legalize the import of opium. Tea – said another rumour – might be bartered directly for opium, so that no silver would leave China. In terms of Confucian morality this was improper – to sanction by law something admittedly evil was an outrage – though to foreign traders the plan might sound like commonsense, and it certainly appealed to some high

Chinese officials as the easiest way out of their impasse. William Jardine, the hardest-headed man in the opium business, went on believing for years that legalization must be the favourite option of a strong party in Peking.

There was by now in Great Britain a small but vocal group – of High Church Tories, soon to be joined by Evangelicals and Non-conformists with missionary contacts – who were loud in their public denunciation of opium. A respectable word like 'legalization' might help to stop their mouths. In 1836 drug sales had fetched over £2 000 000 but of this £280 000 had been paid out in bribes. If regular Customs payments took the place of such bribes, the revenue would provide the Manchu court with a solid reason for tolerating the opium traffic, instead of harassing it with Edicts. And up inland trade routes where opium went – legally, at last – other British merchandise might follow. To Jardine, planning retirement, there was also no doubt the private hope that 'legalization' might take the stigma off the enormous fortune he was taking back home with him.

Peking had as a matter of fact considered but discarded several proposals for legalizing opium. Ignorance of each other's language and culture, and lack of diplomatic contact, sealed Chinese and British off from each other, so the foreign trading community had only a wishfully distorted idea of the debate on the drug problem which went on throughout the Chinese Empire from the middle 1830s onwards.

Hsu Nai-tsi, formerly a criminal judge at Canton, was one high Peking official to advocate legal import by barter. Hsu wanted also to encourage home-grown opium. His plan evidently was to get the narcotic under official control, so it could be effectively forbidden to civil servants and soldiers.

In May 1836 Jardine wrote optimistically to one of his captains in the coast trade, 'We have lately had a chop from the Emperor, ordering the authorities here to report on the propriety of admitting opium as an article of trade under the name of medicine – on payment of a small duty. The general opinion is in favour ...' Elliot, writing to Lord Palmerston, described Hsu's memorial as 'a public confession that the Chinese cannot do without our opium'. But the British were giving too much weight to a local man who happened to say what they wished to hear. The debate inside China was going against 'legalization'.

The new Viceroy of the Two Kwangs, who took office early in 1836 – Teng T'ing chen – was also believed to support legalization, but events proved otherwise. Teng, a cultivated man of 60, and really more interested in poetry and philology than administration, was shrewd enough to see early on which way Chinese opinion was turning. He began enforcing the law to such effect that the customary bribe of thirty dollars to get a chest of opium ashore at Canton doubled to over sixty dollars. In December 1836 Teng issued a public leaflet headed, 'The smoke of opium is a deadly poison', having already arraigned nine notorious foreign opium dealers – seven British, including Jardine, one American called Whiteman, and one Parsee. They were peremptorily ordered to leave China. No doubt all this zeal was well regarded in Peking, though three years later at least six of the nine were still in Canton, and merrily trading. But real trouble was coming.

The Manchus, always well aware of being a foreign minority of three million imposing their will on hundreds of millions of Chinese, put the safety of their dynasty before everything. They had woken up fully to the opium menace by 1832, when a secret society known as the Triads, powerful in and around Canton, had put up as rival to the Manchu Emperor a pretender called the Golden Dragon King. The rebels managed to defeat an army sent against them by the Viceroy of the Two Kwangs, because government troops were disheartened when rain stopped them lighting their opium pipes for a whiff of Dutch courage before they went in to attack. If the army failed, the dynasty was lost. The Viceroy responsible was exiled to Urumchi in Central Asia, and the use of opium by the army was again severely punished.

Expenditure on wars against rebels, combined with the drain of silver, were also fast emptying the Manchu treasury. When Lord Macartney visited Peking, the Imperial treasure house had held seventy million taels of silver. By 1820 this silver reserve was reduced to little more than ten million taels, and the export of silver during the 1830s was four times what it had been in the 1820s.

Chinese and foreigners alike were beginning to agree that the total of opium addicts – usually men between 20 and 55 – was also by now to be reckoned in millions. The Viceroy of Hupeh and Hunan estimated in 1838 that there must be over four million opium addicts. Another Chinese scholar reckoned that the 40 000 chests due to enter China that same year would supply eight and a half million smokers. Toogood Downing, a well-informed English physician with experience in Canton, had calculated two years before that the quantity of opium imported in 1836 would make when prepared for smoking about 33 200 000 taels of mixture, enough for the needs of 12 500 000 smokers. The figures differ but the emphasis is clear: free trade was spreading opium addiction through China like a plague.

High officials debated what should be done, in the traditional form of memorials to the Emperor. Chu Tsun, Vice-President of the Board of Rites, doubted if China could now supply enough tea to match the vast opium import. If barter was therefore impractical, why not simply stop the drug coming in? 'If it is possible to prevent the exportation of dollars, how can it be impossible', he wrote, 'to prevent the importation of opium?' Lin Tse-hsu, who had made his own calculation of the number of addicts, put the Chinese predicament to the Emperor in a nutshell: '... a few decades from now we shall not only be without soldiers to resist the enemy, but also in want of silver to provide an army.'

'Let the law concentrate, and hit hard at the wealthy and powerful', echoed Viceroy Teng from Canton. By November 1836 the Imperial government finally decided, not to legalize opium, as Jardine and others had been hopefully supposing, but to suppress it altogether. Technically the task would not be easy.

Lintin Island, though legally Chinese soil, was beyond Chinese control. Since 1830, the number of receiving ships finding permanent sanctuary there had increased from five to twenty-five, and the Chinese had no naval force effective enough to shift them.

Teng struck hard at the one link in the smuggling chain that was within his reach – the fast armed galleys which ran the drug from receiving ships to the creek villages around the Bay of Canton. They were Chinese-owned and operated from shore: early in 1837 they were all destroyed.

During the south-west monsoon, when the anchorage at Lintin was unsafe, the receiving ships would shift to shelter in Kam-sing-moon, a bay north of Macao and west of Lintin. In the winter of 1836 Teng had a battery built on shore to command Kam-sing-moon. When the monsoon began, in April, the depot ships had to stay bottled up at Lintin – safe from Chinese guns, if not from the weather.

Elliot was quick to see the coming danger. He warned London on 2 February 1837, 'From a trade prohibited in point of form, but essentially countenanced, and carried on entirely by natives in native boats, it will come to be a complete smuggling trade.' To Lord Auckland, Governor-General of India, he at once wrote, though perhaps in wrong-headed terms, for help from the Royal

67

Navy, arguing that '... visits of men-of-war at this crisis ... would have the effect either of relaxing the restrictive spirit of the Provincial Government, or of hastening onwards the legalization measure, and thus ... releasing the trade from its actual condition of stagnation'. There had been brief repressive campaigns before, but they had always petered out. How was anyone to know that this one would be different?

The difficulty of landing opium and the accumulation of supplies at Lintin and elsewhere caused the price to fall dramatically. At the end of 1837 Patna opium was down to $620 a chest, and by February 1838 a chest of new season's Patna had sunk to the record low of $450. In June 1837 Jardine, Matheson wrote to inform a correspondent: 'We are doing everything in our power to work the article off on the coast and among the islands in European boats.' This renewed push up the coast led at times to armed conflicts. In one 'severe battle' between Chinese war junks and an opium schooner several men were killed – but a cargo of 100 chests of opium was successfully destroyed. By November 1837 Jardine, Matheson were obliged to report that 'the drug market is getting worse every day, owing to the extreme vigilance of the authorities.' The firm sent all the armed schooners they could spare along the coast of Kwangtung and Fukien, and tried to get a footing on Formosa, where the Dutch had introduced opium 150 years before. Elliot reported to the Foreign Office in November that latterly there had never been less than twenty opium ships along the coast, forcing a trade, and added, 'There is every reason to believe blood has been spilt.'

If a display of armed force was effective along the coast, why not use armed British boats in Canton Bay itself and even up the Pearl River? This dangerous experiment was begun by a devout, Bible-reading Scot called James Innes – eccentric, tough, and one of the dealers named in Viceroy Teng's original expulsion order.

Innes, a 'licensed trader' in East India Company days, had often been in trouble before, both with the Company and the Chinese. He was an old hand in the coast trade, combining opium traffic at Fukien with the free distribution to the Chinese there of pious Christian tracts. From *Colonel Young*, the first receiving ship to be stationed actually off the coast, her cargo replenished by *Fairy*, a tender going back and forth to Lintin, Innes was reputed in 1831 to have brought back a third of a million dollars.

During 1833 a servant of the Hoppo – the Manchu head of Chinese Customs, and the second most important man in Canton –

had gone so far as to threaten Innes with a wooden chopper. Innes announced that unless his assailant were arrested before sunset he would take his own revenge by burning the Hoppo's roof over his head. This was no rhetorical threat. Innes arrived on the scene, as the sun went down, with Congreve rockets and blue lights, and proceeded to fire them off at the Hoppo's mansion. Even Lord Palmerston found that hard to swallow – 'tantamount', he remarked severely, 'to piracy' – but Lord Napier spoke up for Innes: 'success', he commented, 'has always attended determination'.

Now James Innes was not merely running opium into Canton Bay, but taking it past the guns of the Bogue Forts right up the Pearl River to Whampoa – in a ship's cutter, flying the Union Jack, and manned with armed lascars. The great opium houses of Jardine, Matheson & Co. and Dent & Co. – who between them accounted for half the trade in the drug – had the resources that smaller men lacked for putting a fleet of armed sailing boats on the Pearl River. The big operators were soon able to pocket the price differential – sometimes as high as seventy dollars a chest – between Lintin and Whampoa which formerly had gone to the Chinese, who manned the rowing galleys. Opium was at times being run in European boats to the very walls of Canton. 'All this is tolerated', wrote Matheson jubilantly, in January 1838, 'only on account of the Viceroy being afraid to interfere with the property of foreigners.'

By July, the naval vessels Captain Elliot had asked for arrived from India – HMS *Wellesley*, a ship-of-the-line, with Admiral F. L. Maitland aboard, in company with a brig, HMS *Algerine*. Viceroy Teng began to patrol the waterways leading to Canton with war junks, and to reinforce the Bogue Forts. Elliot had hoped that the presence of a battleship might intimidate the Chinese at least into accepting a direct communication from him on equal terms, instead of a petition. But the Chinese were in no mood to budge – even over a matter of form.

The usual oriental comedy was played out. A few days after Admiral Maitland dropped anchor, Elliot received from the Chinese mandarin at Macao a document marked with the character *yu*, signifying 'command'. Guessing this must contain an order for *Wellesley* and *Algerine* to leave Chinese waters, Elliot protested against the improper superscription and returned the paper unread. The British warships, as it so happened, had strict orders against the use of force, except in case of extreme necessity – had they not merely been brought here to give silent encouragement to 'legalization'?

Captain Elliot went up to Canton to account in reassuring terms for their presence. His interpreter delivered at the city gate a conciliatory letter to Viceroy Teng. That evening, through the Hong merchants, that paper too was returned unread: it had lacked the superscription *pin*. Diplomatic communication between British and Chinese was wearing very thin. In October 1838, after Admiral Maitland had gracefully presented his Chinese opposite number, Admiral Kuan, with some bottles of a good wine, the British warships left. Silent threats were evidently not going to deflect the Chinese from their campaign against opium.

Early in December 1838, panic spread in Canton among the *han-chien*, or 'treacherous evil-doers' – those Chinese who kept up connections with foreign opium merchants. In one swoop, over two thousand Cantonese opium brokers, pushers and notorious addicts were arrested. At the same time, all over the Empire, known opium-smokers were arrested. 'Not an opium pipe to be seen, not a retail vendor of the drug', mourned William Jardine. Of Viceroy Teng, he wrote, 'he has been seizing, trying and strangling the poor devils, without mercy ... We have never seen so serious a persecution, or one so general.'

James Innes operated his business from an office in the Creek Factory at Canton which was also Jardine, Matheson & Co.'s headquarters. On 3 December 1838 a Chinese Customs official seized on the waterfront near these premises a consignment of boxes containing the equivalent of two chests of opium, which had just come upriver in a ship's boat.

The two Chinese labourers unloading the boxes were arrested and made to confess that the drug belonged to Innes, and had come from the foreign ship *Ki-le-wun*. No foreign ship on the river bore any such name, but a captain called Cleveland had brought the American merchantman *Thomas Perkins* into Whampoa, and that was near enough. Both Innes and the American ship were given three days to leave. An expulsion order had been outstanding against James Innes for the past couple of years, but Innes being the man he was refused to budge an inch.

The Hong merchants were owners of the Creek Factory. They threatened, no doubt under official pressure, to tear the roof down: tit for tat. The foreign community at first supported Innes, but when Viceroy Teng extended Innes' time of grace to ten days, at the same time stopping all trade, their solidarity began to hurt their pockets.

Innes agreed to leave by 16 December, sending Viceroy Teng a statement which cleared Captain Cleveland and the two Chinese

labourers – but he simply went down to Macao and ran his smuggling business from there. Captain Elliot, in the hope this might
improve his standing with the Chinese, agreed later to write at
their bidding to the Portuguese Governor of Macao, asking him
to expel Innes. The unquenchable James Innes retorted that his
opium bore the mark of the East India Company, it was specially
prepared for the Chinese, and he was therefore merely assisting
the British government. Of course, when it came down to brass
tacks, he was right. No civilized relationship with China, formal
or informal, could ever be established so long as the British government secretly condoned the forcing on China of a drug that the
Chinese themselves had by now made up their minds to keep out.
Captain Elliot was the man in the middle. He might privately
detest the opium trade, but officially he dare not act in concert
with the Chinese to abolish or even seriously to hinder it; and this
he knew.

After Innes had left, but before trade was reopened, Viceroy
Teng did his best to give the foreign opium dealers an object
lesson. About 11 a.m. on 12 December a Chinese official came into
the exercise yard outside the Factories at Canton, and his men
erected one of the execution crosses to which criminals in China
were tied when put to death by strangulation. (Of the two current
forms of capital punishment in China, strangulation was regarded
as less shameful than beheading.)

The sentence on Ho Lao-chin, condemned to death for keeping
an opium den, was to be carried out in full view of the foreigners
who had supplied his stock-in-trade. The intention, as Viceroy
Teng put it, was 'to arouse reflection, that the depraved portion of
the foreign community might be deterred from pursuing their
evil courses; for those foreigners, though born and brought up
beyond the pale of civilization, have human hearts'.

The execution cross happened to have been driven into the
ground directly under the 100 ft flagstaff which bore the Stars
and Stripes. The flag was run down by the US Consul, and an
indignant crowd of about eighty foreigners soon forgathered. Ho
Lao-chin arrived, an iron chain hung round his neck. The on-
lookers noticed the mandarin's servant give the condemned man
one last and merciful pipe of opium: meticulous consistency was
never a Chinese virtue. Ho's outstretched arms were about to be
lashed to the cross when up came a crowd of seamen from the
former Indiaman, *Orwell*, on shore leave and ready for any mischief.

The Jack Tars in no time smashed up the execution cross, and
then began laying about them at the nearest Chinese heads with

broken chunks of it, one of them exclaiming, 'I say, Bill, we don't get such a lark as this every day!' With help from a few of the foreign merchants, the mandarin hustled away his prisoner. A Chinese crowd had also, of course, gathered, and were watching the knockabout amiably, until some of the younger foreigners, brandishing their walking sticks, began trying to 'clear the square'.

Then the trouble began. The Chinese mob started throwing stones. The seamen riposted with broken bottles, a missile never popular with barefoot Cantonese. The merchants retreated hastily towards the cover of the Factory buildings, and soon were besieged there. By now the Chinese crowd numbered about 8000. Some of the more hot-headed foreigners were looking around, inside, for weapons, and there was talk of an armed sortie, when two young Americans, William Hunter and Gideon Nye Jr, decided they had had enough.

They clambered over the Factory roofs to Hog Lane, and thence to the warehouse of Howqua, the senior Hong merchant – an influential and genial old man, reputed to have accumulated £5 000 000 in foreign trade. Howqua liked trading with Americans, whose freewheeling methods he delighted to copy, and knew very well that he might be made personally responsible for the riot, so he got a message off to the Governor of Canton. By six in the evening the clash of gongs warned the rioters that mandarins were coming. Chinese police appeared, whip in hand; some of the mob panicked across the wharf and fell into the river, the rest quickly dispersed into the night. The trouble was over.

Captain Elliot, ten miles downriver at Whampoa, who got news of the riot at four that afternoon, had risen to the occasion dramatically – as he generally did – by organizing an armed landing-party to follow him to Canton. He put his men under the command of Captain Marquis of *Reliance*, and set off ahead. Luckily for everyone, Captain Elliot reached Canton too late; the violence was over.

Though Innes had been sent out of Canton, armed foreign boats continued bringing opium up the Pearl River, and the Hong merchants refused to carry on trade until they were stopped. The tea trade was at a standstill, and, as Captain Elliot reported, 'within the space of one year ... there would have been at least three hundred armed and lawless men carrying on this business in the very heart of our regular commerce'.

Since armed boats were their best way of keeping the opium business alive, the smugglers at first ignored Elliot's written warning. On 23 December 1839 Elliot communicated directly with Viceroy Teng, proposing Chinese cooperation in clearing the smugglers out of the river. Teng decided not to stand on ceremony this time, since the Superintendent of Trade was for once helping to enforce Chinese law. Elliot went to Whampoa and, with the backing of Chinese officials, got his prohibition enforced. By 31 December he reported that all British opium boats were gone from Whampoa, and on New Year's Day trade was resumed.

On the same day William Jardine made a thoughtful appraisal of his business. This anti-opium campaign had spread to every province of the Chinese Empire, and Jardine gave it as his considered opinion that if the campaign were kept up for another twelve months, opium consumption was likely to decline by two-thirds. His armed boats had been forced out of the river, and even the coastal trade was failing to produce results, Jardine, Matheson & Co.'s captains reporting that 'every part of the coast had been visited by vessels with opium, but without any success worth mentioning'. By the end of January, Captain Elliot was obliged to inform London that 'the stagnation of the opium traffic ... may be said to have been nearly complete for the last four months'.

The subsidized poppy fields of India, however, went on producing opium by the ton. Three years before, Indian opium shipments to China had been more than 30 000 chests for the first time. In this coming year of 1839 shipments were to exceed 40 000 chests. But, as production soared, the big market was fast disappearing. Had opium really been a 'free trade' as the smugglers were fond of claiming – dependent, that is, solely on the free play of market forces – it would soon have dwindled away, as Jardine feared.

But both British and Indian governments had an important vested interest in opium. Both were drawing a considerable revenue at one corner or other of the trade triangle: opium–silver–tea; indeed, Far East trade was now very largely financed by Chinese silver. The Chinese authorities were unaware that those 'three hundred armed and lawless men' on the Pearl River had been supporting on their shoulders an inverted pyramid of trade in many other commodities, spanning the world from London and Liverpool to Boston and New York.

That traders might influence or even control governments was a concept an educated Chinese would have found hard to grasp. In China, merchants were social inferiors. That by suppressing the Canton opium trade their Imperial Commissioner would throw down a challenge to the entire British Empire would also have seemed extremely far-fetched.

Americans trading in Canton knew better. Some began shrewdly to follow the example set for them by Olyphant & Co. On 27 February 1839 the outstanding American firm of Russell & Co. sent their customers a circular, declaring that they had 'resolved to discontinue all connection with the opium trade in China'. But opium financed tea. To their London agent, Russell & Co. wrote sanguinely, 'if the export of teas is kept up, new sources must be opened to procure the means of paying for them'. That, however, was easier said than done.

On the last day of the old year – the day before trade was officially reopened in Canton – the Chinese Emperor had appointed a High Commissioner there 'to investigate port affairs' – a euphemism for stamping out the drug trade. A High Commissioner was an exceptional appointment in China – created to meet an emergency, and granted special powers. The man chosen was 53-year-old Lin Tse-hsu, who as Viceroy in Hupeh and Hunan had handled the local opium problem with great success.

Commissioner Lin in the days before he left Peking had nineteen successive interviews there with the Emperor. There was no reason to believe that the ruling Manchus would falter in their campaign against opium, whatever the consequences.

Of all the high officials with a Confucian training who in their different ways tried to resolve the problems inflicted on China by the arrival of the 'seaborne barbarians', Lin is the most sympathetic. His father had been a poor teacher in Fukien – the tea-growing province north of Canton, and a notorious market for the coastal trade. By now over 70 per cent of the population in Fukien smoked opium.

Lin Tse-hsu was a plump man of medium height, with a heavy black moustache and a thin beard, renowned then and since as a poet, and nicknamed, on account of his moral uprightness, Lin the Clear Sky. Lin belonged to a modern literary school in China which interpreted the teachings of Confucius so as to justify the reforms that obviously were needed. Lin and his collaborators made a conscious effort all their lives to understand economic and social problems, and to improve their knowledge of the world outside China.

Lin was well known as the man who had once put down a

peasant revolt single-handed and without bloodshed. In 1823, when the Sung River flooded and the people rose in protest, the local Governor sent for troops. But Lin, then the Governor's aide, crossed the river in a boat alone to discuss their grievances with the rebels face to face. He had been ever since the high official Peking sent to cope with particularly difficult situations.

A fortnight before Lin's formal arrival at Canton – in a state litter, borne by twenty bearers, and with an escort of six men-at-arms – he had stirred things up in advance by naming to the local authorities fifty-four Cantonese notorious in the opium racket who had so far not been touched – most of them being corrupt officials who were being protected by their superiors.

Lin set up his headquarters at the Yuen-hua Academy, conveniently near the foreign Factories. He began by publishing four Edicts. One required teachers to stamp out opium-smoking in the schools, and their pupils to form groups of five, mutually guaranteeing themselves not to use the drug. The next Edict pointed out caustically to the 'gentlemen, merchants, soldiers and peasants' of Canton what a bad name their province had by now for opium-dealing. Quoting his own recent experiences in central China, Lin sought to convince the Cantonese that even a man addicted to opium for many years was not a hopeless case, but might be helped to a cure. (Not long after, Lin got in touch with the Medical Missionary Society – of which, ironically, William Jardine had latterly been Vice-President – asking if Western medical science could help in finding a prescription to cure opium addiction.)

Lin's third Edict condemned the marines on the coastal patrol boat as a pack of weaklings, who pilfered opium captures in order to smoke the drug when off duty. His fourth Edict extended the system of guarantee groups to the villages under the control of village elders.

Lin then wrote the first version of his famous letter to Queen Victoria – appealing to the Queen of England, over the heads of her local officials, to work with the Chinese in getting rid of opium. One fallacy runs all through Lin's letter – his assumption that in Great Britain the use of opium as a drug of addiction must be illegal, as it was in China. That opium should be freely imported into Britain by a company chartered by the Crown – the Honourable East India Company – and sold there without hindrance to dismal factory operatives and harassed mothers of large families would have strained Lin's credulity to breaking point.

'There is a class of evil foreigner', he wrote confidently, perhaps a little arrogantly, to Queen Victoria, 'that makes opium and

75

brings it for sale, tempting fools to destroy themselves merely in order to reap profit. Formerly the number of opium smugglers was small; but now the vice has spread far and wide, and the poison penetrated deeper ... we have decided to inflict very severe penalties on opium dealers and opium smokers ... this poisonous article is manufactured by certain devilish persons in places subject to your rule. It is not of course either made or sold at your bidding ... I am told that in your own country opium smoking is forbidden under severe penalties ... it would be better to forbid the sale of it, or better still, to forbid the production of it ... What is here forbidden to consume, your dependencies must be forbidden to manufacture ... When that is done, not only will the Chinese be rid of this evil but your people too will be safe.'

Lin's first difficulty was to get a letter of this importance adequately translated into English. The official interpreter on the Chinese side made such a dog's dinner of it that Lin sought help from the best American linguist in Canton, Dr Peter Parker – a former stonemason, who after studying theology at Yale and medicine in Philadelphia had for the past four years been running an eye clinic for poor Chinese in premises given him by the enormously wealthy Chinese merchant Howqua. Dr Parker did better as a translator, but not much. The surgeon of *Sunda*, shipwrecked on Hainan, was brought with other survivors to Canton. When given Parker's translation of Lin's letter to read and improve on, he admitted, 'Some parts of it we could make neither head nor tail of.'

To make play with the pompous formalities of Chinese official phraseology, or with comic mistranslations, became later a commonplace way of scoring points off China, especially in Parliamentary debate. But the surviving draft of Lin's letter, pruned of its bits of nonsense, advances an argument well worth treating with respect. In fact, the long-term interests of both Britain and China would best be served by suppressing the opium traffic and, as Lin surmised, a decision to end it could be taken only by the British government. There were no regular diplomatic channels, however, for conveying such a letter to Queen Victoria, so Lin was obliged to look round for an Englishman who might sympathize with the Chinese point of view.

In Peking a new Imperial Edict of unprecedented severity had been issued against opium. Everyone involved in the drug trade from broker to opium-den operator, from the farmer who grew the poppy to the policeman who took a bribe, was to be ruthlessly punished. Those who gave up their opium voluntarily would be pardoned. Addicts were given eighteen months' grace – time to seek a cure. For the first time, the principal foreign opium dealers became liable to beheading, and their Chinese accomplices would suffer death by strangulation – this, as it happens, was a clause Lin had particularly asked for.

By 12 May 1839, 1600 Cantonese violaters had been arrested, and 42 741 opium pipes had been surrendered. (Lin evidently knew something of an addict's fetishistic attachment to the tools of his vice: to compel the surrender of a favourite opium pipe was a simple blow struck at a daily habit.) 28 845 catties of opium on sale in Canton – the equivalent of 2900 chests – had also been impounded by the authorities in the first onslaught. During the next seven weeks 11 000 more catties of opium were surrendered.

But compared with the huge quantity accumulating offshore at Lintin, this was nothing. Captain Elliot, in a letter to the Foreign Office, estimated that nearly 20 000 chests of opium had already arrived in China and waited there unsold. To these must be added 'upwards of 20 000 in Bengal, 12 000 in Bombay ... upwards of 50 000 chests ready for the market, and the crop of the current year ... soon [to be] added to this stock'.

The enormous local stock of the drug Lin now planned to seize and destroy. He expected that from a loss like this the smugglers would never recover. Had they merely been smugglers, he might indeed have managed to put them out of business. But, as the shrewdest traders were beginning to figure, with such an opium glut building up in India, to destroy the stocks held at Canton might turn out to be a blessing in disguise.

Lin forbade the foreigners at Canton to leave for Macao, and went on to warn the Hong merchants that, having connived at opium-smuggling, they must now mend their ways. Howqua and his colleagues must either find a convincing way to persuade the foreigners to surrender all that opium stored in their hulks at Lintin, and get their solemn promise not to import any more, under penalty of confiscation and death, or a couple of the Hong merchants could expect to have their heads chopped off.

Eventually, after being convinced that the lives of the Hong merchants were in real danger, the drug traffickers agreed to offer up a token amount of their opium – 1036 chests, some of which in point of fact belonged to the Hong merchants themselves. Lin was not to be taken in by symbolic gestures. 'This is a mere fraction', he replied. 'There are tens of thousands of chests.' He then ordered that Lancelot Dent ('He alone has 6000 chests') should be brought into the walled city of Canton.

Possibly Lin had in mind sacrificing Dent as an example: beheading him. The foreign opium merchants had not yet taken in that they were liable under the recent Imperial Edict to the death penalty – but when the idea came home to them they refused to let Lancelot Dent take a risk on their behalf.

Dent himself temporized, asking the Chinese for a safe conduct. Next day Howqua and Mowqua, another rich Hong merchant, appeared at the Factories each deprived of rank and with an iron chain hung round his neck, as a token that his life too was in jeopardy. Robert Inglis, a partner in Dent's firm, went in his place into Canton with three others and had a discussion with high officials in the Temple of the Queen of Heaven. But next day Lin implacably repeated the demand for Dent himself.

Lin intended to enforce Chinese law, but the ambiguous nature of the opium smuggler was evidently not yet clear in his mind. By bringing the drug to Chinese waters in unauthorized armed vessels, under threat of force, the smuggler broke not only Chinese but International Law. A British or indeed any other naval vessel, doing duty as a policeman of the seas, would have been right to apprehend him on sight, or sink him if he resisted. At the same time, the opium smuggler was a valuable, if irregular, instrument of British policy – the last buccaneer. Dent, Matheson, Innes and the rest of them, though men of great personal audacity, were always comfortably aware that if things got too hot, the British government would come to their rescue. And this is just what happened.

On 24 March 1839 Captain Elliot arrived dramatically at Canton in *Larne*'s gig, rowed by four blue-jackets, and wearing his full-dress uniform, having dodged the Chinese blockade on the Pearl River. Elliot ran up the Union Jack, amid hearty British cheers, took Lancelot Dent into his own headquarters, and put him under his personal protection.

Lin had come up against his real antagonist, at last – an anomalous personage, neither merchant nor officer, but with the British fleet at his beck and call. Events during the coming months became a duel between the two personalities: Commissioner Lin, the poet, the experienced administrator at the peak of his career, the intellectual doing his best to hack a way out of the prison of stereotyped Confucian thought; Captain Elliot, with a romantically adventurous sea-going career behind him but his reputation still to make, a sensitive man who never managed to disentangle his own humane instincts from his formal duty to obey all orders without question as a naval officer should. Elliot was a victim not only of the personal attitudes he was prone to strike – as if to explain himself to himself – but also of the clever, hard-headed, commercially successful men around him, who did their best always to edge their Superintendent of Trade towards compromising decisions.

For all his intellectual curiosity – he had foreign newspapers translated, and extracts made from foreign geographies and polemical attacks on the drug trade – Lin was never quite able to make out what the foreigners he had to contend with were really like. His weakness was usually to give the British credit for nobler motives than they chose to show.

Another siege of the Factories now began. The servants all left 'as if running from a plague'. On 28 March three of the four streets down which the British might leave were walled up by the Chinese. Great gongs sounded all night through, making sleep impossible, and the waterfront was crowded with Chinese troops. The foreign merchants were supposed to be deprived of food and limited to two buckets of spring water a day – in fact the guards, who were supposed to maintain this blockade, cheerfully smuggled in quantities of food and drink.

Deprived of their servants, the merchants contrived to discover or invent how to boil an egg, but made a gruesome mess of cooking rice. Although effective use was later made of the tale of their sufferings, they treated the siege as a lark. As James Matheson (who was to help finance this kind of propaganda in London) mockingly remarked, 'They suffered more from an absence of exercise and from over-feeding than from any actual want of the necessities of life.'

The merchants amused themselves playing cricket and leapfrog in their exercise yard. Looking out across the Pearl River they could see three concentric lines of boats, in which 300 Chinese soldiers, armed with matchlocks, guarded their way of escape with much waving of flags, blowing of conches and threatening gestures. (Chinese soldiers were carefully trained in threatening gestures.) One Yankee seaman shinned all the way up the 100 ft flagpole, to everyone's applause. The real danger to their lives, as the merchant community were not slow to grasp, came not from those picturesque Chinese men-at-arms, but from the offchance that the thousand or so foreign seamen at Whampoa might take it into their heads to follow Captain Elliot's gallant example, and cut their way through the river blockade on a rescue operation. Then the blood would flow in buckets.

For Elliot to cooperate honestly with Lin – as during the last trade embargo he had, briefly, with Teng – to help in suppressing the opium trade was really out of the question, though all his earlier professional experience, against piracy and slavery, tended to push him that way. By coming up to Canton in *Larne*'s gig and protecting Dent he had committed himself – though Elliot did his best to obscure the real issue. From now on he began seeking around almost desperately for points of conflict which might sound more reputable than opium. Great Britain – as well as her representative – had a bad conscience about the real ground of conflict with China and has had one ever since.

Opium dealers when it came to the push had no real objection to parting with their shiploads of unsaleable opium on the orders of a Crown representative. A claim for compensation against the British government was better than a dead loss. In any event, Lin was forcing on Elliot this degree of cooperation. Only after their opium stocks were given up would he lift the siege, so that this year's tea crop could be got moving.

Elliot told British subjects to surrender their opium to the Chinese, and on his personal responsibility guaranteed that they would be indemnified later. On receiving the glad news of this capitulation, Lin at once followed the accepted policy of 'soothing the barbarians' – who, to Chinese bewilderment, notoriously craved large meals of meat – by sending 250 livestock into the Factories. The American share was 2 sheep, 4 pigs, 10 fowls and 16 geese.

Explaining the inwardness of what had happened, to Jardine and Abel Smith, in London, James Matheson pointed out sagaciously, '... the Chinese have fallen into the snare of rendering themselves directly liable to the Crown'. He went on to announce ironically, 'To a close observer, it would seem as if the whole of Elliot's career were expressly designed to lead on the Chinese to commit themselves, and produce a collision.' Putting the secret hopes of their partnership once more into words, Matheson had already suggested, 'I suppose war with China will be the next step.'

Lin's intelligence service told him that local stocks of opium amounted to 20 000 chests – in fact, a very close guess. He gave the besieged merchants his programme. When a quarter of their opium had been landed – at Chuenpi, near a Bogue Fort, on the coast opposite Lintin Island – their Chinese servants would be allowed back in the Factories. When half had been landed, passage boats would run once more down to Macao. The trade embargo was to end when three-quarters of the drug had been sent ashore,

Treaty of Nanking in 1842

Treaty of Tianjin in 1858

Opium Wars

Nullification

Antebellum Politics: The Controversy

The Rule of Acbar: "The Great Mughal"
over India

The Peace of Utrecht

and when all 20 000 chests had been handed over, life would go completely back to normal.

The receiving ships at once began sailing from Lintin over to the Bogue. Consignments of unsaleable opium that had only just arrived were hurriedly included in the surrender. In all, 20 283 chests were given up at Chuenpi, at a market value, in normal times of between two and three million pounds.

Lin then required every merchant to give a bond to abide by the law and pledge not to smuggle in more opium. Chinese law had – made foreigners who smuggled opium liable to the death penalty. This gave Captain Elliot a chance to shift his ground. Let the gravamen of the argument be, not opium, but whether British subjects should be liable to Chinese courts. With melodramatic emphasis, Elliot declared that he would rather give his own life than sign such a bond.

He had a fair case. Punishments under the Manchu code had a touch of brutality – beating with the light and the heavy bamboo, transportation, banishment and death by strangulation or decapitation. In cases of homicide or robbery, two modes of torture were allowed by the code – though they were used almost only on hardened criminals – an instrument that crushed the ankle bones, and one that squashed the fingers. In everyday practice the law was applied leniently – most death sentences were reprieved, women escaped most punishments, near relatives were not punished for concealing crimes, and a magistrate resorting too readily to the bamboo or to torture was regarded as professionally incompetent. But when all was said in its favour this was not British justice. Ever since 1784, when the Chinese had executed the unlucky gunner off *Lady Hughes,* no British subject on a capital charge had been put in risk of a Chinese court. Indeed, for the past fifteen years foreigners had practically managed to escape Chinese jurisdiction altogether. Now the Chinese were trying to get their hands on Lancelot Dent and make an example of him. He was, to all appearances, an eminently respectable merchant, and the Chinese might try to chop his head off. Elliot had a point of principle, at last, which British public opinion would undoubtedly rise up and support.

Commissioner Lin – who believed, as did Peking, that his confiscation must have given the drug trade a mortal blow, had on 30 March been the happy recipient of a gift of roebuck venison from the Emperor himself (signifying *'promotion assured'*) – not to mention a scroll with *good luck and long life* written out calligraphically by the Emperor's own hand in Imperial vermilion. (To these gifts, in the privacy of his own apartment, Lin respectfully burned incense and kowtowed three times.)

James Matheson set up his office out of reach of the Chinese, on the receiving ship *Hercules*, anchored off the barren island of Hong Kong. He was well aware that there were still addicts in China craving to buy their daily supply of the drug whatever the risk, and this demand Matheson set himself to satisfy. When surrendering his own 6000 chests, he had prudently kept 500 in reserve. However much opium Lin was managing to destroy, the rules of the game were unchanged. The Chinese coast, undefended by a navy, was wide open to a bold man and, in the long run, the market was insatiable.

Matheson sent Jardine's nephew Andrew to organize a branch of the firm in Manila, and he opened negotiations for floating a loan in London for the Philippine government, through the good offices of John Abel Smith, MP. The Philippine government demonstrated its gratitude in advance by halving the import duty on opium admitted for re-export. (In fact, the London loan never materialized.) Six fast and armed Jardine, Matheson clippers based on Manila began running the drug to old contacts on the China coast, and fresh stocks were built up.

When word of Lin's success reached Singapore and India the price of opium there fell dizzily. If the Chinese market were sealed off, where on earth could the vast accumulation be sold? New season's Malwa opium went down in Bombay to a derisory $200 a chest. To buy cheap opium for his Manila operation, James Matheson shipped $100 000 to Singapore.

The most spectacular coup in Singapore was brought off by Captain Joseph Pybus, in his schooner *Time* (140 tons), an exceptionally fast little ship built in Shoreham for the Mediterranean fruit trade – one of the crack ships from all the world over which had been bought up for the opium fleet.

While the opium surrender was actually in progress, Captain Pybus came into Canton Bay with twenty chests aboard and, discerning a way to make his fortune, quietly slipped off, making for Singapore. There he discharged his twenty chests on shore at a time of day when the Bund was crowded with opium dealers. The sad spectacle of the drug actually and visibly coming back from China caused the local price to collapse. Captain Pybus proceeded to buy 700 chests through an agent discreetly. He bought at an average price of $250 per chest, and sold all 700 at the famine price of $2500 per chest making a gross profit of a million and a half dollars. The schooners Jardine, Matheson sent up the coast were meantime regularly selling opium bought at $200 for $800, though only at the cost of coping with an increasing and violent resistance from the Chinese, which the year following culminated in at least one pitched battle. The clipper *Hellas* (209 tons) lay becalmed north of Nan-ao, and running foul of some fishing stakes was unable to bring her broadside to bear when eight war junks and three larger open boats attacked her. In the hand-to-hand fighting that followed – until a breeze sprang up which enabled *Hellas* to sheer off – all fifteen Europeans aboard were wounded, her Yankee captain J. Jauncey had his jaw smashed by a large musket ball, and the schooner was set afire. The opium trade was coming very close to open piracy.

Though separated by thousands of miles, William Jardine and James Matheson were actively collaborating to give their transactions an air of respectability in the one place that politically now mattered – London. All the firms surrendering opium at Chuenpi had levied one dollar per chest, for a fund to help Jardine in London make sure of their compensation. 'You will not, however', Matheson reminded his partner, 'be limited to this outlay, as the magnitude of the object can well bear any amount of expense ... you may find it expedient to secure, at a high price, the services of some leading newspaper ... we are told there are literary men whom it is usual to employ ...'

Whether Samuel Warren, a barrister of great literary talent and later famous as author of the Victorian best seller *Ten Thousand a Year,* was spontaneously inspired to defend the Jardine, Matheson viewpoint in his *The Opium Question* or whether money passed, must now be a matter for conjecture. Warren's pamphlet is the most cogent and explicit statement of the opium smugglers' political point of view, and an interesting early specimen of 'public relations' – the costly but effective technique for purchasing good opinions which Jardine, Matheson & Co. were among the earliest commercial firms to employ. Arguments set on foot by Warren have coloured the history of the first Opium War ever since.

Subsidized or not, sensational pamphlets and news items multiplied. All London was rapidly made aware how honest British merchants in Canton had been besieged, imprisoned, deprived of food, and actually threatened with death. The arch-villain, Commissioner Lin himself, was accused of having 'some thousands of

acres laid down to poppy plantations' – implying Lin had destroyed British opium only because it competed with his own.

Lin in fact, by the middle of May 1839, with over 20 000 chests
of opium on his hands, was in a delicate position. He had taken
every precaution against fraud and theft – organizing twenty teams,
each supervised by a military and a civil officer, so that each team
handled a maximum of 100 chests, which were sealed and marked
on receipt. Knowing that high-ranking mandarins were not universally regarded as incorruptible, Lin decided at first to wash his
hands of the problem, by shipping the drug to Peking for inspection
and destruction there. But a censor in the capital was quick to
point out that 40 000 porters would be needed to carry the chests
overland, from Canton, over the mountains, and 100 large boats
with a thousand or so crew would need to be found to ship them up
the Grand Canal. The expense and the opportunities for pilfering
would be enormous. Accordingly, on 30 May 1839 an order came
from the Emperor that the drug should be destroyed on the spot.
Lin, in anticipation, had already composed a prayer to the God
of the Sea, advising all sea creatures to hide somewhere safe when
the poisonous drug was run off.

There were some, the Reverend Doctor Karl Gutzlaff prominent
among them, who remained to the last incredulous that Commissioner Lin should have had so much portable wealth actually in
his hands, and not kept some for himself. But the evidence goes
to show that the drug was all destroyed.

Near the coastal village of Chen k'ou three large trenches were
dug, a hundred and fifty feet long, seventy-five wide and seven
deep. They were lined with flagstones and timber, and surrounded
by a bamboo fence. The balls of opium, broken open, were thrown
in a trench, then covered with two feet of water. Quantities of
salt and lime were tipped in, and the decomposing sludge stirred
and drained off into a creek which ran down to the sea. The heat
and stink were appalling. Five hundred labourers were supervised minutely by sixty trusted civil and military officers. One
coolie who tried to filch a piece of drug was executed on the spot.

As witnesses to the act of destruction, Lin invited among others
the American merchant C. W. King, representing Olyphant &
Co., the firm occupying Zion's Corner which scrupulously had
never handled opium, and Elijah Bridgman, the first American
missionary to China and an editor of the *China Repository*.
Bridgman later wrote: 'I cannot conceive how any business can be
more faithfully executed.' King, a Quaker, pointed out sententiously, how 'while Christian governments were growing and farming

this deleterious drug, this Pagan monarch should nobly disdain to enrich his treasury with a sale which could not fall short of $20 000 000.'

From his carpeted pavilion at Chen k'ou, hung with scroll paintings and choice examples of calligraphy, Lin kept the work of destruction in full view. C. W. King was called over for an interview – the Quaker manfully withheld his consent to the kowtow but conceded Lin a dignified bow. King described the Commissioner afterwards as short, rather stout, and vivacious, with a clear voice. Commissioner Lin asked King who among the Hong merchants was most straightforward, and laughed when the Quaker was unable to give a frank answer. Lin went on to inquire about the prospects for legitimate trade. When King warned Lin that the British were planning to use their new-fangled steam-boats as gunboats, the Emperor's Commissioner frowned. By now the more intelligent of the mandarins saw a long way into the technical reasons for Britain's power at sea, and China's helplessness.

Lin's private opinion – a measure of his ignorance of the economic forces now pressing on China from the world outside – was that foreign trade had grown too large to be beneficial, and should be cut back closer to what it used to be: 40 ships a year instead of 120, tea instead of opium.

With the opium destroyed there remained outstanding the vexed question of the bond. This time it would be, not a meaningless document, like the bond the Hong merchants had once given to cover William Jardine, but a promise which meant what it said and carried penalties. The British merchants trading at Canton were on the whole happy that Captain Elliot intended to refuse on their behalf. They had no serious intention of ever giving up their immensely profitable opium business. American merchants, less committed to opium, signed the bond in an ingeniously modified form, minus the death clause. Lin was happy to introduce this wedge between British and Americans; moreover, the Americans themselves were not slow to see the commercial advantages of a neutrality that leaned slightly in the direction of China.

Now that Captain Elliot had committed himself to their interests, the free-traders in Canton were ready to follow his lead, even if grudgingly at times. Elliot's first step was to deprive the Chinese of any future possibility of using the British as hostages. He ordered his countrymen to quit Canton. Though he had no means of enforcing such an order, by 27 May all British ships and most British subjects had left the Pearl River.

Some of the Americans had been unenthusiastic about the opium surrender. Russell & Co., despite their circular publicly forswearing the drug trade, still had sixty chests of Turkish opium hidden away in stock. They now had no intention whatever of leaving Canton – since it was obvious they would soon inherit the business the British were leaving behind. Captain Elliot begged Robert Forbes, the manager of Russell & Co., to leave with the British, telling him, 'if your house goes, all will go, and we shall soon bring these rascally Chinese to terms'. Forbes – a typical Yankee trader – later spoke of the satisfaction it had given him to reply that he had not come to China for health or pleasure. 'I should remain at my post so long as I could sell a yard of goods or buy a pound of tea.'

In the coming months only the American presence in Canton enabled the British to sail out their vast tea purchases – often in British ships nominally transferred to the Stars and Stripes. Freights, of course, were enormous. While the boom lasted, the Americans in Canton charged more to transport tea and silk the fifty or so miles by water from Whampoa to Lintin than formerly to ship them 12 000 miles from Canton to Boston. Some Americans started discreetly supplying Lin with modern guns; the business of gun-running was to have a long history henceforward in China.

The inevitable weaknesses of Lin's policy were already being pointed out by his many rivals in Peking. Censor Pu Chi-t'ung put in a memorial criticizing Lin's attempt to make the foreign merchants sign a bond. Even if they did guarantee under pain of death not to bring opium into Canton Bay, he pointed out, what was to stop them transferring the drug to Chinese ships out at sea? As Matheson was already demonstrating from Manila, on the high seas the British could do what they chose.

For the time being, Captain Elliot, however, had no warships to call upon. Even the little sloop *Larne* – whose gig he had borrowed, to reach Canton – was away to Calcutta with despatches. For the present Elliot trod carefully, proposing despite Portuguese misgivings to base British trade for the time being on Macao, the small peninsula where the Portuguese were so submissive that, as Lin once reported to the Emperor, 'they are practically Chinese'.

(The Portuguese had prudently sent their own 3000 opium chests away to Manila.)

Elliot's luck was turning. On 7 June an armed merchantman, *Cambridge* (1080 tons), owned by her master, James Douglas, dropped anchor off Macao. Having heard in Singapore that Lin was destroying opium, Douglas had sold his cargo of the drug there at a loss, and loaded cannon instead – twenty-six 18-pounders, four long-twelves (in addition to *Cambridge*'s normal armament of six 18-pound carronades). Douglas had taken on powder and shot and extra crew to work the guns, and, on arrival at Macao, was at once offered by Captain Elliot a fee of £14 000 for eight months' hire of *Cambridge*. Three days later, Elliot appointed Douglas to be commodore of the British merchantmen which had come down from Whampoa – most of them now at anchor in the sheltered deep water between the island of Hong Kong and the Chinese headland of Kowloon.

By 10 June, Captain Elliot, more confident after this accession of strength, began once more to jostle Commissioner Lin. His first complaint was that the war junks off Kowloon Point – the local fleet which under Admiral Kuan was keeping the British merchant flotilla under observation – had been obstructing the British there from buying food ashore. Hunger, he warned, might lead the crews to take a rash step.

Lin replied suavely that no order had been given to cut off supplies, and he would have the war junks anchor elsewhere for five days. By then the foreign ships must either put to sea, or make a Customs declaration and proceed up the Pearl River to Whampoa – otherwise those war junks would go into action against them. Such a threat was mere bluff, as Lin well knew. Under the guns of *Cambridge*, the British merchantmen rocked safely in their anchorage and two months later British and Chinese were still confronting each other, at Kowloon — the war junks keeping cautious watch, the British ships, just to the south of them, busily loading wares fetched down for them at fancy freights by their American cousins up in Canton.

By mid-July, the smuggling of opium organized from Macao and Manila was reported as once more being in full swing along the entire coast of Fukien – Commissioner Lin's birthplace.

An incident on 12 July screwed the antagonism up a notch. A party of about 30 British seamen and petty officers off *Carnatic* and *Mangalore* – ships for which Jardine, Matheson & Co. and Dent & Co. were agents – took shore leave at the Chinese village of Chien-sha-tsin on the Kowloon side of the Hong Kong anchorage.

After being so long cooped up aboard, the Jack Tars were in a lively and eventually vindictive mood. Horseplay began with the demolition of a Chinese temple, and ended with some of their number beating up a Chinese called Lin Wei-hsi, who died next day. Which of the numerous blows struck by various hands had killed him?

The Chinese never took homicide lightly: their code exacted a life for a life. Elliot knew how serious this might become. He sailed across to the village, and started handing out money: $1500 for the family of the dead man, $200 as a 'reward for evidence convicting the real murderer', $100 to distribute at large among the villagers, and $400 to bribe local officials. This money was later charged off amicably to the drug-smuggling firms responsible for *Carnatic* and *Mangalore*.

Commissioner Lin's riposte was to placard Macao – where the minority of foreigners was outnumbered ten to one by native Chinese – pointing out that he would have ordered the immediate execution of any Chinese who happened to strike and kill a foreigner. He reiterated the Chinese principle: 'He who kills a man must pay the penalty of life.'

If Elliot wanted to change the ground of their dispute to the right of jurisdiction of a Chinese court over a British subject, here was a case much less to his liking. His bribes had neither silenced the villagers, nor yet produced a scapegoat. One of those seamen had undoubtedly killed Lin Wei-hsi – but no Briton had been handed over to a Chinese court on a capital charge for over fifty years. Had Elliot yielded to Lin's demand – fair and just though it might have sounded by Chinese standards – public opinion at home would never have stood for it.

Elliot tried to settle the matter with a show of justice, in case a public performance of that kind might satisfy the Chinese. Invoking an unused British law that few were quite clear about, Elliot brought the six likeliest suspects to trial on 12 August aboard *Fort William*. The Chinese authorities ignored their invitation to attend. A bill for murder against Thomas Tidder, the boatswain in *Mangalore*, was thrown out by a jury of merchants that included James Matheson. Two seamen convicted of rioting were fined £15 and given a sentence of three months' imprisonment, to be served on their return to England. Three convicted of riot and assault were fined £25 with six months' imprisonment. (When these convicted men eventually got back to England they escaped scot-free, since Captain Elliot had exceeded his jurisdiction.)

On 17 August Commissioner Lin sent Captain Elliot a peremptory demand that the murderer be handed over. Lin had every reason for pressing hard. Destroying those 20 000 chests of opium had not brought the drug business to a stop; far from it. Dealers lately arrested had confessed that opium-smuggling organized from Macao was again becoming prevalent under Lin's very nose, in Canton Bay. With this murder case as a popular pretext, Lin intended making Macao too hot to hold them.

The British in the next few days began leaving the Portuguese city to take up less comfortable quarters in the ships at anchor off Hong Kong. Macao's carefree days as a pleasure resort were over. A letter from George Chinnery, the old painter, to James Matheson reflected the mood of foreboding. He was now, said Chinnery, as he looked round the studio from which after so many years he was about to be uprooted, 'living in the greatest misery ... I should like to paint a few pictures (at least try at it) before I'm put to the sword. Rely on it, something serious if not dreadful is coming ... I do not go out again, I think, until I cross the beach.'

The Portuguese Governor of Macao sent a confidential warning to J. H. Astell, formerly Lord Napier's secretary but now working for Dent & Co., the big drug firm. On the night of 25 August Astell was warned the Chinese had a plan to surround every house in Macao where a British subject dwelt. They would all be taken prisoner. The Portuguese were perhaps desperately trying to get rid of unwelcome guests; anyway, the rumour worked. Captain Elliot speeded up embarkation, and by 25 August all fifty-seven families of the British community, men, women and children, had gone to live afloat. Lin reported, with satisfaction, to the Emperor, that the British would soon find themselves deprived of the greasy meat dishes which they ate with such pleasure. To any follower of Confucius, a diet of beef was repugnant: the ox was entitled to respect because it pulled the plough.

Help was coming. Three days after the last Briton had left Macao, the floating community was immensely cheered to see the sails of the 28-gun frigate *Volage* (Captain H. Smith) lift above the horizon. The 18-gun *Hyacinth* was not far behind. Elliot began to think he might now be strong enough to force delivery of supplies from the Chinese shore.

On 1 September, Lin had found a breathing-space to answer a list of hair-raising questions from the Emperor, which had waited on his desk since July. They all concerned the habits of foreign barbarians, and suggest very exactly the atmosphere of ignorance at Peking in which Manchu rule must have been carried on. Lin's replies are, by comparison, sensible and accurate. Is it true, asks the Emperor, that foreigners buy thousands of Chinese girl child-ren? For black magic? Lin replied soberly that unemployed Chinese workers were sometimes recruited for service abroad in mines and plantations, but they generally came back after a few years. One or two youngsters might be employed as pages, but not for black magic.

Was foreign opium, asked the Emperor, mixed with human flesh? It might, said Lin cautiously, be mixed with the flesh of crows. He had ascertained that certain foreigners (he had in mind the Parsees in Bombay who shipped Malwa opium) had a ritual of exposing their dead to let the crows peck away the flesh. There must evidently in Peking have been important personages looking around for evidence that the inexplicable narcotic effect of opium was caused by sympathetic magic, with human flesh as a vital ingredient.

Two days later, to underline that the Portuguese held Macao not as a possession but under lease from China, Lin paid the town a formal visit – arriving at the Barrier in a sedan chair with eight bearers. He was met by Don Adraio Accacio da Silveira Pinto, the Governor, and by 100 Portuguese soldiers drawn up as a guard of honour. To the Portuguese officials Lin gave presents of silk, fans, tea and sugar candy; and to the soldiers a blow-out of beer, mutton, wine, not to mention $400 in silver. Lin continued to find the appearance of foreign devils very odd, noting in his diary: 'The bodies of the men are tightly encased from head to toe ... they look like actors playing the part of foxes ... They have heavy beards, much of which they shave, leaving only one curly tuft ... indeed, they do really look like devils.'

Captain Elliot, with two frigates at his disposal, intended sticking it out at anchor near Hong Kong since a retreat 640 miles to Manila would make shipping out the tea crop too difficult, even with American help. Lin was willing enough to let the British return and trade, but only licitly and on Chinese terms. After Elliot had refused to give up Lin Wei-hsi's murderer, all supplies of food and water from the shore had been denied to the floating community. There were a couple of thousand to be fed, including Elliot's wife and child, so on 4 September the Superintendent of Trade chose three small armed sailing vessels, able to operate close inshore – his cutter, *Louisa*, the pinnace which served as tender to *Volage*, and the small, schooner-rigged *Pearl* – and with Gutzlaff for interpreter made for Kowloon. Three large junks showed up, with the mouths of their cannon painted red. On shore, at Kowloon village, was a Chinese coastal battery.

Gutzlaff, unarmed, went ashore by boat to deliver the two letters he had written for Captain Elliot in Chinese. One was addressed to the mandarins, and threatened reprisals if the merchant fleet were not supplied with food. The other was intended for ordinary Chinese living along the coast, and implored them not to poison the springs of fresh water. The mandarins who met Gutzlaff on shore said they lacked authority to accept any such letters. At 2 p.m. Captain Elliot sent them an ultimatum: if the British did not get supplies within half an hour, they would sink the junks.

Those British boats to the mandarins' eyes were much smaller and less impressive than the fearsomely painted war junks. They let the time of grace expire, and Captain Smith, in the pinnace, fired a gun at the nearest junk – the first shot in the war.

A youngster called Elmslie, brother to Captain Elliot's secretary, was present at the action – much as Elliot himself had served, as a mere boy, in the devastating bombardment of Algiers. Young Elmslie later wrote to his family in London, telling them exactly what happened next.

... the Junks then triced up their boarding nettings, and came into action with us at half pistol shot; our guns were well served with Grape and round-shot; ... they opened a tremendous and well directed fire upon us, from all their Guns (each Junk had 10 Guns) ... the Junk's fire Thank God! was not enough depressed, or if otherwise, none would have lived to tell the Story. (19 of their guns we received in the main-sail.)

... The battery opened fire upon the English at 3.45 p.m. and their fire was steady and well-directed ... At 4.30, having fired 104 rounds, the cutter had to haul off as she was out of cartridges. The junks immediately made sail after the *Louisa* ... We ... gave them three such Broadsides that it made every rope in the vessel grin again. We loaded with Grape the fourth time, and gave them Gun for Gun ... this is the first day I ever shed human blood, and I hope it will be the last.

The action was broken off at sunset. The British, though fighting boldly against odds, had failed to overawe the Chinese, or force them to deliver the needed supplies. Elliot's despatch next day to London shows his uneasiness at having perhaps overplayed his hand. 'The violent and vexatious measures heaped upon Her Majesty's officers and subjects will I trust serve to excuse those feelings of irritation which have betrayed me into a measure that I am certain, under less trying circumstances, would be difficult indeed of vindication.'

Later that September, Lin told the people of Kowloon to go armed and get ready to resist a possible British landing. On 22 September he inspected eighty Chinese ships-of-war – junks and fireships – in the mouth of the Bogue. The Chinese eighth month was traditionally the time for going up to a high place, to look at the moon and write a poem. Lin climbed as far as the mirador at the top of Shakok Hill near Chuenpi, to admire the moonlight. He could see Admiral Kuan's fleet at anchor. His poem began: *'A vast display of Imperial might had shaken all the foreign tribes, and if they now confess their guilt we shall not be too hard on them ...'*

At the 'Battle of Kowloon' so-called, the Chinese had on the whole the upper hand, though the official Chinese report to Peking inevitably made of the affair a 'great victory' – a two-masted ship sunk, fifty British casualties. To dress up a report is a temptation to which officers of other nations too have at times succumbed – but this was going much too far. The passionate anti-foreign sentiment being aroused in Canton by the scholars who followed Lin's lead was from now on to hail any major setback to the foreign devils as a Smashing Blow. All popular wars fall, of course, into this trick of optimistic hyperbole, but accounts of imaginary victories reaching the Chinese rulers in Peking must have made any sober appraisal of their enemy exceptionally difficult.

Even Lin, after the 'Battle of Kowloon', began acting as if his war junks might after all be strong enough to expel the British ships by force. The Chinese saw this conflict as a police action in which the morally superior would inevitably be the victors and this became a mental handicap. The very conception 'war' – not to mention the ruthless techniques now essential in a war between nation states – had for thousands of years been alien to Chinese experience. There might have been local rebellions or barbarian raids, but for thousands of years in China there had never been a war between states. The one great moral justification for the Chinese Empire (as, in its own day, for the Roman) had been that whatever its technical backwardness or social oppressiveness, within its own vast borders it kept the peace.

The new postal service through the Mediterranean and across the Isthmus of Suez was faster than the old packet-ship round the Cape of Good Hope, but even so, Captain Elliot's apologetic report of the engagement at Kowloon and Lord Palmerston's encouraging reply were bound to take months to go and come. If the government in London changed, so might the policy. Captain Elliot had every reason to be worried. His nominal job was to superintend trade – but after committing the British government to a bill for several million pounds in compensation for the confiscated opium, he had just fired the first shots in an undeclared war which he had neither the force nor the authority to sustain. What would Lord Palmerston say? What would the British Parliament say? He had the cordial approval, so far, only of the opium smugglers.

4 Playing at War

*'O just, subtle and all-conquering opium! that, to the hearts of rich
and poor alike, for the wounds that will never heal, and for the pangs
of grief that "tempt the spirit to rebel" bringest an assuaging balm.'*
De Quincey: *Confessions of an English Opium Eater*

As an Irish peer, Lord Palmerston was free to sit in the House
of Commons. He had become a Member of Parliament when only
23, in 1807, and he was to sit in the House – with one small interval
– for fifty-eight consecutive years. His career began with nineteen
years as a minister at the War Office – in the time not only of the
military campaigns which led up to Britain's victory over Napoleon,
but of the social distress, which followed.

Palmerston differed from certain of his colleagues in grasping
the need to head off criticism by making small concessions. In
those days for example, the standard punishment in the British
Army for serious offences was flogging with the cat-o'-nine-tails.
In one year alone – 1814 – over 18 000 British soldiers were flogged,
and this began to cause a public outcry. Though required by his
job to defend this form of punishment in Parliament, Palmerston
was in favour of deflecting criticism by cutting down the maximum
sentence a court martial could award from 300 strokes to 200.
It made no practical difference, but would sound like a concession.
His readiness to shift his ground like this to gain a tactical advantage meant that Palmerston was distrusted by the diehards of
his party. In the reforming 1830s he found it not too much of a
wrench to move over to the Whigs.

As the Whigs' Foreign Minister he made for himself a major
reputation – aggressive, skilful, opportunist. Indeed Lord Palmerston set his mark so firmly on the mid-nineteenth-century Foreign
Office that, even when he was out of office, the permanent officials
who saw eye to eye with him would edge a Minister of a different
party towards a Palmerstonian policy. Officials like Sir George
Robinson, in Canton, who took some other Foreign Minister's
mildness too literally were apt later to find themselves dumped.

Though no orator, Lord Palmerston knew how to make a jaded House of Commons smile, and voters at an election laugh and cheer. He could clinch a debate with a joke, leaving his opponents to drown upside down in their own unanswerable rhetoric. Palmerston was perhaps the first politician of his class to grasp the cynical truth that giving more and more people the right to vote need not matter so much, if accomplished demagogy could somehow slant their choice.

Palmerston was fond of boxing and field sports, light verse and light women. He lived permanently in debt, and the spectacle of old Lord Palmerston, in his white top hat and dyed sidewhiskers, taking horse exercise down Piccadilly and into the Park, was for years one of the familiar sights of London. But when a deputation of cotton spinners came up to London, to urge on him a policy that might ultimately be good for their business, Palmerston always knew what they were driving at. Masked by his affable worldly witticisms was a rigorously trained mind: his teacher at Edinburgh had been Professor Dugald Stewart, friend and interpreter of Adam Smith. To Lord Palmerston the arguments of Adam Smith about the virtues of free trade not only corresponded with Britain's real interests but were intellectually unanswerable.

Frivolous and unscrupulous though Palmerston might be thought, he kept a grip on economic reality, as is shown in what he wrote during January 1841 to Lord Auckland, Governor-General of India, to explain why he was pushing China into war. Here, as Palmerston saw it, is British policy for the next few years in a nutshell:

The rivalship of European manufactures is fast excluding our productions from the markets of Europe, and we must unremittingly endeavour to find in other parts of the world new vents for our industry ... if we succeed in our China expedition, Abyssinia, Arabia, the countries of the Indus and the new markets of China will at no distant period give us a most important extension to the range of our foreign commerce.

On 16 September 1839 John Abel Smith, MP, managed to arrange an interview at the Foreign Office for his client the multimillionaire China merchant, William Jardine. The Foreign Minister failed to show up. Did Lord Palmerston have no sense of urgency about the situation in China?

As Jardine wrote with some irritation to his partner, James Matheson — busy at about that time reorganizing the firm's damaged drug business from his floating office aboard *Hercules* — 'His Lordship appointed Saturday at the Foreign Office ... many people there, but no Lord Palmerston. Parties connected with India and China are becoming very impatient . . . the delay is very provoking.'

A week later, however – on 21 September – word had reached the Foreign Office at last of Lin's behaviour in Canton during the previous March – the time when the merchants had been besieged in the Factories until they agreed to yield up their opium.

Since despatches took months to arrive, Lord Palmerston was still without news of the events of the long summer, which had led up to the 'Battle of Kowloon'. In that time of slow communications he had to judge for himself what might have happened since; but as a politician he could see that the news already come to hand might be adequate as a pretext for bringing military pressure to bear on China.

Palmerston's chief difficulty was not to find troops and ships for his war – they could be provided from India, over which Parliamentary control was indirect. He must find a way of convincing a Parliament in which the government of the day had only an uneasy majority that this recent pretext for going to war with China was overwhelmingly valid. The less emphasis on opium the better.

Lord Palmerston told Abel Smith on 22 September that he was 'desirous of seeing Mr Jardine, as he had many questions to ask', and added: 'I suppose he can tell us what is to be done.' But he was evidently still gathering information and feeling his way. Abel Smith's impression, as reported later by Jardine, was that Lord Palmerston 'was convinced serious notice ought to be taken of the gross insult and of the robbery of our drug, but would not commit himself further even to him with whom he is on intimate terms'.

William Jardine now had the chance of expounding, at the centre of real power, that view of what should be done in China which he and his partner Matheson had been spending so much hard cash to advocate.

Jardine had not long to wait. On 27 September he was invited to call at the Foreign Office, and this time took with him not only Abel Smith, MP, but also Captain Grant, for a long time commodore of the Jardine, Matheson clipper fleet. William Jardine had valuable information to offer which the British Admiralty was anxious to possess – his maps and charts of the China coast, showing the navigational secrets his firm had accumulated during its long experience in the contraband trade.

Jardine spread out these charts 'that his Lordship might have a clear idea of the country with which we must cope'. Then they got down to business. 'The extent of armament, number of troops necessary, number of shipping, all were discussed', Jardine reported, 'but with no direct avowal made to coerce if necessary.' Lord Palmerston kept the charts to show the Cabinet when it met on the Monday following.

Parliament was not to sit again until the New Year, so the immediate problem was to help the Cabinet see the question in a proper light. Jardine went off to help orchestrate pressure from the northern manufacturers and City merchants, who, over recent years, had been brought to believe that they might profit handsomely when a larger market was forcibly opened in China.

The political reaction from carefully organized pressure groups was prompt. On 30 September a letter was put in Lord Palmerston's hands from thirty-nine Manchester firms, pointing out that since the beginning of 1839, cotton goods to the value of £46 200 had been shipped to Canton. This trade was now in jeopardy. The day following, ninety-six London merchant houses with interests in China, and fifty-two Liverpool firms, spokesmen for the port from which cotton textiles were mainly shipped, petitioned Lord Palmerston to interview a delegation of their representatives (one of whom turned out to be none other than John Abel Smith, MP). Other petitions soon followed, from the textile city of Leeds and the port of Bristol.

This campaign was joined by many honest, God-fearing men, manufacturers and merchants alike, who in recent years had been squeezed out of their European and American markets, as other countries industrialized, and were now optimistically looking for a second India in China. Many of the signatories would no doubt have repudiated any wish whatever to foster the opium traffic, had the question been fairly put. The arguments they responded to may have been specious but they found themselves committed, and many like them have preferred to believe, ever since, that the war against China in fact had nothing much to do with opium.

By 13 October, the decision had been taken – so far as one can judge from Jardine's letters, it was taken actually before the Cabinet had 'made up its mind'. To Captain Elliot in Canton, Lord Palmerston sent a secret despatch encouraging him with the news that an expeditionary force, proceeding from India, could be expected to reach Canton about March 1840.

On 23 November, Elliot was sent a further secret despatch, indicating in some detail the diplomatic negotiations he would be expected to carry through, once China had been brought to heel.

Palmerston's instructions went further than most moderate-minded men in Canton, including Elliot himself would have thought necessary. But his lordship's policy corresponded very closely to what the big opium houses had long advocated, and what Jardine on 26 October 1839 had presented as essential in a long memorandum.

Jardine, perhaps a little carried away, sent Palmerston the next day another private memorandum, offering all Jardine, Matheson's opium clippers for service as an auxiliary fleet. He suggested sending to China 'one ship of the largest class of First Rates ... the appearance of such a concentrated force may tend to convince the Chinese of our strength, and their weakness. From such a vessel when at anchor in a safe harbour, many of the small opium vessels might be equipped and placed under the command of Lieutenants of Her Majesty's Navy – their masters, officers and crew (who are generally well acquainted with the coasts and Islands) serving under them.'

As always with Jardine, there was practical good sense in this suggestion. The naval force that eventually reached China did combine three ships-of-the-line, possessing tremendous fire-power, and a flotilla of smaller warships able to work closer inshore. But Jardine had ignored the obvious political difficulty. Getting Parliament to accept as Her Majesty's ships-of-war a drug-smuggling fleet would require sophistry that might well have deterred even Palmerston.

By and large, however, Lord Palmerston used William Jardine's detailed indications as his brief. Early in November 1839 Jardine's suggestions were sent on to the Admiralty, Palmerston emphasizing that they came from 'persons possessed of much local knowledge'. As the naval force Jardine and Palmerston had discussed in such detail – 16 men-of-war, 4 armed steamers, 27 transports carrying 4000 Scottish, Irish and Indian troops – sailed on its way, the First Lord of the Admiralty wrote exuberantly to his friend the Governor-General of India: 'After all, it is nothing more nor less than the conquest of China we have undertaken.'

Two months earlier, on 7 September 1839 a total of thirty-eight sea-going British merchant ships could still be counted at anchor in Hong Kong Bay, and twenty-eight British firms were represented aboard them. Men had their families in those ships, merchants their offices. Housekeeping was uncomfortable and expensive, shore beckoned, and the longer it lasted the slacker became the hold over the floating merchant community of Captain Elliot's personal authority. Of those business houses only a third – though the largest and most influential – had in fact handled the opium to which the Chinese were taking exception. The smaller fry began wondering what the chances might be of an accommodation with the Chinese on business terms. After all, the new season's tea crop was soon due.

Elliot had tried to regain the foothold the British had lost in Macao, but the Governor, da Silveira Pinto, was unwilling to let them even store their goods ashore. Though Macao's annual revenue of about £20 000 was almost all derived from opium, with Lin's troops massed on the far side of the Barrier the Portuguese were unwilling to risk their neutrality.

On 18 September, Elliot, who now had HMS *Volage* and HMS *Hyacinth* to protect the merchant fleet, told Captain James Douglas that the services of his armed merchantman *Cambridge* would no longer be needed. In lieu of the agreed sum of £14 000 for eight months' hire, Captain Douglas had to be content with £2100 for two and a half months; he was not very pleased.

Captain Douglas took the guns out of *Cambridge*, and sold them off to the British authorities. The ship herself passed to the American firm of Delano, at a price of £10 700. She was renamed *Chesapeake* and towed upriver: and early in the New Year Commissioner Lin bought her from the Americans. The Chinese now had one modern ship-of-war.

For overcoming China's military weakness, Lin adopted a twofold policy with curiously modern overtones. He was 'arming the people' – not only raising militia levies at the charge of local landlords, until every Cantonese village had its corps of 'Braves', but also recruiting military and naval irregulars. Five thousand unemployed tea porters were recruited at $6 a month – paid by the Hong merchants – and trained as makeshift soldiers. They could join if they were strong enough to lift over their heads a five-foot spar with a granite wheel at each end, a weight of 133 lb. In August Lin had formed a volunteer fleet of fishermen, and sent them off in their own small boats to patrol and raid, paying them also $6 a month – $12 if they had families. This was good money for fishermen, who in China were so poor they were exempt from taxation. At the same time, Lin made strenuous efforts to copy Western military techniques.

At Fatshan – the great metal-working centre of South China, and a focus of anti-foreign sentiment – a foundry began turning out 5-ton guns to a European model, and under expert foreign superintendence – probably American. In January 1840 Lin began fitting out the Bogue Forts with two hundred modern cannon bought abroad and shipped into Canton – turning 'free trade' to his own advantage. His new purchase, the 1080 ton *Chesapeake,* was moored in the Pearl River to reinforce a blockade of rafts and sunken stone barges which protected the approaches to Canton.

Banners now flew from *Chesapeake*'s mainmast with the symbols Yang and Yin, and the Chinese character signifying *Courage.* A crew was signed on of lascar and Filipino seamen, and local Chinese with ocean-going experience. *Chesapeake* was armed with thirty-four guns bought in Singapore and made in England. When, the year following, a British boarding party had the chance of inspecting her, Captain Hall of *Nemesis* reported that it was 'surprising to see how well the Chinese had prepared for action, the guns being in perfect order, fire buckets distributed about the deck and everything clean and well arranged'. The Western powers still had immense technical superiority in waging war, but it was to be a slowly wasting asset.

On 13 October 1839 Captain Elliot received his first clear hint that he might not be able to carry the dissidents in the floating British community with him much longer: a merchant ship, *Thomas Coutts,* arrived that day off Macao, owned and chartered by men who had no love for the opium business. Her consignee, called Daniell, had once been on the East India Company's Select Committee in Canton, and knew the local scene. Captain Warner, commanding *Thomas Coutts,* had taken a legal opinion in Calcutta as to the validity of Captain Elliot's order which had been keeping British ships out of the Pearl River. He was advised that in English law the ban had no force. (So far no one at Hong Kong knew that an expeditionary force would eventually arrive.)

Lin's offer was still open: the British were as free to trade as the Americans, but they must accept his terms. Any ship guaranteeing that it carried no opium – any merchant signing a bond not to trade in the drug – could proceed freely up to Whampoa. In the hope of undermining Captain Elliot's authority, Lin had gone even further, sending word through the Chinese magistrate in Macao, at the end of September, that if the British found the death-penalty clause in his bond offensive, they could sign a differently worded document, as the Americans had done, and thereafter trade freely in the mouth of the Bogue under the guns of Chuenpi Fort.

Elliot was not wholly unwilling to let the merchants sign the bond in this amended form, but the concession had been coupled with a renewed demand that the murderer of Lin Wei-hsi be given up to Chinese justice. Elliot went through the formality of increasing to $2000 his announced reward for the capture of the murderer – the Chinese themselves had no doubt of the real murderer's identity – but staunchly refused to yield up either the five British seamen who had accepted his sentence, or anyone else.

Both sides were fumbling for yet another formula – the British not to sign the bond, but to have a right to trade outside the Bogue, providing their cargoes were first examined – when Captain Warner of *Thomas Coutts* (1334 tons) knocked the bottom out of all this. He let Daniell, his consignee, simply sign Lin's bond in its original form and sailed up to Whampoa to load tea. Opium was not his business, so he had nothing to fear. Other merchantmen at anchor in Canton Bay, obliged to pay fancy freights to the Americans, took serious note.

Here was an Englishman whom Lin had reason to think might be honest. Promptly he entrusted Captain Warner with his letter to Queen Victoria. In January 1840 Captain Warner acknowledged receipt of the letter, and promised to deliver it. By next June in London, the influential banker Thomas Coutts, who had an interest in the ship named after him, had the letter in his possession, and wrote to Lord Palmerston for an interview. The Foreign Office answer, on 15 June 1840, was a refusal. The British wanted an improved diplomatic contact with China, but only on their own terms.

For Captain Elliot however the situation was touch and go. If others chose to follow the example set by *Thomas Coutts* – and there were signs already of dissatisfaction – the authority he had managed to impose on all these ships during the opium crisis would dwindle. Lin at that moment was very close to getting all he wanted. But, unluckily for him, five days after *Thomas Coutts* entered the Bogue, on 20 October 1839, Captain Elliot opened the seal of the secret despatch from Lord Palmerston, telling him that by June of the year following, 1840, 16 warships and 4000 troops would arrive in China. So while waiting he could afford to be provocative.

Incompatible accounts are given by British and Chinese sources of exactly what came next, but the order of events would appear to be something like this. Since Elliot had refused to trade at Chuenpi on the terms he offered, Lin gave the British an ultimatum: their ships must either start doing business or leave China. He announced that any British captain not signing the bond must quit Canton Bay in three days' time. Captain Smith of *Volage* riposted with a demand, on behalf of the British, to be allowed within three days to live ashore and buy supplies. A second British ship, *Royal Saxon* (Captain Towns), in from Java with a cargo of rice, was said to be ready to sign the bond.

On 2 November 1839 in the mouth of the Bogue lay a Chinese fleet of 26 ships – 15 war junks and 14 fireships – commanded by formidable old Admiral Kuan. To any British merchantmen who might now choose to go upriver, those Chinese ships-of-war hinted at protection, yet also they implied a threat. What if those fireships made an attack one night on the rest of the British flotilla, now under orders to quit, and crowded with refugees?

Captain Elliot's despatch reporting what happened to Lord Palmerston left *Royal Saxon*'s probable intentions out of the account. The Chinese say that on 3 November 1839 *Royal Saxon*, having signed the bond, was peaceably making towards the river mouth, to proceed up to Whampoa and unload her duty-free cargo of rice, when HMS *Volage* fired a warning shot across her bows. Southward from Chuenpi, the Chinese war junks had anchored in line, offering cover to *Royal Saxon* and any who might choose to follow her example.

What seems likely is that Admiral Kuan, under pretext of helping *Royal Saxon*, might have been watching his chance to attack the British merchant fleet with his fireships so as to enforce Lin's ultimatum. Kuan may also have intended boarding the ship in which Lin Wei-hsi's murderer was known to be serving, so as to seize and carry off, if not the murderer himself, at any rate an expiatory victim.

Captain Elliot himself had spent the last two nerve-racking days with Captain Smith aboard his frigate, and between these two experienced British naval officers a difference of opinion was emerging. Smith had already written to Admiral Kuan, warning those junks back into their anchorage at the mouth of the Bogue. Admiral Kuan – whose experience of the effect of modern gunfire, at Kowloon, had been somewhat unconvincing – replied confidently: '... all I want is the murderous barbarian who killed Lin Wei-hsi. As soon as a time is named when he will be given up, my ships will return into the Bogue. Otherwise, by no means whatsoever shall I accede.'

Captain Elliot, conciliatory towards the Chinese except when he lost his head, wanted to give Admiral Kuan an answer in writing, but Captain Smith had had quite enough of diplomacy. Once night fell, how could *Volage* and *Hyacinth* possibly stop Kuan's fireships from slipping past and wreaking havoc? In Captain Smith's professional opinion, the time for argument was past. Either the Chinese junks went back as they were bid, or they must be forced back.

At noon on 3 November, since Kuan had not shifted, Captain Smith hoisted the signal to engage. The twenty-nine Chinese ships of war were still strung out in line, north and south, with the wind easterly and the sea moderate. The 28-gun *Volage*, with the 18-gun, flush-decked *Hyacinth* following her, bore away northwards, both ships with the wind on their quarter, favourable for coming sharply about. They commenced the action by giving the hulls of the Chinese junks their starboard broadsides at a range of only fifty yards. The answering shot from the Chinese guns – as usual when they were closely engaged – flew high and harmless. At the end of the line the British ships-of-war put about, and on their return gave the Chinese a hammering with their port broadsides.

This unequal encounter, later called the Battle of Chuenpi, lasted three-quarters of an hour, Admiral Kuan himself, according to Elliot's report, 'manifesting a resolution of behaviour honourably enhanced by the hopelessness of his efforts'. Kuan's valour aroused so much real admiration in the British that when, smashed up and waterlogged, he broke off the action in the hope of limping back to shore, *Hyacinth* was ordered not to sink him. Three war junks were sunk already, one had blown up when her powder magazine was hit, many were badly hulled. There had been unimportant damage by high-flying cannon-balls to the frigate's rigging, and one British seaman was wounded. At the Battle of Chuenpi the largest Chinese naval force that could be handled as a unit had been knocked to smithereens by two rather small British warships.

Captain Elliot's authority over his countrymen was satisfactorily re-established by the action. Three weeks later he received from Lord Palmerston the second secret despatch, which gave him in clear outline the diplomacy he was to follow, and defined the terms to which the Chinese were to be reduced, once the expeditionary force had done its work.

At the beginning of December, thirty-two British ships were at anchor off Hong Kong, but still managing to trade surreptitiously despite the order sent by the Chinese Emperor on 19 November that the British were to be 'cut off from their rhubarb and tea'.

The large export of Chinese rhubarb, a purgative root, from Canton to Britain had long fascinated the Chinese authorities. Peking was even toying with a theory that a purge of rhubarb must be physically essential to the British, or else, with their repulsive diet of greasy meat and boiled vegetables, would they not all become hopelessly constipated? Depriving the British of their rhubarb might bring them to their knees.

On 6 December 1839, following on the action at Chuenpi, Lin stopped trade with Britain 'for ever'. During the first six months of 1840 no foreign flag was hoisted at Canton, though a dozen or so foreign ships stuck it out at Whampoa. About a fortnight after the secret despatch from London had arrived, rumours about an expeditionary force from India began to reach the Chinese. Lin was sceptical, the Americans less so, but all concerned began to get ready for the eventuality. Lin pressed on with buying his guns and strengthening his forts. The Americans shipped out every chest of tea and bale of silk they could lay hands on. Between 1 October 1839 and 18 June 1840 a total of 24 826 599 pounds' weight of tea intended for Britain was freighted down by American businessmen.

In these months of waiting the system of anti-opium repression along the coasts of Kwangtung and Fukien became more efficient, and the coastal trade less profitable, until by June 1840 a cargo of the drug arriving from Singapore was on offer at the give-away price of $268 a chest. Lin might be making so many difficulties along the coast that the drug had become hard to dispose of, but in Canton Bay a use was being found for it. The Chinese bumboats that brought fresh vegetables to the British merchant fleet from shore were extorting high prices, so the British began paying them off in pieces of opium. The fishermen Lin had armed made a fire-raft attack on these supply boats, and claimed to have burned twenty-three of them.

When Captain Elliot was driven to violent action against the Chinese he commonly had misgivings soon after. He gave them clear expression in his despatch to Lord Palmerston of 16 Novem-

ber 1839, written directly after the action at Chuenpi, but discussing – significantly – the topic of opium. No man, Captain
Elliot informed the Foreign Minister, 'entertained a deeper detestation of the disgrace and sin of this forced traffic on the coast of
China'. He admitted seeing 'little to choose between it and piracy
... as a public officer he had steadily discountenanced it by all
the lawful means in his power, and at the total sacrifice of his
private comfort in the society in which he had lived for years.'

Someone as emotionally case-hardened as Lord Palmerston
could hardly be expected to feel similar qualms, but such misgivings as Elliot's were indicative of the unease felt on the spot
by a number of men of goodwill – including merchants and professional men, British as well as American. The special circumstances of the drug trade, that is to say the secret patronage it
enjoyed because of its connection with the Indian revenue, forced
upon the Canton merchants – as on Elliot – a series of hideous
dilemmas. Opium was also on Britain's conscience, and the Parliamentary debate on the coming war would afford a moment for
self-examination.

William Jardine and Lord Palmerston were men of a similar
age, both formed in the wars against Napoleon, and both sharing,
despite their differing backgrounds, the same brute grasp upon
reality. The extent to which smuggler and statesman saw eye to
eye over China is given confidential expression in Jardine's letter
to his partner Matheson of 14 December 1839. Reporting that
finally the Cabinet had 'made up its mind to act a decided part,
and demand reparation', Jardine admits that he has that day sent
Palmerston 'a paper of hints'. Jardine's personal view of the armed
force required in China turned out to correspond very closely with
the force actually sent (except that Jardine stipulated for 7000
soldiers, only 4000 arrived, and the campaign went awry for
lack of men on the ground).

The guidelines for Elliot's diplomatic pressure on the Chinese
were also recognizably close to what the big drug traffickers had
always wanted. Therefore following Palmerston's policy to the
letter, as Captain Elliot must have known from the start, would
make him an instrument of the very drug traffickers Elliot so
detested. As a servant of the Crown all his life, Elliot was condi-
tioned to obedience, but from this time on, in his official actions,
hesitation shows, and punches are pulled.

Though other officers might sneer behind his back, Elliot
after this is lenient with the Chinese whenever he gets the chance,
thereby managing to mislead them into supposing that the British

lacked a strong aggressive purpose. At the end of the account the Chinese paid an unwarrantably high price for Captain Elliot's good intentions.

British and American commentators at the time and since have strongly urged the view that in 1839 the real issue was not opium but extra-territoriality – or, sometimes, the Open Door in China. The argument is respectable, but it must be recognized that the British government laid down from the start a policy and a strategy which corresponded very closely to the declared needs of the big opium smugglers. The war, in taking its course, was bound to define more sharply all other points of contention between China and the maritime powers. But to begin with, as Lord Palmerston civilly admitted to John Abel Smith, MP, once the fighting was over, 'To the assistance and information which you, my dear Smith, and Mr Jardine so handsomely afforded us, it was mainly owing that we were able to give our affairs naval military and diplomatic, in China those detailed instructions which have led to these satisfactory results.'

Lin, with approval from Peking, had been trying to sow dissension between the British and other foreigners at Canton, especially the Americans. Opium, after all, came mainly from British territory, and the time was propitious, since Britain and the United States were already publicly at odds over the boundaries of Oregon and Maine.

But though a slightly pro-Chinese neutrality had been paying them so handsomely, American merchants in Canton were beginning to waver. They had no wish to pick the losing side, and if it came to war, who could expect the Chinese to win? But if the British won their war with no help from the United States, might they not be tempted in the peace settlement to exclude their main competitor from the markets of China?

Until now, Imperial China had admitted foreign traders on equal terms, but there was already serious talk in Peking of doing what the Japanese had done, and barring foreign trade altogether. (The Japanese ban against opium importation and use was also rigorous and effective.) If Britain did succeed in forcing open the door to China – and what was to stop her? – had not America better get a foot inside quickly?

Some Americans, however, were openly on China's side. For instance, Caleb Cushing, a clever lawyer whose family had done well, at one time, out of the opium trade (though they had later renounced it), stood up in the House of Representatives on 16 March 1840 to voice this warning:

I trust the idea will be no longer entertained in England, if she chooses to persevere in the attempt to coerce the Chinese by force of arms to submit to be poisoned by opium by whole provinces, that she is to receive aid or countenance from the United States in that nefarious enterprise.

The other side of the question was put in a memorial to Washington from American merchants in Canton which called out for armed intervention on a scale that might cramp the style of the British. If only France, Britain and the United States – they said – were jointly to blockade the Chinese coast, a treaty could be obtained, without bloodshed, which would put foreign trade on a safe footing. (In fact, as time was to show, if Great Britain won her war, the United States had more to gain than lose.)

Consul Delano wrote to Lin on 26 April, warning him that a British fleet was due by June, and would undoubtedly blockade Canton. Could not the clearance of American ships from harbour meanwhile be speeded up? Lin, still trying to convince himself that no British fleet was going to arrive, answered with annoyance that Canton was a Chinese city – so how could the British blockade it? He reminded the Americans tartly that they were not subject to Britain any more, and that since the British left Canton they had been making more money than ever. The rift was showing.

So far Lord Palmerston had been able to keep his critics in the dark, and thus preserve his freedom of action. The war with China was badly needed, among other reasons, because of the generous promise Captain Elliot had made to compensate those whose opium had been destroyed.

Elliot had put the government in debt to the tune of over £2 000 000. Possibly his hand had been forced. Certainly, the big opium houses had connections in London influential enough to make serious political trouble were this pledge dishonoured. Party discipline was less operative in those days, and the government in which Palmerston served was chronically unsure of its majority. The opium men could make trouble, but any proposal to compensate them with a cool two million of public money was even more likely to upset the apple-cart.

Suppose, however, that the two million could be extracted from the pockets of the Chinese themselves? What if a war in the Orient could be made to pay for itself? By the time the House of Commons got to hear, the expeditionary force would be poised for

107

action – and, whatever its merits, a war once begun is never easy for political critics to bring to a halt.

Questions in Parliament by 12 March 1840 were getting uncomfortably close to the real point, but Lord Palmerston skilfully prevaricated, his tongue in his cheek, as he nudged what confused memories his hearers might still retain of the Macartney and Amherst Missions, by saying coolly that the object of the expedition was 'not to commence hostilities, but to open up communication with the Emperor of China'.

During the next few days criticism both open and private of the government's China policy became sharper. Tories were reminded of the fiasco involving the late Lord Napier, for which Lord Palmerston was personally responsible, and which had earned him the cutting rebuke from their leader, Wellington. Lord Palmerston would have to deal not only with Tory critics on the benches opposite but with certain doubters in his own ranks – humanitarians who had heard from missionaries about the horror of the opium dens, and spokesmen of merchants doing a legitimate business with China, who considered that ever since the East India Company's monopoly had ended, the British in Canton were being needlessly provocative.

Sir Robert Peel, the astute leader of the Tory opposition, decided to introduce a motion of censure in such terms that Palmerston's critics on both sides of the House might be tempted to vote for it. Facts were lacking about the threatened war; Peel's motion criticized Palmerston's handling of the China situation. There were several lines of attack.

Sir James Graham opened the debate for the Opposition with a well-informed but monotonous speech that went on for more than two hours. He reminded the House that a sixth of the public revenue in Britain and India, taken together, came from the China trade, in the form of tea tax and opium profits. Though Captain Elliot had repeatedly asked for instructions to regulate the opium traffic, none had ever been sent.

Thomas Babington Macaulay, who at 39 was Secretary of State for War, and already celebrated for his *Essays*, made a slashing and high-flown reply. As a member from 1834 to 1838 of the Supreme Council for India, Macaulay was better placed than most others in the House to explain frankly, if he chose, the equivocal basis of the opium trade, but in speaking for the government he concentrated on the vivid and the colourful, as if he were standing on his feet and making up an essay as he went along. Macaulay's peroration concentrated with immense effect upon

Captain Elliot's glorious action in running up the Union Jack the moment he arrived at the beleaguered Factories in Canton after having dodged the river blockade.

... the victorious flag was hoisted over them ... reminded them that they belonged to a country unaccustomed to defeat, to submission or shame ... I beg to declare [Macaulay went on] my earnest desire that this most rightful quarrel may be prosecuted to a triumphal close ... that the name not only of English valour but of English mercy may be established.

Sidney Herbert, from the Tory benches, in a chiding riposte, pointed out that '... we are engaged in a war without just cause ... we are endeavouring to maintain a trade resting upon unsound principles, and to justify proceedings which are a disgrace to the British flag'. But Macaulay's oratory, if it had clarified few issues, had made pulses beat faster.

By far the most interesting, accurate and cogent speaker was William Ewart Gladstone – who, at 30, had not long since been described by Macaulay as 'the rising hope of the stern unbending Tories'. Gladstone's speech in this debate marks a turning-point in his career. Somewhere at this time of his life the severe young Tory, who but a few years earlier had voted unhesitatingly for flogging soldiers and excluding Jews from Parliament, began to move off at the tangent which took him, later, to the leadership of the Liberal Party, and, over Ireland, some long way beyond.

John Gladstone, his father, a Liverpool merchant of Scottish origin, had founded his huge fortune by speculating successfully in corn during the bread shortages of the Napoleonic Wars. As peace approached, John Gladstone invested heavily in sugar plantations worked by slaves. There was a slave rising in 1823 on his Demerara estate after which twenty-seven leaders were executed, most without trial. But this equivocal background, though no doubt psychologically omnipresent in the relations between father and family, were physically a long way distant from the pleasant Lancashire country house where William Ewart Gladstone and his sister Helen had been brought up with their ponies and flowers and piety and music.

At Christ Church, where he took a double first, and in the House of Commons, to which he was elected when only 23, young Gladstone, though a serious, talented, devout, and eloquent man, never developed much beyond the opinions to be expected in someone of his background. But Indian opium cast an irrational shadow over his as over many other Victorian homes.

Helen, his lively and beloved sister, had been given laudanum for a minor ailment, and soon found in doses of opium what she lacked in life. By 24 she was a hopeless and scandalous addict. Gladstone when he rose to speak in the Opium War debate had not long recovered from a nervous crisis, during which he had taken his addicted sister abroad, in the vain hope of a cure. He spoke as one who had mastered the subject, yet with an undertone of passion.

'Does he know that the opium smuggled into China', Gladstone asked the House, in reference to Macaulay, 'comes exclusively from British ports, that is, from Bengal and through Bombay? . . . that we require no preventive service to put down this illegal traffic? We have only to stop the sailing of the smuggling vessels . . . it is a matter of certainty that if we stopped the exportation of opium from Bengal and broke up the depot at Lintin and checked the cultivation of it in Malwa and put a moral stigma on it we should greatly cripple if not extinguish the trade in it.

'They gave you notice to abandon your contraband trade', he went on. 'When they found you would not do so they had the right to drive you from their coasts on account of your obstinacy in persisting with this infamous and atrocious traffic . . . justice, in my opinion, is with them; and whilst they, the Pagans, the semi-civilized barbarians, have it on their side, we, the enlightened and civilized Christians, are pursuing objects at variance both with justice and with religion . . . a war more unjust in its origin, a war calculated in its progress to cover this country with a permanent disgrace, I do not know and I have not read of.' Gladstone curtly rejected Macaulay's flagwagging, in one phrase. 'Now, under the auspices of the noble Lord, that flag is become a pirate flag, to protect an infamous traffic.'

When Lord Palmerston rose in reply, he knew that both the moral and the severely practical issues which Gladstone had invoked were not necessarily relevant to the power situation he had to face. A Parliamentary debate where important speeches dragged on eloquently for hours could be a boring as well as a serious occasion, even to Victorians.

All Palmerston needed was a majority of votes. To get it, he adopted a bantering tone, emphasizing Macaulay's clever irrelevancies, but to clinch his argument he had a couple of extra aces in his cuff.

'I wonder what the House would have said to me', Palmerston asked genially, 'if I had come down to it with a large naval estimate for a number of revenue cruisers . . . for the purpose of preserving the morals of the Chinese people, who were disposed to buy what other people were disposed to sell them?' Palmerston went on to remind his audience that ending the Indian opium monopoly would simply increase the Turkish or Persian crop, then he played his two strong cards.

The Foreign Secretary read out the memorial that American merchants in Canton had sent to Congress, asking for a joint naval force from Britain, France and the United States: making it sound as if the vital issue there might not be opium, but the problem of bringing China into the comity of civilized nations.

The House was also informed by Palmerston of a petition just come to hand, signed by representatives of important British firms trading to China, which bluntly declared that 'unless measures of the government are followed up with firmness and energy, the trade with China can no longer be conducted with security to life and property, or with credit or advantage to the British nation'. This petition was headed, as it happened, with the signature of one William Jardine.

But the sleight-of-hand served its purpose. The House divided 262 votes against 271 – a close-run thing. Peel's motion of censure was lost by only nine votes, but, for the government of the day, nine votes was a majority.

On 9 June 1840 another 28-gun frigate, HMS *Alligator*, joined HMS *Volage* in Canton Bay. The threatened blockade of Canton could now begin.

William Jardine, in his 'paper of hints', had asked for two ships-of-the-line. These were battleships powerful enough to bombard coastal cities to destruction from deep water, though far too large for work close inshore. He thought these big ships should be supplemented by twelve frigates, two river steamers, able to move in shallow waters independently of wind and tide, and the transports necessary for 7000 men.

Jardine had gone on to advise a blockade of the Peh-ho River – the water-route to Peking – which would bring pressure to bear directly on the Imperial Court. An offshore island should be captured, both as a military base, and as a pawn when it came to bargaining with the Chinese over terms. The destroyed opium must of course be paid for, and further ports opened to trade. Jardine had suggested Amoy, Foochow, Ningpo and Shanghai.

The naval forces that arrived in *Alligator*'s wake were stronger

111

than Jardine had stipulated. There were three 74-gun ships-of-the-line (*Melville, Wellesley* and *Blenheim*), two first-rate frigates (*Druid* and *Blonde,* 46 guns), five 28-gun frigates, eight corvettes and brigs of ten to eighteen guns, and four armed steamers belonging to the East India Company. Three thousand six hundred fighting men – Scottish and Irish infantry, and Indian troops from Madras and Bengal – arrived in twenty-seven transports. The Indian troops had as usual been mutinous about their orders to serve overseas. Later on in the Indian Army a stock threat to sepoys was, '. . . and you will be sent to China, and there you will be killed'.

The opium business, when the Navy arrived in such force, was at once reorganized on its old footing. The receiving ships took station at Lintin, and fast smuggling galleys began to run the drug ashore in broad daylight. Opium prices were openly published in the *Canton Register*, and wherever the British fleet went the opium clippers followed them. Three ships in the fleet now assembling in Canton Bay came from the squadron, based at the Cape of Good Hope, which normally had the duty of patrolling the West African coast to put down the slave trade. One curious outcome of the first Opium War was that slave-traders to Brazil and the southern United States had an easier run for their money.

Flying his flag in *Melville* was Captain Charles Elliot's cousin, the Hon. George Elliot, who as a Rear-Admiral not only outranked the Superintendent of Trade, but had it so happened been appointed Senior Plenipotentiary, with Captain Charles Elliot as his junior. Admiral Elliot, a veteran who had done praiseworthy service under Nelson, was subject as his memoirs show to few of those impulses of sympathy or misgiving which Palmerston must by now have noted in Captain Elliot's attitude towards the Chinese.

Captain Elliot, however, did not let this snub deter him from making whenever possible his careful distinctions in favour of China. He proclaimed when hostilities began that the expedition was not against peaceful Chinese, but had been caused simply by Lin's bad treatment of the English, who in their turn now proposed to act only against the mandarins, and the officers and soldiers of the government. Captain Elliot invited the Cantonese to continue trading – this evidently was how, after his years as Superintendent of Trade, Elliot continued to see his task: to maintain business as usual in the intervals of bombardment. Even when, later, a British army was threatening the City of Canton with assault, Captain Elliot went out of his way to remind

112

the British General that 'the protection of the people of Canton and the encouragement of their goodwill towards us are perhaps our chief political duties in this country'.

Outside the Gate of Eternal Purity (which also, significantly, led to Canton's execution ground) Lin had established in May 1840 a refuge for confirmed opium smokers who sought to break the habit. Lacking the resources of modern medicine, the cure he offered was necessarily painful – a course of pills taken in solitary confinement. Of smokers who would rather persist with their habit, the official Chinese view was: 'Those who are unwilling, or cannot leave off, must wait till they die of the disease they themselves have engendered.'

To animate the spirits of his men and to lay his hands on hostages, Lin also put up a prize-money list. The reward for sinking a 74-gun ship-of-the-line was $20 000. A naval commander captured alive was worth $5000; dead, he would fetch only a third; Captain Elliot was priced at a flattering $50 000. White rank-and-file were good for $100 a head, but the sepoys, or 'black barbarians', were rated low, at $20. The sepoys soon earned a bad reputation for violence against Chinese villagers and their womenfolk, but appear also to have shared somewhat in an odium directed against the Parsees, for many years past conspicuous in Canton by their tall caps and flowing robes. Parsees were the acknowledged agents for Malwa opium.

On 24 and 25 June 1840 the greater part of the British fleet moved off and out of sight, leaving only three familiar vessels, *Volage, Hyacinth* and *Larne,* backed up by a first-class frigate, *Druid,* to maintain the blockade of Canton. Lin was tempted to take it for granted that his much-improved river defences, including those hundreds of modern cannon, had deterred the British, and diverted them to the north. Lin's American informants soon warned him that the British warships had gone north so as to threaten the island of Chou-shan.

The British authorities in London had been enlightened as to the strategic potentialities of Chou-shan – an island fifty-one miles around, which grew tea and made rice wine, and was placed off the mouth of China's largest river, the Yangtze. Chinese taxes were paid in grain, which was shipped every year in enormous quantities up the 1000-mile-long Grand Canal, to feed Peking. In a typical year – 1831 – over a quarter of a million tons of grain had been moved up the Canal in thousands of junks, by a workforce of 64 000 men. From a base on Chou-shan, this traffic on the Grand Canal could be threatened.

The opium smugglers had got a footing on Chou-shan several years before. In 1836 Jardine had written to one of his clipper captains, John Rees: 'How would it answer to send a vessel to the Chou-shan group? ... with perseverance and good management, not neglecting bribes, or fees, to the Mandarins, we must I think succeed to some extent.' In January 1838 he sent Captain Jauncey in *Governor Findlay* to Chou-shan with a cargo of Malwa opium, and orders to take raw silk in exchange. Of late years, while the drug habit was thus being implanted among them, the Chinese on Chou-shan so identified foreign ships with opium that when, as part of the invasion fleet, HMS *Modeste* made her landfall there, a bag of dollars was thrown on deck. Not long after, up bobbed the head of a local drug smuggler, expecting to buy supplies.

The capital of Chou-shan Island was the port of Tin-hai – a small city of about 50 000 inhabitants, facing a land-locked harbour. Tin-hai was enclosed within a five-sided wall – twenty-two feet high and fifteen feet thick, with defensive towers at intervals – and protected on four sides by a canal. The fifth side was overlooked by a steep hill with a joss-house on top and this hill was a point of weakness in the defence – a hostile battery installed there could command and bombard the city.

The normal garrison of Chou-shan was a militia of 1600 men. Since, in China, the soldier's trade had for thousands of years been despised, military service there, as indeed in nineteenth-century Britain, was left to a rank-and-file of misfits, scallywags and the very poor. On Chou-shan the local militia – usually poor fishermen or sailors – assembled once a year, drew their spears, bows-and-arrows and matchlocks from the armoury, went through their exercise a few times, and dispersed.

As the British fleet moved leisurely into position offshore, there were about 800 of these ill-trained and worse-armed Chinese militia on the vital hill with the joss-house, which was defended by six guns. These were not Lin's modern weapons, but old-style Chinese pieces, wedged into stone embrasures so that they could neither be levelled nor trained. The local powder was so bad that Chinese roundshot appeared sometimes merely to roll down the bore and tumble out.

Many native craft had been drawn up for safety at the water's edge. Defending them, eleven war junks had formed line, between

114

the British fleet and the shore, their red-muzzled guns aimed seaward, and their coloured streamers flaunting. The Chinese Admiral's flagship could be identified by a badge representing three tigers' heads, astern. Along the wharf, 600 more militia had formed up, behind an improvised rampart of grain bags.

On the evening of 4 July, the Chinese commander, Brigadier Chang Ch'ao fa, came out in a boat, and boarded HMS *Wellesley*. Interpreting for Colonel, later Major-General, George Burrell, recently promoted from the Royal Irish to command the British force, was the Rev. Dr Karl Gutzlaff. Brigadier Chang was allowed to inspect at his leisure the overpowering broadside of the British battleship, and Gutzlaff then called upon him to surrender by dawn next day. Chang acknowledged the unaccountable force that confronted him, but added: 'Still, I *must* fight', and was rowed ashore.

Ranged at anchor across Tin-hai harbour, their broadsides loaded with grape and ball, and trained on the Chinese town and its fortifications, were *Wellesley* (74 guns), *Conway* and *Alligator* (28 guns), *Cruiser* and *Algerine* (18 guns) and ten brigs each mounting ten or more guns apiece. As the sun came up, there was no sign from the Chinese of a white flag.

By 2 p.m. the troops, who all morning had been clambering down from the decks of their transports, to fill ships' boats at the rear of the men-of-war, were ready for their landing. They were in light order, carrying weapons and ammunition and one day's cooked rations. The boats formed into two lines. As with dipping oars the blue-jackets rowed the soldiers ashore, a broadside from *Wellesley*, aimed at the joss-house on the hill, announced the overwhelming bombardment. All the shore guns and war junks made answer – a brave but entirely hopeless answer – to the scientific crescendo of fire.

After only nine minutes a succession of fifteen broadsides from the warships had smashed Tin-hai into helplessness. 'The crashing of timber, falling houses and groans of men resounded from the shore', said an eyewitness of this bombardment. '... even after it ceased, a few shots were still heard from the unscathed junks ... we landed on a deserted beach, a few dead bodies, bows and arrows, broken spears and guns remaining the sole occupants of the field.'

The Chinese Admiral had his legs shot off, and died soon after. The Chinese Magistrate and several of his subordinates committed suicide in despair. The Madras Artillery got four of their guns ashore, and within two hours had them mounted on the hill; at a range of 400 yards they began systematically firing into the now defenceless town. As night fell, thousands of Chinese civilians could be seen, streaming out of the gates, headed for the countryside, sped on their way by a dropping fire from the British artillery. None of the British had so far been wounded.

British officers arriving ashore were not long in discovering that Tin-hai was stocked to the brim with jars of *samshun* – a potent rice wine, flavoured with garlic and aniseed. They promptly began smashing jars, until the streets ran with liquor. But after rowing the troops ashore, the seamen from the fleet had been allowed to stay there. There was no keeping Jack Tar from the rice wine: soon drunken soldiers and sailors were roaring through the flaming wreckage of the desolated town and its suburbs, for the time being utterly out of control. No person, no property, was safe. 'A more complete pillage', reported the *India Gazette*, 'could not be conceived ... the plunder ceased only when there was nothing to take or destroy.'

This was the occasion after which the Hindi word *lūt* – previously used in an English form only hesitantly, and with inverted commas – became firmly established in the language, as *loot*. In taking Tin-hai, two thousand Chinese were killed. British losses, at the end of the day, were nineteen. Gutzlaff came ashore, with an entourage of mainland Chinese who would do his bidding, and was installed as Civil Magistrate.

David Jardine and Donald Matheson, representing the family firm, reached Chou-shan by clipper on 11 July, but the Admiral, perhaps under the influence of his cousin, was so far refusing to let opium vessels into harbour. The opium traders were not to be fobbed off. Lin's intelligence agents on Chou-shan had soon to report that the British were unloading some of their opium there at the astounding price of $100 a chest: a bargain offer to encourage new customers. With war under way, the drug trade was reviving. Between August and November 1840, 43 vessels were reported as being engaged in opium smuggling – 16 larger ships mounting 6–16 guns, and 27 smaller brigs and schooners mounting 4–12 guns. Supplies were flowing in; at the change of the monsoon, 12 000 chests of opium had reached China from India and 30 000 more were in transit.

Drug traffickers on Chou-shan were followed not long after by the missionaries. William Lockhart, of the London Missionary Society, set up a clinic there, under the protection of the British troops: opinion latterly had swung towards medical missions as the most impressive way of opening the Chinese mind to the superiority of Christian doctrine. The clinic was badly needed: 1600

Chinese patients were admitted between September and the end of the year.

The British on Chou-shan had, as it turned out, less to fear from their Chinese opponents than from their own commanding officer. Though thousands of empty houses, not to mention temples and public buildings, were available as billets in Tin-hai, the troops were put under canvas on a fever-ridden site amid paddy fields – Colonel Burrell giving as a reason his unwillingness to upset Chinese religious prejudices.

With the temperature going over 90 degrees in the shade, Colonel Burrell continued to insist that his men wear their serge coats tightly buttoned up to the neck. At the end of the account, he lost 448 men from dysentery and intermittent fever. The plenipotentiaries sent to India for a more experienced officer to replace him.

The damage, however, had been done. Sir Hugh Gough, arriving late in the day from India to take over, had his style badly cramped for lack of effectives. The Cameronians, for example – a regiment with a good record for health and morale – had left their barracks at Fort William in India with 28 officers and 902 other ranks, and only 6 reporting sick. At the end of 1840, only 110 Cameronians were fit for duty, and 240 were dead. As one senior officer commented bitterly in a letter home: 'We are playing at war, instead of waging it.'

In 1837 Thomas Love Peacock, the satirical novelist and hater of modernity who had been Shelley's friend, gave evidence to a Parliamentary Subcommittee on Steam Navigation. Peacock as Examiner at the East India Company was officially an advocate of using steamships imperially in the East – but the other side of his mind flashed out when to one questioner he riposted, 'I am not aware that it would be any benefit to the people of India to send Europeans among them.' As a result of Peacock's professional acumen (not his hidden doubts) five steamers were available in good time for operations in Chinese waters. The most famous of them, *Nemesis*, was launched from Laird's at Birkenhead early in 1840.

She was an iron paddle-steamer of 700 tons, with a 120-horse-power steam engine and auxiliary sails – specially designed to draw no more than six feet of water when fully laden, yet to carry two swivel 32-pounders, five 6-pounders and a battery of smaller iron swivel-guns. *Nemesis* was flat-bottomed, with two sliding keels, a retractable rudder, and a hull divided into seven water-tight compartments, which made her in effect almost unsinkable by Chinese gunnery, not to say fire-rafts.

When *Nemesis* left Portsmouth on 28 March 1840, though commanded by officers of the Royal Navy, she was officially des-cribed as an armed merchantman. Her destination was given as the Russian Black Sea port of Odessa.

Nemesis showed up next at the Cape of Good Hope, where her unusual design and perplexing function earned her the nickname of 'Mystery'. She left the Cape reputedly for Australia, but arrived off Macao – the first iron ship to reach China from Europe under her own steam. The British now had a ship-of-war that could make headway against all predictable opposition up to the very walls of Canton.

Under Lin's encouragement, the local Chinese were, however, learning modern military techniques as if their lives were at stake. Each time the British captured Chinese war *matériel* after an engagement, they would need to take note of some up-to-date detail – a bomb-proof casement, an effective gun-carriage at long last, or an efficient chain-shot. But how could the Chinese possibly imitate *Nemesis*?

A foreign 'devil-ship' was propelled by paddles, and powered by steam. The Chinese had brains and courage, but no industrial base: they therefore built themselves a war junk driven by a large paddle like an under-shot waterwheel – but it had to be worked by human muscle. They had adapted for war a vessel invented in China years before. There was no steam engine, but coolies toiled round and round, moving the capstan bars that worked the windlass that rotated the paddle wheel.

Blonde (Captain Bourchier), sent to Amoy, the seaport on a granite island off the coast of Fukien, with a letter from Lord Palmerston to the Chinese Prime Minister, had delivered it in a manner not entirely diplomatic. Since a boat going ashore with his interpreter was fired upon, Captain Bourchier poured broadsides into Amoy until fort and town were silent, then stuck a bamboo in the beach with the letter attached, and went away without further comment.

The two plenipotentiaries, Captain Elliot and his cousin the Admiral, went north in *Wellesley* (74 guns) escorted by *Blonde* and three other frigates, *Volage*, *Modeste* and *Pylades*, and the steamer *Madagascar*, and came to anchor in Peh-ho Bay. The muddy mouth of the Peh-ho River – the waterway connecting Peking with the sea, up which Lord Macartney's embassy had sailed, years before – was guarded by considerable fortifications, the Taku Forts. Frowning down on them from one of these forts the plenipotentiaries could observe amid ancient Chinese cannon a row of British field pieces on regulation gun-carriages – in fact, the battery Lord Macartney had included among his gifts to the old Emperor in the previous century.

The river mouth was obstructed by a bar, which *Madagascar*, drawing only 11 ft 6 in., managed to get over with a few inches to spare at high tide. Even though the larger ships of war could not enter the river, the Chinese considered these intruders as uncomfortably close to Peking.

This time Palmerston's letter was taken in hand – by 57-year-old Ch'i Shan, a Manchu grandee of Mongol descent, who as Viceroy of Chihli, the province that included the capital, was the most important of Chinese provincial viceroys. For his interview with Captain Elliot, Ch'i Shan for a man in his position was modestly dressed, in a robe of blue silk and white satin boots. His broad-brimmed summer straw hat bore not only the deep red coral button of his rank but also the peacock feather of Imperial favour. Courteous, diplomatic, amenable, oblique, Ch'i Shan was secretly appalled at the danger to the dynasty represented by the arrival of this British naval squadron.

Ch'i Shan had earlier expressed misgivings as to where a strong anti-opium policy might lead. If the Emperor caved in now to this crude and visible barbarian threat, the incipient dissatisfaction all over China with Manchu rule might flare up into revolt. These barbarians must somehow be jockeyed back to Canton, to the Empire's outer edge, and a scapegoat must be found. Since the barbarian passion for meat was well known, Ch'i meanwhile 'soothed' them with large deliveries of mutton, beef and poultry.

The text of Lord Palmerston's letter happened to play into Ch'i Shan's hands. Much of it, inevitably, was concerned with specific complaints against Lin's conduct, and by chance it came under the Emperor's eye on the same day as Lin's own detailed report from Canton. Lord Palmerston had used the phrase, 'to demand from the Emperor satisfaction and redress' but somehow in translation this had been toned down, so that, in Chinese, it read, 'to beg the Emperor to settle and redress a grievance'. If Lin's conduct were the barbarians' only real grievance, that could easily be settled.

'Lin caused the war by his excessive zeal!' the Emperor is

119

reputed to have exclaimed. 'You are no better than a wooden image', the disillusioned Emperor wrote to Lin, '. . . with the speed of flames you should hasten to Peking.'

Admiral Elliot had meanwhile been grumbling at the risks his ships were taking in Peh-ho Bay. His cousin gave way, and the squadron sailed back to the Yangtze, leaving much too quickly for its presence near Peking to have the minatory effect Palmerston had intended upon the minds of high officials there. Instead they tended to interpret the departure as one more instance of barbarian lack of resolve.

I-Liang, Governor of Kwangtung, was named on 13 October to replace Lin at Canton, pending the arrival there of Ch'i Shan, who henceforward was to take over the challenge of 'soothing the barbarians'. Lin's last official act was to supervise a Military Examination – a display of shooting arrows from horseback. Much of his enforced spare time he spent practising calligraphy. The anti-foreign mood he had aroused in Canton did not diminish with his going; when Ch'i Shan got there, he was at once met by a deputation of local scholars and mandarins, imploring him not to yield an inch.

Pending an investigation into their conduct, Lin and Teng were told to stand by and advise Ch'i Shan. There is no sign that Ch'i Shan ever took their advice, but Peking was perhaps having second thoughts, and toying with alternative policies. The effective choices were resistance or concession – but the Manchu were unrealistically looking for ways to keep both options open.

The British government's real intentions were, in the long run, implacable. However, by misinterpreting Captain Elliot's well-meant attempts at deference and conciliation, Ch'i Shan thought the British could be cajoled. The British were being driven to their programme of aggression by what to the Chinese could only have been incomprehensible economic pressures. Traditional 'soothing' of clumsy barbarians by subtle Chinese no longer made sense.

Captain Elliot himself was from now on under an alternation of pressures he was not fitted to withstand. Many of the career officers around him were exhilarated by the walkover their modern ships and weapons had given them. They wanted to edge Elliot forward into a kind of compromising total violence that because of his concern for the Chinese he attempted to resist. But half-heartedness was no way to wage a war of conquest.

Was there in sober fact any obstacle to the British simply imposing their will on China, as in the fairly recent past they had done in India?

Lin was well aware of one awkward fact: China was probably too big for them – weak enough to be defeated, possibly, but too big to be garrisoned.

And the other maritime power busy in the China trade was Britain's rival. To make of China another India, the British would need to contend at the same time with the Americans, just as in India, during the previous century, they had pushed out the French. But during the previous sixty-five years – though nowadays the fact is sometimes politely overlooked – the Americans in their struggle for independence had twice fought the British to a standstill.

By their system of offering rewards, the Chinese had managed to lay hands on a number of foreigners. Peasants on Chou-shan kidnapped, one by one, about half a dozen sepoys who tried to scrounge too far from their tents. An officer in the Madras Artillery, Peter Anstruther, had been pounced on when doing a military survey on 16 September 1840 a mile from the unhealthy British encampment. Tied hand and foot to a long bamboo pole, he had been bundled with the others across the straits to the mainland city of Ningpo.

In Macao, kidnappers managed to make away on 5 August 1840 with a divinity student from Cambridge, Vincent Stanton, as he was taking a bathe on a lonely beach. After he had managed to prove that he had no connection whatever with opium, Stanton was not badly treated, and his captors even found for him a Prayer Book and Bible.

The largest group of hostages captured in September 1840 – survivors off the armed brig *Kite* – included an Englishwoman, a detail which clearly nagged at Elliot's sensitive mind. (When he went across later to Ningpo in *Atalanta* to negotiate the prisoners' return, and was blandly told they might all be handed over in exchange for the island of Chou-shan, Elliot took the proposition in earnest, which to the wily Ch'i Shan must have once again been a sign of British irresolution.)

Kite, a 281-ton Newcastle brig in the India trade, had been commandeered there as a transport. In Chou-shan she was fitted out with six 12-pounder carronades. A party of marines and naval ratings, some of them rather unwell with dysentery, came aboard to work the guns. A naval officer, Lieutenant Douglas, RN, took over command, and *Kite* was sent to join *Algerine* and *Conway* in the dangerous work of surveying the estuary of the Yangtze, her former captain, John Noble, serving as sailing master. His peaceful trading voyage might be at an end, but his wife Ann was still on board, not to mention their 5-month-old baby.

When *Kite*'s draught, of ten feet, was judged excessive for the work in hand, the young parents must have sighed with relief. The brig was sent back to Chou-shan with despatches, but on Tuesday, 15 September 1840, she ran aground.

The baby was trapped in the cabin, and drowned. Lieutenant Douglas and Mrs Noble, with Witt the chief mate and two cabin boys, got themselves into the jolly boat, and were swept away by the tide, leaving twenty-six of the crew clung to the rigging of the capsized brig. All the survivors – officers, crew and Mrs Noble herself – were eventually taken prisoner by Chinese fishermen, and brought to the city of Ningpo.

On first being brought ashore they were given a bad time – chiefly from the flouts and jibes of a Chinese crowd in an anti-foreign mood. They were taken to towns nearby, in small wooden cages, as a patriotic raree-show. The crew were cross-questioned as to whether *Kite* had opium or guns aboard, and the game was over when two of her carronades were found at the site of the wreck. Concluding that their prisoners had been up to no good, the Chinese sent them for the time being to the prison which housed local Chinese opium offenders, whose harsh conditions they were made to share.

Once the possibility was admitted in negotiation of these British prisoners being handed back in exchange for Chou-shan, their conditions began to improve. They were taken to a temple, given warm clothes, granted a measure of freedom, and allowed to write to Chou-shan for necessaries. A plot to rescue the officers and Mrs Noble, organized by a mysterious agent with the *nom de guerre* of Blondel, came to nothing, since, with Mrs Noble's consent, the officers very decently refused, by accepting the chance of escape, to abandon their men.

Captain Anstruther managed to impress the Chinese with his fearless good humour. They much admired his gift for taking likenesses; the fee for a mandarin's portrait was set at one dozen pork pies. Good specimens of foreign handwriting were also much sought after. A number of the marines, who had brought dysentery with them from their foul encampment on Chou-shan, succumbed and died, but the others did not do badly.

A dread of being in Chinese power was an understandable obsession with the British, and may explain, for instance, their dogged refusal to give up the murderer of Lin Wei-hsi. The Chinese were by now shrewd enough to discern and play on this fear. The mandarin who finally exchanged the prisoners, after their five months in Ningpo, did his best for example to persuade them that, if he had delayed two more days, all of them would have been sent to Peking to suffer a lingering death. Anstruther was informed that plans had been made to offer up his heart and liver as a propitiary sacrifice to the souls of Chinese who had fallen in battle: apparently he took this information with a pinch of salt, but of course the warning may have been true. Yu-ch'ien who was appointed acting Governor of Liang-chiang in 1840 – a Mongolian who later impeached Ch'i Shan and I-li-pu for being too easy with the British – certainly had the reputation even among the Chinese for being an exceptional brute. War anywhere gives sadists their opportunity.

When Ch'i Shan arrived in Canton on 10 December 1840, to take over from Lin, he found Vincent Stanton still a prisoner, and busily reading his Bible. Ch'i Shan invited Stanton to his official residence as his guest for a couple of days, and having made a good impression on the amiable young man, sent him back to Captain Elliot – who by now was sole plenipotentiary, his cousin, the Admiral, having gone home in November complaining of heart trouble.

Though Canton was still nominally under blockade, reliable Chinese smugglers were carrying goods down back waterways, on such a scale that the smugglers agreed to an unofficial British suggestion that to avoid confusion they should all fly a blue flag.

Canton's defences had been modernized. Ch'i Shan was to all appearances confident of bemusing the British, perhaps because his view of the war had been formed by studying Chinese official reports in Peking replete with highly imaginative details of 'smashing victories'. Ch'i Shan expressed his policy in simple terms: 'After prolonged negotiation has made the Barbarians weary and exhausted, we can suddenly attack them, and thereby subdue them.' Elliot appears to have taken Ch'i Shan's readiness to negotiate at its face value. 'So far as I can judge', he wrote to Matheson, 'the Court has deliberated on peace or war, and decided that peace is the wisest course.'

Though no one just now was eager to take his advice, Lin saw deepest into events: China's only real hope was to master the means of modern war, and then fight to a finish. 'People may say that our junks and guns', he wrote, 'are no match for the British, and that ingenious diplomacy is preferable to a protracted war. But

O – they do not know!' Ch'i Shan went on being so ingeniously evasive that on 5 January 1841 Elliot felt obliged to threaten him that at 8 a.m. of the 7th hostilities would reopen if concessions were not made. Since he knew about the destructiveness of British broadsides only by hearsay, Ch'i Shan remained unmoved.

To change his mind the British made plans for a demonstration: to destroy completely the outermost Bogue Forts. Around these fortifications about 3000 Chinese troops were entrenched, their flanks protected by field batteries. To shift them, the British proposed to put 1461 men ashore in two divisions under cover of the ships' guns. The troops were to be marines, British infantry, sepoys, and a party of seamen to manhandle the field pieces.

The starboard division was to land under the walls of Chuenpi Fort, which would be hammered meanwhile by the guns of *Calliope*, *Hyacinth* and *Larne*, with the help of four steamers including *Nemesis*, while *Samarang*, *Druid*, *Modeste* and *Columbine* proceeded to soften up the walls of Tycocktow Fort on the other side of the channel.

A seaborne landing on a coast held by enemy troops is accepted to be one of the riskiest and most difficult evolutions in the profession of arms – but with the Royal Navy to blast all opposition and put the troops ashore, landings of this description were made again and again, and for derisory losses, during the China campaigns.

This landing began at 9.30 a.m. At Chuenpi, *Hyacinth* was the first to open fire. Two companies of marines, and the guns, established a beach-head without opposition, the remainder of the division landing in good order soon after. The mud through which the field-pieces had to be dragged did more to slow proceedings than any aggressiveness on the part of the Chinese.

Tartar troops – the *corps d'élite* of the Manchu dynasty – were defiantly waving flags and beating gongs from their entrenchments. Their field batteries opened fire, but were adroitly outflanked by the marines and sepoys. After a short bombardment from the British men-of-war, the guns of the fort were silenced.

The warships having ceased fire, Fort Chuenpi was put to the assault, and taken at a rush. The Tartar brigadier was shot dead while rallying his men – some of whom were becoming unnerved by a type of absolute warfare they had never imagined. Believing a rumour that the British gave no quarter, the Tartar troops refused to surrender. They were jammed between British troops and a naval landing party coming up at their rear – all in a bloody-minded mood. The Tartars were cut or shot down like animals in a knacker's yard. 'A frightful scene of slaughter ensued', admitted an eyewitness, 'despite the efforts of the officers to restrain their men.' By 11 a.m. the blue-jackets in the warships saw the Chinese flag run down from the watchtower ashore, and the Union Jack flutter in its stead. Six hundred Tartars had been killed and only a hundred taken prisoner; the British had thirty wounded, mostly by an accidental explosion.

A flotilla moved off to wreak havoc on the enemy war junks at anchor in the mouth of the river – *Nemesis* setting fire to eleven junks, one after another, with Congreve rockets. The fort of Tycocktow, across the channel, had been blasted by successive broadsides from a range of 200 yards, and was a silent wreck. Old Admiral Kuan, commanding the Chinese forces, sent a physician who spoke a little English to accompany a white flag and ask for a three-day truce, so he could confer with Commissioner Ch'i Shan. Elliot accepted, writing optimistically to James Matheson: 'I hope we shall settle without further bloodshed. The Commissioner knows we can take much more than he would like to lose whenever we please.'

The fighting men expected that Elliot would now let them push on all the way to Canton, knocking the Chinese over like ninepins. Instead, troops were set to the dull task of demolishing the fortifications they had captured, then a truce was declared. Lulls in the fighting went much against their grain.

The French Consulate-General at Manila had two months before sent an attaché called C. A. Challoyé to represent France at Macao. Now the French corvette *Danaide* (Captain Rosamel) turned up in Canton Bay, to keep hostilities there under observation. The British had another rival on the spot. From this time on the French too were to make their presence felt in China. They did comparatively little trade – though tea exports to France had somewhat increased because of an optimistic belief there that tea was beneficial against cholera. The French however had hostages of their own inside China, the 200 000 Chinese Roman Catholics.

Since the British blockade was still nominally operative, *Danaide* was unable to proceed up the Pearl River, but Captain Elliot urbanely invited Captain Rosamel to accompany him personally, in *Nemesis*.

Elliot and Ch'i Shan after the show of force at the Bogue Forts, were slowly coming to terms. They met for their negotiations at

125

Lotus Flower Wall, about twenty-six miles downstream from Canton, Elliot arriving with his interpreters and his French guest, escorted by fifty-six Royal Marines and a fife-and-drum band of sixteen. Ch'i Shan presented the troops with mutton and wine, and they in turn enlivened proceedings with a display of musketry. Elliot and Ch'i Shan then went out to confer on a boat in midstream.

Considering how unsuccessful his troops had been, Ch'i Shan was not forced to concede much by the draft Treaty of Chuenpi. The British would keep Hong Kong, but return the larger and more fertile island of Chou-shan. (In point of fact, though to officials in London Chou-shan may have looked good on the map, it was a place difficult of access to sailing ships during three months of unfavourable monsoon.)

Intercourse between Britain and China was hereafter to be direct and official, and trade might reopen in Canton. China would pay a six-million-dollar indemnity, thereby saving Lord Palmerston from the painful obligation of asking a hostile Parliament to vote increased taxes to pay for an unpopular war. Palmerston had defined the political effect of such huge post-war indemnities as long before as 16 June 1834, in his protest to Russia at the indemnity that was squeezed out of Persia by the Treaty of Durkmanchaya: '... almost as fatal to its Independence as territorial cessions would be, because the resources of the State may be crippled and its freedom of action taken away by the want of pecuniary means, as well as by a curtailment of territorial extent'. The indemnity was, also, a way of softening up China by weakening her central administration.

Both negotiators could justly point out to their superiors the gains that had been made. China got back Chou-shan without firing a shot. The indemnity was heavy, but Hong merchants could always be squeezed for that sort of thing (as in due course they were, $820 000 towards the ransom of Canton being paid by old Howqua alone). Captain Elliot was adding Hong Kong to the British Empire at no expense to the British taxpayer. A reasonable basis for future trade and diplomacy had been agreed upon.

There was only one snag, though neither side yet knew it. The treaty drafted at Chuenpi, eminently reasonable though it might sound, was unacceptable to Lord Palmerston – who saw in it his detailed instructions flouted. And it was equally repugnant to the Manchu Emperor, who raged when word was brought him of this new piece of barbarian insolence. The Emperor was heard to exclaim loudly that the loss of Hong Kong was an outrage.

The rebel, Elliot, should be brought at once to Peking for condign punishment. With a British squadron no longer loitering in the mouth of the Peh-ho River, the Manchu court had regained their nerve.

But, until the bad news was brought home to them, Ch'i Shan and Captain Elliot continued for the next month or so to perform their roles on the public stage, like puppets, deceiving, insisting, demanding, evading. Politically, they were in limbo; their confrontation had lost all reality.

Orders at last came down from Peking for Ch'i Shan's arrest. On 12 March 1841 he was to leave Canton in chains. All his property was confiscated, and the vast extent of it – 425 000 acres of land, 13 500 ounces of gold, a personal fortune estimated at £10 000 000 – gives some notion of the scale on which an eminent mandarin not as disinterested as Lin could exploit, if he chose, the people he was sent out to govern. Ch'i Shan was sentenced to death, a sentence commuted later to hard labour in a military camp on the Amur River, the bleak northern border between China and Russia.

Captain Elliot, too, had cooked his own goose – though since communications with Britain were so slow, he was not to know this for several months to come. When told of the negotiations Lord Palmerston replied acidly, 'After all, our naval power is so strong that we can tell the Emperor what *we* mean to hold, rather than that *he* should say what he would cede.' Palmerston wished to keep Chou-shan, or some island well placed near the Yangtze mouth, to 'give British commodities an easy chance of access to the interior'. He wanted 'admission of opium into China as an article of lawful commerce'. He wanted a larger indemnity; he wanted more trading ports. Her Majesty's Government, Captain Elliot was told bluntly, would not ratify the agreement he had made.

On 20 January, Ch'i Shan had received word from the Emperor that there was to be no more parleying. Thousands of fighting men were on their way to Canton from the interior. Yang Fang, a famous old soldier – over 70, stone deaf, able to communicate only by writing, but reassuringly famous – had been sent to lead the troops. I' shan, the Emperor's cousin, was on his way to retrieve the political situation.

127

The British meanwhile took over Hong Kong. The attractions of this barren, fever-infested island were a deep-water anchorage, and the comparative absence there of a hostile population. (Captain Stead, of the transport *Pestonjee*, landing on Chou-shan not knowing it had been given back, was cut to pieces in no time by angry villagers.) Hong Kong was unprepossessing – someone described it once as looking like a half-demolished Stilton cheese – and many were dubious of its value. One man who immediately saw Hong Kong's potentialities was James Matheson: he moved the firm's headquarters there in January 1841 and began to build a large stone godown, solid as a fortress. Whatever moral defects the opium dealers may have suffered under, they had an excellent grasp of practical reality.

Law and order were soon introduced into Hong Kong, a naval officer being sent ashore from HMS *Modeste* to hear complaints against the local Chinese, while his boatswain stood by to inflict summary justice. 'None of the Chinese ever stood more than six blows of the cat, when they invariably fainted', observed an eye-witness. Possibly they were more inured to the bamboo.

When Ch'i Shan, in the weeks preceding his arrest, showed a certain reluctance about keeping his agreement – this being, of course, before Lord Palmerston's denunciation had arrived – Elliot drove his arguments home by yet another display of force. On 25 February he assembled troops and fleet for an assault on the next group of forts and they were taken with the usual brutal felicity. Captain Elliot himself had a close shave from a Chinese cannon-ball as he sat intrepidly on a hammock-netting to observe the course of the fighting. 300 Chinese were killed, 100 wounded and 1100 taken prisoner. This time among the dead was numbered Admiral Kuan himself, who had fought his country's enemies with a courage that gave the British a chivalrous satisfaction. When the Admiral's family came to fetch the old man's body home, HMS *Blenheim* accorded her distinguished enemy the tribute of a minute gun.

Over the clumps of acacia and bamboo that marked the first bar of the Pearl River, the British as they pushed on to keep up the pressure could see the masts of *Chesapeake* (formerly *Cambridge*) waiting to block their way. 'The enemy made a determined resistance', noted the First Lieutenant of HMS *Modeste*, 'but could do nothing from the terrific broadsides from the ships.' The Chinese encampment was set afire. 'On the mandarins advancing in front of their men, and brandishing their swords, a few guns from *Calliope* checked them.' A boarding party entering *Chesapeake* reported that the 'decks resembled a slaughter house'. She was not long after blown up, by a Congreve rocket, fired into her powder magazine from *Nemesis* (who had steamed upriver with eyes painted awe-inspiringly on her bows, flying a banner with large Chinese characters which declared that Britain was making war only on the Imperial government). The explosion of *Chesapeake* going up into the air was heard thirty miles away.

At last Major-General Sir Hugh Gough made his appearance – a 61-year-old Anglo-Irishman with an estate in Tipperary. A brave, good-natured and efficient soldier, he had won his promotion under Wellington, in the Peninsular War, at the battles of Talavera and Vittoria. In peacetime, after commanding a regiment of infantry against the rebel Irish peasantry, he had gone out to serve in India.

Under Gough's command, boatloads of troops were towed, by shallow-draught steamers, to the very walls of Canton and there skilfully disposed, in the pouring rain, for an assault on this supposedly impregnable city. The troops were on their toes, itching for the profitable thrill of taking Canton by storm, when a deputation arrived in the British lines led by old Howqua, the multimillionaire Hong merchant, and including the American Consul. All the city's authorities, so they said, had disappeared. Ch'i Shan himself had been bundled off in chains to Peking. On Yang Fang's behalf, they pleaded for a truce, and to the disappointment of the entire army, a truce was granted.

Though in the long run the deaf old warrior had no serious intention whatever of keeping the peace, the breathing space then granted enabled merchant ships to make a dash up to Whampoa and load tea. An agreement was made that if any foreigner brought in opium, the drug might be seized by the Chinese authorities, but the man was to be let go: there were to be no more bonds with death penalties attached; and Lin's zeal against opium was, by tacit consent, to be a thing of the past. This truce lasted precariously until May – by which time twenty-eight million pounds of tea had been shipped out, and Chinese reinforcements numbering tens of thousands had reached Canton.

Yang Fang gave the word for a surprise attack, under the war-cry, *'Exterminate the rebels!'* On 29 May British vessels at anchor in Whampoa were attacked by fire-rafts, manned by crews throwing stink pots and armed with long boarding pikes, and the Factories at Canton itself were looted and demolished by Chinese troops.

Between 21 and 30 May the British were once again obliged to show they meant serious business by moving up the Pearl River in force and menacing once more the walls of Canton.

Captain Elliot was criticized later for not having gone on to take the city by assault and put it to the sack. His own sentiments of humanity may have held him back, but there were military reasons also for sparing Canton. The British had by now only 2200 men, some the worse for fever, and the garrison of Canton was known to be over 20 000. If that small British force got out of hand, and started drinking and looting, but this time inside the walls of an armed city of a million inhabitants, amid a hostile countryside, Canton might prove a baited trap. The British stayed outside the walls, while the city bought its immunity for a ransom of six million dollars cash, to be paid in seven days.

With both sides on the point of repudiating their agreement, the war for the moment was at a standstill. The Chinese had managed to get the British bogged down in the neighbourhood of Canton – which, from their point of view was a long way from the real centre of power, at Peking. The British had got their prisoners back, though it had cost them Chou-shan. They had shipped their tea out, though that transaction had, of course, also been profitable to the Chinese. But there was a quicker way of making money in China: the ransom from Canton had fetched in seven days more than twice the British government's annual revenue from tea.

On 24 July 1841 Captain Elliot picked up the *Canton Press*, a local newspaper published in Macao and strongly under the influence of Jardine, Matheson & Co. From its columns stared out a news item announcing his own dismissal; official word had not yet arrived, but Jardine, Matheson, with their fast clipper service, usually got to know facts and prices ahead of their competitors. The new plenipotentiary was to be a forceful soldier and diplomat in the East India Company's service called Sir Henry Pottinger. One can imagine the pawky satisfaction it must have given someone at Jardine, Matheson & Co. thus to snub an official who had never bothered to conceal his distaste for the biggest business in Canton.

When he got back to London Elliot published a memorandum to vindicate his conduct. 'It has been popularly objected to me', he wrote, 'that I have cared too much for the Chinese. But I submit that it has been caring more for lasting British honour and substantial British interests to protect a helpless and friendly people ...' Such days and moods in China were over: a country

130

fighting a shameful war is seldom magnanimous. Queen Victoria herself wrote, with scathing contempt, of 'Charles Elliot ... who completely disobeyed his instructions and *tried* to get the *lowest* terms he could'. But some of the Tories showed their approval of Elliot's moderation. The war in China was a Whig war; in 1841 Sir Robert Peel had managed briefly to bring down the Whig Cabinet and Palmerston with it. And family connections still counted: something suitable was done for Charles Elliot. Within a year he was off to the wilds again – as British Consul-General to Sam Houston's independent Republic of Texas.

Lin remained in disgrace, but because of his great abilities, Peking still found him useful when things went badly wrong. Lin too was to undergo a curious apotheosis, appearing in London in the collection of Madame Tussaud, as a waxwork figure done from the life. 'Commissioner Lin and his favourite concubine', announced the catalogue, '... dressed in magnificent Chinese costumes, lately imported.' The artist was an enterprising Chinese pupil of old Chinnery's.

William Jardine did not live long to enjoy his opulent retirement. At the age of 55 he took his seat as MP for Ashburton, and for the next two years continued a loyal supporter in and out of office of Lord Palmerston, but in 1843 he died, by all accounts of a lingering and atrocious illness. (All through the nineteenth century a superstition was current among British seamen that those who prospered in the opium trade were doomed to suffer in some other way, and Jardine's was a much-quoted case.) But his partner James Matheson made old bones. On his retirement from Canton, Matheson was duly elected to Parliament for Jardine's former seat. In 1843 James Matheson married, and in 1844 he bought an island off the Scottish coast. There at an outlay of £514 000 he built Lews Castle, a dwelling described as 'fabulous'. His name figures with Gladstone's and Pottinger's among the donors who endowed the Chair of Chinese at London University. From 1847 to 1868 he sat as member of Parliament for Ross and Cromarty. James Matheson died in Mentone, childless, in 1887 at the age of 91.

Under entail his anti-opium nephew Donald eventually inherited island and castle. Donald Matheson had gone to China in 1837, as a boy of 18, and eventually became a partner, but by the age of 30 could stick the unsavoury trade no longer. In 1849 he resigned and went home, and in course of time his opinions travelled full circle. As a devout and philanthropic Presbyterian he took office in 1892, when an old man, as Chairman to the Executive Committee of the Society for the Suppression of the Opium Trade.

5 Soothe the Barbarian

'I must now only hope to meet you as well and somewhat richer than you are now, some years hence when you return to us as a mandarin with a first-class button and loaded with the spoils of China.'

Lord Minto, First Lord of the Admiralty, to Rear-Admiral Sir William Parker on his leaving to take command of the East India Station, 1841

The British chain of command when the war began anew sounds uncomfortable. The expeditionary force came under the ultimate authority of Lord Auckland, Governor-General of India, who had provided the troops and who was to give Sir Hugh Gough his orders. The fleet – now commanded by Sir William Parker, in his day Nelson's best frigate captain – came directly under the Admiralty. The new plenipotentiary, Sir Henry Pottinger, had been chosen by the British Foreign Office, and was there to carry into effect Lord Palmerston's instructions.

Luckily the three leaders resembled each other strongly in background and temperament – sharing an exuberant, boyish aggressiveness – so that this unlikely sounding arrangement worked well. Afterwards, the Duke of Wellington, who probably knew more about war than any man living, praised their campaign as being 'without parallel as the joint work of a fleet and an army ... a revelation of amphibious power'.

Both Gough and Pottinger were Anglo-Irishmen, who had first put on uniform as boys, during the Napoleonic Wars. Henry Pottinger was sent to sea when he was 12, and at 15 had been lucky enough to obtain, through political influence, a cadetship in the Indian Army. He had risen eventually to Colonel. Gough was commissioned in the Limerick Militia when only 14, and at the ripe age of 15 was adjutant to the 119th Regiment of Foot.

Sir William Parker had the great Admiral Lord St Vincent for an uncle, which no doubt meant his services at sea were never entirely overlooked, but his successful naval career had been based on ability. He entered the service at the age of 12, and by 31 was able to retire in the rank of Captain with 'a competent fortune' in prize-money. He bought an estate near Lichfield, and spent the next fifteen years as a country gentleman before going back to sea.

'Old Billy Parker' was a disciplinarian – combining high professional skill with the kind of dotty fixed ideas that exact a wry affection from the men obliged to suffer them. He would never, for instance, keep in his ship's company any officer who smoked tobacco. He had a well-known fad about the utility of the peaked cap; the way to win his favour was to buy and wear one. The Chinese referred to him as Pa; they called Sir Hugh Gough Ko.

Though Sir Henry Pottinger's job was political, he too relished the exhilaration of getting right up in front when there was action, and this made him popular. He had known India when British military prowess there was high. After mastering native languages, young Lieutenant Pottinger had risked his neck doing intelligence work over the border in Baluchistan and Afghanistan. He had served in the Mahratta War, but his name was put forward to Lord Palmerston as the right man for China because of the reputation he made when political agent in the province of Sind: Henry Pottinger had a gift for imposing his will forcibly on native potentates.

Though Sir Henry had a gusto for violent action, he was rather inert as an administrator: when he moved on he usually left problems behind. He knew how to bully the Chinese into doing what he needed, but they could sometimes outwit him.

Sir Henry Pottinger and Admiral Sir William Parker arrived together at Macao on 10 August 1842, in the steam frigate *Sesostris*, having made the trip from England in the record time of sixty-seven days. From London, William Jardine wrote, reassuringly, 'I have had two or three conversations with him of a very satisfactory nature.' Reinforcements had also come to Hong Kong from India, including men of the 55th (Westmorland) Regiment, armed with the new percussion musket – not all of them overjoyed, perhaps, at being sent to China, after eighteen years continuous overseas service, when they had expected to go home.

Sir Henry Pottinger made his mark at once, with a calculated display of browbeating. He began by informing merchants trading to Canton that he 'could allow no consideration connected with mercantile pursuits ... to interfere with the strong measures which he might deem necessary', going on to warn those traders who were British subjects 'that if they put either themselves or their property in the power of the Chinese authorities ... it must be clearly understood to be at their own risk and peril'. Captain Elliot's obvious tactical mistakes were not to be repeated. In Canton the easy-going, half-hearted days were over.

Nemesis was sent steaming up the Pearl River to inform the Viceroy of Sir Henry Pottinger's arrival, but when on 18 August the Prefect of Canton came down to Macao with a retinue to bid Sir Henry welcome – a large concession from the protocol-bound Chinese – the plenipotentiary chose to give these Chinese fellows a measure of his own importance by not receiving them in person.

The fleet was soon on its way north again, convoying twenty-one transports carrying 2700 fighting men – 1350 having been left behind to garrison Hong Kong and keep an eye on the turbulent Cantonese. This time the first British objective was Amoy – a seaport on a barren granite island, a couple of miles off the coast of Fukien. There were only a few cultivated fields on Amoy, trees were rare, and meat had to be imported. The town lived by fishing, but did a good deal of illicit trade with Singapore, and was frequented from time to time by pirates.

The two British commanders, taking Sir Henry with them, went aboard the steamer *Phlegethon*, and ventured recklessly close inshore to observe Amoy. Lin and Teng had by now left their mark on Amoy: the coastal defences were modernized. *Phlegethon* cruised along the thousand-yard façade of a battery recently built of granite blocks, faced with earth, and Parker, Gough and Pottinger counted ninety-six embrasures. This battery defended the entrance to Amoy harbour. Across a 600-yard channel, on Ko-lung-su Island, the strategic key to Amoy, was another battery of seventy-six guns, many of them modern and smuggled in from Singapore. The citadel of Amoy itself mounted forty-two more guns, and the garrison numbered 10 000, of whom the best troops were Tartars manning that long granite battery.

The morning of the assault was hot and sultry. At first the sailing ships of the British fleet lay becalmed, but towards midday an encouraging breeze filled their sails. Three frigates, *Blonde, Modeste,* and *Druid,* were detached to engage the Chinese guns on the island of Ko-lung-su, while the long granite battery covering Amoy harbour was hammered at 400 yards' range by crushing broadsides from two ships-of-the-line, anchored out in deep water.

The paddle-steamers were kept busy, towing the troops ashore in ships' boats. Sir Hugh Gough was put on the beach, at the head of his men, by *Nemesis,* at 3.45 p.m., near the flank of the long battery. HMS *Modeste* and HMS *Blonde* made use of the breeze to get inside Amoy harbour. They there engaged, and quickly silenced, five defensive batteries. They put paid also to twenty-six war junks drawn up at anchor, including a large new one, mounting thirty-six guns, which had been given the exact armament of a British frigate.

After seventy-five minutes of cannonade the batteries of Ko-lung-su Island had been silenced, and the entrenchments above them were cleared. Though the fall of Amoy was now inevitable, guns were still firing from the long granite battery defending the harbour approaches. This battery managed to withstand a pro-digious three-hour bombardment from the two British battleships, and eventually had to be taken at the bayonet-point by troops attacking from the rear, which Sir Hugh Gough led in person.

The few Tartar artillerymen who had matchlocks fired them off when Gough attacked, and then took flight, carrying away their wounded. The Tartar commander waited until he could see that his men were clearly beaten. He then climbed through an embrasure, made his way down the beach, and deliberately walked into the sea towards the enemy ships, until water closed over his head, and he was drowned. This gesture was reported back to Peking as a notable deed of courage. The Tartar General had 'rushed out to drive back the assailants as they landed, and fell into the water, and died'. It was an imaginative suicide, but as an instance of heroism, the British found it perplexing.

The long battery the Chinese had built did impress them how-ever; they admitted it to be 'a most masterly piece of masonry'. The battleships 'might have fired until doomsday'. No cannon-ball had gone in deeper than sixteen inches. From the captured battery the British soldiers also made a collection of jettisoned opium pipes.

The Chinese, by ingeniously copying the enemy, were overcoming their technical backwardness in the material techniques of war, though they had still not shed the non-combative habit of mind which Chinese tradition tried to make second nature.

To overawe rebels or frontier barbarians there had as a last resort to be soldiers, even in China. But they were not, as in Europe, a disciplined and efficient force, ruthless when necessary and used at regular intervals by a state power to wage a war on its commercial or political rivals. Even under the minority rule of the Manchus the Emperor's army was chiefly a means of psycho-logical intimidation, since, in the recesses of his mind, any rebel was bound to be more or less in awe of Imperial authority. A rebel might as likely be won over as crushed: this was the logic behind the irritating term that Chinese officials so often used, about 'soothing the barbarians'.

In the old days, before Lin modernized the forts along the south China coast, a cannon had been a noisy piece of magic – a bang intended to terrify. A Chinese soldier was trained to make grotesque stylized gestures and to pull nightmare faces, as if his real job were frightening naughty children. In a sense, so he was, since any rebel against Imperial power would normally feel in his heart that he was offending the filial duty to which all Chinese were bred up.

To this traditional distaste for soldiering had lately been added a mistrust among ordinary Chinese of the soldiers from Tartary who had brought the Manchu dynasty to power, and kept it there. Tartar soldiers, though quartered within the walls of Chinese cities, were feared and despised by the Chinese themselves as foreigners.

The three British leaders had lived by war since childhood. Their troops were professionals, who had chosen to leave behind the society that bred them, and live out their lives in the regiment. Some were Indian sepoys, serving the white man's Raj. The rank-and-file in the British regiments were men shaken loose from society, who had taken the Queen's shilling to elude the Poor Law in England, or escape hunger in Ireland, or depopulation in the Highlands. Men of this stamp were about to enjoy in China a sequence of easy victories, over a people with no heart for fighting, whom many of them found it psychologically gratifying to despise.

Any private soldier at Amoy envying his comrades the fun they had had thirteen months before, at the taking of Chou-shan, got a sharp reminder from Sir Hugh Gough in an Order of the Day, that 'private property was to be held inviolable, and that which in England obtains the name of robbery deserves no better name in China'. Camp-followers at Amoy who did try their hand at looting were condemned to death on the spot.

Though looting by the rank-and-file might be deprecated, the British commanders themselves were keen as ever on prize-money – then regarded in war as legitimate. But to their chagrin the local treasure slipped through their fingers. Thousands of silver dollars were smuggled out of Amoy just before it fell, hidden inside hollowed logs, and carried off by officials pretending to be wood-merchants.

By 1 October 1841, in the teeth of the north-west monsoon, the ships of a British expeditionary force had once again intruded into the harbour of Tin-hai and Chou-shan Island fell soon after. During the past year the Chinese had tried to make a better job of fortifying Tin-hai. A battery a mile long now extended from joss-house hill to the city wall. Observers in the ships counted 270 embrasures, but only eighty guns had so far been mounted. Around this battery the Chinese made a stiff resistance. General Keo and his staff were killed where they stood, and when he saw himself defeated the Tartar Commander-in-Chief cut his own throat. This time Sir Henry Pottinger announced emphatically that 'under no circumstances will Tin-hai and its dependencies be restored to the Chinese government, until the whole of the demands of England are not only complied with, but carried into full effect'.

The Chinese usually went out of their way to help shipwrecked men, even in time of war, but survivors from two armed British ships wrecked one after another on Formosa were treated very badly.

The first ship lost there was the army transport *Nerbudda*, carrying 243 Indian camp-followers, and a detachment of the 55th Regiment, including an officer and a colour-sergeant. When *Nerbudda* went aground off Formosa on 30 September 1841, and began to fill with water, there were not enough boats for all those Indians. Holding them off at bayonet-point, the white men on board, led by the captain and two mates, got into a couple of the ship's boats, and staved in the hull of the third, so no one else could follow.

They had left behind the ship's gunner, a Filipino. He loaded a gun, threatening to sink the departing boats unless they came back for him. The captain rowed alongside and took off the gunner, but at the same time dropped all his ammunition overboard, so the same trick could not be played twice. An opium coaster, *Black Swan*, picked up the survivors soon after, and took them to Hong Kong, where the discreditable facts leaked out. *Nerbudda*'s captain was arrested, and HMS *Nimrod* was sent north to see what could still be done, but the wreck had gone to pieces.

More than half the Indians – sweepers, bearers, hospital assistants – after lingering five days on the waterlogged wreck, had managed to get ashore on rafts. They were soon captured by local Chinese soldiers, who stripped them and imprisoned them in chains, fifteen or more to a cell. The following March the men off

Nerbudda were joined in prison by the surviving crew, fourteen of whom were British or American, of the brig *Ann* (Captain Denham) which had gone aground when heading south with a freight of silver after selling off a cargo of opium in Chou-shan. *Ann*, nicknamed 'skimmer of the seas' on account of her turn of speed, had started her life as a Spanish slaver called *Tangador*, but was made prize by the Royal Navy off Sierra Leone with 250 slaves aboard, then sold by auction and acquired for the opium trade.

The use of opium as a narcotic had prevailed on Formosa since the Dutch were there – long before it reached China – and all these shipwrecked prisoners, American, British and Indian, were to suffer in consequence. Everyone on Formosa to whose arbitrary power they became subject – not only prison guards and common soldiers, but every official from mandarin and high military commanders, down – was apparently an opium smoker; capricious, and neglectful of duty, sometimes cruel.

Corrupt though they seem to have been, the high Chinese officials on Formosa were under the same pressure as their colleagues on the mainland coast to show zeal in the war. So Yao Jung, the Governor, in complicity with the Tartar General Ta-hung-a, decided to gain a false reputation by claiming these two wrecks, *Ann* and *Nerbudda*, as foreign warships they had defeated in combat. The trick worked. The two officials received praise and rewards from Peking, but to keep up the deception the unfortunate survivors had, of course, to be treated as prisoners of war. They were also highly inconvenient witnesses to the truth of the matter, so their lives were at risk.

The miserable existence of these prisoners on Formosa was for some long time not known to the British, and when they did find out it was almost too late.

From their base of Chou-shan Island the British intended this time to carry the war to the heart of China. There were two possible directions of attack. They could go the way the Chinese authorities were expecting them to take – straight for Peking. But as Captain Elliot had found out the year before, only ships drawing less than twelve feet of water could hope to cross the bar at the mouth of the Peh-ho River – the water route direct to China's capital. A few thousand British infantry, if unsupported by cavalry or by the guns of a fleet, might come to grief if they met, say, Mongol cavalry on the plains of north China.

But there was an indirect approach. A couple of hundred miles up the Yangtze – where the river was still a mile wide and capable of floating the entire British fleet – lay the great city of Nanking. From near Nanking the Grand Canal ran north to the Peh-ho River. Rice from the fertile paddy fields of central China was carried up the Grand Canal every year in junks to feed Peking's three million inhabitants. The British leaders decided that a ship-borne attack up the Yangtze to Nanking, by indirectly threatening the food supply to his capital, might well put enough pressure on the Emperor to bring him to terms.

The city of Ningpo, across the straits from Chou-shan Island, was picked out as an accessible mainland base from which to develop this attack on Nanking. Ningpo lay twelve miles inland and was protected at its river mouth by the fortified town of Chen-hai – ringed by three miles of castellated walls, and overlooked by a citadel on a rocky spur. There were 3000 Chinese soldiers inside the walls of Chen-hai, and 700 more in the citadel.

The British attack on Chen-hai began at dawn on 10 October 1841, and took its usual course. Broadsides from two battleships and two frigates shelled the Chinese out of the citadel. A landing party of marines and seamen escaladed the city walls and by 2 p.m. the fortified city had fallen, for a cost of three British dead and sixteen wounded. The Chinese lost several hundred men, and 157 guns were captured, some old, some brand new, and one an exact Chinese copy of the British carronades which had been taken by fishermen out of the wreck of *Kite*. Commissioner Yu, having lost the city entrusted to him by the Emperor, committed suicide.

When warships from the African anti-slavery squadron had left the Cape of Good Hope for service in China, the Jack Tars had promised their Cape Town sweethearts to send them back China-men's pigtails as souvenirs. Now came their chance. Prisoners taken at Chen-hai were lined up, to have their pigtails hacked off with sailors' jack-knives: to the Chinese, a public humiliation. Sir Hugh Gough soon put a stop to it.

With Chen-hai gone, the fall of Ningpo was certain. This was the city where Captain Anstruther, and the survivors from *Kite*, including Mrs Noble, had been paraded about to the public gaze in small cages. On 13 October, Ningpo – a city of 250 000 inhabitants, inside a five-mile wall, and famous for its wood-carving, silk and embroidery – fell to the British almost without a fight.

Sir Henry Pottinger had written a high-spirited letter just before to the Foreign Secretary announcing incautiously that

139

'he looked forward with considerable satisfaction' to 'plundering Ningpo as a reprisal for the maltreatment there of British prisoners'. But the Tories were again in office and, though Pottinger did not know it, the Foreign Secretary was no longer the congenial Lord Palmerston, but his schoolfellow at Harrow and life-long rival, Lord Aberdeen.

On receiving this jubilant proposal to sack Ningpo, Lord Aberdeen, a man of scruples, was so distressed that he overlooked Sir Henry's recent advancement to the rank of baronet, in annotating his despatch: 'The worst proposal I have seen from Mr Pottinger ... it ought not to pass unnoticed.'

Sir William Parker and Sir Hugh Gough were not keen on sacking Ningpo either. They pointed out sharply to Sir Henry that the terms on which the city had capitulated would make giving it over to be plundered by the troops a breach of honour. Admiral and General were also no doubt well aware that in taking on an empire numbering hundreds of millions with a disciplined force of less than ten thousand men, they dare not let their troops get out of hand.

Ningpo was soon bled of its wealth, but more circumspectly. The city's public treasure, amounting to $160 000, was carried off by British prize agents 'under the protection of an armed party'. Memories of the sack of Tin-hai were still fresh in Ningpo: a 'ransom' was willingly paid by the inhabitants to the value of 10 per cent of all the property within the walls and 10 per cent of all cargoes moving up the river.

The troops soon ensconced themselves in winter quarters, making free, as soldiers will, of what they found there. A mob of Chinese scallywags, who followed the army everywhere, for what they could pick up, began terrorizing the city, looting the citizens of whatever the British soldiers had neglected to take. Though Ningpo was not officially 'plundered', the high standard Sir Hugh Gough had tried to set at Amoy was beginning to deteriorate.

The Rev. Dr Karl Gutzlaff, the Prussian missionary-linguist, his swivelling glance half-concealed under his big straw hat, went ashore with the British when they occupied Ningpo, and was appointed magistrate to control the local population. He encouraged peasants from the surrounding countryside to bring supplies to market, and had soon hired an intelligence network of Chinese willing to spy for the British.

Sir Henry Pottinger went south to Hong Kong: winter was when the all-important tea crop had to be shipped. War in the north; business as usual at Canton. The river at Ningpo froze, and snow fell. There were skating and snowballing, officers went duck-shooting, and forty or so British stragglers were kidnapped by the Chinese and carried off to Hangchow, often after being made drunk. Some of the kidnappers, when caught, were sentenced by Gutzlaff to work in the quarries of Hong Kong, in chains. The British made occasional raids into the neighbourhood; spies accumulated intelligence; by and large the army passed a happy and healthy winter.

A few days before the fall of Ningpo, a 13-year-old orphan called Harry Parkes arrived at Macao, after travelling out from England alone. Harry's sister Catherine had just married Dr Lockhart, who ran the missionary clinic on Chou-shan, and his dead father's cousin, Mary, was Karl Gutzlaff's second wife. The missionaries agreed to do something for young Harry, but it would mean learning Chinese.

To begin with he was found a berth as clerk to John Robert Morrison, son of the first Protestant missionary to China, and author of *A Chinese Commercial Guide* (Canton 1834) which gives helpful directions to the novice opium dealer. J. R. Morrison was at present secretary and interpreter to Sir Henry Pottinger, at a salary, then thought very ample, of £1800 a year. Morrison spoke and wrote Chinese so well that later on, during treaty negotiations, the mandarins could not believe he was British, and suspected him of being a renegade Chinese.

Harry Parkes, a small, fair boy with blue eyes and an intense, terrier-like earnestness, was set to work grinding at Chinese, which he found much harder than his Latin lessons of the year before, at King Edward's School, Birmingham. Young Harry soon became a prime favourite with Sir Henry Pottinger who had his own memories of being flung out into the world at the age of 12.

When Sir Henry went north in *Queen* next spring he took the boy along, to give Gutzlaff a hand with administration and intelligence. Like Kipling's *Kim*, Harry Parkes was being groomed for what might come later.

There is fair reason to suppose that Rev. Dr Karl Gutzlaff – who much preferred the Christian name of Charles, and was known to the Chinese as Kuo-shih-li – must have dabbled in espionage, officially or unofficially, for at least nine years. In 1832, when knowledge of the Chinese coast had been at a premium, Dr Gutzlaff managed to procure from a Chinese scholar a chart of the inner

141

reaches of the River Min (which flows past the port of Foochow, and is particularly tricky to navigate on account of its eighteen-foot tide). As an intelligence-gatherer for the British in Ningpo, he was now showing considerable mastery in this sordid if inevitable business.

Gutzlaff had appointed for his Chief of Police a local man called Yu Te-ch'ang, aged 34, whose previous occupation had been 'selling singing-girls'. The British authorities were furnished by Yu with the names of local Chinese who might be rich enough to squeeze for a share of the city's 'ransom'. Yu helped recruit a network of forty agents to spy on troop concentrations near Hangchow, where a build-up for the recapture of Ningpo was optimistically being organized by the mandarins. We know all this because when caught later by his fellow-countrymen, Yu tried to save his own neck by denouncing all forty of his agents.

Another of Gutzlaff's spies was Ch'en Ping-chun, a Chen-hai man who had done military service in Canton, and worked afterwards as a quack doctor there. He helped guide British warships into Chen-hai during the attack. Later on he was captured by the Chinese when spying at Yu-yao, thirty miles north of Ningpo. Ch'en had the great luck to be actually standing trial there when the British troops arrived, so for once he got away scot-free.

Ch'en was the spy who procured for Gutzlaff the exact date and time of the planned Chinese counter-offensive, but his luck ran out soon after. On 15 March 1842, while gathering intelligence west of Ningpo, Ch'en was once more caught by the Chinese, and that was the last of him.

The Chinese General entrusted by the Emperor with the difficult task of recapturing Ningpo was 48-year-old I-ching, who had done good service when still in his thirties against Moslem rebels in Sinkiang.

Interesting sidelights on the way General I-ching organized his counter-attack are contained in a report of the campaign written by a 30-year-old scholar called Pei Ch'ing-chiao – one among 144 volunteers who came from Soochow to help drive the barbarian invader from the soil of China. Pei had joined the army in an exalted mood, bearing a sword and a patriotic poem, both given him at parting by his old father. The reality of war, as usual, was rather a let-down.

Pei was sent off by the Chinese command to Ningpo itself, to pick up information. His first sight as he approached was dis-heartening: a chopped-off head at the city gate under a placard which read: 'This is the head of the Manchu official Lu T'ai-lai who came here to obtain military information.' Pei was questioned at the gateway, but he managed to get inside.

Much of the military intelligence this well-intentioned Chinese poet and amateur spy picked up in Ningpo, when checked against British records, is inaccurate and wishful. Pei reported the presence in the city of only two warships and 300 men. But at least 2000 men must have been wintering there, and many more were due to arrive.

Pei's next job at Chinese headquarters was to supervise the making of 500 mortar rockets – copying an ancient model which resembled an illustration in *The Firedragon Book*, a seventeenth-century artillery manual. So concerned was the Chinese staff about the spies Gutzlaff was known to be sending amongst them that all reports had to be made, not aloud, but in ink on an ivory slab, and wiped out as soon as read. This slowed everything up.

The young staff officers, though inexperienced in war, were all highly cultivated. A painter called Wang Ch'eng-feng had for several months been engaged on a picture about the army's activities, entitled *All Proceeds According to Plan*. He presented this painting to the General, who asked his young men to embellish it by inscribing upon it their own poems.

The contrast in mood between the two camps is extreme. The British in occupied Ningpo were led by men accustomed all their lives to the disciplines of war. Whatever their occasional inner misgivings at the sight of blood ('I am sick at heart of war, and its fearful consequences!' General Gough would exclaim, in his racy Irish brogue, before plunging anew into the fray) war was for all of them a normal human activity.

Most of the leaders on the Chinese side, by contrast, were literary intellectuals, victors in the national examinations, their minds impregnated with Confucian texts and traditional com-mentaries. They had been trained to think of power not in terms of arbitrary command and unquestioning obedience, but as a projection of mild paternal authority, culminating at the apex in the ritual prestige of the Emperor. Of course, authority in China was often arbitrary and sometimes violent – but everyone saw in such bad behaviour a defiance of principles.

Now this age-old society of organized social equilibrium – in which men of their class had always been the beneficiaries – was visibly cracking up around them. At times, these high principled and cultivated men are at a loss – they lapse into dottiness, anguish, self-deception, suicidal gallantry, sometimes into cruelty. The marvellous subjective consolation – the slow dreaming suicide – of opium is always available. Taking into account the psychological, as well as the practical, handicaps under which they laboured, Chinese intellectuals like Pei and his fellows did well and acted bravely. It is hard to imagine how, faced with an enemy challenge so unfamiliar, so technically omnipotent, they could possibly have done much better.

At the Chinese New Year, General I-ching went to the Temple of the God of War, to pray for victory. He took omens, and a significant message came to hand – a snatch of verse, which read:

> If you are not hailed by humans with the heads of tigers
> I would not be prepared to vouch for your security.

Three days later some aboriginal warriors turned up from the Golden River. They wore a fantasy uniform: yellow garments with black spots or stripes, and a cap resembling a tiger's head. In no time, tiger-skin caps were all the rage. Into the Dragon's pool – evidently the local Loch Ness – a tiger skull was thrown, on the offchance that the Dragon reputed to live in its depths might oblige the army by surfacing to attack the barbarians' fire-belching devil-ships, which otherwise were invincible.

The timing of the Chinese attack – a night assault on 10 March 1842 – was decided in the event less by pedantic military considerations than by War Magic: the twenty-eighth day of the first Chinese month (a Tiger month) and at the hour of the Tiger (between 3 and 5 a.m.). So how could they lose?

Ten days before the attack, the General invited his staff to a competition. They were to compose in advance their reports of the anticipated victory. A promising young officer called Miu Chia-ku won the day, with an account which attributed to various well-known personalities in the army the heroic deeds that, when the time came, they were bound to perform – a kind of prophetic anticipation not wholly unknown in modern war journalism.

A threefold Chinese offensive was intended. There would be a serious attempt to recapture Ningpo, with Chen-hai as a sideshow; and 276 small craft were to make an amphibious attack on Chou-shan. The seaborne venture was a predestined disaster. The

Chinese flotilla cruised about for a month, not daring to land. Undeterred, its commander, Ch'en T'ing-ch'en, claimed a fake naval victory, producing some British wreckage as proof, and before the truth leaked out, he had been awarded his Peacock's Feather.

By 9 March, Gutzlaff had got together a fairly convincing picture of the Chinese counter-attack on Ningpo. His difficulty lay not so much in procuring intelligence, as in getting over-confident British commanders to take any notice. That night no patrols were sent out beyond the walls of Ningpo, to make contact with an approaching enemy, though officers were tipped off to be a little more strict than usual in their nightly rounds. Luckily the rank-and-file had been alerted, thanks to a private source of information. The British privates, as soldiers will, had made pets of a number of Chinese orphans. From these quick-witted Chinese boys no military secret could be kept for long. Having found out somehow that General I-ching's offensive was due, they began twitting their soldier pals – making rude gestures, as of a Tartar firing a matchlock, or a Chinese executioner chopping off a barbarian head. So a number of the men were forewarned, and slept in their boots.

A detachment of Chinese soldiers, dressed up as civilians, had already managed to enter the city, and were waiting for the Hour of the Tiger. At 4 a.m. the vanguard of a Chinese force numbering in all about 5000 men made violent attacks on the south and west gates of Ningpo, while others tried to scale the nearby walls. As dawn lit up the scene, many of the Chinese assault troops were seen by the British to be obviously under the influence of opium.

The attack on the West Gate was led by the aborigines from the Golden River. They had discarded the pikes, swords and matchlocks issued to them, in favour of their traditional long knives, and came on wearing tiger-skin caps. Their rush was met at the West Gate by men of the 18th Regiment, under Lieutenant Armstrong, who from the parapet of the bastion poured down upon the Golden River men volley after volley of musketry. A few Chinese soldiers managed to scale the wall up ladders, or by driving pegs between the crevices of the masonry. They were fought off the parapet hand to hand. The West Gate was held, over 100 Golden River men lying shot dead there.

With help from the men they had previously smuggled in, the Chinese managed to break open the South Gate. In a dense, enthusiastic mass the victorious Chinese soldiers poured down the long, straight street that led from the south gateway to the market-place in the centre of Ningpo. But they ran headlong into a British howitzer, brought up by ponies and quickly unlimbered. Captain Moore, commanding the howitzer, waited until the range was the length of a cricket pitch, then poured in grapeshot. Fire from the gun tore terrible holes through a dozen bodies in succession. The front ranks were pressed on from behind, and had no chance whatever of escape. As the howitzer fired again and again, the street became choked up with dead and dying. Before the Chinese broke and ran, the piled blockage of mutilated flesh was fifteen yards deep.

In a street at right-angles to the only Chinese line of escape, British infantry had been drawn up with loaded muskets, waiting to take them at close range in the flank. As an endless mob of Chinese soldiers, driven back by the howitzer, fled past and ran for the gate, they were smitten with platoon fire. This was the mechanical, terrible musketry of the pitched battle – when the front rank fire in unison at a nearby target, then file promptly by right and left to reload at the rear, while the second line fires its volley, and the third, and the fourth, until the front rank is ready to fire once more.

No British were killed that night, but over 500 Chinese dead were counted. All units of the Chinese army which had been in action at Ningpo were permanently demoralized, from the effect on their minds of grapeshot and musketry at close quarters. Henceforth, against any European army, they were defeated in advance.

Pei, stationed that night with Chang Ying-yun, the general commanding the reserves, heard the howitzer in the distance. Aware that his own side, so as to save Ningpo from damage, were not using artillery, Pei knew that this repeated gunfire must be British. General Chang, the Commander-in-Chief's right-hand man, had been given the duty of moving up the reserves, once a city gate was open, so as to reinforce the attack. But General Chang was an opium addict, and the tension of his moment of responsibility proved too much for him.

As they both waited, Pei could see the craving come upon the General. As the first of the Chinese vanguard came running past in headlong retreat, Pei, waiting for orders that never came, was forced to watch over his commanding officer, sprawled out in a narcotic daze, a pipe between his lips. At last, when it was nearly all over, the General managed to stagger to his own litter, and was carried away to safety. Pei, one of the young scholars who from

146

patriotic motives were contemptuous of opium, goes on to assert what can scarcely have been true, even if Chinese soldiers acted on the belief: that the British showed special favour to opium smokers, never put one to death, and would willingly release any addict they took prisoner.

Not one of the Chinese plans had worked, not even the more far-fetched ones. The scheme to throw monkeys carrying fire-crackers into the rigging of anchored British warships came to nought, because no one had the nerve to row close enough. A macabre proposition worthy of the twentieth century – to sell the British animals infected with smallpox – had been vetoed by General I-ching as discreditable. The sideshow – an attack on Chen-hai by troops armed with spears and knives – was an inevitable fiasco. For his failure to take Ningpo, General I-ching was sentenced to death, but in 1843 he was reprieved, and given a disagreeable post on the Central Asian frontier, at Yarkand in Turkestan.

In April and May, when reinforcements of infantry arrived, together with more river steamers, the British again took the offensive. Most of the cities threatened with assault were from now on to be given the option of buying their safety with a cash ransom. But later it was discovered that the Chinese expression for 'ransom' meant 'money paid to kidnappers', so the word 'indemnity' came into favour.

The expeditionary force captured, in turn, Cha-pu, Wu-sung and Shanghai, all without much opposition. Karl Gutzlaff was familiar with the terrain, having been on an expedition to Shanghai ten years before as a Christian missionary. Cha-pu fell in the manner of other Chinese cities – to the firepower of ships' guns, the disciplined aggressiveness of professional soldiers, and a General who knew how to outflank.

The Tartar troops who defended Cha-pu did not disgrace themselves. Three hundred of them made a memorable stand in a joss-house outside the city wall. They held up the capture of the city for hours, so enraging the Royal Irish that (until prevented by their officers) they proposed killing the sixty survivors instead of taking them prisoner. The prisoners in the end were tied together in groups of eight or ten, by means of their pigtails, and marched off, having gained their lives at the expense of their dignity. These Tartar soldiers lived together in a special quarter of the city. The British, when they broke in, found that all the Tartar womenfolk had hanged or poisoned themselves, rather than fall into the hands of an enemy. Many of the defeated Tartar soldiers who escaped death in battle cut their own throats to avoid humiliation. Rather than survive defeat, the mandarins serving in Cha-pu also committed suicide, after killing their families.

Wu-sung and Shanghai were taken almost without resistance. Three hundred and sixty guns were captured there, and nine tons of gunpowder. Shanghai paid a ransom of $300 000 for its immunity from sack, though the British commanders, no doubt with the best will in the world, were unable to repress freelance looting there.

To judge by eyewitness reports, the unofficial plundering of Shanghai – as of other cities captured later – went through two stages. First came a certain amount of inevitable picking and stealing, usually from their billets, by British soldiers. ('The contents of the houses in which their billets chanced to establish them were always', said Lieutenant John Ouchterlony of the Madras Engineers, '. . . carried off as legitimate "loot".') The second stage, more devastating, was the systematic plunder of the disorganized city by a mob of Chinese thieves. ('Much property valuable for its rarity as well as for its intrinsic worth', adds Ouchterlony, 'was of necessity left behind, and of course abandoned to the gangs of Chinese marauders which always hung upon our rear when the evacuation of a city was going on.') Defending the habit that British troops had fallen into, of looting the houses they occupied, Ouchterlony adds with pawky logic: 'The practice of the Chinese, of plundering whatever we abstained from touching, would have speedily removed all scruples.'

On 8 July 1842 there was a total eclipse of the sun – to the Chinese always a portent of national disaster.

What an educated Chinese was up against when his city was occupied by 'barbarians' may be glimpsed in the diary of Ts'ao Cheng (who spoke of himself as an 'impractical old bookworm' and lived in a suburban house inside a walled courtyard). It began when foreign soldiers beat down the courtyard gate with their musket butts. They came in and plundered the house of all its valuables, but particularly wanted to know where Ts'ao had hidden his money. They pulled back his head, held a knife to his throat, and repeated a useful Chinese expression they had picked up somewhere: *'Fan ping! Fan ping!'* meaning *'foreign cakes'* – the current expression for silver dollars.

'My wife', added Ts'ao, 'had had nothing to eat for three days . . . presently Neighbour Wang came through the rain, bringing

148

me half a roasted chicken. This was splendid ... A band of local brigands now arrived ... there were twenty or thirty of them ... everything the foreigners had not taken they made a bundle of, and took away ... they had left not a single farthing, or a single grain of rice.'

Ts'ao had two small boys, as well as his wife, to provide for. Early next day he took a basket 'like a monk with a begging bowl', and went round the city, managing to cadge some rice. He reported, 'the foreigners have contented themselves with loot and rape, but as the city fell without resistance there has been no general slaughter ... they are pressing the people into their service to do all their heavy work, such as shifting gun emplacements and gunpowder ... They take anyone ... Buddhist monks, notables, and well-known people ...'

Before the army left Shanghai, Sir Henry Pottinger thought it well to issue a proclamation, reminding the inhabitants that the British were in fact fighting not the Chinese people but the Imperial government.

The British expeditionary force by this time grouped about 12 000 fighting men, of whom 9000 were armed with the latest percussion musket. The plan was to deliver them up the Yangtze, by ship, as high as Nanking, so as to interrupt traffic on the Grand Canal and thus bring pressure to bear on Peking. In fact this year the Chinese, forewarned, had got their grain fleet up the Grand Canal as early as 26 June and only after did the British discover that as a matter of high policy the Chinese never kept less than a three-year rice supply in their capital. Therefore, by their indirect offensive the British could reasonably expect only to intimidate not to paralyse the Chinese government. In real terms their successive victories were neither as overwhelming or as final as at the time they seemed.

Admiral Parker had decided to take one battleship up the Yangtze – HMS *Cornwallis* (74 guns) – as the most powerful element in a fleet of eleven frigates and corvettes, besides five steam frigates and five armed steamers, and nearly fifty miscellaneous troopships and transports. He organized his force into three divisions, each separated by a mile of water, and led by a warship.

Such an endlessly strung-out line of shipping, making way mostly under sail up a river imperfectly charted, gave the Chinese

149

a sitting target. One well-placed and efficient battery, in a shot-proof casement, manned by efficient artillerymen and guarded by obstinate infantry, could have jammed the Yangtze with wreckage, but on the Chinese side there were no such batteries, and no such men. Lin's policy was by now discredited. The Manchu rulers had anyway been putting their best resources into fortifying the approaches to Peking.

For all their tone of bouncing confidence, the British commanders were taking an enormous chance. They speculated on the demoralization and incompetence of the Chinese army, but the gamble was forced on them. The British could go on winning only in so far as their ships-of-war could deliver and protect their fighting men. Lin had understood this, when on being sent into exile he advocated a popular war based on China's vast interior. Taking 10 000 men only a couple of hundred miles inland would stretch British sea-power to the limit.

Twenty miles downstream from Chinkiang – a fortified city hampering the approach to Nanking – the first British convoy encountered a Chinese 6-gun shore battery so placed that, if worked with a will, it could have raked the leading ships from end to end. The six Chinese guns were fired only once, then the gunners were seen to run for it across country, as if unable to bear even the thought of a British warship's answering broadside.

The French were still keeping events in China under cautious observation. Two French warships, *Erigone* (44 guns, Captain Cécille) and *Favorite* (18 guns, Captain Page) had arrived at Wu-sung soon after the British occupied the city – a silent reminder that though Great Britain might take the brunt of the fighting, her French rivals and her American competitors expected a share of the spoils. The British were to go on intoxicatingly from victory to victory; the likelihood of 'conquering China' was further off than ever.

At 7 a.m. on 21 July, as British troops were landed from their ships under the walls of Chinkiang, the day was already appallingly hot. By evening, twenty men from one regiment alone, the 98th, had died of sunstroke. The city was ominously silent. Most of the Tartar garrison had formed up to give battle from entrenchments, outside and beyond the city walls.

Peter Anstruther of the Madras Artillery, now promoted to Major, got his field-guns up, to gall the Tartar trenches. British infantry were sent in under cover of the guns to make a frontal attack, and the Tartars ran for it. (The new percussion musket turned out to be a satisfactory weapon, less prone to misfire because of damp, but the shorter bayonet that went with it was an inferior article, likely to bend when thrust home.)

Those Tartar troops still inside Chinkiang and strung out along the walls, began to fire at the advancing British assault columns with their matchlocks and gingalls – the latter an antique-looking large-calibre musket, fired from a tripod. The British, sweltering in the enormous heat, brought ladders up. Under covering fire from their own light troops, a storming party of grenadiers of the 55th, led by Captain Macleane, made a successful escalade near a gate, up the face of a square bastion which gave adequate cover from the Tartar fire.

The gate was forced, the defenders bayoneted, and as sepoys of the 2nd and 6th native infantry poured into the city, the Tartars retreated in good order towards their barracks firing as they went. The other city gate under attack held out until 11 a.m., when it was riskily but successfully blown in with three bags holding 160 lb of gunpowder.

The Tartar quarter of Chinkiang, where 2300 picked troops of the garrison had formerly lived in barracks, was now the usual shambles. The Tartars had killed their own wives and children by strangulation, sword or poison. The Tartar General, Hai-lin, chose a bizarre but symbolic way to meet his death. Making a huge pile of official papers, he sat on top and set them alight, making of his own office archives a funeral pyre. ('Worthy', remarked Sir Henry Pottinger sententiously, 'of a nobler and a better fate.')

The poet Chu Shih-yun lived outside Chinkiang, on a bank of the Grand Canal. His diary, in describing General Hai-lin's behaviour before the British attack, indicates clearly the mood of vindictive despair now shown by the Manchus. Interpreting Chinese resentment against them as 'treachery', they were striking out wildly.

'The Lieutenant-General', writes Chu, 'was in a very excited state. All over the town he arrested harmless people on the ground that they were in league with the enemy. He handed them over to the Prefect to imprison and flog ... it was only at the four gates that he had a cannon pointing outwards. Inside the city his whole activity consisted in arresting passers-by ... on suspicion of their being traitors. Whenever women or children saw Manchu soldiers they fled in terror, upon which the soldiers ran after them and slew them, announcing to Hai-lin that they had disposed of traitors, for which he gave them rewards.'

On 15 July, General Hai-lin 'made a brief tour of inspection, came back, and wept until his eyes were swollen'. Plunder by

151

roughs and bandits had already begun, but Chu managed to get his family to safety across the river. On 17 July, says Chu, five foreign ships arrived, and the bombardment began. Meanwhile, inside the city, Manchu troops continued to search the streets for 'traitors', shooting on sight anyone they could not identify. On 21 July the British attacked.

Chu reveals himself in his diary as one of the many educated Chinese who were beginning to dislike the Manchus rather more than the British, and his account of the way the Tartars fought at Chinkiang badly underrates them as soldiers. On 24 July – to follow Chu's account – the British in Chinkiang executed two sepoys and put up a placard which warned against rape and looting. After 16 August there was to be no more commandeering of goods without payment. (Lieutenant Bernard, serving in *Nemesis*, writes of seeing the streets of Chinkiang littered with plundered silks and furs, and of pickets put at the city's four gates, stopping any soldier who tried to bring out his loot, and taking it from him to augment the official prize-fund.)

Twelve days later, according to Chu's diary, the foreign soldiers began selling back for silver dollars, from a market stall, the clothes they had previously looted. On 5 September the British put up a placard, announcing that peace negotiations had begun. The inhabitants of Chinkiang (who by then would have been in dire need of some artificial consolation) were at the same time advised to go to Sui-shan 'where opium is on sale very cheap – an opportunity not to be missed'. The opium ships had followed the Royal Navy up the Yangtze.

Yang-chou, a city between the north bank of the Grand Canal and Nanking, tried to buy its immunity. Morrison, Pottinger's interpreter, set the price at $600 000, but that was apparently asking too much. The merchants of the official salt monopoly, who were given the job of collecting Yang-chou's ransom, managed to scrape up only half. Since it was late in the day, the British took what was offered – terming it an instalment of an overall indemnity they proposed to extract from the Chinese authorities by treaty.

Nanking, a city as big, in those days, as Paris, and enclosed within a red, sandstone wall thirty miles in circumference, was where the last native dynasty, the Ming, had capitulated to the Manchus. As the British came near, they saw flutter from the parapet a large white flag. Word came that I-li-pu, a high-ranking

Manchu with a name for probity, whose service included the post of Viceroy at Nanking, was imminently expected on the scene, with powers to conclude peace.

Young Harry Parkes was by this time established with Sir Henry Pottinger as a firm favourite. Already he had a useful smattering of Chinese, which it amused Sir Henry to hear him try out on notabilities. At the age of 13 he was about to watch, at close quarters, how an experienced, hard-headed British official intended to impose his will upon the suppliant Chinese. At the capture of Wu-sung, young Harry had already encountered bloodshed. ('I counted fifteen dead men in a short space.' He wrote: 'This is my first sight of the horrors of war.')

Sir Henry's plan was not to give the Chinese any scope whatever for guile or finesse. He had no intention of risking the fruits of his spectacular conquest by magnanimity, and he soon showed it.

On 9 August, I-li-pu was unable to present satisfactory credentials. Sir Henry Pottinger at once threatened to reopen hostilities. Nanking, he warned them, would be attacked on the 10th. To show he meant business, the 74-gun *Cornwallis* and the frigate *Blonde* were moved close to the city walls, an infantry brigade was disembarked, and a battery of eight-inch howitzers put ashore. The Chinese begged for time, and this was the more willingly granted when the British found that the place they had chosen for making a breach in the city wall was exceptionally difficult for their soldiers to get at.

Three Commissioners were appointed by the Emperor, and, with the fullest credentials, hurried down to Nanking. They were led by Ch'i-ying, a high official who was a member of the Imperial clan, and the Emperor's close personal friend.

The Commissioners at once wrote back from Nanking, warning the Emperor of the stark reality which over-optimistic war reports, and the knowledge that this year's rice was safely up the Grand Canal, may well have concealed from him: 'Should we fail to ... ease the situation by soothing the barbarians, they will run over our country like beasts, doing anything they like.'

Since the Chinese spokesmen were in no condition to haggle, the treaty Sir Henry Pottinger managed to extract from them tallied very closely with Lord Palmerston's original instructions, and William Jardine's hopes – except that, on the spot, Pottinger could see the superiority of Hong Kong, with its deep-water harbour, over Chou-shan, with its unfavourable winds and hostile population. So on his own authority he took and kept Hong Kong.

The indemnity to be paid by the Chinese was assessed by Sir Henry at the enormous sum of $21 000 000 – about half the total Chinese revenue in any given year. This mass of silver was to be paid in instalments, over three years, Chou-shan and the islet dominating Amoy being kept as security, until payment was complete. The sum demanded would amply meet the cost of the war, not to mention paying off the drug traffickers for their destroyed opium.

The Chinese Commissioners were found, at first, to be innocently under the impression that the ransom of $6 000 000, paid previously to Elliot when he refrained from sacking Canton, had been China's compensation for the destroyed opium. 'How can payment be extorted,' they complained, 'a second time?'

Dent & Co., whose principal, Lancelot Dent, was so narrowly rescued from martyrdom, had been the firm used by Captain Elliot to remit the Canton ransom to London. They had evidently been under a similar illusion, to judge from the way they handled the money. Before passing on the ransom, they had deducted £63 265 18s. 4d. from the silver on their own account, as 'payment' for the 500 chests they alleged Captain Elliot had 'bought' from them, to make up the total Lin demanded. Dent & Co. did well for themselves; other opium dealers merely got certificates for the amounts of drug they had surrendered, and were compensated at a more modest rate, as well as having to wait a long time for their money.

With the Nanking indemnity, there was to be no such monkey business. The silver would be sent home by warship (a profitable duty and an indirect reward for the captains concerned, who were allowed to deduct one per cent of the value of specie that was carried in a warship a distance over 600 leagues).

The British consented to withdraw from under the walls of Nanking, as soon as the first instalment was handed over, and by 12 October HMS *Blonde, Modeste, Herald* and *Columbine* were on their way home, with another six million silver dollars under hatches.

On coming to power in 1841, Peel found he had inherited from the Whigs a chronic budget deficit, persisting since 1837, of over two millions annually in a total revenue, mostly from indirect taxation, of about £50 000 000. This shortfall reflected Britain's loss of markets in America and Europe, which Lord Palmerston was trying to put right by a policy of aggression in China. To Peel in 1842 – a year of slack trade and social distress – the arrival of Chinese silver was a gift. In 1843 the gross deficit had risen to three and a quarter million pounds, of which £750 000 was happily met from the Chinese indemnity. As late as 1845–6, when the revenue went into surplus at last, China was still feeding into the British budget a very welcome half a million sterling. Pottinger's rapacity at Nanking has its own explanation.

In the terms of the treaty, the Chinese also accepted that they must henceforth negotiate with the British, not as tribute-bearing barbarians obliged to kowtow, but on equal terms. Amoy, Foochow, Ningpo and Shanghai were named as additional ports open to trade. All those Chinese who might have 'cooperated' with the British – Gutzlaff's spies for instance – were to be amnestied.

The Treaty of Nanking, in a Chinese and an English text, expressing what the British had fought the war to obtain, and the defeated Chinese had been forced to concede, was signed on 29 August 1842 aboard HMS *Cornwallis*. The Chinese pleni-potentiaries, as if to indicate silently that there had been no meeting of minds, appended their names to the text without even bothering to read it. The signatories went on to toast the health of Queen Victoria in cherry brandy. During these celebrations, Ch'i-ying 'insisted on Sir Henry's opening his mouth, while he with great dexterity shot into it several immense sugar-plums'. This, so the British were informed, was an old Manchu custom, demonstrating a high degree of mutual confidence. 'I shall never forget,' remarked an eyewitness, 'Sir Henry's face of determined resignation.'

I-li-pu, as one of the Chinese Commissioners signing the Treaty, asked the Emperor to punish him for submitting to the English: he was banished as a common convict.

Pottinger, when writing to Lord Palmerston the previous October about the intended attack up the Yangtze, had announced confidently, 'Either Peking must give in, or the Maritime pro-vinces will be at our disposal.' He went on to hint that it might then rest 'with the Queen of England to pronounce which ports, or portions of the seacoast of China, shall be added to Her Majesty's Dominions'. But outright conquest of this sort in China was hampered by the presence of rivals. Captain Médée Cécille, of the French frigate *Erigone*, had come up the Yangtze in a hired junk, manned from his own ship's company. He went aboard HMS *Cornwallis* uninvited, and asked to be present when the Treaty was ceremonially signed. Sir Henry, less urbane than Captain Elliot, would have none of it. But the French presence, nearby, was a silent warning to the British that they could hardly expect to have it all their own way, in China.

The French, like the Americans, had hitherto not been quite sure what stance to take. There had not long before been Anglo-French tension over the annexation of New Zealand, and there was soon to be conflict over Tahiti. Rumour asserted that in the previous February, a French representative had made secret overtures to the Viceroys of Canton, offering to modernize the Cantonese Navy, and to build warships equipped with modern guns and torpedoes, for use against the British. Patience, and perhaps the sporting chance of being able to play one foreign power off against another, were evidently China's remaining diplomatic resources.

At Shanghai, before taking the British expeditionary force up the Yangtze River, Sir Henry Pottinger had held a secret conference with the Roman Catholic Bishop of Nanking – a priest of French origin who came aboard HMS *Cornwallis* dressed as a Chinese. One side effect of the British campaign, as Lieutenant Ouchterlony points out, was that 'a number of Catholic missionaries took advantage of the general confusion, and of the temporary dispersal of the mandarins, to follow in our wake . . . for the purpose of penetrating in the guise of Chinese . . . into the heart of the Empire'.

On one important matter, alone, the British failed to get their own way. The Chinese, despite their overwhelming defeat, refused to include in the Treaty, or even to discuss during the official negotiations, any proposal whatever for regulating the opium trade. This brave obduracy of theirs on the very issue about which (in their own eyes, at least) the war had been fought and lost was a portent. Having put their names to the Treaty of Nanking under duress, the Chinese, in years to come, meant whenever possible to dodge its obligations.

Lord Palmerston had given Sir Henry Pottinger precise written instructions about opium. He was 'strongly to impress upon the Chinese plenipotentiaries . . . how much it would be to the interest of that Government to legalize the trade.' But the Emperor's reply showed him still intransigent: 'Gain-seeking and corrupt men will for profit and sensuality defeat my wishes, but nothing will induce me to derive a revenue from the vice and misery of my people.'

Though they would not come to terms about opium, or even publicly discuss it, the Chinese Commissioners sent Sir Henry a reply to the long written memorial he submitted to them. 'Our nations have been united by friendly commercial intercourse for two hundred years,' they argued. 'How then, at this time, are our relations so suddenly changed, as to be the cause of national quarrel?...from the spreading of the opium poison. Multitudes of our Chinese subjects consume it, wasting their property and destroying their lives ... how is it possible for us to refrain from forbidding our people to use it?'

Still hoping to find some indirect way to force 'legalization' upon them, Sir Henry decided to ask the Commissioners for a private and unofficial interview. Their conversation apparently began by the Chinese spokesmen asking him point blank why the British did not forbid the growth of the poppy in India. According to the American merchant, Gerald Nye, who had contacts on both sides, Sir Henry's argument went along familiar lines: the British government were constitutionally unable to forbid the cultivation of the opium poppy in India, and, even if they did, it would continue to be grown elsewhere.

'If your people are virtuous, they will desist from the evil practice,' Sir Henry is reported to have argued (no doubt tongue-in-cheek, since after his period of service in Sind, on the export route for Malwa opium, he can hardly have failed to be aware that the drug was addictive). 'If your officers are incorruptible, and obey your orders, no opium can enter.'

'Your people will procure the drug', he went on to warn them, 'in spite of every enactment. Would it not be better to legalize the importation?' The Chinese at last managed to bring home to Pottinger that their Emperor might agree to anything else – but never to this.

Sir Henry Pottinger's first failure with the Chinese, over opium, was followed by another and less conspicuous one, later, in the Supplementary Treaty. They hoodwinked him about the regulation of shipping between Canton and Hong Kong, leaving a measure of control in Chinese hands: a source of trouble to come. According to later gossip among old China hands, these blunders were what lost Sir Henry the peerage he might confidently have expected for services rendered; though in 1845 Parliament voted him a pension for life of £1500 per annum.

With the fighting at an end, the harbour on Chou-shan Island was crowded with shipping. 'A goodly array of opium clippers,' said an observer, 'occupied the inner tier off the suburb of Tin-hai, busily plying the much-abused trade in the drug, which here found a ready sale, the Chinese shipping it over in large quantities to the mainland, in boats, running their cargoes with perfect impunity, as the power of the mandarins had for some time been in complete abeyance.'

157

Armed opium ships were anchoring in the Pearl River, at Whampoa, for the first time since 1820, as if to remind the Cantonese in the most pointed manner of China's defeat. Alexander Matheson, now running the family opium business, reported complacently, 'The drug trade continues to prosper.'

But the volatility of the Cantonese had still to be reckoned with. In November, when the fighting was over, several ship's captains at Whampoa caused offence against the traditional rules by taking their wives upriver with them – a provocation enough to bring the Cantonese mob surging out on the streets.

An angry crowd converged on the Factories. They began by burning down the British flagstaff. American merchants held them off their own quarters at the point of the gun, killing five. Chinese troops tried to disperse the mob, and failed. A treaty, enumerating concessions to the 'foreign devils', might have been signed by the Manchu Emperor's representatives at Nanking, but Canton had a mind of its own.

Sir Henry Pottinger was granted one last proconsular moment, when by brandishing at the Chinese the threat of renewed warfare he made them jump to obey him. The luckless prisoners on Formosa – survivors from *Ann* and *Nerbudda* – had been taken out of gaol at the very moment the plenipotentiaries were negotiating over on the mainland. In the presence of an excited Chinese crowd, they were decapitated one by one. By a fluke, a handful of them – hostile witnesses to the dirty work on Formosa – had their execution postponed, and by his quick threat of war Sir Henry Pottinger undoubtedly saved their necks. Viceroy I-liang hurried over from the mainland, to investigate, and the high officials held responsible for the various acts, on Formosa, of cruelty and deceit were handed on to the Board of Punishments in Peking.

The Tories, now forming Britain's government, had when out of office used the opium question as a stick to beat the Whigs. In their ranks, particularly among High Anglicans like Gladstone, a sentiment against the opium trade was strongly persistent, and on 4 January 1843 Lord Aberdeen made it clear to Sir Henry Pottinger that 'the British opium smuggler must receive no protection or support in the prosecution of his illegal speculations'. (An injunction phrased like this would, of course, no longer apply, if the Chinese later showed themselves willing to 'legalize' the drug.) An Order in Council, empowering 'the British Plenipotentiary to forbid the opium traffic in Hong Kong', also helped placate those anti-opium critics who were still in earnest.

Some months later Sir Henry Pottinger responded to this

pressure from London, the character of which he evidently well understood. It was high time. Between August 1841 and January 1843 forty-seven vessels entering Hong Kong had informed the harbour-master that their cargo was opium. On 1 August 1843 Sir Henry proclaimed in Hong Kong that 'opium being an article the traffic in which is well known to be declared illegal and contraband by the laws and Imperial Edicts of China, any person who may take such a step will do so at his own risk, and will, if a British subject, meet with no support or protection from HM Consuls or other officers'.

Gratifying though this proclamation may have been to critics of the opium trade in Britain, the firm of Jardine, Matheson & Co. were unperturbed; they knew their man. Matheson reported as follows to London: 'The Plenipotentiary had published a most fiery Edict against smuggling, but I believe it is like the Chinese Edicts, meaning nothing, and only intended for the Saints in England. Sir Henry never means to act upon it, and no doubt privately considers it a good joke. At any rate, he allows the drug to be landed and stored at Hong Kong.'

Ellenborough, the new and ebullient Governor-General of India, had previously written to check Lord Aberdeen, reminding him that Her Majesty's Government should do 'nothing to place in peril our Opium Revenue. As for preventing the manufacture of opium, and the sale of it in China, that is far beyond your power.' When Captain Hope, RN, of HMS *Thalia*, was so literal-minded as to take the official pronouncements against opium at their face value, and one day stop a vessel he judged to be illegally carrying the drug, he was told sharply 'not to interfere in such a manner with the undertakings of British subjects', and ordered back to India. Lord Aberdeen managed eventually to stifle his humanitarian impulses to the extent of minuting a despatch to Pottinger: 'I think Sir Henry Pottinger may be permitted to suspend the exclusion of opium from the waters and harbours of Hong Kong for the present, if he should think expedient to do so.' The fine gestures were over; the drug trade had never stopped for a moment.

Soon, in addition to their big, fortress-like granite godown at Hong Kong, stacked with opium, Jardine, Matheson & Co. had an 866-ton receiving ship *Comanjee Hormusjee* permanently at anchor in the harbour. They were operating eleven receiving ships in all, to supply six coastal runners, and their stocks were brought from India by five crack clippers: this fleet cost them annually a quarter of a million sterling. By 1850, when opium imports into China were at least double what they had been in the year of Commissioner Lin's ban, the government of India was receiving £5·5 million sterling, out of its total revenue of £27·5 million, from opium. And this, of course, was what really mattered.

In 1843 yet one more Parliamentary attack on the trade had been mounted, this time by Lord Ashley (later the Earl of Shaftesbury), the philanthropist, whose punning aluminium statue as Eros is the familiar centrepiece of Piccadilly Circus. Ashley for some years to come was to act as spokesman in London for those who condemned the opium traffic. Lord Ashley was an impassioned Evangelical, haunted all his life by the thought of unnecessary human suffering – of which, like not a few of his class then and since, he had met with more than his fair share, in childhood. A Tory on entering politics, he briefly held office under both Wellington and Peel – on one occasion acting as Commissioner for the India Board of Control.

In 1830 he married the daughter of Palmerston's mistress, Lady Cowper – she was arguably Palmerston's natural child – and Palmerston (who married the widowed Lady Cowper in 1839) welcomed Ashley warmly into his own home. But this curious friendship between saint and cynic did not deter Lord Ashley from throwing over his ministerial career, to become a thorn in the side of both Whigs and Tories.

Ashley's main targets in Parliament had so far been the hard-faced industrialists and coal-operators of the north, who filled mine and mill with little children, and worked them to death like small animals. Cotton-mill owners were most often radical allies of the Whigs (though the Tory leader, Peel, inherited a fortune made in cotton). Many Tory peers on the other hand were bene-ficiaries of coal royalties, so Ashley soon got used to being shot at from both sides, and taking a line of his own.

In a leading article of 3 December 1842 *The Times* had for once urged the government to wash its hands of all responsibility for the opium traffic, and do without the Indian revenue. 'We owe some moral compensation to China', the paper had declared, 'for pillaging her towns and slaughtering her citizens, in a quarrel which could never have arisen if we had not been guilty of this national crime.' This utterance, though no doubt sincere, was not simply a revulsion of conscience. *The Times* was skilfully voicing an opinion, then current among businessmen, that China's good-

ust somehow be gained, if she were to become a large market
gitimate exports – and that opium-smuggling was likely to
their pitch.

'hile Pottinger, in China, was carrying through his tariff
iations, Lord Ashley rose in the House of Commons, in
rt of petitions presented against the opium monopoly by a
of Quakers, and by the missionary organizations of the
yans, Congregationalists and Baptists. Members on the floor
e House critical of the opium trade were numerous enough
eat a motion to adjourn. Ashley's argument that opium would
the market for other British exports was listened to attentively;
scribed the trade as 'utterly inconsistent with the honour
uty of a Christian kingdom'.

ut, as time was to show, the Chinese had no burning wish
y the textiles which then comprised four-fifths of Britain's
ts, preferring their own homespun. Ashley's basic argument
d him a short-lived sympathy in a Parliament where the
e industry was well represented, but in the long run was
ading.

ne effective speaker in the debate was a ghost from the past –
eorge Staunton, long ago the 12-year-old prodigy on Lord
rtney's embassy, now a bachelor in his sixties with a landed
e in Hampshire. Though in the past Sir George had wavered –
izing the opium trade in 1840, but supporting the merchants'
to compensation, and so committing himself to the war
inevitably followed – this time he was forthright. 'If there
een no opium smuggling, there would have been no war,' he
red.

r George correctly traced the alarm of the Chinese authorities
e growth of opium addiction back to the bad old decision of
ast India Company – of which he himself had been a high
l – to increase enormously the supply of opium, and lower
rice. When Baring the banker – speaking what the House
rstood to be the mind of Sir Robert Peel, the Prime Minister –
red there was no remedy but legalization (implying that for
hinese the problem had got out of control) Sir George Staunton
ted, 'The Chinese government could and did stop the traffic
ually, for four months previous to the seizure of the opium.'
r Robert Peel aborted the debate with his usual skill by
g his Parliamentary critics to believe, through Baring, that by
very next mail news was confidently expected that the
eror of China had agreed to legalize opium. Peel very possibly
is subordinate put this point of view in good faith. He could

161

hardly have supposed that, over legalization, Pottinger
fail in the end to get his own way.

Lord Ashley's protest in 1843 was far from being the
Parliamentary denunciation of the opium trade. Ashley ma
to get the question raised again in 1855. In 1857 he succeed
extracting from the law officers of the Crown their opinion
the opium trade was at variance with the spirit of the Trea
Nanking, and 'with conduct due . . . as a friendly power bound
treaty which implies that all smuggling will be discounten
by Britain'. But not much practical use could be made o
admission, since, by 1857, what the Chinese themselves r
as the second Opium War had already broken out.

The British campaign against the opium traffic went
through the nineteenth century, resolutions in one form or an
being put and lost in the House of Commons in 1870 (151 vo
47), in 1875 (94 votes to 57), in 1886 (126 votes to 66) and i
(165 votes to 88). The minority finally carried the day – a
sistent minorities will – but Britain's trade with China in I
opium did not officially come to an end until the Manchu dy
was on the point of extinction, between 1908 and 1913, durin
lifetimes, and, indeed, within the living memory, of some
present leaders of China.

The traffic – this time in opium derivatives, like her
revived enormously with the Japanese invasion of China. I
the late 1930s the normal annual recorded import of heroi
all China, including Manchuria, had been of the order of
kilograms. In 1938–9, 2400 kilograms of heroin were consign
the Manchukuo Monopoly Bureau, in Japanese-occupied
churia.

The *Manchester Guardian* of 25 April 1938 reports: 'D
1936, the traffickers set up clinics at village fairs, adver
their skill in curing tuberculosis and other diseases. The me
sold was always the same: heroin or morphine. The countr
were ignorant of what was happening to them. When the
of the medicine wore off, feeling worse than ever, they ret
to the clinic for advice. They were told they must persist wit
treatment . . .'

In 1938, similar small clinics advertising cures – one m
with a Red Cross – were opened in Peking itself, by then in Jap
hands. Anyone seeking treatment was perfunctorily register
suffering from disease, and after that could buy as much l
or morphine as he liked. By 1941 there were 51 664 regi
addicts in Mukden, the Manchurian capital, and there were

in every village. By April 1944 the opium poppy was being
:ly cultivated in twelve of the sixteen provinces into which
huria had been divided. Addicts in Manchuria at the time of
Japanese defeat were estimated to number 13 000 000 (or
hird of the population). This was the measure of the social
em the Chinese Communists inherited, and have apparently
ed.

6 Pirates and Rebels

'... thanksgiving to God for the war between China and Great Br
and for the greatly enlarged facilities secured by the treaty of
for the introduction of Christianity into that Empire.'
From a resolution passed unanimously at a meeting of the Lc
Missionary Society in Exeter Hall in 1843

'... I am in dread of the judgement of God upon England f
national iniquity towards China.'
From the diary of W. E. Gladstone, 14 May 1840

During 1842 Sir Henry Pottinger came back to England, on
and was banqueted at Manchester by men in the cotton
With his customary optimism he assured them that victo
China had 'opened up a new world to their trade so vast th
the mills in Lancashire could not make stocking stuff suff
for one of its provinces'.

For a year or two, British merchants went on believing
kind of assurance. When the cotton trade fell slack, men in
cashire would tell each other optimistically, 'If every Chin
buys a cotton nightcap, our mills will be kept going.' Lc
unlikely merchandise poured into the Treaty Ports of C
much remaining unsold. A Sheffield firm, which evidently
never heard of chopsticks, sent the Chinese an immense
signment of cutlery. So many pianos arrived that every B
family in Hong Kong was soon able to afford two, at cut p
and the rest mouldered in a warehouse. But for the next f
years of turbulent armed truce between Britain and China
trade that really mattered – in cotton textiles – remained stag
Not only did the Chinese go on wearing their own cotton home
but they cleverly managed to increase fivefold their expc
Britain of silk (from 10 727 bales in 1845 to 50 489 bales in
Silver ceased to flow out, and the balance of trade turned ag
China's favour.

For British traders the real money was in opium. Si
young man came out to China intending to make his fortu
five or six years, and then go home and live like a gentlema

164

lexities of the textile trade had little appeal. According to *Times*, by 1857 – when war broke out anew – the British situation had become exasperating. In that year, the Chinese ted to Britain tea and silk to the value of £15 million. This requited in China by opium sales worth about £7 million, nents of raw Indian cotton of about £1·5 million, and an rt of British manufactures into China that had stuck fast out £2 million. The £4·5 million trade deficit had to be made but this time, by the British – in shipments of silver.

ghai – the treaty port which gave access up the Yangtze to al China – was booming. Much silk was exported through ghai, and from Shanghai opium was shipped upriver to the ew market: those inland provinces of China where the habit lot been generally implanted.

he British Consul at Shanghai was Rutherford Alcock – a d army surgeon, exceedingly tall and beaky-nosed, eccentric courageous, who carried rather to extremes Sir Henry Pot's method of impressing the Chinese by pomp. When obliged ld speech with a mandarin, Alcock put on a cocked hat, trousers with a broad silver stripe, and a blue coat, trimmed silver lace, and smothered with the six decorations awarded when fighting as an irregular in Spain. By 1848, Consul k was able to report that twenty-four merchant houses were sented at Shanghai, three of them American – and that four- of the trade there was in British hands (though by 1853 ican tonnage entering Shanghai exceeded British). The b where the foreign merchants traded was flat and smelly, church, a club, an hotel, a racecourse and a cemetery had dy been built there.

acking the silk trade, and neglected by tea exporters, Hong was more directly dependent on the trade in opium. In the nn of 1845 seventy-one opium ships, some of them American, recorded as using Hong Kong, nineteen belonging to Jardine, eson & Co. and thirteen to Dent & Co. The British govern- had phrased its instructions to Treaty Port consuls with it was neither their duty to help opium smugglers, nor to the Chinese carry out Chinese laws against the drug. In quence, as the Governor of Hong Kong reported, 'almost person possessed of capital who is not connected with govern- employ is employed in the opium trade'.

165

Dysentery, boils and fever were so prevalent on the h
little island that in the London music halls, '*Go to Hong K*
became a joke way of exclaiming '*Go to hell!*' After the
Regiment had served for eight years in the garrison, of the ori
arrivals not ten men were left alive. Over 2000 dead fron
regiment were buried on Hong Kong. In the summer of
Hong Kong Fever killed nearly a quarter of the troops i
garrison and a tenth of all the civilians.

The lack of law and order on Hong Kong became a by
The prediction made as long ago as 23 February 1841 by
Hong Kong Register was coming true: 'Hong Kong will b
resort and rendezvous of all the Chinese smugglers, opium sm
shops and gambling houses will soon spread ... the island w
surrounded by floating shameens [brothels] and become a gel
of the waters!' The local police were notorious for incompe
and corruption. Big opium houses hired their own armed gu
and every European and American carried a loaded rev
Crews off American whalers, coming to Hong Kong to refit,
kept things lively – by 1850, ninety American ships were ent
the harbour annually.

Opium was almost respectable in Hong Kong compared
the piracy for which the island soon became the notorious or
zing centre. Marine storekeepers were the key men: they imp
cannon for the Chinese pirates, sold off their booty for them
kept watch on the movements of patrolling warships. Se
from American whalers and British men-of-war were encou
to desert, and hire out their skills to the Chinese pirate fleet
The Times was later to observe, Queen Victoria's new c
had become 'an Alsatia of refuge for all the outlaws and
spirators of the mainland; the resort of pirates ... where
arms and ammunition, the best adapted for their lawless pur
could always be obtained at the lowest cost'.

After a time spent as Chinese Secretary to the Superintende
Trade at Hong Kong, the Rev. Dr Karl Gutzlaff returned t
service of religion. Chinese could go into parts of China no
accessible to foreigners. Gutzlaff's idea was to employ them
time, not as spies, but as colporteurs, trading by retail in Chri
literature, and living as they travelled on the proceeds of wha
they might sell.

Gutzlaff eventually had several dozen of these religious

working for him, and by 1849 the method looked so promising
he returned to Europe, where he went on a preaching tour,
ing his vision of converting all China with much the same
nistic fervour (and to much the same people) as his old chief,
Henry Pottinger, had preached the great opportunity for
ıg cotton goods.

Vhile Gutzlaff was away-in Europe, raising funds, another
estant missionary called Hamberg – who had been sent to
ı a couple of years earlier by the Basel Missionary Society –
me inquisitive. He was not long in finding out that, morally,
laff's colporteurs were not much of an improvement on his
. Most were not even nominally Christian, and some were
n smokers. They spent their money in low dives, and several
criminal records.

ıutzlaff's team of salesmen had outwitted him. When loaded
ɔ make a missionary tour through inland China, they simply
round the corner and sold their bundles of Christian literature
to the printer, at a discount. Far from converting the be-
ɛed mainland Chinese, most of Gutzlaff's colporteurs had
r even left Hong Kong. This disclosure was Gutzlaff's death
. He contrived to marry a third English heiress, called Dorothy
·iel, but soon after, on 9 August 1851, he died of a dropsy.

richest prize a Chinese pirate could hope to run across was an
n ship, freighted either with the drug, or, if a sale had already
effected, with silver. Opium clippers and coasters in these
erous years had good reason, therefore, to put to sea ready
·ouble. As well as an armament of guns, they kept boarding
; in readiness, lashed to the mainmast, and carried a chest of
·d pistols and carbines on the quarterdeck. The command
·itish opium clippers was frequently given to former naval
·rs.

·espite all such precautions, on one day in 1847 the whole
la of opium receiving-ships anchored in Chimmo Bay, between
y and Foochow, was taken by surprise. Crews were massacred,
their stock and treasure pillaged. Shortly after this, the
n schooner *Omega* (178 tons) and *Caroline* (85 tons) were
ked by Chinese pirates when at anchor near Amoy; most
eir officers and crew were killed, and their cargo plundered.
ı the clipper *Sylph*, apart from the Captain and three mates,
,hip's company included an unusually large complement of

167

experienced petty officers, and a very large crew – a couple
dozen men before the mast, including ex-naval-ratings, paid
a month, more than twice the pay offered elsewhere. *Sylph* fo
ship of her size was superbly manned, heavily armed, and co
outsail almost all rivals. Yet Chinese pirates lurking off Hai
got *Sylph* in 1849.

The pirates operating in Canton Bay had a name for impe
nent audacity. In 1844, when the Chinese official commanding
Bogue Forts had been so rash as to menace them, they kidnap
him, cut off his ears, and held him to ransom for $60 000. In
same year they captured a pay-chest of 12 000 rupees, inten
for the British Army in Hong Kong.

Pottinger had been replaced in 1844 as Governor of Hong K
by Sir John Francis Davis, the Chinese scholar and former E
India Company official. Sir John tried to enforce some sembla
of law and order in the colony, but his undisguised dislike of
drug trade made local magnates uncooperative, and the na
officer commanding, Admiral Sir Thomas Cochrane, also drag
his feet when Sir John wanted to use the Royal Navy to hunt d
pirates. Cochrane recommended instead a system of private c
voys, but, as it turned out, the convoy system played into
pirates' hands. An honest merchant needing protection on
high seas would pay an armed ship with apparently good cre
tials, only to discover that papers and flag were not what t
seemed. The Portuguese were reputedly worst, but sea robbery
went on under cover of the Union Jack and the Stars and Strip

There was a sigh of relief from the drug traffickers in
when Sir George Bonham, an easy-going man who wanted no be
than to work his way gently through to his imminent retirem
replaced Sir John as Governor. After a lifetime of service in
East, Sir George was strongly of the opinion that learning Chi
warped the brain; he would never promote a linguist. He
easy-going about opium, but piracy, which made trouble for
big opium houses, with their political influence in London, m
also make trouble for him. Moreover, by undertaking to ha
their pirates, he might hope to improve relations with the Chi
authorities in Canton, at present very chilly. Sir George Bon
persuaded the Navy to act.

Admiral Cochrane's misgivings about using the Royal N
may well have been because he knew that such an operation c
become scandalously expensive. The British Parliament's
of 1825, for *Encouraging the Capture or Destruction of Pira*
Ships and Vessels, which awarded £20 in prize money for

.tical person' captured or killed during an attack on a pirate
, had never envisaged handing out money on the scale likely
rove necessary on the China coast.

ince every junk, pirate or peaceful trader, went armed, any
ese vessel afloat could, at a pinch, be counted by the Navy
pirate, and blown out of the water at a handsome profit. And
is what happened. As an eyewitness called John Scarth reed, 'In many expeditions against pirates, I have no doubt,
bers of innocent people have been killed ... it has too often
the custom to burn, kill and destroy, taking care not to bring
any prisoners.'

nformation was provided by Hong Kong's assistant super-
ndent of police, D. R. Caldwell – a brilliant linguist with many
acts in the island's underworld. (Caldwell later left the police
joined the underworld. On being accused of extortion from
hel-keepers he resigned his rank to become managing agent
Hong Kong's licensed gamblers at a yearly salary, then im-
se, of $20 000.) With Caldwell's help Captain John C. Dalrymple
, RN, mounted an action against Chinese pirates in September
. There were at that time two large and well-organized pirate
s harassing Hong Kong. One, under Chin A Po, was known to
k out of Bias Bay, forty miles to the north and east of the
ny, and the other, under the orders of the legendary Shap Ng
, commanded the westward approaches to Hong Kong from a
somewhere in the Gulf of Tongking.

n the quiet evening of 28 September, Captain Hay, command-
in *Columbine* – an 18-gun brig and 'the fastest ship in the
al Navy' – encountered fourteen junks, sailing in double line
hward. Some distance off, along the Bias Bay coast, could be
a village on fire. When Caldwell hailed the nearest junk, she
ned to be a salt-trader, headed for Hong Kong, but he could
rly discern her nineteen guns being cleared for action. The time
nearly midnight.

Before the wind dropped, *Columbine* had time to manoeuvre
s to fire both her broadsides into the fleet of pirate junks,
eby putting three of them out of action.

In the small hours the pirate junks moved off, propelled by
eps, with the brig limping after. By dawn, they had gained a
and a half, but the P & O steamer *Canton* came in sight round
adland, and took *Columbine* in tow. The gap closed, another
te craft was sunk by gunfire, but after the Chinese managed
ut a shot through *Canton*'s engine-room she had to sheer off for
irs.

Columbine, operating in a bay not yet charted, went agro
on a reef, so Captain Hay sent his ship's boats scurrying after
retreating pirates. As the British clambered aboard the hin
most junk, the pirate captain valiantly blew her up. The suic
action killed four of the boarding party and severely wou
five. *Canton,* now under steam, came as close as she dare to
reef, and managed with some difficulty to haul *Columbine*
The rest of the pirate flotilla had, by now, sought safety in a nat
harbour called Fan-lo-kong, or the Ram's Horn, at the hea
Bias Bay.

At midnight on 1 October the small gunboat *Fury* arri
with a detachment of marines on board. There was no win
fill *Columbine's* sails, but *Fury* towed her into the pirate's s
tuary, where lay twenty-three large junks, each mounting betv
twelve and eighteen guns. Though these pirates had already sh
they could fight with incomparably better will than the old Imp
war junks, even making mincemeat of a heavily armed opi
clipper when the odds were right, they stood little chance aga
the brisk gunnery of British naval ratings who sniffed a fort
in prize money.

The destruction wreaked that night on Chin A Po's fleet
the cost of one British seaman slightly wounded – was devastat
In an action lasting only forty-five minutes, two small docky
and the pirates' arsenal were set on fire, and the twenty-t
junks destroyed. Four hundred Chinese were killed: there
£20 on the head of each one.

On 8 October Captain Hay sailed *Columbine* south-west
company with the gunboats *Fury* and *Phlegethon.* Off Hai
Island, this British squadron met up with eight Chinese war ju
under Admiral Wong, who reported that he had just been wor
in an encounter with the pirate chief Shap Ng Tsai. The Bri
managed, soon after, to capture the pirates' look-out boat.
interrogating the one Chinese who survived, Caldwell learned
the pirate chieftain had anchored his great fleet of sixty-
junks in the mouth of the Tongking River, half a mile beyond
bar – placing the best of them in a semi-circle, broadside on, so
the river entrance would be commanded by an aimed cros
of 240 guns.

The 18-ton brig with her two attendant gunboats mana
to float across the bar of the Tongking River at high water.
apparent odds were overwhelmingly in favour of the Chin
But the flowing tide had shifted the anchored junks so that t
opening broadside, at 600 yards, was aimed less accurately t

Ng Tsai had planned. When the pirates fired off their 240 many of their shot went high and wide, though an un-
ortable number landed on target, *Columbine* taking the im-
of thirty-nine roundshot, and *Fury* of forty-one. Unchecked,
mbine eagerly attacked the Chinese centre, moving in to
ge Shap Ng Tsai's flagship, conspicuous in the sunset by a
lag bordered with gold. Tropical night soon fell. A fusillade
cendiary rockets was poured out from the two little gunboats,
Columbine fired broadside after broadside from her eighteen
at such close range that some shot tore a hole through two
ree junks at once. Ninety minutes after the action started,
Chinese flagship blew up spectacularly, like an immense
sion of fireworks.

hat night in the Tongking anchorage twenty-seven junks
ed to the waterline, and two days later, after a destructive
of runaway junks upriver, a final count could be made.
he pirate fleet – sixty-four vessels mounting a total of 1200
– only six had got away. Since the bounty easiest to collect
that on a dead pirate, it is hardly surprising that 1700 pirates
reported as killed outright. This one operation cost the
sh government £42 425 in 'blood money', and founded the
nes of the small number of officers and ratings taking part.
he suppression of piracy on the China coast – where an
cent trader and a guilty pirate, once dead, were not very
nguishable – cost the British taxpayer the total sum of
243 in bounties, until the law was amended by the *Head*
ey Act of 1850 and the *Naval Prize Act* of 1854. The amounts
were declared 'not only excessive in themselves, but an
cement to wanton and undeserved attacks on the Chinese
; populations'. As Lord Elgin, when plenipotentiary in China,
to write on 1 February 1859, '. . . I fear we do some horrible
tices in this pirate hunting. The system of giving our sailors
ect interest in captures is certainly a barbarous one, and the
nt of much evil.'
. small diplomatic advantage was gained, however, Viceroy
Kuang-chin, writing cordially from Canton to acknowledge
this British action against the pirates would 'gladden the
ts of all men'. Hsu had good reason to be pleased. In Chinese,
and bandit are the same word: a pirate was a sea-bandit,
during those years piracy often had recognizable political
tones. For instance, men lucky enough to escape the des-
ion of Shap Ng Tsai's fleet went inland to join the rebels in
ngsi, who were raising the country people there against the

171

Manchu. The indestructible Shap Ng Tsai himself manage
get away in six small boats with 400 of his men, to open opera
anew, though on a smaller scale, from a base on Hainan – whe
last he was bought off, in subtle Chinese fashion, with a well-
government job as a naval mandarin.

The two British naval actions gave a death blow on the C
coast to organized piracy with big fleets, operating from s
bases like little independent kingdoms. But by 1854 piraci
Hong Kong waters were once again occurring at the rate of
teen a month, and Chinese pirates were to plague the coas
another ninety years. After Captain Hay's spectacular succe
Columbine, Chinese officials were seldom unwilling to ask
help of the Royal Navy in putting down pirates. Mandarins
went on anti-pirate cruises in British warships later on v
Britain and China were once again at war. The British had dr
into giving a helping hand to a dynasty which more and r
Chinese saw as alien and oppressive, and were seeking some
to overthrow.

Though the British did the fighting in the first Opium War,
have taken the blame ever since, the French and the Ameri
were quick to take advantage of China's defeat by forcin
Peking treaties of their own.

The French were not as yet trading much in China, but
had other interests to foster. The Treaty of Whampoa of 1844
intended to establish their right to protect the Roman Cat
community. A growing anti-foreign sentiment had been ma
life more difficult for missionaries who chose to work in the inte
most of them Roman Catholics. During the patriotic camp
in 1840, when the war was raging, the Dominican Mission in
coast province of Fukien, had suffered persecution. On 11 Sep
ber 1840 Father Perboyre was executed in Wuchang. In 18
mob attacked the Vicar Apostolic as he travelled in Manch
and in 1852 a pretext was found for arresting the Chinese
and eight students at the Catholic seminary in Hankow. 7
treaty right to protect missionaries gave the French, there
a motive for armed intervention in China at almost any time
might choose. Making war for the benefit of opium traffi
had run the British into political trouble at home; the French n
elude such criticism by drawing the sword in China for the F

The Treaty of Whampoa, negotiated in October 1844 bet

172

n de Langrené and Ch'i-ying, led to an Imperial Edict which
ed a renewed toleration to 'the religion of the Lord of Heaven'
ng the Roman Catholic term for God. The ban on Christianity,
sed when the Jesuits had been expelled, was thus formally
, but Ch'i-ying apparently had no idea of the gulf separating
ersion of Christianity from another. A similar Edict had to be
ed, a year later, for the Protestants. At the same time,
ying conceded the right of foreign women to enter China. Their
and deportment might be scandalous to ordinary Chinese,
as he advised the Emperor, 'the presence of females at the
', might 'soften barbarian nature and give us less anxiety as
tbreaks'.

he Treaty of Wanghia, 1844, was negotiated for the United
s by Caleb Cushing, the same shrewd Massachusetts lawyer
in Congress, had spoken out with such fervour against the
m War. Cushing was sent to China in a crack American
te, *Brandywine*, which made the passage from Rio to Bombay
e sensational time of eighty days. From Bombay to Macao,
e second leg of the voyage, *Brandywine* raced with the 370-
rig *Antelope*, which carried Cushing's secretary of legation as
nger, and Malwa opium as cargo. Captain Philip Dumaresq,
e little *Antelope*, beat Commander Foxhall A. Parker of
dywine – and a zealous opponent of the opium trade – into
o roads by a margin of several days.

o impress the Chinese, Cushing had been rigged out with a
ial uniform – a Major-General's blue frock-coat with gilt
ons and 'some slight additions in the way of embroideries',
-striped trousers, spurs, and a hat with a white plume. Nature
also blessed him with luxuriant moustaches and an abundant
d. As a negotiator, Cushing turned out to be as impressive
had been made to look, but his interpreters, the missionaries
gman and Parker, let him down rather badly. Their draft of
reaty's Chinese text left so much to be desired that Ch'i-ying
obliged to write apologetically to the Emperor, explaining
the document was 'so meanly and coarsely expressed ... and
was such a variety of errors, that it was next to impossible
int them out ... we were able to polish the passages that were
ely intelligible'.

he Chinese may not quite have grasped the meaning of what
were being asked to sign, but Cushing had in fact made
ious use of his legal training to extract valuable concessions
them of which they were only dimly aware. There was, for
nce, a clause permitting treaty revision after twelve years,

173

which under international law applied equally to other t signatories, including the British. 'Treaty revision' meant th twelve years' time the Chinese would be expected to give still more; the seeds of renewed war were already being pla

After Cushing, in full fig as Major-General, had ceremon signed the treaty, he made a presentation to Ch'i-ying of se guns, including a pair of new-fangled Colt six-shooters, a collection of books on fortification and tactics. Ch'i-ying g declined the gift, but took the broad hint, promising Cu that 'if at a future day there be an occasion to use them, we ought to request your Honourable Nation to assist us wit strength of its arm'. The defeated Manchus were in a half-he way being courted by British and Americans alike.

The Americans in their treaty made one skilful concessi Chinese feeling by publicly identifying the opium trade as co band. Drug traffickers were henceforth to be denied 'any cou ance or protection from the Government of the United St Yet the fastest opium clippers on the coast were American.

Antelope herself was the only square-rigged vessel afloat could beat through the Formosa Channel against the north monsoon, and in the race from India, the fastest frigate ir American fleet had failed to catch her. Neither China no United States had a naval squadron in the China Seas capab enforcing the treaty's pious prohibition.

By 1853, Humphrey Marshall, representing the State De ment in China, was obliged to complain helplessly of 'the whol system of smuggling that is carried on under both the En *and American* flags'. In 1858 his successor, William B. Reed, driven to admit that, despite the Treaty of Wanghia's verbal demnation of the drug trade, about a fifth of all the opium ent Shanghai reached China in American ships. How could Ame diplomats expect to convince Chinese mandarins that their fr ship both in peace and war was sincere, while this sort of t went on?

During these wild years on the China coast all good intent were apt to become tainted. A British law framed with the de intention of wiping out piracy had already come to signify any dead Chinese seaman good or bad might be worth a boun £20. In the same ironic way the Royal Navy's world-wide paign to put down the slave trade had as its outcome a discredit

c, in which living Chinese became worth hard cash as articles
:port – as replacements all the world over for enslaved black
:ans.

:mployers, particularly in America, urgently needed labourers
york on plantations and in construction. Now that the Chinese
rnment was too decrepit either to protect its own citizens
> enforce its own laws, coolies could be shipped to the foreign
ur market, under conditions hardly better than those of the
: trade. By means of fictitious long-term labour contracts,
:d by a thumbprint, the penalties against slave-trading were
:ed; and by getting the coolie into debt on arrival, his term
ndentured labour' could be prolonged indefinitely.

hipping a coolie to California cost $50, the passage-money
g found by the company which held his labour-contract. In
twenty-two out of the seventy ships carrying coolies were
rican.

.ome unlucky Chinese or other, usually but not always a
man, would be hired – or might be kidnapped, the word
:nt was *Shanghaied* – by a professional crimp. When he
vered his wits, he would find himself prisoner in a barracoon,
:where on the coast – the terms as well as the techniques of
commerce being borrowed directly from the African slave
:. Coolies would be crowded unmercifully aboard an outgoing
:l. The legal pretext of 'indentures' prevented the Royal
y from detaining coolie ships as slavers, though in human
.s the difference was imperceptible. Indeed, any naval officer
mpting to stop a coolie ship to make sure the law was being
plied with ran the risk of a suit for damages.

'he Coolie Trade was jocosely known in mercantile circles as
Pig Trade, to distinguish it from the Poison Trade – in opium.
.sh officials anxious to get on more cordial terms with Chinese
.aldom found the Pig Trade a detestable business. John
ring, when British Consul in Canton, wrote on 5 January
to Lord Malmesbury, then British Foreign Secretary, to
m him that 'iniquities scarcely exceeded by those practised
he African coast and on the African middle passage have not
wanting'. He spoke later of 'the jails of China emptied to
ly "labour" to British colonies', and described 'hundreds ...
ered together in barracoons, stripped naked, and stamped or
ted with the letter C (California), P (Peru) or S (Sandwich
ıds) on their breasts, according to destination'.

'he big men in the opium trade, who formed opinion in Hong
g, were not particularly keen on these interlopers, either.

175

To keep in business, the drug traffickers had to maintain g
relations with a network of Chinese dealers and corrupted offic
and coolie kidnapping led directly to trouble. Consul Bowri
son was in Jardine, Matheson's employ, therefore Bowring
first-hand information of the conflict of interest between Po
Trade and Pig Trade. He put forward officially the argument
'the irregular and fraudulent shipment of coolies' might jeopar
'the immense interests both British and Anglo-Indian invo
in the opium trade, giving ... more than three millions ste
of revenue to India'.

The Coolie Trade was a crying scandal, but what could be d
In Californian gold-mines, on sugar plantations in the Caribl
and, soon, in American railroad construction, the demand
cheap and expendable labour was insatiable. The coolie ship
did not always have it entirely their own way. An American
Robert Bowne (Captain Lesley Bryson) left Amoy on 21 M.
1852 with 410 coolies on board, bound for California. The Chi
took over the ship by force, and most of them – accompanie
one Englishman – went ashore on Miyakoshima Retto in
Ryukyu Islands, 300 miles east of Formosa, where the 1
people fed and sheltered them. (One would like to know 1
about that solitary Englishman.) Officers and crew of *R*
Bowne were unharmed, and by 18 April had worked the
back to Amoy. Though the coolies had received great provocati
eight of them, too sick to walk, having been killed aboard *R*
Bowne and thrown into the sea as commercially useless – t
action was officially treated as 'piracy'. USS *Saratoga*, in comp
with HMS *Riley* and *Contest*, were despatched to the Ryu
Islands, the escaped coolies brought back prisoner and har
over for punishment to the Chinese authorities – who dealt
them leniently, sending most of them back to their homes in Ful

In 1852, 30 000 Chinese left Hong Kong for San Franc
alone – and the business of shipping them was reputed to be w
a million and a half dollars. To connect the two ends of the ma
remained profitable even when the death rate was high. On
trip to Havana in the British-owned and piously named *
Calvin*, 135 passengers died out of 298. On a similar voyage in
Duke of Portland, 128 died out of 332. In some American s
more than 40 per cent died before arrival.

British arguments, motivated largely by humanitarian
siderations, but with one eye always on opium revenue, at
produced an attempt to bring the trade under control. The
Chinese Passengers Act was meant at least to improve co

176

shipboard conditions, but its direct effect was simply to drive the trade out of Hong Kong to other ports and other flags.

The least pleasant aspect of the Pig Trade was the traffic in girls. Chinese law strictly forbade the emigration of females, and, by tradition, Chinese women were exceptionally unwilling to leave home, for any inducement. The plantations, however, cried out for women. If only their expensive 'indentured labour' could be induced to settle down and breed, the owners would eventually have no need to import workers. Shipping out females became a profitable branch of the coolie business, but since women could be procured in China only by kidnapping, or by purchase as girl slaves, the farce of 'indentures' was played out.

In 1855 a British vessel called *Inglewood* came to anchor off Amoy with a cargo of slave girls, the eldest of whom was only eight years old. *Inglewood*'s crew were so nauseated by the stench and misery on board that they decided to report the ship's cargo to the British Consul, who managed to find a legal formula enabling him to take action. The girl slaves had been consigned to a British subject with diplomatic immunity as Spanish Vice-Consul. Since the consignee could not be touched, the children were all sent back where they came from, and *Inglewood*'s Captain was fined £100, which may have hurt but could hardly have put him out of business.

In 1859 Harry Parkes, who had been promoted to Consul in Canton, hit on a way of replacing the local barracoons. For the coolie trade to the British West Indies he established an officially controlled Emigration House, pointing out with cheerful cynicism, 'The system will prove so much *cheaper* than that of man-stealing that those foreigners who do not adopt it from motives of morality will do so with a view to economy.' In the same year crimps flagrantly kidnapping on the open street so as to fill a French ship at anchor off Woosung provoked riots in Shanghai. The Pig Trade was a long time dying, but the odium was already more than the English-speaking powers in China wished to bear; in 1862 the Coolie Trade was banned to Americans by Act of Congress.

Inevitably, some of the Chinese reaching California brought their opium habit with them. Drug addiction in the United States on a troublesome scale dates precisely from the days of the Pig Trade – though it got a fillip later from the reckless use of opium derivatives as pain-killers in the Civil War.

By 1846, a total of 117 000 Chinese had been brought to the United States, most as coolies. They were concentrated on the West Coast, and the estimate was that they consumed about half the opium imported into the United States annually, for medical and all other purposes (a total, in 1846, of 228 742 lb of gum opium, and 53 189 lb of prepared opium). But the big days of the Coolie Trade, and therefore of opium importation, were still to come – and in California, the opium habit was not long in spreading from the Chinese to their American neighbours. Though never the principal smugglers of opium to China, American merchants had certainly done well out of the trade there, and drug addiction had now come back to squat on their doorstep.

By 1875, there were reputed to be 120 000 American opium addicts – including the unfortunate veterans initiated in the American Civil War. The total of opium addicts in the United States remained at about this figure, numbering 110 000 even by 1924. Here was a basic narcotics market for spectacular expansion later, as a multi-million-dollar business in the hands of organized crime.

In February 1850 the Chinese Tao Kuang Emperor died, and in his will heaped reproaches on himself for having been a party to the Treaty of Nanking. His heir was 19 years old, and took for his reign the name of Hsien Feng.

By the mid-1850s the young Hsien Feng Emperor was a confirmed debauchee, obsessed by his favourite concubine, Yehonala – a hard-headed but subtle Manchu girl, chosen for her role from among the families of the Imperial clansmen. Yehonala was in cautious moderation an opium smoker. The young Emperor spent half his working day in bed with her, but during what time remained she would help him decide – at first, no doubt, with some prompting from her family – about the thousands of memorials arriving for the Emperor's urgent attention from all parts of China.

The gangs of eunuchs who intrigued to control the Imperial Palace were at last obliged to admit that Yehonala had the ascendancy. She produced an heir, was acknowledged as Empress – and as China's Dowager Empress, ruthless, devious, indestructible, Yehonala was to continue the real ruler of Manchu China until the early years of this century.

A large number of mandarins might be corrupt, but the mandarinate as such – a civil service with common beliefs, open to anyone hard-headed enough to pass the national examinations – was still the backbone of China's slowly crumbling society. So long as the mandarinate remained intact as an institution, effective central government might continue. But in 1838, at the time when silver was fast flowing out of China, the previous Emperor had taken the unlucky step of allowing magistrates in the ninth or lowest grade – still open to merit – to buy their promotion into the eighth grade for 1000 taels of silver, and thence upward to the seventh grade for 2000 taels (at about three taels to the £ sterling of the time).

Once promotion could be bought for cash, ambitious and ill-paid young magistrates had an even stronger motive for squeezing the poor, and, as opium dealers soon found, they became more than ever accessible to bribes. The gap between government and people widened.

When silver was urgently needed for the vast payments demanded under the Treaty of Nanking another fatal step was taken: degrees were offered for purchase outright. For 30 000 taels, a rich man could buy himself the button of a high-ranking mandarin of the fourth class. And while the apparatus of government decayed, to the social miseries of opium-smoking and coolie-kidnapping were added the consequences of a bizarre natural disaster.

In 1856 China's second largest river, the Hwangho, turned off at right angles near K'ai-feng in Honan, so that instead of emptying into the Yellow Sea at about lat. 34 degrees it forced a completely new outlet into the Gulf of Pehchihli, north of the Shantung Peninsula, in about lat. 38 degrees. During the years between 1796 and 1820 the Hwangho had overflowed its banks seventeen times – so that this hair-raising geographical freak, which ruined peasant farms over thousands of square miles, and wrecked the Grand Canal, may indeed have been provoked by official neglect.

With the Canal out of commission, rice for Peking had to be sent round the coast by sea-going junk. The cost of feeding rice-eaters in the capital became extravagantly burdensome. The huge fleet of Imperial canal boats rotted. Sixty thousand canal men were thrown out of work, and drifted into banditry and rebellion.

The most appalling loss of life, however, in these years of distress, came as the aftermath of a well-intentioned Christian movement, which was endeavouring to redeem China – to modernize the country, and transform its ways of thought. From 1850 to 1862, the rebellion of the God-fearing Taipings led into a long civil war, unparalleled for murderousness until the twentieth century, which changed the fertile Yangtze valley into a wilderness, and cost at least twenty million lives.

The wilder of the two provinces administered by the Viceroy at Canton was Kwangsi – lying inland, on the extreme south-western edge of China, a place of mountain and jungle, hard of access. In Kwangsi, as elsewhere in South China, a sentiment of nostalgia for the Ming dynasty was kept alive by the Heaven and Earth Society – more often known among Westerners as the Triad – a powerful secret society, based on a sort of popular freemasonry, whose members were pledged to mutual aid, and to the overthrow of the Manchu régime.

The people of Kwangsi had clearly seen how the recent war with the British had left the Emperor's troops demoralized. ('Formerly,' said an official report, 'they feared the troops as tigers; of late they look on them as sheep.') China's population had doubled in the previous century, while her agricultural resources stayed much the same, so that in a poor province, when official extortion coincided with crop failure, famine soon threatened, and in a turbulent place like Kwangsi revolt came not long after.

There was in Kwangsi a clan of poor people called Hakkas, originally immigrants from the north. Some Hakkas were tenant farmers, but most plied trades which kept them on the move, as itinerant blacksmiths, stonemasons and miners. They spoke a variant of Chinese all their own; and Hakka women differed from other Chinese women in not binding their feet; they worked alongside their men as equals. The Hakkas had a tradition of having been the last people in China to submit to the Manchus – holding out for forty years after the dynasty was installed in Peking. The Hakka people were to become moving spirits in the new religion of God-Worshippers – based distantly on Protestant Christianity – which soon took a militant turn, changed its name to Taiping, and very nearly succeeded in overthrowing the Manchu régime by armed force.

Now that his soldiers were no longer feared, the only grip that the Emperor had on the rebellious folk of Kwangsi was by means of the semi-religious beliefs which gave the throne a moral ascendancy over the common people all through China. Not surprisingly, therefore, the social convulsion of the Taiping Rising began as a moral spring-cleaning – in which all accepted Chinese values were simplified out of recognition, if not rejected. The Hakkas in Kwangsi had the distinction of throwing up from their midst, in Hung Hsui-Ch'uan (1814–64) a religious genius who might be compared in effectiveness with Cromwell, if not with Mahomet or Moses. Materially, Hung's religious movement may have destroyed more than it built, but his insights endowed it with a prophetic originality, enabling the Chinese people thereby to grope blindfold at least a few steps of their way into the future.

Hung's family lived about thirty miles outside Canton. His father was village elder, and for their highly intelligent son his parents dreamed of an official career. The whole village had an interest in Hung's scholastic success, since, when a boy became a mandarin, he was usually a benefactor to his native place.

When Hung, at 11, sat his first examination, he headed the list of fifteen successful candidates in an entry of one hundred. Thereafter he ranked as a Qualified Student, exempt from corporal punishment, and no longer obliged to kowtow to local officials. But in 1830 Hung failed the next step up the ladder, the examination for Salaried Student. After the high hopes invested in him, Hung was obliged to go to Kwangsi as a village schoolmaster. In the years preceding Commissioner Lin's arrival at Canton, Hung sat the triennial Salaried Student examination there four times. Each time, of between five and ten thousand students examined, only about seventy could expect to pass. He saw at first hand the period, instructive for a Chinese, when the flags of the 'foreign devils' on their immensely tall flagpoles could be seen from all over Canton, when opium dealers operated everywhere and local officials were succumbing to corruption. On one of his first visits to Canton, Hung brought a bundle of Christian tracts, entitled 'Good Words to Admonish the Age', but for the time being they stood on his shelf unread.

After public loss of face at his fourth successive failure – in 1843, after China's defeat in the first Opium War – Hung was brought home in a sedan chair, in a state of nervous collapse. He lay in a trance forty days, shouting, 'Kill the demons!' Later he identified the demons who were haunting his mind not only with Chinese idols but particularly with the Manchu dynasty and their Tartar soldiers. During these forty days, Hung also saw visions. In one of them, he was taken off to Heaven, and met there an old man in a long black robe with a golden beard. This old man was

181

God the Father. He gave Hung a sword to kill demons: in Hung's mind, it all began to make sense.

Hung's inability ever to repeat his first success in the official examinations had its lucky side for him. Examinations in China were the accepted ladder to power, but there as in contemporary Europe they squeezed the juice of originality out of all but the strongest minds. Hung was already, as a Hakka born, at odds with the Chinese society around him, and aligned with the poor. He was literate, and with uncommon powers of self-expression, yet not so impregnated with traditional Confucian interpretations as to reject obtusely all that was new and foreign. Hung had seen at first hand the threat of the maritime powers. He could identify his individual plight with that of China.

Turning over at last the bundle of Christian tracts on his shelf, Hung succeeded in identifying there certain personages and symbols from his forty days of vision. 'Good Words to Admonish the Age' included extracts from Genesis and Exodus and the Gospels, quoted from Morrison's translation of the King James Bible – a version often obscure, and sometimes defective. Three-quarters of the text was taken up by an exposition of Christianity as understood by Liang A-fa (1789–1855) – an early convert, who had worked as a typecutter at the missionary press in Malacca, and afterwards frequented Canton, as a colporteur. What Liang A-fa lacked in theological training, he made up in zeal, seeing Shang-ti, the specifically Protestant God, as an Old Testament autocrat – a kind of Emperor – and emphasizing Original Sin. Hung had little difficulty in deciding that Shang-ti was essentially not foreign but Chinese, the old man with the golden beard who had given him the sword.

The Old Testament has more than once served a turn as a revolutionary handbook. The story of a Chosen People – a persecuted but God-fearing minority of liberated slaves who march courageously to a Promised Land – has appealed in turn to German peasants, English yeomen and American pioneers, not to mention modern Zionists. The organizing imagery Hung needed, he found. His genius lay in applying this fragmentary, quasi-Protestant information to the disrupted lives around him, in such a way as to make the poor of Kwangsi confident of their power to withstand the multitude of difficult circumstances that were oppressing them.

Liang in his homilies had condemned the use of opium, and the degradation of women by prostitution and adultery – propositions no Hakka living near Canton would wish to gainsay. Liang went on to speak obscurely in one passage of Tai-p'ing – 'Great Peace'. Hung concluded that this Great Peace would arrive once the Manchu devils had been driven out – his Confucian training bringing him down to earth for once. (Hung was unlikely to have embraced with much eagerness a religion which unequivocally preached – as orthodox Christianity does – a Kingdom not of this world.)

Tai-p'ing was overdue in China – a time when the king would be upright, the ministers loyal, all officials pure, and the people happy in the worship of Shang-ti, this quasi-Imperial deity to whom Hung continued to have miraculous access in vision. The Empire of China and the Kingdom of Heaven would, as it were, become one.

In a torrential downpour, Hung and his cousins baptized each other, and Hung was inspired to write his first Christian hymn. Much of Hung's later success derived from the aptness of his propaganda. For instance, he rewrote the standard elementary-school textbook to correspond with a Taiping interpretation of Christianity. On the other hand, Hung re-phrased the Fifth Commandment so it chimed in better with the sentiments of filial piety; his ban on opium-smoking was assimilated to the Seventh Commandment. Helped by one of his cousins, Hung Jen-kan, and an old school friend called Feng Yun-shan, Hung opened his war on Demons by smashing all the local idols, and breaking up the Confucian tablets on the schoolroom wall. For this he lost his job.

Hung became a wandering scholar, earning a meagre livelihood, in the traditional manner, by selling ink and brushes to other literates, and here and there making converts. The religious toleration allowed by treaty to Christians gave Hung's God-Worshippers a breathing space, before repression began. Most of his early followers were Hakkas – of all classes, from village schoolmasters to charcoal burners. The time was apocalyptic. In the aftermath of war, crops had failed, and the people of Kwangsi were becoming ungovernable.

Hung decided he needed to know more about Christianity, so in February 1847 he sought out in Canton an American called Issachar Jacox Roberts (1802–71) – called by the Chinese Lo-han – a Baptist distinguished from most other Protestant missionaries by living inside the city walls in great simplicity, wearing Chinese dress and speaking Cantonese. Issachar Roberts was from Sumner County, Tennessee, and ten years before he had arrived in China at his own expense. After 1854, Roberts broke his loose affiliation with the Southern Baptist Convention to work independently:

'uncouth and eccentric' was how he was described by another American missionary who had much more worldly success.

A brave but cantankerous man, sometimes wrong-headed, who was to die from leprosy contracted when nursing sick Chinese, Issachar Roberts preached an old-time religion in which fervour took the place of dogma. Whether he knew it or not, the simple theology – of guilt, repentance and redemption – which Roberts began to teach Hung, had historical roots in the radical simplifications of belief made in the sixteenth century by revolutionary German Anabaptists. Similar fundamentalist beliefs had been given expression in Cromwell's army and had marked deeply the democratic faith of the frontiersmen who fought America's Revolutionary War. Though the principles Hung learned from Roberts were to be given a typically Chinese emphasis, they echoed the phraseology and theory of Europe's earliest popular revolutions.

Rev. Issachar Roberts, who later described Hung as being of 'blameless deportment ... gentlemanly in his manners', impressed on him the importance of Sunday Observance, the Ten Commandments and the Lord's Prayer – all of which became important tenets of belief for the God-Worshippers, even though, by a slip in arithmetic, they were to keep their Sabbath on Saturday. After giving Hung instruction two hours a day for two months, Roberts for some capricious reason refused to baptize him. Hung, once more on his own, went back to Kwangsi, carrying on his back a pile of Gutzlaff's Bibles.

The God-Worshippers now centred their activities on Thistle Mountain, a tract of jungle thicket and rocky slope inside a 230-mile perimeter, the territory of blacksmiths, miners and charcoal burners, and a place difficult to penetrate. In Hung's absence their numbers had grown to 2000. They practised a simple puritanism, which condemned adultery and disobedience to parents, and forbade theft, gambling and the plotting of evil. Though their religion sounds innocuous, in China it was, strictly, a form of treason, since only the Emperor could worship God. The God-Worshippers, like their historical counterparts years earlier in northern Europe and the United States, were accumulating by this kind of quiet, repressive self-control a fund of energy for a great historical act of will.

Hung himself was the theoretician – the prophet – and from the ranks of the charcoal burners emerged an organizer of genius in Yang Hsin-Ch'ing (1824–56) a short, pock-marked young man at one time employed in running opium up the Pearl River. Yang was a Hakka, but he began recruiting to the movement the tough

184

drifters of the frontier province – former salt and opium smugglers, Miao tribesmen with their long record of guerrilla warfare against the Manchus.

After October 1849 arrived the survivors, under Lo Tang-kang, of the pirate fleet smashed by the British, many of whom had been Triads. The conversion of these seamen was an authentic rejection of their past – the proof being that so many of them managed heroically to break the opium habit. 'Your opium pipe', Hung preached, 'is like a gun wherewith you wound yourself. How many heroes are stretched dying upon their pillows!' But, in adopting Hung's puritanism, Yang's new recruits had not forgotten their military skills. As their numbers grew, the God-Worshippers, though still scrupulously peaceful, were becoming dangerous to push around.

Most of the Triads in Kwangsi found the Taipings' strict rule of life, especially the forbidding of opium, hard to take, but the two movements went on giving each other practical help. Triads were bound together by solemn oath, and by a simple, freemasonic belief in the harmonious union of heaven, earth and man – ruler, country and individual – which they expressed by secret signs pointing in turn to sky, earth and heart, or lifting a tea-cup with only three fingers.

God-Worshipper rituals were closer to those of formal Christianity. Candles were placed on an altar, and three cups of tea and three bowls of rice offered up – a borrowing from Taoist ritual that was intended to celebrate the Holy Trinity. The crucifix was not employed, and there was no communion. Except for the use of incense, the service was puritanically simple: doxology, creed, lesson, hymns, ending with a recital of the Lord's Prayer emphasized by the explosion of firecrackers.

By 1850, after three successive years of drought, Kwangsi was faced with famine, and the Governor, a sixty-seven-year-old Buddhist devotee called Cheng Tsu-ch'en soon had to contend with a peasant rising, organized by the Triads, under the slogan, 'Plunder the rich to relieve the poor'. Cheng brought to bear all the armed force he could muster against the Triads, beheading wholesale those he took prisoner; but towards the God-Worshippers he was conspicuously lenient. Governor Cheng's simple plan was, of course, to split the opposition, but Hung had the political acumen to know his own turn came next. Almost against the God-Worshippers' will the time was close when armed resistance would be inevitable. Hung celebrated the critical moment in one of his poems:

185

> Lately the vapours are greatly changed.
> I know Heaven has intended to raise heroes.
> China was once subdued, but it shall be no more.
> God ought to be adored, and adored for ever.

Applying the text from St Matthew (xix, 21) 'If thou wilt be perfect, go and sell that thou hast, and give to the poor, and thou shalt have treasure in heaven', the God-Worshippers turned whatever property they had into cash. They created a common treasury, from which all were to draw equally for their needs. Ten thousand came together for safety into encampments, and more were arriving. Hakka blacksmiths hammered out iron pikes and halberds, which were fastened by raw-hide thongs to long bamboos; they had as yet no firearms. Veterans of the fighting against the British began drilling men and women alike.

The alarming news reached Peking that although the Triad rising had been crushed, ten thousand heretics on Thistle Mountain were in arms. The Emperor turned to the man who was good in a dire emergency – Lin Tse-Hsu, who, ten years before, had led the anti-opium fight in Canton, and been rewarded by exile. On 22 November 1850, when hurrying to Kwangsi, the redoubtable Lin collapsed and died, aged 67 – otherwise the attack by government troops on the God-Worshippers in January 1851 might well have been better organized, and less successfully beaten off. The challenge to the dynasty had been forced on the God-Worshippers; after this first armed clash there could be no turning back.

Hung, on the eve of his thirty-sixth birthday, after the God-Worshippers' first military success, took the title of Wang, or King, calling his new dynasty T'ai-p'ing T'ien-kuo (Heavenly Kingdom of the Great Peace). Hung announced himself as King, not Emperor, because God was to be Emperor. He gave five orders to his army. They were to obey the Ten Commandments. They were always to do what they were told by their officers 'in a harmonious spirit'. They were to respect civilians. They were never to quit the field of battle until ordered. Finally, men and women were to be strictly separated from each other. Even husband and wife must live apart henceforth – the womenfolk fighting in their own battalions. The Taiping Army was to become a substitute family, and warfare the believers' way of life, until Tai-p'ing, the Great Peace, had finally been achieved.

Hung himself lived openly, almost ostentatiously with women. He was evidently well aware what the effect would be. Once sexual privileges had been monopolized by a prophet with a quasi-paternal authority, the army became psychologically one family.

Hung no doubt shared with Yugoslav partisans of the Second World War – also advocates of celibacy – the hard-headed but sensible view that a revolutionary army where both sexes fight as equals is no place for pregnant women. But his insights went deeper. Père Clavelin, SJ, one of the first foreigners to encounter the Taiping, wrote discerningly, 'there is something in their relationship ... which justifies these long-haired rebels calling each other brothers. They give the impression of being one family.' The ban on sexual relations for the rank-and-file awakened a kind of incest taboo in the Taiping Army which exalted the Chinese sense of family solidarity to the pitch of an invincible *esprit de corps*.

For the next eight months the amateur soldiers of the Taiping managed to beat off successive attacks by government troops on their stronghold of Thistle Mountain. Their numbers increased to over 18 000, as Taiping encampments became a refuge for Kwangsi folk who had been caught up in the Triad uprising. But for an insurrectionary army, the defensive is fatal; only audacity commands success. On 25 September 1851 the Taiping Army, having chosen yellow, the Imperial colour, for their banners, triumphantly broke through the cordon of red-uniformed government troops. Hung and Yang led their followers, now numbering 37 000, out of the safety of Thistle Mountain and sixty miles north-east, to lay siege to the city of Yung-an.

From the stocks of rice and silver stored in Yung-an they re-equipped themselves, and began to march north-east across China. Though in battle all fought as infantry, the army was organized according to trades. Blacksmiths were the armourers. When a city was besieged, the walls were sapped by battalions of miners. If an attack was made down a canal, ex-pirates captured boats and manned them. The printers' battalion was kept particularly busy, reproducing Hung's writings – which were circulated by Triad members all over China, until there were sympathizers in every city waiting to open the gates to the Taiping.

Hung left the military leadership to Yang and others; his own role was prophetic. The Taiping had already discarded the pigtail – symbol of Manchu rule – and let their hair grow: they became known as the long-haired rebels. A convert was given three weeks to memorize the Lord's Prayer and the Ten Commandments, which were repeated daily in public by the whole army. The sexes were separated, even on the march, the female battalions being shepherded by women officers riding ponies.

Opium was forbidden; adultery was punished at once, with

187

death; the penalty for owning private wealth was also death. Since Hung anticipated that his men would be fighting every day of the year, he replaced the old calendar, with its spattering of unlucky days, by a new and up-to-date Taiping calendar, in which every day was lucky. When one battle, near Changsha, was going badly for a 3000-strong detachment of the Taiping Army, Hung called on his men to pray. As enemy soldiers came closer, and the onset was imminent, the whole Taiping force knelt down as one man, to repeat the Lord's Prayer aloud. The effect was unnerving; with the Emperor's troops almost face to face, they rose from their knees and made a victorious charge.

In a manifesto issued when he had overcome his followers' misgivings, and taken the decision to march on the great city of Nanking, Hung made a public challenge to the dynasty, 'The Manchus let avaricious and corrupt officials spread all over the Empire, to 'squeeze' and impoverish the people ... the minds of the people are seeking for a remedy to the situation, and there are signs that the Manchu will perish ... We have raised a righteous army to inflict the vengeance of God upon those who have deceived Heaven, and to relieve the sufferings of the Chinese below.' As the Taiping headed for Nanking their army grew on the march.

Hung and Yang were both Hakkas, their forefathers having been immigrants to south China many years before from Liang-kwang. Learning this, the Emperor ordered the Viceroy of Liang-kwang to dig up their ancestral graves, so as to spoil their luck. But something stronger than magic was required to check the advance across China of these self-taught but highly-disciplined plebeian soldiers, who pushed aside the demoralized, red-coated, opium-smoking Imperialist troops, and implacably killed off all the Manchus, under the name of Demons, in every city they captured.

Once the Yangtze was reached, the ex-pirates organized a fleet of boats, and the Taiping Army took to the waterways, on 29 December 1852 reaching Hankow. After a swift and unnerving amphibious attack on 12 January 1853, Taiping soldiers blew in the gate of Hankow's twin city, Wuchang, and massacred the Manchu garrison. The rich valley of the lower Yangtze, the heart of China, lay open before them. In twenty-seven months, fighting all the way, the revolutionary Christian army had covered 1400 miles – the distance from Paris to Moscow. Including women, children and the old, the Taiping movement had grown to number half a million.

Conversions on this scale were of course tending to dilute the original fervour. The Taiping movement – this being its inherent weakness – was bound always to remain a minority, because of the narrowness of the very dogma which had originally given it such impetus. The people of China, having seen the Taiping Army, as it passed on its way, execute such oppressors as moneylenders and corrupt officials, might accord the movement their goodwill. But in localities where the long-established facts of Chinese life had not been shaken up by foreign encroachment, too much of what Hung and his followers preached was utterly alien. The segregation of the sexes was repellent. Many sympathizers could not face the hard but necessary choice between the Taiping movement and the opium habit. And though, to most poor Chinese, Taiping actions on the march were praiseworthy, their religion was inexplicable. Nothing so far had been able to stand up against them, but the further the Taiping marched, the more they lost momentum.

On 23 February 1853 the Taiping Army set off in their boats down the Yangtze towards Nanking. A victorious Taiping force of 80 000 veteran soldiers, by now supplied with cannon, began to lay siege to the city, which was defended by a weak force of 7000 Tartar Bannermen (who had 20 000 dependants inside the walls) aided by 6000 Chinese troops. On 18 March, a Taiping miners' battalion successfully exploded a charge of gunpowder under the north-east angle of the city wall. Their yellow-clad fighters poured through the breach, brandishing pike and matchlock, to attack the inner citadel.

Once the city had capitulated to the Taiping, ordinary Chinese families were told to stay at home (like Jews at Passover) affixing to the door a label with the character *shun* meaning *submission*, and placing on the table three cups of tea, as a token of welcome. In the city's open spaces, the systematic slaughter then began of corrupt officials, wealthy individuals with a bad name as money-lenders, and the Tartar garrison – all lumped together as Demons. The bloodshed was atrocious. Over twenty thousand corpses were pitched into the Yangtze, and floated down towards the sea. All the Tartar womenfolk were herded together, and locked up in an empty building. Christian prayers were said in the street outside, the building set on fire, and the helpless women burned to death.

Every suspicious-looking passer-by was stopped on the street by Taiping soldiers, and his head examined. Manchu babies were by custom strapped in a cradle, with the back of the head resting on a hard bag of grain, so as to deform the skull and produce the characteristic Tartar facial expression. A man found in Nanking with a flat back to his head was killed on the spot, with no argument. That sexual distortion leads to cruelty was a truism to which the streets of Nanking in the spring of 1853 bore abundant witness.

On 30 March Hung himself entered Nanking, carried in a yellow sedan chair on the shoulders of sixteen bearers, and followed by thirty-six beautiful women on horseback. He retired at once to the remoteness of his palace, from which he seldom afterwards emerged. He let his beard grow; it was black and bushy. The palace servants, eventually 300 in number, were all women. Hung never left Nanking again, but in voluptuous solitude began to organize a new society – at least, on paper. The Taiping now had a territorial basis for their Heavenly Kingdom of Great Peace. They controlled the richest river valley in China, with a population greater than that of the contemporary United States, and they were to keep Nanking as their capital for over a decade.

The Taiping began to organize state-power – with its inevitable distortions of principle. Millions had been made involuntary and half-hearted 'converts' by the brute fact of conquest, and it was tempting to control them by using man and wife, forcibly separated, as hostages for each other's good behaviour. Eventually, power struggles between the leaders – the sexual monopolists – broke out, to be again repressed by massacre, but this time of believers. Married life reasserted itself, and with it slowly returned a typical Chinese set of values, which tended always to place family interests ahead of a theoretical common good.

Hung's entourage of women shocked Protestant missionaries, and gave opium traffickers a chance to snigger – was this strange Bible Christian, they asked, perhaps following the example of King Solomon? Lurid stories put about by the French of young Catholic virgins being forced into Hung's harem and there violated appear not to have been very generally believed; it was, apparently, not that kind of harem. Though Hung evidently had appetites similar to those of Mahomet, his motives may have been less self-indulgent than they appear. Any Chinese Emperor had the duty of ensuring fertility by ritual. The bevy of good-looking girls dancing attendance on Hung at the very least contrasted favourably with the thousands of eunuchs who tried to manipulate the Emperor in Peking. Women for the first time in China, after years of sometimes cruel domestic seclusion, were given an acknowledged not a furtive role in government.

In Taiping theory there was to have been no renewal of normal family life for the rank-and-file until Peking was conquered. But most of the convinced Taiping veterans had found what they were looking for in Nanking. Hung urged an immediate attack on the capital, but for once failed to carry the other Taiping leaders with him. The expeditionary force sent off to the north was not a wholehearted enterprise, and as the likelihood of capturing Peking became more remote, celibacy was harder to enforce – especially when, as time went on, women in Nanking began to outnumber men. Family life was once more tolerated – but when a puritanical movement has made concessions in principle, the end of its moral authority is in sight.

In theory, opium addicts unwilling to change their ways were to be killed out of hand. But the Yangtze valley was so accessible to Shanghai that local addicts were already numbered in tens of thousands. Dent & Co. tried the expedient of stationing their receiving ship *Nimrod* fifty miles downriver from Nanking – as near as was safe – to develop a trade with addicts in Nanking territory, but after six months' trial they admitted that the venture had been commercially disappointing. But though Taiping leaders wanted to stamp out the opium habit they lacked an efficient therapy. A time limit had to be conceded, to help smokers over their habit. Slowly, clandestinely, opium-smoking too seeped back.

The Taiping began to work out and implement their economic policies. The Bible condemned slavery and usury, and afforded hints towards a kind of Christian communism, but though serving sometimes as a justification for Taiping decisions, Biblical texts were an unsatisfactory blueprint to the technically up-to-date and modernized society of which the most intelligent Taiping leaders are known to have dreamed. Yet what else had they to go on?

Radical changes were attempted at Nanking hinting at an industrial future for China. All industry was concentrated in State workshops – that of the silk workers numbering 14 000. Income from production and trade were put into a State treasury, from which – just as when on the march – the Taiping drew for their needs, as the primitive Christians had done. The Sabbath and the Ten Commandments were strictly enforced. Sex equality was introduced to millions of Chinese women, who, unlike the Hakkas, had hobbled all their lives on bound feet, scarcely ever left home, and sometimes been chattel slaves.

Plans were made, in Hung's 'Land System of the Heavenly

191

Dynasty', to abolish the private ownership of land. A scheme with certain obvious defects emerged for dividing up farmland equitably among the peasants – but in practice this programme of land reform could never be put into effect, because though they managed to hold Nanking as their capital, the Taiping were henceforth obliged to fight all the time for mere survival. They may at first have lifted a burden of landlordism and indebtedness from the peasants' backs, but ten years of continuous war to suppress the Taiping made a desolation of the Yangtze valley.

In May 1853, an inadequately large Taiping expeditionary force had been sent off to attack the Imperial capital, which lay a long way to the north. On its march northward, this army kept open no lines of communication with Nanking, so news of its progress was unreliable, and reinforcement would not be easy.

On their long march the Taiping soldiers had fought successfully as infantry, but now, on the cold plains of north China, they were to encounter a style of fighting which lay outside their previous experience. Their army, lacking horsemen, was about to meet the most effective cavalry in Asia.

The decadent young Emperor had been prompted by bold advisers in this crisis to risk a dangerous expedient. From his allies in Mongolia, beyond the Great Wall, he had called for 4500 horsemen. They were put in charge of Seng-ko-lin-ch'in, son of a Mongol chief, who after education as a Lama priest had married into the Imperial family. A Mongol dynasty had previously sat on the Imperial throne, in the days of Marco Polo, and Seng-ko-lin-ch'in was known to be ambitious – but this was a chance the Manchus were obliged to take.

These slant-eyed Mongol cavalrymen, wearing conical, fur-edged hats, high boots, and loose coats belted over shaggy trousers, were impervious to cold. They were filthy, stinking, lived off melted butter and raw mutton, and spoke no Chinese, but they were astounding marksmen with the bow and arrow, and terrifying lancers. These were the men who, once, had conquered half the known world. To the Taiping footsoldiers, plugging through the winter landscape, the onset of these strange horsemen must literally have seemed like an apparition of Demons.

Though Mongol horsemen were beginning to harry them, the Taiping force by October 1853 had marched to within 100 miles of Peking. Inside the Imperial city there was panic. Famous Generals

Emperor Ch'ien Lung arrives in state for his meeting with Lord Macartney at Jehol *(British Museum)*

Western gate of Peking *(Radio Times Hulton Picture Library)*

Frigates *Andromache* and *Imogene* forcing the Bogue *(National Maritime Museum)*

Macao *(The Mansell Collection)*

Commissioner Lin supervises the
burning of opium *(British Museum)*

The Emperor Ch'ien Lung *(Hong
Kong City Museum)*

His Excellency the Earl of Macartney
(Hong Kong City Museum)

Commissioner Lin *(F. Lewis,*
Publishers)

Admiral Sir Charles Napier
(Radio Times Hulton Picture Library)

The Bridge of Nanking (*Radio Times Hulton Picture Library*)

The city of Nanking (*Radio Times Hulton Picture Library*)

Opium clippers off Lintin Island *(National Maritime Museum)*

The European Factories at Canton *(Radio Times Hulton Picture Library)*

The Royal Navy attack the fort at Chuenpi 7th January 1841
(National Army Museum)

William Jardine *(National Portrait Gallery London)*

James Matheson *(National Portrait Gallery London)*

The Rev. Dr Karl Gutzlaff *(The Mansell Collection)*

Howqua *(The Tate Gallery)*

Whampoa from Dane's Island *(Radio Times Hulton Picture Library)*

HMS *Columbine* attacking Chinese pirates *(National Maritime Museum)*

North Taku Forts immediately after capture 21st August 1860
(Radio Times Hulton Picture Library)

Taku Fort *(Radio Times Hulton Picture Library)*

The bombardment of Canton *(Radio Times Hulton Picture Library)*

Baron Gros *(The Mansell Collection)*

Sir John Bowring
(Hong Kong City Museum)

Sir Henry Pottinger
(The Oriental Club)

Ch'i-ying *(Courtesy Museum of Fine Arts Boston)*

The state entry of Lord Elgin into Peking 1860 *(Hong Kong City Museum)*

The signing of the Treaty of Tientsin *(The Illustrated London News)*

The Summer Palace Peking
(*The Mansell Collection*)

The Eighth Earl of Elgin
(*National Galleries of Scotland*)

A self-portrait of George Chinnery
(*National Portrait Gallery London*)

Prince Kung (*National Army Museum*)

Lord Palmerston (*National Portrait
Gallery London*)

Rear Admiral James Hope
(*National Maritime Museum*)

General de Montauban
(*Radio Times Hulton Picture Library*)

General Sir James Hope Grant
(*National Army Museum*)

feigned sickness, or made excuses to leave. Thirty thousand rich families fled. The Emperor himself was finding reasons to escape to his hunting lodge in Tartary. Down in the south the Cantonese took for granted that the Manchu dynasty was doomed, and acted accordingly – when Seng-ko-lin-ch'in managed to screen the capital with his mercilessly effective cavalry, and began to push the Taiping back, as the winter came on.

Cavalry are the eyes of an army: the Taiping, being foot-soldiers, were forced to operate blindly. They were chivvied away from the capital by men on horseback who could cover country at three or four times their speed. The Taiping were operating 950 miles from their base, and, here in the north, rice was hard to come by. Their numbers started to dwindle. On 6 February 1854 Nanking sent off a small reinforcement of 7500 men to stiffen the attack on Peking, but they were too few and came too late. The high tide mark of the Taiping movement had been achieved; now came the slow ebb.

Put on the defensive, the Taiping in north China turned to guerrilla warfare; and after a long year of it, on 7 March 1855, the Taiping General, Lin Feng-hsiang, was taken prisoner. By 31 May the last 500 survivors had surrendered, and were sent to Peking for public beheading. But though the rebel attack on Peking had failed, by tying up government troops in north China the Taiping expeditionary force there had bought time which enabled Nanking to be organized effectively as a base.

From traditional China emerged a second leader against the Taiping – a Chinese called Tseng Kuo-fan (1811–72), a high official of patience, discernment and conspicuous simplicity of life. He too, agreed the Manchus, might be secretly ambitious, but, as Yehonala pointed out tartly, 'We have to trust someone!' Tseng was a short, dark, stout man with a straggling beard, a celebrated scholar. When the authorities came looking for him – he had retired from his post as Vice-President of the Board of Rites in mourning for his mother – they found Tseng hoeing cabbages on a patch of land in Hunan that his ancestors had cultivated for the past twenty-five centuries.

Tseng intended to fight his war against these strange Christian innovators, not with Imperial soldiers – who had failed dismally everywhere – but with men like his Hunan Braves, a traditional militia drawn from well-to-do and conservative-minded peasants, whose pay was obtained by subscription from the rich. Tseng also began a counter-propaganda to Hung's version of Christianity – with its unacceptable notion of universal brotherhood – by appealing to traditional Confucian values and the established Chinese family.

So far, central China had been little affected by the ideas or habits of the seaborne barbarians, so the province of Hunan provided Tseng with a reliable base. China had two enemies, the Christian foreigners and the Christian Taiping, and Tseng intended to bring them into collision with each other. His policy was slowly to push the Taiping further and further down the Yangtze valley, away from the centre of China, until they reached the sea, and were shoved up against the foreigners in the Treaty Ports. The conflict that might follow could, no doubt, be exploited to the advantage of the Manchu. In October 1854 Tseng retook Hankow, and, not long after, his men had the Taiping Army under observation from a camp almost at the gates of Nanking.

Though their régime may, in time, have lapsed from the level of its early idealistic days, the military skill of the Taiping never left them. Only after eight years of patient diplomacy and persistent fighting did Tseng's policy begin to succeed. At their very last gasp, the Protestant Christian Taiping were to meet their match in an army of foreign mercenaries, commanded by a Protestant Christian officer and gentleman who read and believed the Bible no less fervently than did Hung himself – 'Chinese' Gordon, later to meet a spectacular death in the Sudan.

Once it became plain that the Taiping were not going to rule all China – and that therefore the Manchu dynasty would survive, as a power to be reckoned with – all manner of men, from Jesuits and diplomats to businessmen and even Protestant missionaries, became unanimous that there must be something sadly amiss with Taiping Christianity. Theologians began to notice resemblances to the heresy of Arianism, the simplified Christianity centred on God the Father, which had appealed to the barbarian peoples who looted ancient Rome.

The Taiping anyway, as Chinese patriots, had from the first no intention of becoming clients of the maritime powers. Official emissaries from Britain or the United States were apt to be treated aloofly. The Taiping were groping towards ways of making China strong and modern; the Western merchants were in China to make their fortunes – and the two objectives were incompatible. Strict Sabbath observance and daily Bible reading were all very well and proper – but by sitting astraddle the Yangtze valley, the Taiping blocked the opening up of inland China to foreign trade.

194

The hope was not dead among Roman Catholics who looked ahead of somehow regaining their old ascendancy at the Manchu court; but that meant publicly backing the Manchu dynasty. The Roman Catholic mission was financed in large part by judicious investments in Chinese real estate, and so had inevitable misgivings about a social movement hostile to landlords as a class: in the words of Abbé Huc, at one time Missionary-General of the predominantly French Lazarist Mission in China, 'We do not give the slightest credit to the alleged Christianity of the insurgents.'

But among the more democratic of the Protestant sects, optimism for a while had run riot. After all their years in the mission field, here was the unexpected harvest. As Dr W. H. Medhurst of the nonconformist London Missionary Society exulted in 1853, 'What a moral revolution! To induce 100 000 Chinamen, for months and years together ... to live without dollars, and all share and share alike!' In 1854 another missionary of the same society reported triumphantly: 'Opium smokers and whore-mongers are exterminated. A host united and governed by such rigid rules is a mighty modern miracle.'

To the merchant community, Taiping hostility to the opium habit was not a point in their favour. Great hilarity had been aroused among them by the discovery that one of the four principal Taiping generals had in earlier life been a Cantonese tea-porter. Their sarcastic nickname for the Taiping leaders – the Coolie Kings – is a sign of the times. Thirty years earlier, foreign devils had, by and large, been affably disposed towards the Chinese, if at times perplexed or exasperated by or even in awe of them. Now, after a succession of easy victories, a tone of contemptuous superiority was becoming the fashion. The scallywags in Hong Kong and Shanghai had at last managed to convince themselves that they were essentially superior to the Chinese.

Missionaries who sympathized with the rebels tried to get through the blockade, and find out what this new society in Nanking was really like. They knew the Taiping kept 500 men busy, printing copies of Gutzlaff's translation of the Bible. They discovered that in official examinations in Taiping territory, the New Testament was to take the place held elsewhere by the Confucian Classics. Taiping agents were smuggling Christian literature into the barracks of the Imperial troops, in the hope of seducing them from their duty; the soldiers called them 'Goblin Books'.

On 11 May 1854, Hung, ensconced in his harem, sent word to his old teacher, Rev. Issachar Roberts, informing him: 'I have promulgated the Ten Commandments to the army and the rest of the population, and have taught them all to pray, morning and evening. Still, those who understand the Gospel are not many.' Roberts was invited to go to Nanking and preach, but passing through Shanghai he was stopped in his tracks by Humphrey Marshall, the American Commissioner. Marshall warned Roberts – and all other missionaries with the same idea – that any American joining the Taiping would violate American neutrality, an offence punishable under a statute of 1848 by death. (Roberts finally reached Nanking in 1860, and spent fifteen months there in some state, wearing a crown and yellow robes, but departed disillusioned.)

Of all the foreign powers in China, the United States, with its Protestant ethic and revolutionary origins, its professed friendship for the Chinese people and a declared mistrust of the aggressive British, might have seemed likeliest to take sides with the Taiping. The rebels controlled 400 miles up the Yangtze from Chinkiang, with a fifth of the population of China, but Robert M. McLane, who became American Commissioner in April 1854, decided against American *de facto* recognition of their government. His opinion – no doubt correct – was that the Taiping 'might not fulfil China's treaty obligations to Britain, France and the United States'. In practice, the Taiping whatever their religion would be more unmanageable than the Manchu, and less easy to do business with.

This view was shared by Sir John Bowring, who later in the same year went up the Yangtze in a British warship. He reported glumly that the 'spread of the civil war is cutting up the very foundations of the national prosperity'. Since the Taiping attack on Peking had clearly not gone well, Bowring too judged it better for the British to support 'the existing Imperial government, bad, corrupt and ignorant though it be'.

In terms of their own power politics, these hard-headed diplomats were adequately justified. What the Taiping prophetically sketched out might one day far off become a Chinese reality. But in the short run it was clear to see that when the Taiping were thrown back from the gates of Peking, this lost them their last real chance to impose their curious exotic puritanism on all China – by force if not by persuasion.

The seafaring foreigners who had involved the Chinese in the meshes of the world market also brought in new ideas with their cargoes, though not always useful ones. The only non-Chinese body of doctrine that Westerners at first circulated widely was the Holy Bible, and of this the Chinese, as they groped for a theory to interpret the predicament into which modern commerce had inexplicably plunged them, made consummate use. But rich though the Bible no doubt is in poetry and thought, it can clearly be no substitute for science, technology and a valid economic theory.

Quotations, and sometimes complacent ones, from Adam Smith's *Wealth of Nations,* the Bible of Free Trade, were now and then in the mouths of the Presbyterian drug-merchants at Canton. But though they might suppose Adam Smith gave opium-trafficking an intellectual justification, Matheson, Jardine, Gutzlaff, Pottinger, Parkes and the rest were in no hurry to translate his master-work into Chinese. For that matter, the rival economic theories of Karl Marx had to wait fifty years before becoming accessible to China. But once valid modern political and economic theories, either pro- or anti-capitalist, had come their way, the Chinese were exceptionally quick to apply them to their own condition, while remaining essentially Chinese. They knew what they needed.

The Taiping Rising, if at times cruel or grotesque, was in this way a dress rehearsal for the profounder revolution, misleadingly appearing at first to be one merely of 'Westernization', which when it began half a century later was led, to begin with, by another Hakka, Dr Sun Yat-sen.

During the Middle Ages the dominions of the Mongols, extending from Poland to China, had been the largest Empire the world had ever seen. The disintegration of Mongol power left a vacuum, which the Chinese and Russians proceeded to fill, moving towards each other from opposite ends of Asia. The Russians reached nationhood by a confrontation with what was left of Mongol power. In 1480 they refused to pay their customary tribute to the Mongol Golden Horde, and at about the same time the Mongol dynasty of Yuan was expelled from China, and Chinese ascendancy once more established over the peoples along the border – the Tibetans, Mongols, Turks and Annamese. By 1483, the first Cossacks had moved into Siberia, and by the middle of the seventeenth century the Russians had reached the Pacific.

In thus sharing the defunct Mongol Empire between them,

the Russians and Chinese were bound to collide. The clash came
on China's northern frontier, along the Amur River. In 1650 a
force of Russian cossacks ran into Manchu cavalry, who were
collecting Imperial tribute there, and the Manchus got much the
worst of it. ('The Muscovites', they reported to Peking, 'would
make grid-irons of the parents to roast the children on.') At
intervals for the next fifteen years there were ferocious armed
clashes along China's northern border – a forest war of bow-and-
arrow against musket – the Chinese, though less efficiently armed,
usually managing to overwhelm the Russians by sheer weight of
numbers.

In 1689 there was a diplomatic wrangle at the border, two
Jesuit fathers, Gerbillon and Pereyra, serving the Chinese as
interpreters and advisers. The Treaty of Nerchinsk at last brought
the long frontier war between Russia and China to terms, and
peace was kept between them for the next 150 years. The Treaty
of Nerchinsk was an exception among treaties forced on China
by European powers, in being reasonably fair to both sides, so
that for long afterwards the Chinese were noticeably tolerant
of the Russians. In Peking there were, for example, 300 Orthodox
Christians, including Russians permitted to study Chinese there,
all with their own priest and church.

The Russians kept to their own side of the fence, limiting
their trade with China to a caravan across Mongolia. Two or
three hundred camels carried tea by this route every year out of
China, each camel reaching Kyakhta on the border with four
chests of tea, a burden of about 600 lb: this was the celebrated
Caravan Tea of the nineteenth-century connoisseur. At the height
of this trade, the Russians took out fifty million pounds of tea a
year through Kyakhta.

Ill-informed though the Chinese may have been about world
geography, they were quite well aware, as time went by, of being
encroached upon by land as well as sea. The British had tried
to take over the former Chinese dependency of Nepal as long ago
as 1815, and in Asia the Russians were laying hands on one independent principality after another. A Russian demand, persisted in over many years for a right of navigation along the
Amur River, the frontier established by the Treaty of Nerchinsk,
was therefore sedulously rejected by the Chinese, who had also
refused to let the Russians trade at Canton.

The Russians said they wanted to send boats down the Amur
to supply their outposts in Kamchatka – but it was quite evident
that, in going down the Amur, Russian ships would turn the

flank of the protective Gobi Desert. Once they could reach Chinese ports without first sailing halfway round the globe, there was always the risk that Russia might begin to play the same bullying game as the other foreign powers.

Defeat in the first Opium War having revealed Chinese weakness, the Russians too began discreetly pushing themselves forward. The Governor of Eastern Siberia, Count Nicholas Muraviev, dropped a friendly hint to the Chinese in 1853, in much the same terms as the Americans: 'If Russia became stronger in the East she might even act as Protector of China.' The Orthodox Church in Peking began to be used as an espionage centre. Muraviev forced his way down the Amur River at last, during the Crimean War, with a thousand soldiers in a convoy of forty barges and rafts, and no permission from China, under the plea, 'Necessity knows no law'.

In 1857 Admiral Count Putiatin brought to Peking a firm offer from the Tsar – to help in putting down the Taiping rebels, in exchange for three provinces of Manchuria. The Chinese Emperor would have nothing to do with any such bargain, and refused all discussion of 'frontier rectification'. But the Russians, while pretending to act as honest brokers between China and the Western powers, had shown their hand: they wanted a tract of Chinese land in Manchuria, to the south of the Amur, extensive enough to give them a naval base opening on the Pacific.

Local secret societies sharing Triad ideals took advantage, here and there, of the shock of the Taiping insurrection, to raise local rebellions against the Manchu. On 18 May 1853 Triad members with local help took over the port of Amoy, managing to hold it against all opposition until 11 November. John Scarth, a British trader who spoke Chinese and knew Amoy well, declared of the rising that 'nearly all the people joined'. In Amoy the rebels executed not only Manchu representatives but moneylenders and corrupt officials. 'The bettering of their own condition was their chief aim,' said Scarth.

When Imperial troops retook the seaport on the barren granite island there was yet another massacre. Unsuccessful rebellion was a disgraceful offence in Chinese law – equivalent, since an Emperor was in a paternal relation towards his people, to parricide. In Amoy as elsewhere the Triad, with their romantic, as it were Jacobite, nostalgia for the restoration of the Ming, the last

199

native dynasty, lost their throw and paid for it with their lives.

Since almost everyone in Amoy had helped the Triad to power, the massacre was wholesale. Hundreds of victims were loaded into junks, taken some little way offshore and beheaded, their corpses being tipped by the heels into the water. The Chinese have a peculiar horror of dismemberment – strangulation is less shameful than beheading – and the sight was also too much for Captain Fishbourne, RN, of HMS *Hermes*, who threatened to fire his guns into any junk that went on beheading prisoners.

He also sent a landing party ashore to stop executions in front of foreigners' houses, and on the beach. Even so, 2500 people in Amoy had their heads cut off in that one day. A captured Triad leader was put to death in a way to strike terror: the Emperor's soldiers buried him alive, up to his neck in quicklime, which they slaked, so that the living flesh was burned from his bones. Survivors of the rising in Amoy who managed to get away in boats crossed the strait to Formosa, and they set up in business there as pirates.

From these years of rebellion and repression originates the Western mythology of 'Chinese torture' – still familiar in popular fiction and even in political propaganda. Any minority trying to gain power, or fearful of losing it, is prone to use terroristic methods, as the Taiping had shown at the bloody capture of Nanking. But the ruling Manchu, also, were a tiny alien fraction in China, numbering only one per cent of the population, and their Tartar soldiers were stationed in the cities specifically to intimidate. When a minority turns to a policy of terror, sadists soon emerge from society's twilight zone – where they always exist – eager as ever to fulfil their own unpleasant reveries with official sanction. In this, as the recent history of Western Europe shows, there is, alas, nothing specifically Chinese.

The massacre at Amoy was minor compared with the reign of terror organized in Canton and its provinces by Viceroy Yeh Ming-chen – a curious man, immensely fat, the son of a village apothecary who had risen high in his official career thanks to exceptional intelligence. Yeh was brutal, yet an accomplished poet; he opposed foreign domination with great sagacity, yet consulted the planchette before he took any important policy decision. He had the demeanour of a typically corrupt, acquisitive

Chinese high official – yet when government funds ran low, Yeh was ready to spend his personal fortune in putting down rebellion: a monster, yet an interesting monster.

Yeh boasted freely of having, in and around Canton, put to death a grand total of 100 000 rebels. By all accounts he despatched 70 000 of them in the first six months of 1855, after the British had come to his help by providing warships to break a Triad blockade of Canton.

Foreign help for Yeh was at first unofficial, mainly American. A Canton trader called W. C. Hunter joined with Kingqua, a former Hong merchant, to finance a private navy – command being entrusted to an American seaman called Drinker, who was granted a Chinese commission as Admiral.

Admiral Drinker's filibusters were a mixed and mercenary bunch, of American and British merchant seamen, naval deserters, Portuguese and Filipinos. His flagship was a Macao lorcha, re-named *Hornet*, and he had besides an 80-ton sloop and two half-decked boats of 20 tons apiece, which he christened *Rough and Ready* and *Rough and Tough*.

'Don't shoot the mandarin soldiers if you can help it,' Admiral Drinker's men were warned, as they went into action at Whampoa in November 1854. 'They're our allies – they're there to help us – they wear red coats.' Drinker and 200 of his filibusters had not much difficulty in capturing the fort in Blenheim Reach for Yeh – who paid him $25 000 for his success. But filibustering was a gross breach of neutrality – any British seamen taking part was nominally liable to two years' imprisonment, any American to death. The British persuaded the American Commissioner, Robert M. McLane, to have the irregular navy disbanded.

On 29 December, however, the rebels in the Pearl River managed to beat the Imperialists in a pitched battle at Whampoa. Though Viceroy Yeh liked the foreign devils no better than the Chinese rebels, he was driven in this crisis to ask the Governor of Hong Kong for help, and it was promptly given. The insurrection at Canton was, of course, hampering the export of tea, but this was not the only reason why the British came officially to Yeh's aid. Having decided that the Manchus, with all their faults, would be easier to manage than the rebels, they hoped to soften Yeh into conceding treaty rights which in practice the British had never yet been granted – such as free entry into the walled city of Canton.

In January 1855 – after 200 rebel junks, some of them ex-pirates, had pushed an opposing force of fifty of Yeh's war junks to within three miles of the city gates – Admiral Sterling went up the river with a squadron of five British warships. The rebel junks, knowing from bitter experience that against modern ships of war they stood no chance whatever, were obliged to withdraw, with Canton almost in their grasp. In February the rebel leader Ch'en Hsieng-liang demanded that all Americans, British and French leave Canton within five days, taking their belongings with them. But a breathing space had been won by the warships, and Yeh, the pressing danger over, was already beginning by systematic massacre to crush the Triad movement inside Canton.

Sir John Bowring, Governor of Hong Kong, took his policy of conciliating Yeh so far as to ship across to him, in HMS *Niger*, a large number of Triad sympathizers – 'long-haired rebels' – who had fled for refuge to the island. An earlier British proposal to identify Triad supporters by branding them on the cheek before expelling them had been expressly condemned by London.

Heads of executed rebels were usually delivered to the yamen, or government office, as a proof that justice had been done. But now in all Canton there were not enough baskets to hold the severed heads; the executioners were obliged instead to send Yeh boxes filled with amputated right ears.

Thomas Meadows, the one Chinese scholar in British employ who stood up publicly for the Taiping – as a movement he believed could renovate China – has left a description of one of these mass public executions in Canton.

The official executioner, as usual, wore a bloodstained conical hat, dark clothes, and a chain at his waist like a belt. He cut off his victim's head with a narrow three-foot sword, held with both hands, and brought down with all the force of the body. As the blade became blunted in use, an assistant stood by, to put a new edge on it.

Suspected rebel sympathizers were made to kneel in rows, a second assistant holding up each head, in turn, by the pigtail. At the official signal – the waving of a banner – the executioner's swordsmanship was so rapid that Meadows saw him behead thirty-three men in three minutes by the clock. On this occasion the final prisoner, a captured Triad leader, was pinioned to a cross and 'cut in a thousand pieces' – his flesh, that is to say, being sliced from his living body, like ham.

By the end of the decade the rising in Kwangtung had been subdued, and a million people in the province were dead – from famine, war, pestilence, or the executioner's rapid sword. News that death on this scale was being inflicted in his name at Canton was kept, however, from the Emperor, who in one or other of his marvellous Peking palaces was leading, meanwhile, a life of day-dream and debauch.

The mandarins raised money for their campaigns against rebels by ignoring an injunction of the late Emperor at the time of the Treaty of Nanking, and taxing opium as it entered the Treaty Ports. Opium going up to Shanghai was assessed at twelve taels the chest, and a dozen junks were anchored near the receiving ships at Woosung, flying banners which read significantly, 'Public Committee for Patriotic Collections'. To pay for military expenses at Amoy the unofficial tax on opium was at one time pushed up, as an emergency measure, from $2 to $50 a chest.

Foreigners trading at Shanghai conducted their business outside the Chinese walled city – which on 7 September 1853 was taken over by about 1200 members of the Small Sword Society, an offshoot of the Triads, and with the help of the local people successfully held by them until 17 February 1855. Most of the Small Swords were seafaring men from Kwangtung and Fukien, and one of their outstanding leaders was Lin Li-chu'an, a Cantonese physician, who had made himself popular in Shanghai by treating the poor free.

The rebels took Shanghai with little opposition and less blood-shed. 'The people made no active opposition,' reported John Scarth, adding: 'They were something like the Chartists of England.' The Small Swords were helped by foreign seamen who had deserted their ships, and now manned guns for the rebels. An ex-Royal Marine made fuses and loaded home-made brass shells for them. The European insurrections of 1848 had left sentiments of revolutionary romanticism widely diffused among working men. This was the decade of the Garibaldini; the time when it seemed logical and right for American soldiers sent to invade Mexico to desert their own ranks and serve in the Mexican artillery – as the best way of defending freedom.

The rebels in Shanghai let the prisoners out of the city gaol, and put up placards decreeing the restoration of the Ming dynasty. Although no member of the Small Sword Society was debarred from using opium – a tolerance which made Small Sword–Taiping cooperation uneasy – the Small Swords when they took over Shanghai at once prohibited all trade in the drug. ('It would seem impossible to deny,' the British Foreign Secretary, Lord Clarendon,

203

pointed out glumly to Sir John Bowring, 'their authority altogether to put a stop to the trade in opium.')

The local Chinese prefect, Wu Chien-chang, had been at one time a Hong merchant in Canton. With the connivance of US Commissioner Marshall he managed to escape from the rebel-held city, and got together a mixed force of soldiers and mercenaries, to retake Shanghai for the Emperor.

Hit though they were by the ban on opium, most British and Americans in Shanghai were unwilling as yet to choose sides as emphatically as their counterparts had done in Canton. They knew now that in the long run official Chinese bans made little difference to the demand for opium: addicts would break the law to get the drug. But Shanghai was also the port through which guns were run into Taiping territory, in exchange for silk – a profitable business. In Shanghai neutrality leaning slightly towards the Small Swords might be sensible. The Anglo-Americans raised a volunteer force for the defence of the foreign community, and sat it out.

Imperial troops tried on one occasion to push their way into the foreign settlement, and when at the skirmish known ironically as the 'Battle of Muddy Flat' the volunteers, led by Captain O'Callaghan and Consul Alcock, successfully fought them off, they found they were being helped by a well-timed rebel sortie.

The French, however – and rumour said they were being advised by Jesuits, who owned property at Sicawei, near Shanghai – decided to strike out on a pro-Manchu line of their own by opposing the Small Sword rebels. The small French concession – then amounting only to the premises of the French Consul and his neighbour, M. Rémi, a Paris watch-maker – abutted on the city wall. On 6 December 1854 Admiral Guérin sent an armed party and some workmen to demolish a Small Sword battery there which, he contended, might become a danger. The Small Swords fired a blank shot to deter the working party, and not long afterwards the French warships *Colbert* and *Jeanne d'Arc* rose to the occasion by a systematic bombardment of Shanghai. Dismantling the battery cost the French forty-five men killed and wounded.

While Americans and British looked on unenthusiastically, the French naval guns made a breach in the city wall, and marksmen dominated it by rifle-fire. On 6 January 1855 400 armed Frenchmen were landed from the ships, to cooperate with a large force of Imperialist soldiers moving towards the city, wearing blue sashes to distinguish them from the Small Swords.

Houses inside Shanghai had already been set on fire, and a good many civilians killed. This kind of remorseless naval bombardment had always overwhelmed regular Chinese troops during the recent war, but this time the tough seafaring men who led the Small Swords stood up to it and struck back. Inside the breach there was hand-to-hand fighting which lasted four hours, the Small Swords managing to drive the Imperialist army, stiffened though it was by a large and disciplined French contingent, right out of Shanghai. The French made an orderly retreat, but counted sixty men and four officers killed and wounded, out of the 250 who had managed to enter the breach. The Imperialists lost 1200. When Shanghai fell at last to the Imperialists – on Chinese New Year's Day, 17 February 1855 – it was with the active help of French marines.

After the city fell, Chin A-lin, one of the important Small Sword leaders, and formerly a stable-boy in Shanghai, was hidden from those who sought his blood by John Scarth, who was serving there as Belgian Consul, and later smuggled again to Hong Kong by Scarth in the guise of a servant; from there he escaped to Singapore.

In using their naval power exactly as the British had done, the French were claiming their unmistakable right, in any future plundering of China, to be taken into serious account. The Jesuits might dream of re-establishing themselves as a civilizing force in Peking, but the French authorities were turning their eyes particularly towards territorial annexation in Indo-China.

7 The City Question

'*Coleridge always seemed to live in the dreamy regions of cloudland, and it was difficult to follow him through the mazes of his misty eloquence. At table, his harmonious periods fell from his lips like water from a fountain. Every now and then he was observed to put his finger and thumb into his waistcoat pocket, from which he took an opium pill, which he clandestinely conveyed to his mouth.*'
Autobiographical Recollections of Sir John Bowring, 1877

'*In my box I got out a few books ... Scott's and Byron's Poetical Works – a great part of the latter are, I am aware, very licentious and immoral, but these I shall not study, while some possess much purer sentiment and pathos.*'
Harry Parkes, in a letter to his sister, when interpreter at Foochow, 1846

In 1850 the Chinese were buying about the same quantity of British cotton goods as in 1843; by the year 1854 they were buying less. On 26 January 1854 the Manchester Chamber of Commerce memorialized Lord Clarendon, then Foreign Secretary. The cotton trade badly needed the right to ship goods to the interior of China, and also sought the abolition of those vexatious internal Customs duties – called *likin*, and used to finance the war against the Taiping – which were making it even more difficult for British cottons to price the homespun article out of the Chinese market. Dent, who spoke for the opium traders, later said of such demands that 'to enforce them it would be necessary to conquer and take possession of the entire country'.

This kind of concession was easier talked about loudly in London than negotiated in China. Of recent years the Chinese authorities had been deliberately elusive, avoiding diplomatic contact, and contriving ways to make the post-war treaties imposed on them unenforceable. During all his official life in Canton, Viceroy Yeh, whose job included maintaining relations with the overseas 'barbarians' on Peking's behalf, had never once set eyes on a foreigner. Yeh was astute and immovable, with a gift for masterly inactivity, when it would serve his turn best. The Viceroy of the

Two Kwangs had a civil war on his hands; tens of thousands of local rebels to overawe and decapitate. He might sometimes be glad of British help against pirates or insurrectionists, but he would never concede anything of substance in return.

In Britain the political spokesmen for the cotton trade had for many years been radicals of the Manchester School, led by Cobden, a one-time calico salesman, and Bright, a mill-owner. The political philosophy of these men was peace and free trade – but latterly, as Lord Palmerston had been quick to note, peace and free trade might not, at times, be compatible. Markets might need to be conquered or defended, not only with unbeatably low prices, but with guns.

Lord Palmerston, surprisingly enough, had in 1848 appointed as Consul at Canton a well-known literary radical – a friend of Cobden's and former Secretary of the Peace Society. John Bowring was the man who brought back Lord Byron's corpse from Greece in a puncheon of rum, and he later edited the collected works of Jeremy Bentham (which he took the liberty of toning down, on moral grounds). Though a typical literary man of his time and class – a romantic turned progressive – John Bowring had a more private connection with Lord Palmerston going back many years. During the 1820s and 1830s John Bowring – then a polyglot businessman, never very successful, who dabbled in literary translations – had, in his son's words, been 'a confidential agent of the British government – serving Canning and Palmerston and purveying intelligence.' Despite his domestic fame in Evangelical circles as author of the hymn 'In the Cross of Christ I Glory', John Bowring also cut something of a figure among atheistic radicals on the Continent; and Lord Palmerston often found it useful to have a concealed hand in liberal movements abroad.

In 1841 Bowring was swept into prominence by the anti-Corn Law agitation, and managed to get elected to Parliament for the cotton town of Bolton. In the next seven years he made a name for himself as a radical pacifist and an irrepressible advocate of decimal coinage. In 1848, by an unhappy speculation in a South Wales ironworks, Bowring lost what little money he had, and Lord Palmerston saved him from personal disaster by appointing him Consul at Canton. At the age of 57, Bowring began to learn Chinese.

Palmerston had more than once appointed a prominent radical to a difficult post abroad, and the expedient answered. Such men never scrupled about using the violent methods that, as politicians, they had deplored. Watching a man of well-publicized principle eat his own words must also have given Palmerston, in his old age, a certain impish pleasure.

His new role at Canton chafed John Bowring – a frustrated intellectual, growing old, yet still anxious to make a figure in the great world commensurate with his talents. 'Cooped up in the prison house of the Canton Factories,' wrote his son, 'debarred from all access to higher officials, far removed from the political or literary world, and restricted to the dull routine of purely consular duties, he ... found his position almost unendurable.'

In the year of Bowring's arrival at Canton – 1849 – the right of access to the Chinese walled city, claimed under the Treaty of Nanking, was to have been accorded. Access to Canton implied face-to-face discussion with Yeh, and might bring the Chinese up to scratch. Lord Palmerston's instructions to Bowring had pointed out, however, that entry into Canton of all British subjects need not be pressed, if it might lead to war. (Palmerston was well aware that many of the British ruffians now in China made a nuisance of themselves, forcing Chinese off the pavement, making them go past cap in hand, knocking their market stalls over for fun, and the rest of the schoolboy nonsense.) But the treaty right of a British Consul to enter Canton freely should be insisted upon 'even though menaces and the presence of an armed force were necessary'.

In keeping foreigners outside their city gates, the Cantonese had a respectable case, both in law and good sense. Local people were notoriously so hostile towards foreigners that once inside the city no Chinese authority could guarantee a foreigner's personal safety. (Sir John Davis, who negotiated the agreement granting access by 1849, had diagnosed this hostility as having 'commenced with the violence suffered by their women from the Sepoy troops in 1841'.) But the clause in the Treaty defining this right of access could just as easily be construed in China's favour. The term used in the Chinese text, *kiangkan*, signified port, or mart – in distinction to *ching*, meaning walled city – so the Chinese could argue that this implied a right of access only to the Factory area, down by the river. Gutzlaff, seldom a man to give China the benefit of the doubt, had admitted in 1846 that 'to carry the entrance into Canton city at present, British bayonets would be needed' – as, no doubt, when he sent the Secretary of the Peace Society there as Consul, Lord Palmerston was well aware.

If even a limited access to Canton caused bad feeling, it would not, of course, be good for trade; but the question had already soared high above old-fashioned considerations of profit-and-loss.

To use a word only lately come into general use, the right to enter Canton was by now a matter of *prestige*. Inside the walls sat Viceroy Yeh, virtually China's Foreign Minister, his official residence visible from the crow's nest of a ship in the river, yet inaccessible to pressure, and immune even to argument. And by now John Bowring had worked at Chinese so hard, he was sure he could have argued with Yeh – after a fashion – in his own language.

In 1854 the foreign powers would claim their right to a revision of existing treaties. But so little headway had been made with Yeh that a French diplomat was sarcastically reporting by then, to Paris, 'With all their guns, the English cannot get their treaties executed, and are worse off at Canton today than before the war.' Access to Canton was beginning to take on the value of a symbol. In London it might be seen in due proportion, as an important treaty right, not yet yielded and well worth pressing for. But to the men on the spot the 'city question' had become a pre-occupying obsession.

In March 1852 John Bowring served as Governor of Hong Kong in Sir Samuel Bonham's absence on leave. No doubt to urge his claims to the chair he temporarily occupied, Bowring composed an exceedingly long despatch to the Foreign Office, laying down in emphatic detail what needed to be done in China. As a call to action from a transplanted pacifist, even Lord Palmerston might have thought this despatch showed too much zeal. 'China contributes nearly £9 000 000 of revenue to the British and Indian treasuries', Bowring pointed out, 'and our commercial relations here are undoubtedly capable of immense extension.' The key was access to Canton.

Unluckily for Bowring, his long despatch happened to arrive at the Foreign Office during the brief ten months, in 1852, of Lord Derby's Tory administration. Palmerston, who might have understood what Bowring was driving at, was no longer Minister. The Tories had never shown much enthusiasm for risking an expensive war in China for the hypothetical good of the cotton trade. From the Foreign Office, Lord Malmesbury administered the temporary Governor of Hong Kong a peremptory rebuke, bidding him 'avoid all irritating discussions with the Chinese authorities'. Bowring was to abstain from mooting the entry question or from pressing to be received by the Chinese authorities otherwise than hitherto. This answer, as it rankled, no doubt helped accentuate the devious mood of the British officials on the spot.

Happily confirmed as Governor of Hong Kong, on Bonham's

retirement, and Lord Palmerston's return to office, and granted the knighthood that usually went with the job, Sir John Bowring was once more free to flex his mind imperially. 1854 turned out, in fact, not to be Treaty Revision Year, but the period when hostility between three of the four rivals in China – Russia, Britain and France – drifted towards open war in the Black Sea, the Baltic and the Crimea. France and Britain were both ill at ease with Russia's aggressive expansion into the Turkish Empire and the independent principalities of Central Asia; but in the Far East the differences between the conflicting powers were small. Unless the British and French sent gunboats up the Amur River to bombard the Russian settlements there – a tactic which, though feasible, was never seriously tried – there was hardly anywhere for the antagonists to get to grips; though Bowring thoroughly enjoyed rushing back and forth in warships in search of the elusive foe.

The outcome of the Crimean campaign – Britain's first major war for forty years – did in fact alter the game played in China, by changing somewhat the relative strength of the pieces on the board. The British lost a good army in the Crimea by mismanagement, and to bring the long-drawn-out war to an end, a large French force took Sebastopol at last with very little help from their allies. The British fleet, for so long the undisputed policeman of the globe, was not particularly effective against Russia in the Baltic; but Palmerston – who had a zest for war – was able to come back from his brief political twilight with enhanced popularity. The flourishing middle classes were beginning to prefer the sound of Palmerston's racy demagogic patriotism to the outmoded, low-key, radical commonsense of the peace-mongers.

Bowring's place as Consul at Canton was now held by a young man of 28 – Pottinger's boy protégé, Harry Parkes, a brilliant Chinese linguist. Ever since he was 22, Parkes had been supplying the Foreign Office with confidential information about China – and sometimes about his own superiors – in a private correspondence with Edmund Hammond, who for the next two decades was to serve as Permanent Under-Secretary at the Foreign Office. Hammond was a devotee of a Palmerstonian foreign policy. When Consul Parkes went home, in 1855, with a treaty Sir John Bowring had made with Siam – the Siamese were willing to trade, but strictly barred opium – Edmund Hammond arranged for Parkes to be interviewed as an expert witness on China. The earnest young man made a strikingly favourable impression both on Lord Clarendon, at the Foreign Office, and on Lord Palmerston himself, now Prime Minister. To both of them, the emphasis of Harry Parkes's report had been that 'entry to Canton was the key to the whole difficulty'.

In short, between the two men on the spot – Bowring and Parkes – and the responsible Ministers, a personal understanding had been achieved and a private channel of communication opened up which, at need, could bypass official despatches liable some time or other to be exposed to the scrutiny of Parliament. From now on there need be no explanations; a nod and a wink would do.

In choosing Parkes as his source of secret intelligence, Edmund Hammond had picked cleverly. The young man was ambitious, intelligent, and remarkably single-minded, as talented orphans often are. Harry Parkes was, indeed, almost a model young mid-Victorian: forthright, fearless, religious, self-made, energetic, clever – perhaps a trifle domineering, in the Pottinger manner, towards the unlucky Chinese, though a man in his job had a great deal to put up with. A policy had been followed by Chinese officials ever since the Treaty of Nanking of inflicting petty affronts, sometimes even blows, on foreign consuls, so as to make them publicly lose face. Young Consul Parkes's 'stereotyped hollow smile' was already signalling the nervous irritability that by the time he was 30 would be chronic.

Bowring, since the Crimean alliance, had been expected to cooperate on treaty revision with the French – a new treaty acceptable to Britain being one which opened inland China to trade, legalized opium, and gave foreign diplomats the right of access not only to local governors but to the central power at Peking. The French were well regarded by the Chinese because they had never been identified with the trade in opium – not even furtively, like the Americans. As Roman Catholics, they were also free of the suspicion which adhered to Protestant powers of a hidden sympathy with the Taiping. The French in China had their own secret dream: they hoped to revive, in Peking, the ascendancy enjoyed there centuries before by the Jesuits, thereby becoming the Manchu dynasty's one reliable prop. But the Russians – after well over a hundred years of peaceful trade with China – were hoping for much the same: to become Manchu China's sincere friend. Russia and France intended to anticipate any reward they might eventually earn for this disinterested behaviour by nibbling at the edges of an enfeebled China – Russia in Manchuria south of the Amur, the French in Annam.

The British and French began to fear in 1856, once their war with Russia was over, that unless they pushed hard now for a treaty revision, the defeated Russians might be tempted to recoup their loss in the Crimea by gaining the upper hand in China. The crisis was near.

The French already had a creditable motive for bringing pressure to bear on China. A French priest called Father Auguste Chapdelaine, sent out to China in the service of *Les Missions Etrangères de Paris*, had worked for the past three years in a small town called Hsi-Lin, in the turbulent border province of Kwangsi, the homeland of the Taiping. Father Chapdelaine spoke Chinese, followed the Roman Catholic custom of wearing Chinese clothes, and was known locally as Father Ma. There happened, unluckily, to be a notorious rebel leader called Ma Tzu-nung.

Father Chapdelaine was suspected of having links with the Christian Taiping – no doubt unjustly, since Catholics were seldom in sympathy with the Taiping's eccentric Protestantism. But in the midst of a brutal war against Christian rebels the local Chinese magistrate made no effort to distinguish between one sort of Christian and another. In February 1856 Father Chapdelaine was arrested and put on display in a cage, as the British survivors from *Kite* had been, years before. In accordance with Yeh's policy of striking terror, on 29 February the missionary priest was decapitated and dismembered. Pious subscribers to *Les Missions Etrangères* were later appalled to learn that his heart had been cut out, cooked and eaten, but for the truth of this horrifying detail, evidence is defective.

When the sad news arrived of the execution of Father Chapdelaine, Comte de Courcy, French Consul in Canton, made an emphatic protest to Yeh, who later had the candour to admit, 'He dressed and spoke like a Chinese; nobody thought him to be French.' Consul Alcock, in Shanghai, considered it 'a matter of surprise that a single missionary of the many hundreds in the interior should have been left alive, not that one should have been sacrificed'. But as a justification for the use of force, the good Father's violent martyrdom came at exactly the right time: by September 1856, Lord Cowley, the British Ambassador in Paris, was warning the Foreign Office that the French were proposing to take up the Chapdelaine case with vigour.

The right claimed by the British to a revision of their treaty was due originally to Caleb Cushing's shrewd horse-trading, yet at first the Americans kept aloof. Some leaned towards China – particularly the American house of Russell & Co., which did large business with Howqua, and had not forgotten how profitable neutrality had turned out to be in the earlier war.

Dr Peter Parker, the veteran missionary representing the United States in China, was just then more preoccupied with a notion that the United States ought to annex Formosa. There was a basis already: an American firm had a monopoly of Formosan camphor, steam-coal had been found, and the Stars and Stripes flew over a virtually independent trading settlement there – welcomed by the local Formosans since it discouraged pirates. An American receiving ship in Takoa Bay had an opium monopoly there, and at uncommonly high prices, up to $1500 a chest – the cost of production being about $200 a chest. (In 1859 Dent & Co. introduced competition by sending in their armed clipper *Eamont.*)

But biting off a detached piece of China would have been a needless distraction – as Washington saw it – from the vast but more rewarding task of opening up the American West. By 1857, when the British Ambassador in Washington tried bringing to the President's notice a memorandum suggesting joint action against China, he was sharply put in his place. If the British and French went to war in China, any concessions they won were bound by treaty also to accrue to the United States, under Cushing's skilfully drawn 'most favoured nation' clause. Let them go it alone.

The incident that precipitated the new war was minor but dramatic.

On 8 October 1856, at eight in the morning, three young seamen called John Leach, Charles Earl and Thomas Kennedy sat idly at breakfast on the deck of a lorcha called *Dart*, moored near Dutch Folly, the anchorage on the Pearl River facing the Canton Factories. Two of them were only twenty-one years old, but all three were British – a fact which enabled them to earn $30 a month very easily as nominal 'captains' of Chinese lorchas. John Leach, the host, was 'captain' of *Dart*, Charles Earl of *Chusan* and Thomas Kennedy of *Arrow*. By putting a ship under the command of a British subject and registering her at Hong Kong, a Chinese owner obtained the valuable privilege of sailing under the Union Jack.

The lorcha, a sea-going vessel originated by the Portuguese, was a curious hybrid. The hull was Western, but rigging and sails copied those of a junk, for ease of handling by a Chinese crew. Young Thomas Kennedy, a native of Belfast, was ready to embark for Hong Kong later that morning in *Arrow* (127 tons) which he could see, moored fifty yards ahead of where all three men sat

213

breakfasting, amid a thicket of Chinese junks and sampans.

Kennedy later made oath that, because of his imminent departure, *Arrow* was at that very moment flying both her Blue Peter and a British ensign. This may well have been true, though the master of a Portuguese lorcha, lying not far off, was also able to give evidence that no Union Jack had been borne by *Arrow* for the previous six days. To anyone familiar, day after day, with shipping on that stretch of the river, *Arrow* would not have been conspicuously British, rather the contrary. But her owner had bought the right to fly the flag.

Kennedy idly noticed a couple of large war junks work their way up channel, flying the Imperial ensign. Two boats, commanded by mandarins, and with about sixty uniformed marines aboard, cast off from the war junks and moved towards the shore. To Kennedy's surprise they boarded *Arrow*, quickly took prisoner all her crew – fourteen Chinese – and having tied their elbows behind their backs began dumping them into the mandarin boats. Leach, Earl and Kennedy at once got into a sampan, to row alongside the lorcha *Arrow* and see what the trouble was. Kennedy swore later – the nub of the matter – that he actually saw one of the Chinese marines, in uniform, haul down his Union Jack from the mizzen gaff. This was serious: an insult to the flag.

Kennedy knew a few words of Chinese. To his first shouted protest, the marines replied (as marines will) with an oath; but one of the mandarins was reasonable enough to leave at the young man's bidding a couple of his crew aboard *Arrow* as boat-keepers. The Chinese then bore off the twelve men they had arrested.

All evidence goes to show that, on this occasion anyway, *Arrow* was an honest trader, having come up to Canton only the week before from Macao with a cargo of rice. The lorcha's past, however, was chequered. Originally she had been built, owned and manned by Chinese. After capture by pirates, *Arrow* had served in the rebel fleet against Yeh's war junks. Taken prize by Yeh's men, she was then knocked down at auction to a Chinese, who in his turn sold her to Fong Ah-ming, the comprador employed by the Hong Kong firm of John Bird & Co. Her new owner was a Chinese who had lived in Hong Kong for ten years. The lorcha's original owner, who had lost her to the pirates, still had a claim on her. This was requited by a somewhat elaborate deal which left *Arrow* in Fong Ah-ming's hands, as owner, with a nominal British 'captain', a Hong Kong colonial register, and a right to sail under British colours.

But whether young Kennedy knew it or not, at least one and

probably three men in his present crew were known associates of pirates – one of them having that very morning been identified by a former victim, as he sat on deck. This was why the war junks, on their way upriver, had made the wholesale arrest. It might be argued that all the crew of *Arrow*, whether pirates or not, were under the protection of the Union Jack. The mandarins, however, contended that when they made the arrest, no British ensign had been flown.

Arrow's papers were across the river, at the British consulate. Thomas Kennedy went over right away, and reported the facts to Consul Parkes, who at once boarded the offending war junk, and in his fluent Chinese reminded the officers of 'the gross insult and violation of national rights they had committed'. One of them slapped his face.

As Parkes reminded Sir John Bowring in his report of the incident, all twelve of those suspects – as the crew of a British ship – should according to Treaty have first been brought to his consulate. This offence, in Harry Parkes's official view, could be expiated only by having all twelve Chinese seamen returned formally to his consulate, to the accompaniment of a public apology. But, as Parkes was no doubt well aware, this would mean inflicting a bigger loss of face than the Chinese were likely to find acceptable. Yeh was not a man given to public apologies.

Sir John Bowring at once let Parkes know that he had read between the lines of his report. In an enthusiastic personal letter that came up from Hong Kong with his more prudent official answer, Bowring asked Parkes, 'Cannot we use the opportunity and carry the city question? If so, I will come up with the whole fleet.'

With the Crimean War over, British ships-of-war had been concentrating in Chinese waters to reinforce any arguments Bowring might make on the theme of treaty revision. Lord Clarendon, who had in mind a naval demonstration in the north next spring, perhaps with the support of France and the United States, was just about to send instructions along these lines when news of the *Arrow* incident reached London.

Sixteen warships were available in Hong Kong, including three steamers – a larger force than ever before put at a Governor's disposal in time of peace. But Rear-Admiral Sir Michael Seymour, commanding the fleet, was hard to convince. 'I do not think,' Bowring cautioned Parkes, 'the Admiral will make war.'

Sir Michael's father, and more famous namesake, an Irishman from Limerick, had been a particularly dashing naval officer in the Napoleonic Wars, losing an arm on the Glorious First of June and picking up a title and a fortune in prize money. His son, a worrier by nature, was slower off the mark. His own naval career had been less spectacular: he had run HMS *Challenge* aground off the coast of Chile, but been lucky enough to survive the court martial which followed; he had lost an eye in the recent war, when a Russian mine went off in his face accidentally. Admiral Seymour was a laboriously conscientious commander, who needed to feel his way.

Bowring could be overwhelmingly persuasive; his trick was to start arguing and never stop. This time, with Admiral Seymour, he was also disingenuous. By making sure he showed the honest Admiral only those parts of his instructions which called for a settlement of the 'city question', while by all accounts keeping out of sight the cautions given him by Malmesbury and others, as well as by hammering hard on the 'insult to the flag', Bowring overbore the Admiral's misgivings. He wrote in triumph to Parkes: 'The Admiral has left me in an excellent disposition, and we must write a bright page in our history.' With a fleet to back their words, Bowring and Parkes could be as uncompromising as they chose towards Viceroy Yeh.

On 10 October, Yeh had come out with his own circumstantial explanation. A notorious pirate called Le-Ming-tae – signed on as a member of *Arrow*'s crew less than three weeks before – had been identified aboard the lorcha; hence the mass arrest. Yeh went on to make out an even better case for himself by throwing doubts on *Arrow*'s credentials. He claimed that to provide the comprador with a British register, £1000 had been paid over to Mr Block, manager of John Bird & Co. and Danish Consul in Hong Kong. (Money to this amount had certainly changed hands, but Block insisted it was to clear his comprador's title to *Arrow*.) Yeh announced his willingness to return nine of the arrested men, but this Parkes adamantly refused to accept. He had asked for all twelve seamen, and a public apology, and nothing less would do.

Commodore C. G. J. B. Elliot, RN, who was senior British naval officer in the Pearl River, arrived outside the city on 15 October in the steam tender *Coromandel*, towing behind her a detachment of Royal Marines in the boats of HMS *Sybille*. A reprisal might change Yeh's mind. The tactic agreed on was to detain as hostage an Imperial junk similar to the junk which had borne off *Arrow*'s crew.

Commodore Elliot was soon reporting cheerfully to Admiral Seymour that *Coromandel* had cut out from the mass of shipping

216

moored in the Pearl River a junk which 'carried the Imperial flag ... I am assured she is of the class and very similar to the junk that boarded the *Arrow*'. But, in a less self-confident tone, his despatch went on to admit, 'I understand she has on board a valuable cargo.'

Next day Consul Parkes was obliged to warn Sir John of the blunder: 'Some doubts have now arisen as to whether she be an Imperial junk, or only private property.' Chalking this one up to his own side of the account, Yeh wrote chidingly to that stickler for protocol, Consul Parkes, 'The junk in question is a trading junk ... suddenly involved in trouble by the act of the said Consul. Where, in the Treaty, will he find authority for such proceedings as these?' The Chinese Viceroy did his best at the same time to placate the British by returning to their Consulate all twelve of the arrested men. 'Hereafter, Chinese officers', Yeh conceded, 'will on no account without reason seize and take into custody the people belonging to foreign lorchas, but when Chinese subjects build for themselves vessels, foreigners should not sell registers to them ... for it will occasion confusion between native and foreign ships, and render it difficult to distinguish between them.'

Fortified by the knowledge that both French and American consuls thought he was technically in the right, Harry Parkes stood his ground, reporting to Bowring, 'No officer of rank or letter of apology accompanied them, and I explained to the officer in charge ... that they must be given up in the manner demanded by my letter of October 8.'

Despite his many years in politics, Sir John Bowring appears to have been so carried away by self-generated enthusiasm as not to grasp how thin the *Arrow* incident would sound, as a pretext for 'menaces and the presence of an armed force' in the cooler and more deliberate atmosphere of London. By making a report to the Foreign Office, earlier that year, about Chinese lorchas with Hong Kong registers 'participating in nefarious deeds' he had even spoiled his own case in advance. Yet climbing down now would award Viceroy Yeh yet one more little local victory, and at a time when to force concessions from China had become urgent. Bowring's former friends in the Lancashire cotton trade wanted China opened up; he was fortified by the clearly indicated sympathy of his old patron in shady business, the Prime Minister. It must have seemed best to go on, and somehow link the *Arrow* incident violently to Britain's disputed treaty right of entry into Canton.

Yet another serious blunder came to light. Though Parkes on

the day in question had *Arrow*'s papers in his office, he had failed to observe that her register had expired, eleven days before. In a letter to Parkes on 11 October Bowring was obliged to admit: 'It appears on examination that *Arrow* had no right to hoist the British flag.' But three days later, Sir John was writing to Viceroy Yeh, 'There is no doubt that the lorcha *Arrow* lawfully bore the British flag, under a register granted by me' – a deliberate untruth which, when it came to light, did his battered reputation no good.

The pressure on Yeh to fill Parkes's demands to the very letter was intensified out of all proportion. The day after Parkes had declined to accept the twelve prisoners in the form they were offered him, the British Admiral, on Parkes's suggestion, seized the Barrier Forts, about four miles downriver from Canton, reporting a 'loss of four or five killed on the part of the Chinese, solely arising from their ill-judged resistance to our forces'. Admiral Seymour also ensconced himself in the forts on Honan Island, opposite the city, thereby cutting off Canton's secondary route to the sea, the Macao Passage.

An ingenious way had been also suggested by Harry Parkes for using a warship's firepower to knock sense into Yeh's head. 'Should [Yeh] still be contumacious ... I think that the residence of his excellency, which is not far from the waterside, should also in that case feel the effects of the bombardment.' Yeh called out his Braves – his local militia. The armed confrontation had begun.

Sitting tight would require nerve, but there was not much else Yeh could do. The million inhabitants of Canton – the forty-three million in the two provinces he governed – hated and feared him as an executioner. Though in the creek villages around Canton Yeh had a force of militia, their experience had been gained fighting against their own rebellious countrymen. They lacked heart. The popular fervour once roused by Commissioner Lin had been demoralized by Yeh's mass executions. Yeh also had over 200 war junks, capable of harassing ships of their own type approaching Canton up the waterways, but helpless against modern men-of-war. And word had just reached him that Chinese rebels were advancing in force upon Canton from the north.

Perhaps one foreign power might be played off against another. But though the French had so far shown no willingness to follow this reckless British lead, and though a few individual Americans might privately sympathize with China, there was in sober reality not much chance of foreign powers helping the Chinese or hindering the British, since in one way or another they all stood to gain by a

British victory. But Bowring and Parkes might get into difficulties of their own making. They had already begun to move on a pretext that carried weight with nobody but themselves. They now proposed to break their way into Canton with a force far too small to hold the huge city down once it was entered. Passive resistance – of which he was a past master – might still win Viceroy Yeh a few weeks or months of grace.

Harry Parkes's brutal hint was taken. Access by British officials to Canton having been formally demanded and formally refused, on 28 October the request was underlined by a bombardment. In the river not far from the city wall, and opposite Yeh's official residence, the steam frigate *Encounter* lay at her moorings. At 1 p.m. *Encounter*'s ten-inch pivot gun began lobbing shells over the wall into Yeh's roof-top at monotonously regular five-minute intervals, and went on until sunset. The bombardment was intended to weaken Yeh's nerve, but the tale soon spread through Canton that their terrifying Viceroy was sitting it out in a chair, unruffled, with a faint smile on his face, reading a book. His subordinates had eventually been obliged to implore him to place himself out of danger.

Another rumour was going the rounds: that when the British attacked, the rebels inside Canton planned to rise up against Yeh. No doubt with a sidelong glance at the former British habit of paying £20 for any dead 'pirate' Yeh offered $30, increased by 25 November to $100, for every chopped-off British head, proclaiming: 'The English barbarians have attacked the provincial city, and wounded and injured our soldiers and people . . . Wherefore I herewith distinctly command you to join together to exterminate them . . . killing them whenever you meet them, whether on shore or in their ships.' A British 'commander' was eventually valued at $5000, and on Harry Parkes's head the Chinese had by 1858 put the huge price of $30 000. The French Consul voiced an immediate objection. Since both French and British were clad in similar foreign garb, they would both look alike to angry Cantonese. 'It is not like this', said Comte de Courcy, primly, 'that civilized nations make war.'

By 29 October an adequate breach had been made in the city wall by slow fire from two British guns mounted across the river, at Dutch Folly. (This and other bombardments cost in all fifty-six Chinese lives.) Viceroy Yeh, to gain time, sent a mandarin to parley with the British. Having a shrewd idea of what else might be worrying the Viceroy, Harry Parkes warned his emissary that 'partisans of the revolutionary factions had intimated their wish to cooperate ... in an attack on the city, but that the Admiral had declined all connection with their proceedings'. Bowring, too, had left his Byronic radicalism behind him in Europe. Men were needed outside the walls of Canton to fetch and carry for the troops, but Bowring turned down a request for the help there of 200 Hong Kong coolies, because 'many ... are notoriously affiliated to the secret political societies'. The British wanted a treaty, but would do nothing to dislodge the Manchus.

Late in November the rebel organizations in Hong Kong tried once more to give their comrades moving in from the countryside a helping hand. One thousand five hundred of them, having laid their hands on shipping, crowded into the mouth of the Pearl River, with the idea of attacking Yeh at the same time as the British, and thereby softening up Canton pending the arrival from inland of the rebel army. But British warships under Captain the Hon. Keith Stewart, RN, forcibly kept this rebel squadron from entering the Bogue. Yeh had succeeded in his intricate policy at least to this extent: the British, unasked, were keeping the rebels at bay for him. But could they take and keep Canton for themselves?

The British entry into Canton through the breach their guns had made was not glorious. Though the Chinese had cannon along the parapet, loaded and aimed, their guns did not even fire as the storming party approached. Except for a little desultory sniping from matchlocks, the two columns, of seamen and Royal Marines, clambered up the debris towards the breach in an uncanny silence.

Commander W. T. Bate, RN, of HMS *Actaeon*, was the first man up, at 3 p.m. on the afternoon of 29 October 1856, and stood in the breach, alone, for a moment, waving the Union Jack. His spectacular gesture was imitated, soon after, by James Keenan, the United States Consul at Hong Kong, who took his turn in the breach, accompanied by a seaman who had been instructed to wave the Star Spangled Banner. Since the United States were strictly neutral, Consul Keenan had, of course, no business whatever to be entering Canton in this irregular if picturesque fashion. But Consul Keenan was magnificently drunk.

A British field-piece, dragged up to the breach and unlimbered there, began to fire down the long straight alley towards Yeh's official residence. Then Admiral Seymour put himself at the head of some marines, and marched down the alley, with Harry Parkes at his side – only to find when they reached Yeh's residence that it was empty. Yeh's gamble was coming off. The British had ships and guns, but to take and effectively hold Canton the Admiral was now estimating – somewhat belatedly – that he would need an army of 5000 men. The force he had brought ashore was put together from his ships' crews; they could make a landing but not form a garrison. Nonplussed, the British marched out through the breach the way they had come in.

This hollow victory confirmed in the Chinese mind an illusion that, not long after, was to cost them dear. The barbarians might be invincible when supported by their ships, but if lured ashore and confronted on land in fair fight it began to look as if they might be defeated.

Next day, Admiral Seymour tried to make the best of it by reminding Viceroy Yeh that 'the lives and property of the entire city are at my mercy, and could be destroyed by me at any moment'. This was true. The battery on Dutch Folly commanded Canton. Admiral Seymour could destroy, but he could not administer. Yeh, keeping cool, riposted with a proclamation to the Cantonese, warning them to 'preserve quiet minds, guard your property ... you should not therefore give way to alarm'.

A desultory bombardment of Canton with shot and shell from HMS *Encounter* and HMS *Sampson* killed a few more Cantonese, but failed to break the stalemate. (When details reached London, the more respectable elements of public opinion were reassured by the information that Admiral Seymour had scrupulously refrained from bombarding on the Sabbath.) From inside Canton the Chinese answered, half-heartedly, with matchlock fire.

Of course, no trade was being done. British merchants, rumoured to be heavily over-stocked with tea, drew comfort from the probability of their being, as usual, compensated in cash once the fighting was over and another indemnity had been extracted from the Chinese. Representatives of Howqua and other Chinese merchants – all hard hit – met Parkes in the Consulate on 12 November 1856. They told him that in their opinion the British claim for direct diplomatic access was reasonable, but, reported Harry Parkes, 'their weight as a class both with authorities and people is far less than we suppose ... the people, particularly the rural population, were opposed to our admission'. Since the old East India Company days, the political centre of gravity in and around Canton had shifted.

The managing partner of Russell & Co., the large American trading house which had been keeping Yeh informed, through

Howqua, of British intentions, was a merchant called Sturgis – a strong advocate of American neutrality. To avoid local clashes that might accidentally align Americans with the British, Mr Sturgis persuaded Commodore Armstrong, commanding the US Navy in China, to send away from Canton both American citizens there, and the US Marines who had been sent up to protect them. His plan turned out badly.

A ship's boat from the American corvette USN *Portsmouth* proceeded upriver on 15 November 1856 with Sturgis himself aboard and a very large Flowery Flag fluttering at the jackstaff. Passing the Barrier Forts – dismantled by the British a month before, but quickly made operational again by the Chinese – the boat was fired on, and a roundshot hit the water ten yards ahead. Sturgis, in chagrin, stood up in the stern, and waved the Stars and Stripes. In answer came another Chinese roundshot, this time even closer. At the same moment, the Chinese battery 400 yards away on the opposite bank opened fire with roundshot and shrapnel.

The official American reaction was contradictory. Dr Peter Parker, writing next day to Sir John Bowring, who had invited him to make a joint demand for diplomatic access to Canton, emphasized that 'the Government of the United States is and must remain *neutral* in the controversy', and by 5 December Yeh himself came through with a full apology. But Commodore Armstrong felt it his duty as a naval officer to resent any insult to the flag, Parkes reporting that the Commodore was 'determined to punish this national affront at once, without previously demanding from the Imperial Commissioner [Yeh] satisfaction or apology'. No palaver: a Sunday punch.

The US attack on the Barrier Forts, though not quite as inglorious as the comic-opera entry of the British into Canton, was unimpressive. The armaments of the Western powers were somehow losing their power to inspire awe.

On Sunday afternoon of 16 November two American corvettes, *Portsmouth* and *Levant*, made their way up the Pearl River towards the Barrier Forts. Now, the Pearl River is as big as the Danube, and was, even in those days, a familiar and well-marked waterway for shipping. But USN *Levant* ran aground before she even got into range. USN *Portsmouth*, in tow of a private steamer, stood fire from the Chinese until she came to anchor within 450 yards of the fort on the right bank, which had aimed the first offending cannon-ball. From her sixteen 64-pounder guns, *Portsmouth* buffeted the Chinese fort with a total of 230 shot. 'The forts,' reported

Commodore Armstrong, 'replied with spirit to this heavy fire, and were not silenced until the attack had been sustained for an hour and three quarters.'

By the time the sun rose next morning, both US warships had gone aground, at low water, and were sitting targets for the Chinese. Commodore Armstrong, feeling ill, returned to his flagship, *San Jacinto*, at Whampoa. There, Dr Peter Parker managed to win him round to the idea of a twenty-four-hour truce, to give time for a written American complaint to reach Yeh.

During this cease-fire, the Chinese managed by prodigious effort to reconstruct the batteries and remount their guns. It took three more days of sustained gunnery, and an amphibious landing in which five Americans were killed, to put the Barrier Forts for the second time out of commission. Things had changed since Pottinger's day.

The Americans who finally captured the Barrier Forts found they were built of granite blocks, ten feet thick, and armed with modern 13-inch guns weighing seven or eight tons apiece. Admiral Seymour reported to the Admiralty that the Chinese loss had been 'very heavy, as they made a most determined defence'.

Twenty British subjects still lingered on at Canton, to represent their firms at what would normally be the height of the tea-shipping season, but only Russell & Co. were still doing business. On the night of 14 December that too came to a sudden end. Chinese incendiaries, just before midnight, running to and fro in the darkness with lighted brands, were fired on in vain by British pickets. The tide was low, so that no water could be pumped up or brought to the fire in buckets. By morning, nearly all the foreign Factories had been burned to the ground. The British Factory, which had come off lightly, was two days later again set on fire, only the chapel and the boathouse remaining. Admiral Seymour entrenched the site; it gave him at least a toehold under the walls of Canton.

Yeh found a way not long after to ease the British warships out of the Pearl River. In January, under cover of night, the Chinese floated down towards their anchorage an ingenious modern variant of the traditional fireship – a series of floating explosive machines, one of which, when caught by a British guard boat, was found to be fitted with 3000 lb of gunpowder. A free-lance American mechanic, known to the Chinese as Jen-lei-ssu, and provided with a 'quiet monastery' near the metal-working city of Fatshan for his experiments, had some years before built the Chinese a prototype of such floating torpedoes. They had come too close for peace of mind. Admiral Seymour retired his ships for the rest of the winter down Macao Creek.

Checkmated in the simple procedure for browbeating the Chinese which had always worked so well in years gone by, Sir John Bowring informed Lord Clarendon, in London, that in his opinion, even though it might take the 5000 men for which Admiral Seymour had asked, Canton must be captured before a treaty revision could be successfully negotiated.

The Chinese irregulars, meanwhile, were managing to kill off stragglers, and the British discouraged them usually by burning to the ground all the huts in the nearest village. On 30 December 1856 the small steamer *Thistle* which brought mail up from Hong Kong was found drifting, afire, with eleven decapitated European corpses in the hold. The Chinese crew, having brought *Thistle* into the Pearl River, had stripped off their working clothes to display underneath the badge of Yeh's volunteer militia. The Chinese passengers that morning were also soldiers in disguise. At a given signal they had killed all the British aboard, and carried off their heads to collect the bounty, by now increased to $100 *per capita*.

By this time Sir John Bowring was not a popular man in London. Though obliged to defend him in public, his political masters were clearly aware that he had opened hostilities on an almost indefensible pretext. He had not managed to carry with him either the Americans or the French. The fleet, which might soon have been employed to threaten the seacoast near Peking, was bogged down indefinitely at Canton. And, as *The Times* was not slow to point out, 'a state of war with China costs us £10 000 000 a year in home revenue and commercial profits'. Harry Parkes and Sir John Bowring, between them, had a great deal to answer for.

Criticism of this new undeclared war with China centred in Parliament, and brought together some uneasy comrades-in-arms. Some were not deeply concerned about China, but all had motives for opposing the government led by Lord Palmerston. Lord Derby, the greatest landowner in Lancashire, and leader of the country gentlemen in the Tory Party, proposed in the House of Lords a motion similar to that moved in the Commons by Richard Cobden, the Manchester radical, Corn Law Repealer and peacemonger during the Crimean War. Gladstone, most effective of the Peelites, spoke and voted in accord with Disraeli, a man he mistrusted all

his life, whose wittily bitter attacks on Peel had broken the old
Tory party in two. Against Palmerston's government the Radicals
and Peelites could expect to carry seventy votes.

John Roebuck, an independent member of Canadian origin
who sat for Sheffield – the man whose attack on incompetent
management in the Crimea had confirmed Palmerston as Prime
Minister – was now in opposition. Lord John Russell opposed the
government on China, though he had represented it at the peace
conference after the Crimea. But this unity was makeshift. There
were Tories who objected to starting a war with China for the
benefit of the cotton trade, and pacifist radicals not yet come to
terms with a world situation in which Lancashire might have to
fight for markets. Though all Evangelical newspapers but one
this time supported the new China war, some critics were High
Churchmen or Evangelicals whose flesh crawled at the thought
of the opium trade. Others were simple-minded backbenchers
who years before had detested the sound of Bowring's voice as he
held forth about decimal coinage.

The British Parliament of 1857 – elected on a limited franchise –
still represented by and large the British upper classes in general,
the men of wealth and power. Conflicts of interest among land,
trade and manufacture were never so fundamental as to menace
the property system itself. Given this essential common ground,
the tone of Parliamentary debate was civil, intelligent and frank,
since there was no mass electorate with votes but no property to
be courted. Lords and Commons were not playing to the gallery –
not yet – so their debates on the *Arrow* scandal were outspoken.

Though the mess Bowring had blundered into at Canton must,
of course, imply on Palmerston's part some degree of connivance,
this trouble in China was unlikely to diminish the Prime Minister's
reputation in the country at large, as a war winner. As people had
come to discover after forty years of it – peace was dull. To enjoy
vicariously the horrors of a war abroad by propping *The Times*
against the marmalade pot before putting in a strenuous day at the
counting-house had been exhilarating. So Palmerston could afford
to speak out, as many of his opponents dare not, in a tone that
deliberately echoed the patriotic fervour of Trafalgar and Waterloo
– a tone not then so much resorted to in politics, though later in
the century it was to become commonplace, until hopelessly
sullied at last in the mud of Flanders.

A Blue Book was made available, indicating the course of
events in China by means of documents, and only mildly edited in
the government's favour – the section listing *Insults from China,*

as was widely pointed out, did not bear scrutiny. Official veils put up to conceal the realities of British policy in China were torn to pieces in the debate. Though the political alliance against Palmerston's government might be so ill-assorted as to be almost disreputable, the tone of the argument was, by and large, cogent and sober, as if at one more dimly apprehended turning-point in Britain's history. And rightly so. This watershed once passed, English Tory was to become an imperialist, British radical as likely as not a jingo, and annexation be looked upon not as shameful but splendid.

Lord Derby – high-mettled, accomplished, indolent, a former Prime Minister who had won £94 000 on the Turf – set a high tone for the Opposition in the Lords. 'I am an advocate for weakness against power,' he asserted, 'for perplexed and bewildered barbarism against the arrogant demands of over-weening self-styled civilization.' Derby characterized the *Arrow* incident as 'the most despicable cause of war that has ever occurred'.

Lord Derby's speech carried weight, though his implied condemnation of his own country may have irked the diehards. The bishops' vote in a close-run thing like this would be worth consideration. Though only six Anglican bishops were in attendance, they would have proxies in their pockets for a dozen more. But bishops in a State church, depending on the government for preferment, were politically timid – and for ten years Church patronage had been in Whig hands. Lord Derby therefore brought all the powers of his eloquence to bear on 'the servants of Him who came to bring "peace on earth and goodwill among men" ... the especial guardians of religion and virtue'.

Edmund Hammond was officially available in the House to help out his Minister, Lord Clarendon, during anxious moments in the debate. After noticing how Derby's appeal had gone home to the representatives of the Church, Hammond scribbled Clarendon the following note: 'A report judiciously circulated as to the declining health of the Archbishop of Canterbury would probably neutralize the effect of Lord Derby's wordy peroration as regards the Bench of Bishops.' With a vacancy likely to occur at the very top, no worldly-minded bishop would risk giving a vote disagreeable to the government. With cheerful cynicism Hammond's note went on: '... a similar report, contradicted on Friday, as to the contemplated appropriation of vacant Garters might not be

without its effect'. However immense his rent-roll and exalted his
hereditary rank, a peer was usually susceptible to the Order of the
Garter, the most highly regarded of royal honours: the vague promise might conjure a handful of votes.

Lord Shaftesbury, the philanthropist who years before had
denounced the opium traffic to such effect, this time gave his vote
to Palmerston, though he had misgivings, noting in his diary:
'A sad result. Right or wrong, the government must be supported
to bring these matters to a satisfactory close. Hope and believe
that God, having employed P [Palmerston] as an instrument of
good, would maintain him. But his ways are inscrutable.' Palmerston had latterly given Shaftesbury the final word on ecclesiastical
appointments – and though Shaftesbury might fervently believe
that 'opium and Christianity could not enter China together' the
secret influence he had been enjoying over the appointment of
bishops proved enough this time to make him hesitate.

The Earl of Clarendon, on whom the brunt of answering
Derby fell, was a clever, hard-working Minister – eventually, he
worked himself to death – who shared Palmerston's ideas on
foreign policy heart and soul, and had been his protégé. Indeed, a
quarter of a century before, in 1831, Clarendon and Bowring had
been sent together on a confidential mission to France. Later
Bowring made it his business to procure for Clarendon the bottle
of Jordan Water with which all Clarendon's children were baptized
(and, for that matter, purveyed to Queen Victoria herself a bottle
of the same invaluable fluid). But Clarendon was, for a diplomat,
a little over-inclined to let the mask slip, and blurt out what
actually was in his mind. (His career was almost blighted, for
example, when word reached Queen Victoria that Lord Clarendon
was in the habit of referring to her jocularly as 'the Missus'.)
Lord Clarendon made a brave try at mustering what arguments
the government could decently employ in its own defence -- mainly,
an appeal for loyalty to the men on the spot – when, impulsively,
he let his real opinion show: 'In dealing with a nation like the
Chinese, if we intend to preserve any amicable or useful relations
with them, we must make them sensible of the law of force,
and must appeal to them in the manner which alone they can
appreciate.' Though Palmerston might think the same, he would
dress it up better.

The lawyers had their long, technical and inconclusive dispute
about *Arrow*'s right to be treated as a British ship, then Malmesbury,
formerly the Tories' Foreign Secretary, made a telling attack
upon Bowring's common honesty, pointing out exactly how he had

misled both Yeh and Admiral Seymour as to the facts. In a House where personal honour was not yet an outworn notion, this argument struck home.

Lord Ellenborough, who had warned the British government to keep its hands off the opium trade when he was Governor-General of India in Pottinger's day, now kept up this personal attack upon Bowring. But he took it too far. Bowring during his years as a part-time spy had been accorded an honorary doctorate by Göttingen University, for his 'services to literature'. Bowring would much rather it had been an Ll.D. – in fact, he wore Ll.D. robes when negotiating with the King of Siam – and he had always clung, rather pathetically, to the unEnglish title of Doctor. Ignoring Bowring's recent elevation to the order of knighthood, Ellenborough with savage petulance called him 'Doctor' in every second sentence. This sounded unfair, and robbed Ellenborough's important argument of its impact: 'He has disregarded the instructions of four successive Secretaries of State, supported, as I suppose he is ... by an influence with the government which I cannot comprehend.'

Ellenborough went on to explain, from his Indian experience, exactly how war with China would dislocate not merely British but international trade: 'The cotton of America, the staple of our greatest manufacture, is paid for by bills upon England. Those bills are taken by the Americans to Canton, where they are paid away for tea. The Chinese give them to the opium merchants, by whom they are taken to India, there exchanged for other commodities, and they furnish ultimately the money remittances of private fortunes and the funds for carrying on the Indian government at home.' So much for any hope the Chinese might still have of cutting themselves off from a hostile outer world!

One of the bishops – Samuel Wilberforce of Oxford – spoke and voted for Derby's motion, and he also voted two proxies. The rest of the bench of bishops cast votes and proxies solidly for the government. How many suffrages were privately obtained by dangling the Garter is hard to ascertain. The motion was lost in the Lords by 110 votes to 146, but the government's nerve was shaken.

When Richard Cobden put his motion in the House of Commons, he was sensitive to the taunt of having turned against Bowring after a political alliance of twenty years – but who could have supposed Bowring would turn, overnight, from pacifist to imperialist? Cobden argued shrewdly that if *Arrow* had been moored at Charleston instead of in the Canton River – Americans in South

Carolina having, not long since, claimed the right to board British ships in harbour there to recapture runaway slaves – any British consul acting as high-handedly as Parkes had done would have been disowned.

From his scrutiny of the Blue Book, Cobden drew the same inference as Lord Ellenborough that 'the check previously held over our representative was withdrawn', adding perceptively, 'something must have taken place to lead our Plenipotentiary to suppose that if we got into conflict with the Chinese on the question of entering Canton, it would not be unfavourably regarded at home'.

The Peelites kept up a fire on the opium traffic, Sir James Graham describing the inhabitants of Hong Kong as 'the off-scourings of the opium trade' and Sidney Herbert pointing out, reasonably enough, that although Yeh might have flouted Britain's treaty right to enter Canton, the British themselves were 'in the habitual violation at this moment of a treaty which says that all our efforts shall be used for the suppression of the opium trade'. Roebuck, the Canadian radical, emphasized ironically that the Chinese were civilized, but 'their civilization is of a peculiar kind ... they have not applied their intelligence to the art of war'.

Brickbats in the debate were all aimed at Bowring and Parkes. In the public mythology Admirals were sacrosanct – a sentiment that did little for naval efficiency – so Sir Michael Seymour came out of the hurly burly unbruised. Samuel Gregson, MP for Lancaster and Chairman of the East India and China Association – a pressure group directly influencing about twenty MPS of all parties – introduced a letter from twenty-nine China merchants, and indignantly denied that a single one of them was involved in the opium trade. He had already told Clarendon at a private interview what his members would regard as a suitable treaty with China. (Some of them, from Manchester, wanted to annex Shanghai.)

Opium had, of course, its own distinguished representative in the House: Sir James Matheson, Bart., MP for Ross and Cromarty, but Matheson chose neither to speak in the debate, nor to vote. His kinsman and business associate, Alexander Matheson, MP for Inverness, kept his own counsel, but voted with the Noes.

Robert Lowe, Paymaster to the Forces, who had started his political career in Australia, tried to echo Macaulay's famous speech in the earlier Opium War debate, but badly overdid it, describing the piece of bunting hauled down (if indeed it was) from *Arrow*'s mizzen gaff as 'this very flag brave men had held to their breast and glued there with their best heart's blood rather

229

than surrender it on the field of battle even to a gallant enemy'.

Though critics of the government had the best of the argument inside the House, in the longer run their stance was politically vulnerable, since they appeared to be scoring points off their own country for the sake of what, to most middle-class voters of the Pecksniff or Podsnap type, was a remote, slightly comic and possibly despicable Oriental Empire.

Gladstone – who since the bad news came from Hong Kong had been in a state of intense nervous excitement – gave expression in his powerful two-hour speech to the inner thoughts of the more conscience-stricken MPs. Gladstone made a complete job of fastening responsibility not on the eccentric behaviour of Bowring and Parkes, but on the secret intentions of the government. 'The policy for which Sir John Bowring has clumsily chosen his opportunity for carrying into effect was a policy not unknown to Her Majesty's Government, or by them disapproved ... in case of need, the force of the British fleet was to be available.' Gladstone soon gave voice to his preoccupation with opium. 'Your greatest and most valuable trade in China is ... in opium. It is a smuggling trade ... it is the worst, the most pernicious, demoralizing and destructive of all the contraband trades that are carried upon the surface of the globe.'

Palmerston as he rose to reply was not at his best. He had a cold and was suffering from gout. In his seventy-third year, and in office for nearly half a century, he was a unique political survivor of the generation which had fought and defeated Napoleon. Palmerston had about him still the air of an ageing Regency buck; much of this new-fangled moral earnestness went past his head. This time he misjudged the tone of the occasion, and his habitual little jokes fell flat.

He twitted his radical opponents mildly by praising Bowring as 'essentially a man of the people' who had raised himself 'by his own talents, by his own attainments, by his own industry, by his public service'. Yeh, by contrast, was 'one of the most savage barbarians that ever disgraced a nation ... guilty of every crime which can degrade and debase human nature'. He typified Cobden's speech as saying, in effect, 'everything that was English was wrong' and did his best by attacking Cobden to split some of the Tories away from their incongruous Radical allies.

To throw the anti-opium hunt off his track, Palmerston trailed a large and impudent red herring. The war, he implied, was not in favour of the present drug traffic, but against it. But for the hostilities provoked by Yeh in Canton 'we should have been in communi-

230

cation with the Government of France – and I think the United
States would have joined with us – with a view to sending a friendly
diplomatic mission to Peking ... for securing more extended
commercial relations with them ... The existing restrictions on our
commerce are one cause of that trade in opium to which [Sidney
Herbert] so dexterously alluded last night for the purpose of
catching some stray votes ... we can pay for our purchases only
partly in goods, the rest we must pay in opium and silver.'

Disraeli's speech for the Tories was devoid of any emotion,
pious or patriotic, but full of political acumen. To him the peaceably inclined back-benchers of his own party were rather stupid
fellows, unable yet to grasp their Imperial responsibilities, and he
proceeded to enlighten them, at the same time as damning the
government as incompetent in what it had set out to do.

Disraeli saw the trouble at Canton as an attempt, with government approval, 'by force to increase our commercial relations
with the East'. But was force the way to succeed? 'Since the time
when our Clives and Hastings founded our Indian Empire ...
great Powers have been brought in contact with us in the East.
We have the Russian Empire and the American Republic there,
and a system of political compromise has developed itself like
the balance of power in Europe ... you are as likely not to extend
your commerce, but to excite the jealousy of powerful States, and
involve yourself in hostilities with nations not inferior to your
own.' Disraeli's approach was not clearly distinguishable from
Palmerston's. He too wanted 'a policy of combination with other
powerful European states ... to influence the conduct of the
Chinese by negotiations and treaties'.

Sensing already that the debate was won, and the government
liable to fall, Disraeli taunted Palmerston, 'Let the Noble Lord
not only complain to the country, let him appeal to the country ...
I shall be most happy to meet him on the hustings ... I should
like to see the programme of the proud leader of the Liberal Party.
"No Reform! New Taxes! Canton Blazing!" '

The uncongenial bloc of Radicals, Peelites and Tories managed
to carry their vote of censure by 263 votes to 247 – a majority of
16. Forty-eight Liberals from the Radical wing of the party
had taken Cobden's side; twenty-five Tories had voted against
their party leaders in favour of what no doubt seemed to them
the patriotic side of the question. Palmerston dissolved the House,
having decided, with brilliant cynicism, to fight an election on the
Arrow incident. He knew he had one strong card. Arguments in a
British General Election are never on such a high moral and

intellectual plane as were speeches in a mid-nineteenth-century Parliament.

Gladstone himself described that vote of censure in his diary afterwards as 'doing more honour to the House of Commons than any I remember'. But Queen Victoria, 38 years old and eight months pregnant, was reported by her beloved Prince Albert to be 'grieved at the success of evil party motives, spite, and total lack of patriotism'. She was glad of Palmerston's decision to force an election, since its alternative, a prolonged reshuffling of the Ministry, in which she would have to play a constitutional role, would have been most exhausting.

Palmerston held to his course undeflected, asserting on 5 March 1857, with a touch of the combative pluck which endeared him to ordinary Englishmen, 'There will be no change, and there can be no change, in the policy of the government with respect to China.' Palmerston was well aware that underlying all the speeches in Parliament that defended China – sometimes from generosity, sometimes on a calculation of political advantage – lay one huge fallacy: that the Chinese, having signed the Treaty of Nanking under duress, were willing to keep its pledges. He knew that the Chinese wanted to avoid diplomatic contact, and to evade treaty provisions. They simply did not regard European civilization as a model to follow, nor its rules of conduct as binding.

What Bowring and Parkes had so clumsily begun in Canton, objectively considered, at least gave the maritime powers the chance they had manoeuvred for: to force open yet more widely the door into China. Let the British bear the blame for their violent clumsiness – through that door would pass the opium and missionaries and manufactured goods which were bound, in time, to break up China's traditional economy, enfeeble the spiritual basis of the Emperor's sovereignty, and even – as opium addiction spread – weaken China's physical and moral power to resist. Disraeli had pointed out the way things would go: Manchu China a semi-colony, nominally intact but broken-willed, and with her resources and riches at the easy disposal of a consortium of foreign powers.

Even before he was sure how votes in the General Election would be cast, Palmerston had confidently ordered troops from Mauritius and Madras to China. Not wholly trusting his ally, the Emperor Louis Napoleon, he expressed a certain unwillingness for 'the new Enfield rifle' to be sent to China, in case the French might discover how good it was. Palmerston also picked out carefully a new plenipotentiary, one more acceptable to Parliament. Bowring could count himself lucky to be left to govern Hong Kong.

Britain's paramount representative in China would be henceforth the Earl of Elgin and Kincardine, a Scottish peer, a college friend of Gladstone's and, latterly, a conspicuous success as Governor-General of Canada.

Communications between Canton and London now went twice as fast as they had in Lord Napier's day. The electric telegraph ran from London to Alexandria and Basra, and spanned India from Bombay to Rangoon. Trains would soon run across the Isthmus of Suez, and P & O steamers from Calcutta carried to China not only passengers, but valuable cargoes of small bulk like silver and opium, and at speeds which broke all the records set up by the famous clippers. Not only could British officials in China be kept on a shorter rein, but what the Chinese did was more quickly known in London. News of a spectacular terrorist act in Hong Kong, for which Viceroy Yeh was promptly given the blame, though it failed to sway the vote in Parliament, was to influence powerfully the election which followed.

Chinese rebels had used Hong Kong for years as an uneasy sanctuary – a place where their revolutionary societies were well organized, and Yeh's writ did not run. But Yeh could bring a certain influence to bear on the island, by combining threats to those Chinese who still had relatives on the mainland with an appeal to anti-foreign sentiment. After the attack on Canton, the Chinese servants on Hong Kong began, at Yeh's prompting, to withdraw their labour, leaving the foreigners in a state of domestic helplessness. There was even anxious talk of the island's food supplies being cut off.

Hong Kong at the New Year of 1857 was in an apprehensive mood. However disreputable their business might be made to sound in London, Jardine, Matheson & Co. had no difficulty in borrowing from the Royal Navy an armed force of blue-jackets and marines, to guard their valuable opium stocks against surprise attack. Men went about their business armed with a Colt revolver, and, on 15 January, to all the homes on the island came panic. Four hundred Europeans, who that morning had eaten bread supplied by the E-sing bakery, were taken ill: each four-pound loaf contained nearly a grain of arsenic.

Nobody in fact died as a direct result of poison, since the dose was too large to be kept down. The master baker, Cheong A Lum, had left for the day to Macao, but came back and stood trial – his

233

own family were poisoned, too. Eventually Cheong was acquitted for lack of evidence, only to be re-arrested on leaving court. He was clearly not the culprit.

But somebody had poisoned the bread. As well as giving Palmerston a deafening electoral argument – that the Chinese were 'a set of kidnapping, murdering, poisoning barbarians' – this act of terrorism provoked an ugly panic on Hong Kong amid the European minority. Fifty-two of the baker's men were put under arrest – Bowring, to his credit, standing out against a vociferous demand to have them lynched. Before being brought to trial, guilty and innocent alike were made to suffer. On a plea that other cells were full, all fifty-two prisoners were crammed into a room fifteen feet square and twelve feet high – forty-two of them, those against whom there was least evidence, being kept in this 'Black Hole of Hong Kong' in an intermingled mass of sweltering flesh for nineteen days. The police surgeon put his foot down, at last, about the risk of infection, and they were moved to cells. Ten stood trial, forty-two were released – only to be re-arrested, like Cheong, at the police station door, as 'suspected persons', though eventually set free (after a petition signed by British and Chinese alike) on condition they left the colony. While the panic ran its course, over 500 arrests were made – 204 of 'suspicious-looking characters' and 146 on 'secret information'. A total of 167 Hong Kong Chinese were transported to the island of Hainan.

In reply to American and French consular protests about the mass poisoning attempt, Viceroy Yeh washed his hands of it. He blandly told Dr Peter Parker that 'doubtless there are many Chinese whose hatred against the English has been much increased ... but to poison people in this underhand manner is an act worthy of detestation'. With Comte de Courcy, Yeh finessed, declaring: 'Whoever he is, the author of this poisoning is an abominable creature, but since he is in Hong Kong I find it difficult to proceed against him.'

Reacting to this breakdown in the rule of law, ordinary Chinese left Hong Kong *en masse*. In 1857 the total of voluntary Chinese emigrants, many of them prosperous and most going to California or Australia, increased to 26 213, or nearly half the island's population. The British fleet had been pushed away from the walls of Canton, and was waiting irresolutely in back waterways for the artillery and troops which Admiral Seymor had told Calcutta were essential. The British had lost the initiative; on Hong Kong they had even, at one moment, lost their nerve. Yeh's policy of masterly inactivity was thus far a success.

In the British General Election of 1857 rational considerations, never prominent in any electoral campaign, were for once almost totally lost sight of in skilfully conjured-up myth. Palmerston was developing a high-spirited pantomime style of electioneering to bewilder and bemuse inexperienced voters as they became enfranchised, which served its turn as a handy way of winning votes at least until the Khaki Election of 1919.

Palmerston used Yeh as an Aunt Sally. His election address in Tiverton – circulated in thousands of copies and quoted everywhere by Liberal candidates – hammered into the heads of voters that 'an insolent barbarian wielding authority at Canton has violated the British flag, broken the engagements of treaties, offered rewards for the heads of British subjects in that part of China, and planned their destruction by murder, assassination and poisons'. Would the Opposition now 'follow the logic of their argument', he asked the City of London, 'rebuild the forts of Canton with cannon from Woolwich, and pay for the arsenic in the bread of Hong Kong?'

After their breakfast-table thrills during the Crimean War, strong sensation went down well with middle-class voters, and this they got in good measure. A medical man called Dr Gourlay, writing to Lord Clarendon from an address in Regent's Park, offered his services to persuade George Cruikshank, the celebrated cartoonist – who had a known relish for scenes of cruelty – to help the Liberal cause with engravings showing the atrocities that the Chinese practiced upon one another. By 24 March Dr Gourlay was able to report to the Foreign Office: 'I have much satisfaction in informing you that our modern Hogarth Mr Geo. Cruikshank is now busily engaged in sketching some of the Chinese legal barbarities ... illustrating their punishments of Starving to death, Disjointing, Chopping to Pieces, Tearing the Body asunder by pullies, Skinning alive &c &c.'

Against emotive catch-phrases, sadistic images and blood-curdling atrocity stories not much headway could be made by such commonsense arguments as Sir James Graham put forward at Carlisle: 'The real object is to drug the people of China with opium, and the effect of it here is to enhance the price of tea.' Sensing the public mood, Cobden spoke less and less about China, and tried to change his tune. He lost his seat at Huddersfield, even so, as Bright, Milner-Gibson, and Layard lost theirs: by their opportunistic alliance with the Tories, the most prominent radicals were swept clean out of Parliament. Lord Palmerston had a majority over all his opponents put together of eighty-five seats, in the greatest landslide since the Reform Bill, twenty-five years before.

In China national issues were clarified by a mode of discussion not far inferior to a Parliamentary debate, and, for all its Court manoeuvring and stylized deference to the Emperor, rather more scrupulous than Palmerston's electioneering.

Any mandarin could exercise his right to submit a memorial on public policy to Peking, and many did. Missives from important officials in high office of course got most attention, but from this varied inflow of educated opinion Peking could modify its policy. Memorials were sifted by the Grand Council, a number of them came under the Emperor's eye, and some received notation from his Vermilion Pencil. (To judge by these written comments, the young Emperor, for all his debauchery, was more sharply anti-foreign than some of his officials.)

When Parliamentary debates on China later reached Peking in translation, the Chinese – who were used to discussing policy more discreetly – concluded, quite wrongly, that the British must be bluffing: 'Those who make war keep silent about their proposed movements; everything is talked over and done in secret.'

The Chinese had a much clearer idea by now of the countries pushing open their door. Geographical information was much more complete than in Commissioner Lin's day – partly thanks to Lin's own efforts – and foreign newspapers were eagerly sought after. Nations who came to China on business were easily accounted for, but the French were a puzzle. They have 'no great concern with trade', went on one confidential report, 'but are active in propagating Catholicism. Their soldiers are able, and their cannon effective.' Only 'after persistent enquiry' in September 1855 did Viceroy Yeh manage to discover why the French bought so little tea in Canton: 'It has been found that this country's everyday hot drink is called coffee.' The Chinese decided, wrongly of course, that the French – whom they knew had in their time helped the Americans against the British and the British against the Russians – must simply be mercenaries: 'Whenever any western country takes up arms against anyone, these barbarians hire themselves out.'

If Imperial Edicts that were made public had an unyielding tone, this was not necessarily because high Manchu officials were ignorant, but because they knew themselves powerless. 'Although these barbarians have all the characteristics of human beings', a memorial declared, 'they are unusually cruel and cunning, and depend on the strength of their ships and the superiority of their cannon.' For China, disrupted by civil war, an efficient modern army obviously implied a thriving modern economy. Until that day came, Chinese statesmen had only two resources against the barbarian at the gate. They could take the risk, as Lin had done, of stimulating popular armed resistance. Or they could try, somehow, to limit the impact of the maritime powers, by playing off one against another, following the classic principle: 'Use barbarians to curb barbarians.' In this hope they were to be frustrated, since however much the foreign powers might differ with each other elsewhere in the world, they all agreed in wanting to exploit China.

There was also by now a minority of Chinese who prospered directly by foreign trade, and had secretly changed their allegiance from China to the foreigner. They, of course, saw concession as inevitable and resistance as impossible. But what foreigners in the late 1850s came to regard as a clear-cut War Party and Peace Party in Peking appear rather to have been shifting groups of high officials, differing at a given moment about the possibility and timeliness of resistance.

Chinese efforts to lay their hands on modern weapons were, in any event, being outstripped all the time by the development in the West of newer military techniques. A couple of years later, when the Chinese were desperately trying to hold up the advance of a modern European army equipped with Armstrong guns, breech-loading rifles and incendiary rockets, a memorial reporting supplies despatched to the front has a pathetically improvised air: 1000 fusiliers, 1000 archers, 2300 remounts from the Imperial Stud at Shang-tu, 1000 fowling pieces levied, 1000 bows, 50 000 arrows, 1000 quivers. There was no better to be had, and high Chinese officials knew it. Behind a façade of ancient ceremonial and tactical concession, their policies had a realistic core. There were differences of emphasis on the best way to fight back, but no Chinese statesman of the time did other than mistrust the West.

Lord Elgin, the new plenipotentiary to China appointed by Parliament in 1856 to replace Bowring and placate public opinion, had been at Christ Church, Oxford, not only with Gladstone, but with 'Clemency' Canning, son of the former Prime Minister.

(Canning's nickname was earned when, as Governor-General of India, he refused to let sepoy mutineers be lynched or tortured. The less polite label attached to the handful of Englishmen who took a similar stance was 'white niggers'.) Sidney Herbert, the conscience-stricken politician who helped Florence Nightingale push through her drastic reform of army medical services, was another of Lord Elgin's Oxford contemporaries.

Theirs was a generation of earnest, pious, highly intelligent men, bred on mathematics and the classics, heirs, some of them, to wealth made in the cruel pioneer days of the Industrial Revolution, and therefore to the sense of guilt that went with it. They were affected by the intense High Anglicanism prevailing at Oxford in their time, and all were deeply influenced in their student days by the philosophical insights of Coleridge as to a proper relation between Church and State.

Coleridge, who mistrusted the utilitarian money-grubbers bred in such numbers by industrialism, had called, in his *On the Constitution of the Church and State* (1830) – the one significant addition to Conservative political theory since Burke – for a self-sacrificing and cultured elite: the 'clerisy', men who would be equal to the crisis of their times. The motive, secret or declared, of Elgin's confident and pious young Oxford contemporaries, was to impregnate politics with the spirit of Christianity. Though obliged to accept that business interests now had a preponderant weight in the British power structure, they were inclined to think businessmen too shortsighted and too greedy to govern a great empire with effective humanity.

Though Elgin's tone in public, like Canning's, was patrician, Lord Elgin had come across the seamy side of life rather early. His eccentric and hideously disfigured father, the seventh Earl, a former Ambassador in Constantinople, had almost bankrupted the family estate by borrowing ready money from Levantine usurers at high interest, so as to purchase Greek marbles – particularly the sculptures of Phidias, which he caused to be hacked off the façade of the Parthenon. The Elgin Marbles were eventually bought in for the British Museum at about half what they had cost him, and to escape his creditors Elgin was obliged, in 1820, to cross the Channel to France. The present Lord Elgin, as a boy in Paris, had sharpened his wits, perfected his French, and braced himself for a lifetime of thrift. (Despite the coalmines on their Fifeshire estate, his father's debts – and this in the heyday of coal – were not paid off until 1870.)

Young Elgin grew up – and, at 14, was sent to Eton – at a

time when Byron's scathing and damning verses in *Childe Harold* about his own father were not infrequently on men's lips:

> ... the modern Pict's ignoble boast
> To rive what Goth, and Turk, and time hath spared:
> Cold as the crags upon his native coast,
> His mind as barren, and his heart as hard
> Is he whose head conceiv'd, whose hand prepar'd
> Aught to displace Athena's poor remains.

In Broomhall, the family seat, rebuilt in the Greek style fashionable at the end of the eighteenth century, hung like permanent reminders the sword of a heroic ancestor, Robert the Bruce, as well as certain marble fragments too insignificant to reach the British Museum, which were used as paperweights. The glittering prizes of a political career promised Elgin most, but the Scottish peerage he inherited in 1842 gave no automatic right to a seat in the House of Lords, yet blocked him off from a career in the Commons. Elgin was lucky enough, at the age of 30, when badly in need of a paying job, to be appointed Governor of Jamaica, and the success he made of it sent him up the ladder to Canada.

Elgin was an astute diplomat, with a knack of detaching himself from the parties in a conflict, and imposing his will finally, as arbiter. In Canada, where his instinctive use of French reassured the Québecois, he caused a mild sensation by inviting to dinner the French-Canadian radical Papineau, who earlier had raised an armed insurrection against the British ('a very well-bred, intelligent man', Elgin informed his wife). This was no Henry Pottinger: Lord Elgin was about the best that Britain could send.

In London there were, apparently, misgivings about his nerve (which Elgin later went out of his way to contradict by keeping unnecessarily close to the fighting) so that, though he threatened to resign over the issue, Lord Elgin was not to have the troops in his full control. The plenipotentiary would decide when force might be necessary, and the military commanders were to carry through the operation. Elgin was also forbidden by his instructions to move troops inland, away from the ships. This would prevent him, for example, from marching on Peking, since gunboats could make their way up the Peh-ho River only as far as Tientsin.

Having decided to avenge the martyrdom of Father Chapdelaine, the French agreed to continue their armed alliance with Britain, begun in the Crimea. Napoleon III sent out as his special representative Baron Gros, an expert professional diplomat with a long career behind him in Latin America. Gros made a good impression in China. Elgin got on well with him, and the Chinese observed at once that his ears were of a particularly lucky shape.

Lord Elgin travelled to China the quick way – he was the first passenger of note on the new railroad across Suez – but Baron Gros, sent out by warship, was obliged to pitch and toss his way uncomfortably around the Cape in a large but ill-designed French screw-frigate, *Audacieuse*. Elgin therefore reached Hong Kong in July, three months before his French colleague. And he arrived empty-handed – without the troops that Admiral Seymour had so urgently demanded.

In May 1857, when he called into Ceylon, rumours had reached Elgin of a mutinous outbreak, three weeks before, among sepoys in the Ganges valley. His first idea was to hurry through his China mission, and go to Canning's aid later. But at Singapore, Elgin was met by an urgent cry for help. In the 750 miles between Agra and Calcutta, reported Canning, there were scarcely 1000 European troops. The mood at Singapore, too, was nervous: among the Chinese there had been anti-British disturbances – there were 70 000 Chinese in Singapore, and not one European who could speak their language.

India came first. Elgin at once diverted to Calcutta the 5th Regiment, due from Mauritius, and the 90th Regiment, coming out from England; 1700 men in all. Before leaving Singapore, Elgin satisfied his curiosity by visiting an opium den. 'They are wretched, dark places,' he wrote on 8 June, 'with little lamps . . . The opium looks like treacle, and the smokers are haggard and stupefied, except at the moment of inhaling, when an unnatural brightness sparkles from their eyes.'

Reaching Hong Kong a month later, Lord Elgin did not find himself in very congenial company. His instructions were to go north to the Peh-ho, along with any other diplomats who might be willing to follow his lead, but the appointed representatives of France, America and Russia were not due in Hong Kong for some months, and men on the spot, enraged by Yeh, thought that he should be dealt with first. Henry Parkes's view was that Victory at Canton was a necessary preliminary to negotiations in the north: 'With the fall of that city – a punishment upon it long wanted – hostilities may end, and the Emperor . . . consent to receive a representative at Peking.'

A cutting-out exploit in Fatshan Creek, cleverly led by the dashing Commodore Keppel, in which over a hundred of Yeh's war junks had been captured or destroyed, had so exhilarated Admiral Seymour that he was 'strong on the point that Canton is the only place where we ought to fight'. An address presented on behalf of eighty-five local merchants by Dent the opium magnate stipulated that there should be negotiations with Peking only after the capture of Canton, and urged 'the complete humiliation of the Cantonese'. As Lord Elgin wryly noted in his journal, '. . . there is here an *idée fixe* that nothing ought to be done till there has been a general massacre at Canton'. But though he could see the problem clearly, without troops he was helpless.

Lord Elgin to begin with fought shy of Harry Parkes ('clever, but exceedingly overbearing in his manner to the Chinese'), though later he came to acknowledge the young linguist's unusual ability. Parkes for his own part did not at first consider Lord Elgin a great man. 'He may be a man that suits the government well, very cautious, having ever before him Parliament, the world, the public etc.' These private notions of Harry Parkes's carried weight; he was not long afterwards reporting confidentially to Hammond at the Foreign Office that the Chinese were misinterpreting Lord Elgin's leniency.

The most insupportable person at Hong Kong was Sir John Bowring – criticized, superseded, but still holding an office which in his view gave him the right to deluge Lord Elgin with torrential monologues of advice. Elgin was resisting, in his own mind, this local bloody-mindedness. His duty as he saw it was to get his new treaty with the smallest loss of life and the least damage to the Chinese Imperial régime. Meditating the bad news of the Indian Mutiny, and its probable effects on his China mission, Elgin had written in his journal – his safety-valve, where the cautious diplomat could be frank with himself – 'Can I do anything to prevent England from calling down on herself God's curse for brutalities committed on another feeble Oriental race? Or are all my exertions to result only in an extension of the area over which Englishmen are to exhibit how hollow and superficial are both their civilization and their Christianity?'

Rather than fritter away more time in Hong Kong, Lord Elgin having sampled opinion there decided to knock together a scratch force from the fleet – 300 marines, and a naval brigade of seamen – and go in person to Calcutta, in the 50-gun *Shannon*, where the unexpected arrival of reinforcements from oversea might have a strong moral effect. This naval brigade and a battery of *Shannon*'s 68-pounders were later to be successful in keeping open lines of communication on the great Indian rivers, up to Allahabad and Delhi.

1857 was the year in India when the exuberant confidence of Pottinger's day turned on at least one occasion to blue funk. Lord Dalhousie, the Governor-General whom Canning had come out to replace, was a monster of logic and energy. British India represented a huge market for cotton goods; the quicker it could be unified by railroads, telegraphs, proper law-courts and an anglicized educational system, the better the needs of progress would be served. But all this rapid modernization, by shaking them out of their ancestral mode of life, roused the prejudices of millions of Indians. Christian missionaries were, at the same time, driving hard for converts, so Dalhousie's modernization seemed to portend also the extinction of India's traditional religions, Moslem and Hindu. In the spring of 1857, after Dalhousie had left, the day of reckoning came.

India had in a military sense been held down cheaply. Since Moslem and Hindu were, historically, always at odds – with neither Moslem nor Hindu sparing much love for Sikh or Gurkha, either – it required only a moderate skill in deployment for rule in this vast country to be enforced with a minimum of expensive white regiments. Indian policed Indian; but Dalhousie, a parsimonious administrator, pushed this kind of economy beyond its limits. He had not realized that the reverse might also be true: if Moslem and Hindu regiments somehow discovered common ground, the British grip on India would be lost.

Indian opponents of modernity began to conspire with this in mind – particularly the entourage of the recently deposed King of Oudh, and Moslem puritans of the Wahabi sect, operating from the opium city of Patna. As their agents tried to work on the minds of sepoys of both religions, the British Army command in its blindness provided them with a grievance Moslem and Hindu could share.

Brown Bess, the British Army's old smooth-bore musket, had in the Crimean War been outmoded by a weapon with a rifled bore which shot further and hit harder. The Enfield rifle, now to be issued to the sepoy army, worked on the muzzle-loading principle, like the old musket, but the cartridge had to be greased to ease it down the rifling. A bazaar rumour circulated that this grease was specially concocted from both beef and pork, so as to contaminate the religious purity of Moslem and Hindu both at once. Protestant Christianity had no food tabus: once ritually unclean, Moslem and Hindu, said the rumour, would be open to conversion. The disturbing prospect was enough to unite the sepoys of both religions in mutiny. The longstanding belief in British invincibility had already been shattered by a humiliating defeat fifteen years before in Afghanistan. With bewildering quickness, the military basis of Britain's century-old authority in India was put in jeopardy.

The sepoys were prompted to fortify Delhi and to install there the last representative of the old Moghul dynasty. What had begun as an army mutiny took on the aspect of a rebellion. For a few critical months in 1857, India might have been sliding from Britain's grasp. Peking took note, and those Chinese who believed in the possibility of armed resistance came to the fore.

Lord Elgin arrived in Calcutta with his naval brigade not long after Panic Sunday, 14 June, when on a false and improbable rumour of a sepoy rising at Barrackpore, the city's entire white population had either rushed for safety to Fort William or got hastily aboard shipping in the river. 'There was hardly a countenance in Calcutta,' Elgin noted, 'save that of the Governor-General, Lord Canning, which was not blanched with fear.'

Tales coming down the Ganges valley, especially from Oudh, had emphasized sepoy atrocities, and given them highly alarming sexual overtones which though fascinating to the Victorian mind were in almost every case untrue. Even to professed Christians the most cruel riposte seemed justified. That upright man Colonel John Nicholson, the hero of Delhi, wrote thus to his brother-in-arms, Colonel Edwardes, in May 1857: 'Let us propose a Bill for the flaying alive, impalement or burning of the murderers of the women and children at Delhi. The idea of simply hanging the perpetrators of such atrocities is maddening.'

Colonel James Neill, a strict, 47-year-old Presbyterian commanding the 2nd Madras European Regiment, on each night of his march towards Cawnpore filled his journal with detailed but imaginary accounts of the rape and mutilation of Englishwomen. When ordering Indian prisoners on 25 June 1857 to clean out the cell at Cawnpore where Englishwomen had been murdered, Colonel Neill felt it his duty to specify that as each prisoner in turn was put to work, 'the task will be made as revolting to his feelings as possible'. One Moslem lawyer ('an officer of our civil court') was first flogged, then made to lick up English blood from the floor, then hanged.

Neill's subordinate, Major Renard, hanged twelve Indian villagers because their faces were 'turned the wrong way' when his troops marched by. At each halt on the march the Major had his men burn the nearest Indian village to the ground, as a matter of course. Renard hanged forty-two men at the roadside in two days – these gross actions, though extreme at the time, were generally speaking tolerated by an inflamed European public opinion.

'Your bloody off-hand measures are not the cure for this sort of disease,' was 'Clemency' Canning's curt answer to an officer who sought permission to intensify the terror. 'It would greatly add to the difficulties of settling the country hereafter,' he pointed out, with sober understatement, in the confidential circular which earned him his nickname, 'if a spirit of animosity against their rulers were engendered in the minds of the people.'

To Lord Elgin – who in his own years as colonial Governor had done his best to be fair-minded and even benevolent – this introduction to another aspect of Empire came as a moral shock, and one which afterwards was to affect his conduct in China. To his wife he wrote from Calcutta: 'I have seldom from man or woman since I came to the East heard a sentence that was reconcilable with the hypothesis that Christianity had come into the world. Detestation, contempt, ferocity, vengeance, whether Chinamen or Indians be the object.' Many of the soldiers who went on to serve with Elgin in China formed their view of 'inferior races' in India during the Mutiny.

On 20 September 1857 Lord Elgin returned to Hong Kong, where, in the words of one of Yeh's spies, he betrayed his impatience day after day by 'stamping his foot, and sighing'. During Elgin's absence at Calcutta Sir John Bowring had taken it upon himself to make a private communication to Yeh, in defiance of orders. 'The way he dodged and insinuated,' said Elgin, after taxing him with it, 'revealed to me more than I had before seen of the man's character. ... It is impossible to put the slightest trust in him.'

Baron Gros arrived in *Audacieuse* at last on 17 October, to be given a 29-gun salute, and taken in a palanquin borne by five Chinese to see Sir John Bowring. Baron Gros soon regretted it. 'Bowring gave it him for four hours,' Elgin noted. 'I found him ... ready to make almost any concession, rather than entertain another assault of rhetoric.' Gros, too, wanted not a revengeful massacre at Canton but moderation and effectiveness. This suited Elgin, and since troops were now available – though not in the numbers Admiral Seymour had asked for – the French and British worked out a common plan. October was too late in the year for successful campaigning on the river approaches to Peking; the waterways there would soon be frozen a foot deep. It would have to be Canton.

To avoid Bowring, Elgin had stayed as long as possible in quarters aboard a P & O steamer in Hong Kong harbour. Boils and dysentery were distressingly prevalent in the colony that autumn, and the garrison troops were sick, as usual. Elgin was glad of an invitation from Dent ('One of the merchant princes of China. He is very obliging') to stay in his house at Macao. Because robbers were so in evidence when he got back to Hong Kong, Lord Elgin bought himself a Colt revolver, and got his hand in at target practice.

In November the American plenipotentiary William B. Reed also arrived, after an excellent run of 115 days from New York in the huge 1000 horse-power steam frigate *Minnesota* – an impressive 50-gun warship which unfortunately was too large to operate anywhere close inshore. Reed, a personal friend of President Buchanan's, was a lawyer who for six years had taught American history at the University of Pennsylvania. The President's instructions to him had gone so far as to define Anglo-French objectives in China as 'just and expedient' but he was to emphasize to the Chinese that the United States had no vested interest in opium 'legalization'. Reed was also to cultivate friendly relations with the Russian envoy, and watch for a chance to act as mediator. The diplomatic course Washington had set William B. Reed – of preserving a semblance of friendship for the Chinese, but not missing any pickings that might be available after an Anglo-French victory – was not easy for any man to follow without loss of dignity. At the outset, Yeh refused point blank to meet William B. Reed – the first of several snubs he was obliged to digest.

In November the Russian Minister also turned up, with news from the north. He was Admiral Count Euphemius Putiatin, a veteran of the Crimean War and subsequently Governor of Amur. Count Putiatin entered Hong Kong harbour in a little 6-gun paddle-steamer called *Amerika* – a vessel built in the United States and sent round Cape Horn during the Crimean War to strengthen Asiatic Russia's naval potential. Count Putiatin, after sailing *Amerika* down the Amur River, had lingered for some time at the mouth of the Peh-ho, in the hope of being invited up to Peking. But the Chinese were enforcing the strict rule that Russians could arrive at their capital only by the overland route across Mongolia. Putiatin had made it clear that he would refuse to kowtow – in accordance with Russian precedent – and this had been made the pretext for not having direct conversations with him, though he had brought to Peking a secret offer to help crush the Taiping Rebellion, in exchange for Manchuria. The Chinese, not tempted by this offer, curtly refused to discuss 'frontier rectification'.

Putiatin, subtlest of the diplomats now in Hong Kong, stayed as guest of the American merchant house, Russell & Co. Elgin cultivated his acquaintance, not least because Putiatin had brought with him as interpreter in *Amerika* a priest from the Russian Ecclesiastical Mission, which had been established in Peking since 1727 (though it had no diplomatic status there). The Russians had a virtual monopoly of intelligence from Peking, though two Roman Catholic priests were also at work in the city, clandestinely and in disguise. The Russian used his sources of intelligence to sway and sometimes to mislead his colleagues. Putiatin did not conceal his opinion that Canton was a sideshow, and that (as Elgin reported to Clarendon on 14 November) 'nothing could be done with the Chinese government unless pressure were brought to bear upon Peking itself'. Mandarins near the capital were openly boasting, according to Putiatin, that foreign warships could not navigate the Peh-ho, but with shallow-draught gunboats he thought it could be done.

The Russians, too, had their programme. They would support Anglo-French pressure for an extension of trade, and liberty of conscience for Chinese Christians. But Russia also had in mind to obtain a naval base in Chinese territory, south of the Amur River, as a counterpoise to Anglo-French naval preponderance in the Far East. The plan was secret, though Lord Palmerston already had his suspicions.

Since Russia and China had been at peace for so many years, the Chinese at first were affable towards the Russians, at least in public, but soon the Viceroy of Chihli was obliged to point out that the Russians 'were actually tied up with the British and French barbarians firmly and inseparably, and their initial professions of help and mediation cannot be relied on'. His suspicions were justified.

Men were returning from India. On 1 December a hundred survivors of the 59th Regiment came back from Calcutta, with 300 Royal Marines. On 10 December the French Admiral, Rigault de Genouilly, announced that he was ready to participate in a joint attack on Canton. Two days later his aide-de-camp, Lieutenant Ribout, in *Dragonne*, accompanied by a British gunboat carrying Wade, the interpreter, who was now one of Elgin's secretaries, delivered an ultimatum from Baron Gros to Viceroy Yeh, which informed him that 'France and England ask nothing which is not equitable -- nothing which is not founded on their rights'. They wanted punishment for Chapdelaine's murderer, indemnity for losses, and entry into the city. Under the eyes of an immense Chinese crowd, a mandarin boat came out, took the foreign documents, and scuttled back with them to Canton.

The British ultimatum echoed the French but skated lightly over the *Arrow* question ('A scandal to us, and is so considered, I have reason to know', Elgin wrote, 'by all except the few who are personally compromised'). By 17 December, aboard HMS *Furious* and on his way up the Pearl River, Elgin was noting in his journal that Yeh's answer was 'very weak, and reads as if the writer were at his wits' end'. Baron Gros, too, had felt obliged gravely to point out to Viceroy Yeh that his reply to the French ultimatum, 'not being serious . . . must be held equivalent to a formal refusal'.

Yeh's stonewalling policy was coming to a sad end, and he must have known it. With his fleet destroyed, his army demoralized and the local population mistrustful, he could make no serious resistance to these foreign ships of war. But Cantonese who might sympathize with the rebels were still within his grasp. As the Allied fleet moved up the Pearl River, Yeh beheaded another batch of prisoners – 400 of them – and adorned the city walls with their severed heads.

The multitude of Chinese river-boats between Honan Island and the city had disappeared. One after another a column of foreign warships came to anchor there – four British steam sloops and four gunboats, the steam tender *Coromandel*. Larger French vessels had been left at anchor downstream, their crews being towed up the river in boats with rifle and knapsack. French seamen were specially trained for operations on shore. The French had four gunboats under the walls of Canton, *Dragonne*, *Avalanche*, *Mitraille* and *Fusée*, and the corvette *Phlégéton*. Across the river at Dutch Folly a shore battery was established, and for unlimbering and carrying ammunition sixteen Chinese were attached to each gun. These men wore pointed caps, and uniforms like those of Chinese soldiers, but had been recruited into British service in the Coolie Corps. A total of 671 coolies served in the assault on Canton, most of them were Hakkas, and some had contacts with the rebels.

Rear-Admiral Seymour, as Commander-in-Chief, proclaimed his serious determination 'to discountenance and prevent all looting and plundering both as demoralizing and as subversive of discipline'. On 21 December Lord Elgin, who intended to be present at the attack, conferred with Baron Gros and the Allied commanders aboard *Audacieuse*. The diplomats were observed to lack the enthusiasm shown by the military men for bombardment as a cure-all. Before making a target of Canton they stipulated that Yeh was to be given a forty-eight-hour warning, unlikely though he was to respond. Elgin, though his public face was grimly set, expressed in his journal his inner misgivings at being anchored within two miles of 'a great city doomed I fear to destruction by the folly of its own rulers and the vanity and levity of ours'.

On Christmas morning Royal Marines on Honan Island cut down green branches to imitate holly, and tried their hand at a plum duff that might distantly resemble Christmas pudding. Parkes was sent to placard the walls of Canton with notices in Chinese, warning the inhabitants to 'leave'. A pork barrel was hoisted to the truck of *Nimrod*'s mainmast, and a seaman stood in it, to signal the effect of the impending fire. When the time of grace ran out, on 27 December – the Eve, as Elgin noted sourly in his journal, of the Massacre of the Innocents – a slow fire was begun on the city's twenty-five-foot-high wall from the battery and the moored warships, and went on for twenty-seven hours, a hundred rounds being fired from each ship, supplemented by incendiary rockets at night and mortars by day. Only two shots were returned by the Chinese from the walls. Two hundred Chinese were killed, Canton was ablaze, and the civilian inhabitants had stampeded. The prevailing opinion was that the length of this bombardment was vindictive: the city might as easily have been stormed after a three-hour cannonade as one lasting twenty-seven hours.

The Allies put 5679 men ashore for the assault, but most of them came from the fleet. There were 900 French naval ratings trained for land service, and 2500 British Marines supported by 1500 British seamen, but there were only 800 regular troops, including sepoys, and a handful of men from the unlucky Hong Kong garrison.

Once ashore, the men advanced along narrow paths between ricefields. Under cover of suburban tombs, Chinese troops waved red and yellow flags at them defiantly, and fired off musket-balls and arrows. Some of the Chinese were armed with gingalls – large-bore firelock muskets with a range of a hundred yards. Gingalls were seven and a half feet long, and were worked by a pair of men – one offering his shoulder for a gun-rest while the other fired. The man on whose shoulder the gingall rested was usually knocked down by the impact: this made the sailors laugh.

They bivouacked through a clear but chilly night in the Criminals' Cemetery ('the spaces between the graves affording excellent shelter'). British Headquarters were established in a temple near the cemetery, all the religious statues both there and everywhere else being sedulously disembowelled, since a characteristic rumour had spread among the Jack Tars that, during the first Opium War, treasure had been found in the belly of a temple idol.

At dawn next day 15 000 Chinese were to be seen, crowding the nearby hills – out of range, but in clear sight of the action. They had the demeanour of neutral spectators; no one was willing to die for Viceroy Yeh. While Royal Marine marksmen made sure that any Chinese musketeers who might still be on the city wall kept their heads down, the French, led by Admiral Rigault de Genouilly in person, dashed forward with scaling ladders, and were soon up the wall and showing the flag there, with a British assault force close on their heels. By 10 a.m., Tricolor and Union Jack fluttered out from the Five-Storey Pagoda just inside Canton, and a cheer went up from the Allied force. The Allies had captured all the positions outside the city that dominated Canton, and they now commanded the city's gates and wall.

The Admirals wanted a second bombardment, but Elgin put his foot down. He accompanied General van Straubenzee on a reconnaissance in force along the city walls, and not a hostile shot was fired. The British had lost a hundred men altogether, killed and wounded: the French three killed and thirty wounded. Total Chinese casualties were 450. Thousands of surviving Chinese soldiers – looking like animated period-pieces in round hat, breast-plate, dangling cartridge-box and long musket, or bow-and-arrows – were already scuttling away to the hills for their lives. After this victory rain fell without stopping for seventy hours.

At last, on 5 January, hesitations were overcome and the city entered by a force of 3000 men. Elgin had been right about the needlessness of further bombardment: there was no Chinese opposition. A party of Royal Marines under Colonel Lemon marched off smartly to take possession of the silver in the Imperial Treasury. Fifty-two heavy silver-boxes and sixty-eight packets of ingots were carried down to the river for them – the coolies were paid a wage of a dollar a head in copper cash – and specie to the value of $300 000 was soon safely under hatches aboard HMS *Calcutta*. A force of a hundred blue-jackets, led by the irrepressible Harry Parkes, tracked down the Viceroy himself, who had tried to cover his tracks by having another mandarin impersonate him.

Since Harry Parkes had never seen Yeh face to face, he took the precaution of carrying a portrait. The real Yeh was captured in the act of getting over a wall. The coxswain twisted Yeh's pigtail in his fist, and led him off captive to a sedan chair. Hakkas in the Coolie Corps caught a glimpse of the huge and terrifying Viceroy, with his sensual slab of a face, as he was hustled off to the river. They made mocking gestures in his direction, as of a rebel captive having his head cut off. Yeh was kept prisoner aboard the steam-sloop *Inflexible*. His archives, contained in the 'Management of Barbarian Affairs Yellow Chest', were also seized, and slowly translated. The Allies now had access to the concealed motions of Chinese diplomacy.

Despite Admiral Seymour's pronouncement, sailors had been coming back to their ships waving Chinese banners, wearing mandarin hats, and with their knapsacks stuffed with plunder. On 2 January Lord Elgin wrote: 'My difficulty has been ... to prevent the wretched Cantonese from being plundered and bullied. ... There is a word called "loot" which gives unfortunately a venial character to what would, in common English, be styled robbery. Add to this that there is no flogging in the French Army, so that it is impossible to punish men committing this class of offences.' The same day a deputation of Chinese merchants had arrived, led by old Howqua's son, begging for some kind of government that would put down disorder.

The victors' difficulties were beginning to show. In the entire Allied force there were only three men – Parkes, Wade and a French officer, Captain Martineau des Chenetz – who spoke Chinese. (Parkes also had the services of a bilingual Chinese 'traitor' called Wang Tao-ch'ung, hated by his compatriots, who wore Western clothes and supervised the intelligence service.) Sir John Davis, the famous Chinese scholar who previously governed Hong Kong, and had perhaps been exasperated out of his wits by the behaviour, then, of the Cantonese, had advised Lord Elgin that he should make of the city 'a heap of blazing ruins'. (As to which, Lord Elgin reassured his wife, 'no human power shall induce me to accept the office of oppressor of the feeble'.) By now, nine out of ten houses in Canton were empty, the people having panicked and fled as the foreigners came in. All the merchants, Chinese and foreign, wanted the city's economic life to revive: there was a tea crop to be shipped.

Elgin decided he had no alternative but to confirm in office the city's Chinese Governor – an intelligent and capable man called Pih-kwei, who had held posts in the Kwangtung province for twenty years, and was inevitably nicknamed Pickwick by the troops. He would work under the vigilant eye of an Allied commission including Consul Parkes and Captain Martineau. Since the alternative to Allied occupation of Canton might well be the capture of the city by a rebel army, Pih-kwei uneasily agreed. At least the British and French had made it clear they had no intention of overthrowing the Manchu dynasty. 'If Pih-kwei was removed or harshly dealt with', Elgin explained in a despatch to London, '... we should be called upon to govern a city containing many hundred thousand inhabitants ... with hardly any means of communicating with the people.' A joint Allied–Chinese police force was organized, and kept law and order in a way that gave great satisfaction to the propertied classes.

On 28 January Yeh's residence had been intentionally flattened by gunnery from the French gunboats *Mitraille* and *Fusée*, and the site earmarked for a Roman Catholic Church, to be built as the first charge on the French indemnity once Peking had paid it over. The editor of *Annales de la propagation de la foi* saw in the 1857 bombardment of Canton a punishment of God for Chinese blindness towards missionaries, an opinion that cannot greatly have consoled the surviving relatives of the several hundred Chinese civilian victims. Seventeen war junks, under a mandarin, were lent by Pih-kwei to Admiral Seymour, to help on the Pearl River in putting down 'pirates' – or, as the case might be, seaborne rebels. Yeh's reign of terror was over; Canton had begun to revive.

But as early as 27 January 1858 a secret Imperial Edict had been despatched to Pih-kwei, telling him: 'The only thing to do is mobilize the soldiers and militia and fight them ... the Canton gentry have a sense of justice and the courage of the people can be relied on.' An Edict made public on 15 February struck the same note: 'Canton is captured, and still the Cantonese have not risen *en masse* to deliver it. We assume this is because Yeh Mingch'en's obstinate self-sufficiency has dissipated the hearts of the people.' Another secret Edict was sent at the same time on a roundabout route to Pih-kwei: while helping the Allies govern Canton he was also 'to consult about arousing the village irregulars ... when the barbarians see that mass fury cannot be denied they may restrain their ferociousness somewhat'. In the ninety-six villages around Canton the militia – indistinguishable at other times from ordinary peasants working in the fields – began to give the foreigners trouble.

There were some ineffective attempts to rescue Yeh from captivity by bribing British seamen; his evil spirit still haunted Canton. 'The presence of Yeh', wrote Elgin, 'tends to disquiet the public mind, and to render the task of restoring peace and confidence in the neighbourhood more difficult.' A decision was taken to ship him off in HMS *Inflexible* to exile in Calcutta, where the panic of the Mutiny was over, and the British Raj impressively restored. Yeh was provided with a house in Calcutta, next door to the deposed King of Oudh.

Though he had been the third most powerful official in China, with power of life and death over tens of millions, Yeh was a man of simple habits. He was by all accounts faithful to his one wife, ate mutton and detested beef and had worn the same blue quilted tunic for the past ten years. He abhorred opium, preferred tea to wine, and could hardly conceal his boredom when Christian tracts were forced upon him: they were written in such execrable Chinese. Though considerately furnished with a Bible in Calcutta, Yeh spent much of his time there reading translations from *The Times* – especially of Parliamentary debates.

Yeh kept his self-possession to the last. When, to sweeten his prisoner's exile, the Lieutenant-Governor in Calcutta invited Yeh to a ball, he gently declined this opportunity of cutting a public figure, for the ironic reason that he understood, at a ball, gentlemen spent their time embracing each other's wives, and standing first on one leg, then on another. Yeh lasted out a year of exile. The following poem, written in Calcutta by this erudite and intelligent 53-year-old mass executioner, hints at his mood of boredom philosophically borne:

> While my heart is disturbed by
> Leaping tigers and the insistent bugle's blast
> I watch the white-throat blackbirds
> Until they disappear with the sunset;
> Only the Spring returns as of old,
> Everywhere are cotton-flowers, red against the wall.

When, at his death, the British proposed to bury Yeh in Calcutta's Chinese cemetery, the Chinese community objected that the other ghosts might not like it.

In captured Canton twenty-one million pounds of tea awaited despatch. Admiral Seymour – who seemed at times to behave like the ghost of his own gallant father, perseveringly maintaining the Continental Blockade against Napoleon – had angered the merchant community, particularly the Americans, by establishing a blockade of Canton. His action was not only illegal, since war had not been formally declared, but ineffective, because small shipments could fairly easily be made down back creeks. It came to Lord Elgin's notice that some British naval officers had been tempted by a monetary inducement to turn a blind eye: China invariably corrupted.

On 10 February Admiral Seymour was induced to lift his blockade, and the tea chests got moving at last in bulk down to Whampoa. By mid-April, tea worth £8 000 000 had changed hands. Trade was freed, but martial law continued to be imposed on the city and its suburbs, where a Chinese resistance movement was flickering into life. The Ambassadors of France and Britain wanted their merchants now to take up residence inside the city walls – wasn't that one reason the war had been fought? But they all preferred transacting business on the old site along the waterfront.

In March 1858 the 70th Sepoy Regiment arrived, and to their great satisfaction – having been called 'niggers' in India – were assigned 200 Chinese to keep their quarters clean. The day after they landed, three of them were shot by the French police, for looting.

Lord Elgin was meanwhile engaged in the difficult business of getting the other three Ambassadors – French, American and Russian – to follow his lead northward; and in the even trickier task of getting his own Admiral to back up his endeavour. Since the capture of Canton, when a pet plan of the Admiral's for landing troops had been overruled as unnecessarily dangerous, Seymour and Elgin had not been on the best of terms. Count Putiatin had let it be supposed, not quite truthfully, that the countryside around Peking might be too hot by May for successful campaigning. The drift of his advice suggests that he wanted Russia to profit from new treaties, but would rather she continued to be the only foreign power officially represented in Peking; but what he said, true or not, made a move north sound particularly urgent.

Putiatin was in favour of moving a force of shallow-draught gunboats up the coast to the mouth of the Peh-ho, pointing out that if only they got there quickly enough, they could stop the rice-tribute which fed Peking, and had to be taken round the coast by junk, now that the Grand Canal was damaged. Baron Gros, too, was willing to cooperate fully, and this despite growing Anglo-

253

French tension in Europe – of which Palmerston's government, so recently brought to power with a staggering patriotic majority, was soon to fall victim. The radicals could play the same 'patriotic' game as Palmerston, and did – threatening to bring tens of thousands of working men by railway train from all over England to the West End of London, to denounce Palmerston as a traitor and his Aliens Bill as pro-French. Eighty-four Liberal MPs, after a speech by Milner-Gibson, deserted Palmerston on the Bill's second reading. From being the idol of the crowd, Palmerston was this year hooted when he took his daily horse exercise in Hyde Park, and several unfortunate Frenchmen were ducked in the Serpentine. A jingo mood, though easy to rouse, was evidently hard to master.

With Lord Derby on the point of becoming Prime Minister, Clarendon wrote warningly to Elgin: 'I have not the remotest idea how our successors mean to deal with the China question, upon which they committed themselves so violently.' To defeat Lord Palmerston in the *Arrow* debate, Lord Derby had spoken as 'an advocate for the feeble defencelessness of China against the overpowering might of Great Britain'. He might not have meant this literally, but, even so, there was no sense in wasting time about finishing this unpopular war. Seymour might mutter on about the need for a full-scale blockade of the Yangtze – oblivious of the fact that it would imply an all-out, full-scale war against China – but Elgin simply wanted to get his gunboats as quickly as possible up the Peh-ho River as far as Tientsin. That was close enough to Peking for the Chinese to be forced to negotiate.

Early in March, Lord Elgin gave Rear-Admiral Sir Michael Seymour a sufficient and timely warning of the need to collect a force of gunboats at Shanghai for service further north. He then moved up along the coast himself, on a tour of inspection of the Treaty Ports, planned to bring Ambassadors and boats all together at about the same time in the estuary of the Peh-ho River.

The Admiral, a man who saw clearest what was exactly under his nose, was in no special hurry to move his gunboats north. He was not even making good use of those he proposed to leave behind at Canton. When the gunboat flotilla went leisurely off, those that remained were all anchored, to Harry Parkes's despair, under the city walls, with orders that 'not a gunboat was to move from before Canton'. But Chinese militia in the creek villages were becoming actively hostile, and General van Straubenzee, as Parkes pointed out, could not move a man out on a punitive expedition except with naval aid: 'Gunboats should patrol the rivers and creeks, which in China are the roads.'

In March, Parkes had warned his superiors: 'Pih-kwei is playing off braves and villages against us – no one is safe one mile from the city.' Van Straubenzee, a Crimean veteran known affectionately to his men as Old Strawberry Jam, though his army grew to 3000 regular troops supplemented by 1500 French and British sailors, allowed them eventually all to be pinned down around Canton 'by some 8000 or 10 000 ragged "braves" '. Harry Parkes went on urging rigour; punitive raids; patrols; but this was not a type of warfare that Old Strawberry Jam, who had fought gallantly hand-to-hand in the fog at Inkerman, was accustomed to. The time was not far off when Harry Parkes, drawing in his own mind a despairing contrast with 1841, when 2300 Englishmen at Canton had dictated to a Chinese army of 40 000, would think of chucking it all up to go sheep-farming in New Zealand.

On 5 March 1858 Elgin landed at Swatow. This was an illicit port of trade, not stipulated in the Treaty of Nanking – a shortcoming he hoped to put right in his own treaty. Years ago there had been an opium receiving station offshore on Nan-oa Island; soon, receiving ships were boldly anchoring in the river mouth, and at last, by bribing mandarins, the opium dealers got a foothold five miles upriver in Swatow itself. According to the merchant John Scarth, bribery there was so advantageous that one mandarin 'paid $7000 for the office he holds, though he knew he was only to have it for 10 months'. Foreigners at Swatow even paid their rents in opium.

The mercantile community at Swatow consisted, Elgin wrote, 'mainly of agents of the two great opium houses, Dent and Jardine, with their hangers-on'. There was also 'a considerable business in the coolie trade – which consists in kidnapping wretched coolies, putting them on board ships where all the horrors of the slave trade are reproduced, and sending them ... to such places as Cuba'.

The French, though they had clean hands where opium was concerned, were as deep as the Anglo-Americans in the Pig Trade, as Elgin soon discovered. 'The coolies in a French coolie-ship rose', he wrote. 'The master and the mate jumped overboard, and the coolies ran the ship on shore ... On this, a French man-of-war ... proceeds to Swatow, which is fifty miles from the scene of the occurrence, and informs the people that they will bombard the place immediately, unless 6000 dollars are paid.' Armed force was simply a mechanism for getting money out of China.

On 11 April, aboard HMS *Furious*, Elgin noted gloomily in his journal: 'We are in the midst of the Yellow Sea, going about eight knots, dragging a gunboat astern to save her coal. This is the only gunboat I have got.' By 14 April Elgin was anchored in the rough water of the Gulf of Peh-ho, about five miles out from the bar obstructing the river mouth; there was about eleven feet of water on this bar at a high spring tide. Elgin needed a dozen gunboats, but by now he had only two. Flat-bottomed rice junks were passing into the river at the rate of fifty a day, and though Elgin knew Peking was running short of rice – that year, only a tenth of the needed supplies arrived – he had no force to turn the screw tighter by stopping those junks. As usual, he relieved his feelings about Admiral Seymour into his journal: '... he must be in his dotage. It is stupidity beyond anything I have ever met with in my public career ... He does not even seem to read what is written to him.'

Of the five weeks' exasperating wait that followed, Elgin's private secretary noted ironically; 'We became wonderfully expert at games with rope quoits.' In the bright, cold sunlight – interrupted by unpleasant storms of wind and blown dust – the Chinese could be seen ashore, busy throwing up earthworks and sandbag batteries, to strengthen the five mud forts that commanded the river mouth, and driving piles along the muddy estuary shore to check an Allied landing. Over the forts flew angular banners, blue or yellow, with scalloped borders. Eighty-seven guns could be counted, but they were only a fraction of the total the Taku Forts could bring to bear on ships entering the river.

'The flag of France', wrote Lord Elgin to his wife, on 29 April, when according to Putiatin their best time for campaigning was fast running out, 'is at this moment represented by two gunboats *within the bar of the Peiho River*, that of England by two despatch boats *on top of it aground*.' He went on: 'I have a perfect driveller for an admiral, a general not much better, and a sot for a commodore ... I am like a person in a bad dream.' On 24 April Admiral Seymour put in an appearance – in HMS *Calcutta*, which drew twenty-five feet of water, and was accompanied by one extra gunboat only. Admiral and plenipotentiary were by now hardly on speaking terms.

Throughout late April and early May, gunboats British and French showed up one by one. Meanwhile, Baron Gros had arrived on 20 April, and he and Lord Elgin were already in diplomatic contact with the Chinese, using whatever time-wasting tactic their wits could devise. On 24 April a joint letter, in Chinese, was sent off by all four foreign representatives. T'an, Governor of

Chihli Province, announced that he was empowered to negotiate, but his credentials gave him no authority to conclude a treaty; this deferred action a little longer. As late as 11 May, Admiral Seymour was still advising a full-scale blockade of the Yangtze, and had even managed to infect the intrepid French Admiral, Rigault, with his own misgivings. Rigault and Seymour said they had too few ships to attack such formidable forts, and had not been given enough time to reconnoitre. Elgin's response to Seymour was blistering, and the Admirals changed their tone.

Eventually, by the third week of May, a flotilla of sixteen British and ten French gunboats had been assembled in the mouth of the muddy Peh-ho. All four plenipotentiaries were on the spot, and anxious to move. The actual attack on the Taku Forts would be left to the Anglo-French, but once the forts had been knocked out, the Russian and American Ambassadors were to follow on, up the Peh-ho River, in the little steamer *Amerika*. Count Putiatin had thoughtfully arranged for Palladius, Archimandrite of the Russian College in Peking, to come down to the fleet on some pretext, keeping his eyes open as he travelled.

The priest confirmed the rice shortage in Peking. The young Emperor had for a long time been sick, and was now so irritable that none of his mandarins dare talk to him about foreign affairs; he thought of fleeing to Tartary. The Archimandrite had been sent down from Peking in a closed conveyance; even so, he managed to form an estimate that between Taku and the capital there were 10 000 soldiers blocking the way. He was also able to tell the Admirals exactly where the river passage was blocked by moored junks and a boom. The intelligence the Archimandrite Palladius gave Admiral Seymour apparently relieved his worst fears. The Allied onslaught on the Taku Forts was decided for 20 May 1858.

8 Taku Back and Forth

'As long as China remains a nation of opium smokers, there is not the least reason to fear that she will become a military power of any importance, as the habit saps the energies and vitality of the nation.'
Consul Hurst to the Royal Commission on Opium, 1895

'It is true that the Japanese armies were well armed and well led, but it is also true that the Chinese armies were so demoralized by the use of opium as to be incapable of offering a resistance to any army whatever.'
Prince Galitzin, observer with the Chinese armies during the China–Japan War, speaking in Edinburgh, 1895

The countryside defended by the Taku Forts was uninspiring – a dead-level alluvial plain a few feet above the tide-line. From a distance, the five square mud forts looked as if they, too, were natural formations that had somehow been heaved up out of the mire. At high tide the sea at Taku encroached upon the land. After a heavy rain, even wider stretches of land were covered with water – and distinguishable from the sea itself only where conical Chinese tombs poked up to break the surface, and ancient causeways ran, like stone catwalks, between thatched villages built on mounds.

All through the irresolute five-week pause, while the foreign gunboats arrived offshore one by one, the Chinese soldiers had been seen, improving their earthworks. The navigable channel into the Peh-ho was only 200 yards wide, and Chinese shore-batteries were mounted four hundred yards or more to left and right of it, ready to take any approaching enemy in a crossfire. On 20 May 1858, at ten in the morning, Chinese artillerymen on duty by their guns could see the flotillas of French and British gunboats begin to make their way across the line of turbulent shallow water, five miles out, where fishing nets hung on stakes marked the bar. The gunboats got across safely, and steamed in line up the estuary towards the next obstacle – the heavy boom hung across it, made of five 7-inch bamboo cables, twisted together and floated on buoys.

The timing of the attack was unexpected. The Chinese had taken for granted that foreign ships – even gunboats – could get across the bar only at high tide, but Admirals Seymour and Rigault had sent their gunboats over as soon as there was water enough to float them, and while the tide was still rising. The Chinese guns had been aimed, long in advance, to hit squarely any incoming vessel which approached the bamboo boom at high tide. This was a tactic similar to that used years before by the pirate fleet at anchor in the mouth of the Tongking River – and the old pirate chief, now a blue-button naval mandarin at Ningpo, may well have suggested it. But this time, also, the trick failed. The British and French gunboats reached the estuary long before the tide was full, and all the Chinese shot flew high – whizzing overhead, and making reiterated white splashes in the water of the bay a long way off.

Coromandel steamed up to the bamboo cable at top speed. Her bows smacked into it, and she burst open a gap for the boats that followed to enter. The French gunboats *Mitraille* and *Fusée* accompanied *Cormorant* to attack the two northern forts. The three forts on the southern bank, with their long connecting-line of sandbag batteries, were bombarded by *Nimrod*, and by the French craft *Avalanche* and *Dragonne*. *Leven* and *Possum* towed in the French landing parties. From seaward embrasures in the forts, where 140 guns were mounted, the Chinese kept up a useless if deafening fire for an hour and a half, while, unscathed beneath this hail of shot, the gunboats aimed their fire at the points ashore where they intended to land troops.

The Chinese did manage to do a little damage – with their gingalls, ranged in banks of 200, and independently aimed. *Mitraille* got her screw twisted in a fishing net, and was nastily knocked about by gingalls for a quarter of an hour. Apart from that one brief sitting-target, the busy foreign gunboats seemed almost magically immune to Chinese gunfire, and this had its moral effect. Even before the French and British landing parties had begun plunging through the mud, weapons held high, towards the perimeter of the first fort, Chinese troops could be seen, quitting Taku in masses.

About 100 Chinese had been killed by fire from the gunboats. The British lost five killed, and the French counted six killed and sixty-one wounded – but most of them by accident, when a magazine blew up. The parting shot of the fleeing Chinese was to send fifty traditional fireboats down the Peh-ho, but they all ran aground at a bend in the river, and burned out. The Chinese guns were found to have been firing 8-inch hollow shot and canister, cleverly copied from British models. The mandarin who had commanded the Taku Forts cut his own throat in the Temple of the Sea God, and the Viceroy of Chihli was banished to the northern frontier, for conducting 'operations without plan or resource'. It was all a little too much like one of Pottinger's 1840-style victories to ring quite true.

Lord Elgin – his prematurely white hair contrasting oddly with his healthy red face – was in high spirits, and ready for anything. Two days after seeing the Chinese cut and run from Taku, he confided to his diary: 'twenty-four determined men with revolvers, and a sufficient number of cartridges, might walk through China from one end to another'. Lord Elgin had good reason to get his business over quickly: by the end of the week, he was noting the arrival of a despatch from Lord Derby's new government in London, 'giving me latitude to do anything I choose, if only I will finish the affair'.

In temperatures up to 100°F in the shade, Elgin pushed on to Tientsin, trying not to become irritated at the way *Cormorant* ran aground. (Thirty-two times in thirty-six miles; but *Fusée* beat this: forty-two times.) Chinese crowding the river-bank were always willing to tow the gunboat off – and would take no money for it, though they were glad to be given ship's biscuits. The sight of boats making their way upstream at this rate was astonishing. Rice junks crept up to Tientsin with the tide, making nine miles a day. A rumour began to spread among the Chinese that a new foreign dynasty was arriving, to chase out the unloved Manchu. When Elgin's gunboats reached Tientsin the local mandarins turned up in force, expecting that these were trading vessels, loaded with opium and Manchester goods.

On 4 June 1858, as he began conversations for a new treaty – the Treaty of Tientsin – with Imperial Commissioners sent down hurriedly from Peking, Lord Elgin felt able to congratulate himself on having 'complete military command of the capital of China, without having broken off relations with the neutral powers, and without having interrupted, for a single day, our trade at the different ports of the Empire'.

Kuei-liang, the senior Chinese representative, dignified, amiable, placid, was 74. He wore a tippet of rich maroon silk over his shoulders and arms, and his hands shook with age. His younger colleague, Hua Shana, was 53 and a Mongol. Discussion for a thorough revision of the treaty made years before at Nanking went on for three weeks, the Chinese negotiators fighting hardest to withhold two concessions that the British regarded as essential – permission for foreigners to travel freely through inland China, and consent for Ambassadors to reside at Peking.

The Imperial Commissioners insisted that giving way on these two points would be more than their lives were worth. Baron Gros, won over by Count Putiatin, was inclined to concede that there was hardly any need for an Ambassador actually to reside in Peking, so long as he might visit the Emperor's capital whenever he chose.

This put Elgin in a quandary. Lord Malmesbury, now Foreign Secretary, was known to hold the view that 'Peking might be a rat-trap for the Envoy if the Chinese meant business,' but no one had forgotten how Yeh in Canton had nullified all forms of indirect diplomatic approach. No longer should China be able to fob off foreigners who had a grievance by keeping them at a safe distance from the central government. In negotiating with the Chinese, Elgin from the first day decided to put on his angriest expression, writing to his wife, 'I have made up my mind, disgusting as the part is to me, to act the role of the "uncontrollably fierce barbarian".' He left much of the actual face-to-face bullying to his interpreters, Wade and Lay, who enjoyed that sort of thing, abetted by his younger brother, Frederick Bruce, and by Laurence Oliphant, his private secretary.

Elgin's ultimate threat (though in fact he had no military force adequate to back his words) was to march on Peking unless he got his way. Fierceness worked; objections vanished; the British were granted their right to travel in the interior, and to have a representative at the Chinese capital.

The Treaty of Tientsin also stipulated that the Chinese should avoid the expression 'barbarian' in future – though in China the word translated as 'barbarian' meant little more than 'not speaking Chinese'. Hankow, Tientsin and Nanking were named as future Treaty Ports. (Since Nanking was still the capital of the 'long-haired rebels', this meant that Britain had tacitly made known her readiness to help the Manchus crush the Taiping rebellion.) Lord Elgin was pleased that his treaty cost only twenty British lives, and had been so quickly agreed upon ('the announcement was received by a yell of derision by ... baffled speculators in tea'). Baron Gros, always more alive than the British to the risk of oversetting the dynasty, had warned Lord Elgin that 'the concessions demanded are exorbitant, and perhaps even dangerous for England' as well as reminding him that his country will 'be obliged to use force to secure the execution of concessions obtained by force alone.' In the long run, Gros was right: to any Chinese having in mind the Confucian injunction, 'This was a forced oath: the spirits do not hear such', an agreement made under duress was never morally binding.

The British Treaty – the Chinese text of which was sluggish in emerging, because the official copyists were all opium addicts – was signed on 3 July 1858, to the music of a ship's band, by the light of three large paper lanterns, in the Temple of Oceanic Influences, after which the Chinese complacently entertained Elgin's party to tea and savoury dishes, and Lord Elgin was presented by Hua Shana, the younger Commissioner, with a set of his poetical works. The French, who signed their own treaty next day, did things on a grander scale yet. They enclosed the French text in a splendid blue silk cover, bound with gold, which they had brought out for the purpose from Paris. Baron Gros handed over a list of Chinese Christians in prison all over China, and pointed out that they were to be freed. The French then returned to their gunboats by torchlight, with their Admiral in full-dress uniform on horseback – at which British Jack Tars manned the yards and cheered, and French marines let off fireworks. The British Treaty extracted two million taels of silver (about £650 000) for 'losses at Canton', and a further two million for the cost of the war. The French also got an indemnity of two million taels – or 16 000 000 francs.

Elgin, who knew from experience that Chinese soldiers, and even high officials, were seldom able to draw their pay, was not happy about these indemnities. In a despatch he warned, 'everything we saw around us indicated the penury of the Treasury', and he advised the unwisdom of driving the Chinese government 'to despair, by putting forward pecuniary claims which it could satisfy only by measures that would increase its unpopularity and extend the area of rebellion'. His argument made no impression on politicians in London, who when estimating the cost of their China war had already taken the indemnity into account.

In the process of coming to terms with his conscience about the negotiations at Tientsin, Lord Elgin recorded: 'Though I have been forced to act almost brutally, I am China's friend in almost all this.' Elgin had so far deliberately chosen, for example, to disregard that part of his instructions from Lord Clarendon which specified that he was to 'ascertain whether the Government of China would revoke its prohibition of the opium trade'. William B. Reed, ordered for his own part to press for the extinction of the drug traffic, reported to Washington that Elgin felt 'a strong if not invincible repugnance ... to introduce the subject of opium'.

Lord Elgin was not lacking in advice on the topic. Messrs Jardine, Matheson & Co. went on record as believing that 'the use of opium is not a curse, but a comfort and benefit to the hardworking Chinese'. Baron Gros's aide-de-camp, after a little research, discovered that habitual smokers of eight pipes a day were expected to die within five or six years, modest smokers of one pipe a day had in Chinese opinion an expectation of twenty years from first pipe to last, and most opium users were dead by fifty. An opium smoker who worked for wages normally spent two-thirds of his pay on the drug: he smoked his opium at his family's expense. The French were very glad not to be implicated in the opium traffic – though they had insisted on a clause in their treaty 'legalizing' the trade in coolies. Russian and American draft treaties both had clauses specifying opium as contraband. The British again found themselves isolated.

The consoling but fallacious idea had entered William B. Reed's head – or been planted there – that with the Mutiny over and East India Company rule coming to a final end, the British government was likely to step in and 'control opium-growing' in India. He took a high tone at first, advising Lord Elgin to 'stop the growth and export of opium from India' – a course of action not in Elgin's power – but changed his ground rather quickly on discovering the extent to which prominent Americans, too, were involved in the drug traffic. ('Until recently,' Elgin had reported to Malmesbury, 'US Consuls in both Canton and Shanghai had been partners in a merchant house trading very largely in opium.') The way opium led to social corruption so horrified Reed that he, too, defied his instructions, urging Lord Elgin to press, after all, for legalization, and explaining back to Washington that 'most honest men concur that nominal prohibition is in fact encouragement, and that the only remaining chance of restraint is making the drug dutiable'.

Elgin was in a dilemma familiar to men of high principle who accept a political role. Loathsome though the opium traffic in China might be to him personally, he was not an eccentric nobleman, crusading against entrenched vested interests, but a career diplomat with his father's debts still to pay off. He rather feebly washed his hands of the problem, leaving it to be tackled by his subordinates, and put the onus for accepting 'legalization' on the Chinese. Laurence Oliphant was told by Elgin in negotiating a new Customs tariff that he was from the beginning to make it clear that the British would not 'insist on the insertion of the drug in the tariff, should the Chinese government wish to omit it'. As a gesture this was something, but not much.

Oliphant reported back to Elgin that 'China still retains her objection to the drug on moral grounds, but the present generation of smokers, at all events, must and will have opium. To deter the uninitiated from becoming smokers, China would propose a very high duty but ... opposition was naturally to be expected from us in that case.' The Chinese wanted a tax on opium of sixty taels per chest, the British proposal was thirty taels per chest, about 8 per cent *ad valorem*, and a tax proportionately less than that placed on innocuous Chinese silks and teas in the British Customs. Covert pressure from the immensely influential drug interest prevailed, as on such a point of detail it was bound to. The tax was fixed at thirty taels, which would bring in revenue but deter no one.

The old freebooting days were over. With opium accepted as 'legal' there was nothing to discourage the Chinese themselves from growing the poppy openly, and on a large scale. Though India's opium exports – mainly to China – almost doubled from 1860 to 1880 (58 618 chests to 105 508 chests), opium merchants soon began to look back with regret on the times of restricted competition, smuggling, bribe-taking and high profits. The bankruptcy of the princely merchant house of Dent was only a few years away.

Since the Yangtze River – and therefore inland China – had been opened up by his treaty to trade, Lord Elgin decided to demonstrate to all concerned that the British meant business by sailing a flotilla 600 miles up the great river, to Hankow, taking with him HMS *Retribution* and *Furious*, a survey-boat, HMS *Dove* and two gunboats. Much of this was Taiping country, devastated by civil war. Elgin's treaty – which among all else denied passports to missionaries wanting to visit rebel areas, while granting them to the Manchu-controlled interior – sounded the eventual death-knell of the Taiping movement. The rebels were an obstacle to trade, and whatever other merits their social movement might have, they had no way of withstanding Western military technique.

As Elgin's ships approached Nanking, the rebel capital – where, after seven years of endless fighting, the women by now outnumbered the men two to one – a Taiping battery apparently ill-informed about the rights granted the British under the new treaty opened fire, and was silenced at once by the gunboat

Cruizer. Elgin's flotilla then gave the men on shore the benefit of a one-and-a-half hour's bombardment. At Wuhu, Elgin sent off his representatives – they were strongly pro-Manchu – to report on the local situation. ('Wade has been on shore', Elgin noted on 23 November 1858, 'to communicate with the chiefs, who are very civil, but apparently a low set of Cantonese.')

Lord Elgin's aristocratic disdain for the Taiping movement happened to fit in very well with long-term British policy. He listened attentively to the bad that was usually reiterated in foreign circles about the Taiping ('brutal ... objectless,' he noted, 'they systematically murdered all ... of the dominant race'). Of what could be said in their favour – chiefly by missionaries – he was sceptical. The Indian Mutiny had made all forms of rebellion even more than usually odious to men of Elgin's class. (He sometimes found it interesting, on the other hand, to swap notes with Chinese landowners as to what sort of income they managed to derive from their tenantry.)

The commercial information reaching him was not encouraging, either. A Taiping deserter – evidently anxious to get downriver to a place where the drug was freely on sale – admitted that, by now, a third of the rebel population smoked opium when they could get it, though the Taiping diehards still strongly condemned the vice. Inside Nanking some Manchester calico and a quantity of red cloth imported from Russia were on offer – but local, handloom-woven Chinese cloth was twenty-five cash a yard cheaper than similar cloth from Manchester. Elgin reported that to drive Chinese homespun – in this case, Taiping homespun – off the market, 'British manufacturers will have to exert themselves to the utmost'. When he arrived at Hankow – inaccessible hitherto to seaborne trade – Elgin's private secretary, Laurence Oliphant, found the drug habit implanted, but only inferior, Chinese-grown opium was on sale this far inland. The Treaty of Tientsin would soon change that.

Under a new Viceroy called Huang, the Cantonese had been making more trouble than ever for the foreign soldiers occupying their city. 'Go forth in your myriads, then,' Huang had exhorted, 'and take vengeance on the enemies of your Sovereign ... imbued with public spirit, and fertile in expedients.' By July 1858, when many Allied ships and men were absent in the north, though General Van Straubenzee still kept Canton under martial law, the skirmishing around the city was making life there so uncertain that the British Consulate moved down to Whampoa. In July a Chinese field-piece in the hands of irregulars opened fire on British headquarters. On the night of 21 July 1858 – after the news of the treaty had reached them – the Chinese made a midnight attack on Canton itself. These isolated deeds of valour were met in the way Harry Parkes had recommended – by punitive raids.

After achieving victory in the north, Lord Elgin put his foot down, insisting to the Imperial Commissioners that Viceroy Huang be dismissed, and his War Committee dissolved. Elgin judged that removing from the resistance movement its official and patriotic sanction might take the heart out of it. But shortly before the steam-frigate *Furious* brought him down from the Yangtze to the Canton River, early in February 1859, the Chinese irregulars chalked up their most remarkable success in the country-side outside Canton by ambushing 700 marines. This could not go unpunished.

General van Straubenzee led a column of 1500 men to the Chinese guerrilla stronghold at Shektsing, seven miles outside Canton. This position, mounting three batteries totalling twenty pieces, had been cleverly chosen and fortified, with a swamp covering each flank, and an approach up a causeway dominated by the guns. Men of the Naval Brigade made an unexpected amphibious attack along a creek, to take the Chinese position in the flank; Shektsing was destroyed. An Imperial Edict meekly did what Elgin said and dissolved the War Committee, and the Cantonese irregulars hung up their weapons – at least, for the time being.

In Peking those high Manchu officials believing the foreign powers could somehow be resisted by armed force had grouped themselves around Prince Seng-ko-lin-ch'in. They were given encouragement, and even a promise of 10 000 rifles and fifty cannon, by the Russians. Prince Seng was the masterly leader of Mongol cavalry who in 1854 wore down and broke the Taiping column that had been sent north to take Peking. In Seng-ko-lin-ch'in British troops were once more to encounter an enemy they could admire. They nicknamed him Sam Collinson – and a characteristic rumour spread like wildfire through the ranks that this Sam Collinson was no ordinary Chinese, but a rebellious Irish marine who had changed his allegiance.

Seng-ko-lin-ch'in might have liked to get his hands on Russian weapons, but like most Asiatics he mistrusted Russian patronage. This arms offer was made in 1858, but not responded to seriously until two years later – and then only on terms that the Russian instructors should not enter China, but hand over the guns and explain their use in the border town of Kyakhta. When Russian diplomats in Peking urged the Chinese to 'stir up trouble in India' they were given this bland rebuke: 'The Heavenly Dynasty, in dealing with the outer barbarians, has always emphasized truthfulness. It never resorts to plots leading to war.'

Lord Elgin, having negotiated a treaty, left for home, his younger brother Frederick taking over as Minister in China. Frederick Bruce confronted a situation so ambiguous – with Manchu China secretly unwilling to accept an extorted treaty, the long-haired rebels preparing to fight for their lives, and Russia fishing for trouble – that Lord Malmesbury, at the Foreign Office, warned him on 1 March 1859 to look out for treachery. The Treaty of Tientsin would become a dead letter unless ratifications were exchanged with the Manchu régime within a year. Bruce proposed to go up to Peking with the French representative, de Bourbelon, for the ratification ceremony, using the right to visit the capital that had been expressly granted them by treaty.

A fortnight earlier, Harry Parkes, with typical forthrightness, had written Frederick Bruce a similar warning: 'Seng-Ko-Lin-Chin and other ignorant Mongol blusterers did not I fear see enough of us in Tientsin in '58 to feel assured that we had strength sufficient to compel the strict execution of the Treaty.' Had Lord Elgin let the Chinese down too lightly?

His brother Frederick had been Colonial Secretary at Hong Kong in 1844, and later had served as Lieutenant-Governor of Newfoundland when Elgin himself was Governor-General of Canada. Bruce seems to have been a plodder – travelling on his more famous elder brother's coat-tails, and best at doing what he was told.

He reached the Peh-ho on 18 June 1859 – with not much time left to get his ratified treaty up to Peking. The new American Minister, John E. Ward of Georgia, had also arrived – on 21 June, in USN frigate *Powhatan* (Commodore Josiah Tattnall) – an American warship that, as usual, was too big to proceed close inshore. Ward planned to go up to Peking in a little hired steamer, *Toeywhan*. He intended to have an audience of the Emperor of China – though America's right to do so was not written expressly into her treaty.

De Bourbelon – a fiery little Frenchman, reputed to share some of Bowring's left-wing views – had brought up only two warships to represent France, the rest of the French fleet being occupied just then off Indo-China. The naval force in the Peh-ho estuary this time was nearly all British – sixteen ships of war, of which thirteen were gunboats. The Chinese might well have tolerated a modest military escort at the ratification ceremony, but in revolutionary times a victory parade up the Peh-ho River to Peking – and what else did a fleet that large imply? – might be risky for the dynasty. The British fleet was now commanded by Rear-Admiral James Hope – a very tall, very large, very aloof officer of 40, a veteran of the naval war against the Russians in the Baltic, and a man with a low opinion of Chinese fighting capacity. Hope had taken over from Seymour in April.

Since the Ministers were keen to exercise their new right of access to Peking, they had already refused a Chinese offer to ratify in Shanghai. De Bourbelon had tried to persuade Bruce that the Chinese must be acting in bad faith – that they were deliberately trying to keep the Allies out of Peking – but in this he was mistaken. In a proclamation of 18 June the Grand Council had ordered three buildings outside Peking's Eastern Gate to be got ready for Treaty Ratification Embassies, and a despatch from Ignatieff to Moscow dated 7 July 1859 confirms that this was actually put in hand.

The Imperial Commissioner at Shanghai had stated the Chinese position accurately in a memorial sent to Peking shortly before: 'while the barbarians' temper is antagonistic it is very difficult to get a handhold for managing them. Only when China's army is efficient, supplies adequate, artillery effective and ships strong can we do as we please and repudiate anything. Speaking for the present we can only eliminate the worst, and call it a day.' Court officials may have been hoping somehow to pass off the mass arrival of triumphant foreigners in Peking as a visit from 'tribute-bearing barbarians', and a few may even have plotted to exact a kowtow, but a visit of some sort from the foreign Ministers was accepted as inevitable.

Seng-ko-lin-ch'in, who had been making a great effort to strengthen the Taku Forts and the Peh-ho River defences, was anxious that the foreign diplomats as they arrived should be directed further up the coast, to Pei-t'ang, as their port of entry. On 14 April he had written, in a memorial, 'If the barbarians insist on coming to Peking to exchange ratifications ... at the port of Taku arrangements have been kept strictly secret; not only can they not be allowed to pass through, but they can not even be allowed to spy ... from the port of Pei-t'ang, by going up the river ... one can also reach Peking ... have the barbarian ships, large and small, all anchor outside the bar, and use local boats to carry them up.' To the Chinese, this detour sounded reasonable – Pei-t'ang was only eight miles further north – but Bruce and de Bourbelon, with a large naval force at their disposal, were unlikely to compromise.

Four successive booms – the outer ones of 3-foot timber baulks lashed together – had by now been placed across the river-mouth near the forts. Admiral Hope, hove-to offshore with his ships and his diplomats – and with the time for ratification almost expired – asked the local Chinese authorities that these obstructions be removed. Getting no satisfactory reply, the Admiral turned to Bruce and de Bourbelon for permission to break his own way through. On 21 June 1859 consent was given. Admiral Hope expected at first that a boat party under Captain G. O. Willes, RN, would manage to open a passage, but though Willes cut the outer boom and damaged two of the inner ones with powder charges, the Chinese managed to repair the damaged ones overnight. What else was left but a frontal assault?

At 9 in the morning of 25 June – a calm, clear day – Bruce then eight miles out to sea in *Magicienne* received a letter from Heng Fu, Viceroy of Chihli, sent by two junks which also brought the fleet a gift of fresh supplies. Heng's letter proposed the detour via Pei-t'ang. But Rear-Admiral Hope was due to make his attack that very morning, an hour later, at 10 a.m. Admiral Hope, having made only a sketchy reconnaissance, was not well aware that the stretch of water beyond the first boom was commanded by forty Chinese guns. Given the will, there might have been time that morning to check Admiral Hope, since he made an uncommonly late start – the gunboat, *Opossum*, did not get off her mark to ram the first boom until two in the afternoon. But after all, every British naval action against the Chinese since Captain Weddell bombarded the Bogue Forts in 1627 had been a walkover. *Lee, Haughty, Plover* flying Admiral Hope's flag, *Duchala* flying the Tricolor, steamed in behind *Opossum*. They ran straight into a trap.

Plover's guns went into action at 2.30 p.m. – Admiral Hope, conspicuous in his gold braid, standing on top of her cookhouse, to get a clear view. At 3 p.m. a Chinese roundshot took a piece out of 'the fleshy part of his thigh'. Hope bravely had his wound bound up in order to fight on – but by now there were only nine others in *Plover's* ship's company still fit for service. Her Lieutenant commanding and eight men had been killed, and twenty-two men were badly wounded.

Admiral Hope moved his flag to *Opossum*, taking up his stance

269

once more on the cookhouse roof. This time, because of his wound, he steadied himself with one hand on the mainstay. But an enemy shot took away the mainstay; the Admiral fell down and fractured his ribs. He was taken to *Cormorant,* and there at 4.20 p.m. yielded up his command to Captain Shadwell, RN.

All gunboats inside the boom were disabled, though Bruce, eight miles offshore, and unable to see the fighting for smoke, still assumed the attack was going well. The rest of the flotilla had moved up to help. By the time evening approached and the three-hour gunnery duel tailed off, six out of the eleven British gunboats engaged were out of action, most of them with heavy casualties, four having gone aground on estuary mud within potshot range of the Chinese gunners in the forts. But one outer bastion of the south fort had been enough battered by naval gunfire to make an assault on it feasible. At 6 p.m., Captain Shadwell decided to press the attack.

When the news reached Josiah Tattnall in *Toeywhan* at 5 p.m. that Admiral Hope was wounded, and his boat disabled inside the boom, the American Commodore got permission from his fellow-Southerner, the American Commissioner John E. Ward, to steam to the rescue. Commodore Tattnall interpreted this permission liberally. To the scene of action near *Cormorant* he towed a junk full of armed marines, who were Admiral Hope's fighting reserve, and exclaimed as he anchored *Toeywhan* aft of the French gunboat, 'Blood is thicker than water. I'll be damned if I'll stand by and see white men butchered before my eyes.'

American blue-jackets had disliked being taunted at Canton with standing by while others fought. Disregarding the artificial restraint of American 'neutrality', they swarmed into nearby gunboats and began helping the French and British seamen to work their guns. In one way or another about 200 of them were reputed to have taken an active part in the battle at Taku.

The tide as it fell narrowed the waterway, exposing a broad strip of estuary mud between water and shore. At 7.20 p.m., with darkness approaching, Captain Shadwell managed to put an assault party as far as the seaward side of the broad fringe of mud near the damaged fort, his men there including Royal Marines and a detachment of French seamen under Commander Tricault. For the men still in the ships, the scene ashore was lighted up overhead by Chinese 'fireballs' – extravagantly bright fireworks.

As they struggled thigh-deep through the mire – they had by now a hundred yards of glutinous mud to cross – the landing party came under a heavy fusillade from Chinese gingalls and

270

firelocks. Then came two more obstacles: wet ditches, fifteen feet wide, five feet deep, and 'extremely difficult to cross from the tenacity of the mud ... I thought I should never get out', reported Major Fisher, of the Engineers, one of the handful who survived.

Of the 150 men who got to the brink of the second ditch unscathed, hardly more than one man in three crossed it and came under the fortress wall. 'We squatted with our legs in the water,' Major Fisher's report continues, 'waiting for the bridges and ladders to be brought up ... but it became evident before long that the attack must fail; the bridges were shot to pieces ... There were about sixty of us in the front ditch, and perhaps half-a-dozen serviceable rifles ... an order was sent to remain under cover ... till the tide should rise, when boats would be sent to bring us off.' Boats came for the survivors at half past one in the morning. Captain Shadwell himself, as well as the commanders of the seamen's division and the marine brigade, had been disabled; Commander Tricault was dead. Of 1100 men led into action that day, 434 had been killed or wounded. Three gunboats, *Lee, Plover* and *Cormorant* were a total loss. *Kestrel* was sunk, but later recovered.

Veterans of the Crimea were heard to say they would rather fight the desperate action of Balaclava three times over than have another go at the Taku Forts. 'Had the opposition they expected been that usual in Chinese warfare,' confessed Admiral Hope, in a revealing passage of his report to the Admiralty, 'there is little doubt that the place would have been successfully carried at the point of the bayonet.' The Chinese, for centuries regarded as almost ludicrously peaceable, at last were learning to fight.

Those Chinese in Peking who believed the 'barbarians' could perhaps be held back by force of arms were much encouraged, but on 5 July Prince Seng-ko-lin-ch'in gave wild optimists this warning: 'Their resentment must be deep. Most of the barbarian warships which came up the river were damaged. They are sure to go to Canton and Shanghai, collect warships and plan revenge.' Reporting the victory at Taku to the Emperor, Prince Seng emphasized that Americans too had taken part: 'Although the starting of hostilities was by the English barbarians, France and America's cooperation in the mêlée is also inescapable.'

Prince Seng was convinced he had living proof that the Americans were only making a pretence of neutrality, and had been even more deeply implicated at Taku than Commodore Tattnall's *beau geste* implied. Seng was misled in this but for a curious reason. Two Allied prisoners had been taken by the Chinese at Taku, one a severely wounded Englishman. The other was a

Canadian called John Powers, who had fought in a regular way under the British flag, but decided to tell his Chinese captors he was an American so as 'to get clear'. This mild deception by one prisoner tangled up matters thoroughly.

A special category of foreigner called 'Canadian' – either English or French, and living in America, yet not, as the Chinese understood the meaning of the word, 'American' – this strained Seng's credulity beyond all normal limits. When S. Wells Williams, the American missionary-interpreter, tried to mend matters by a full and honest explanation, Prince Seng wrote scathingly: 'He was not even willing to acknowledge the American barbarian captured ... he stated ... that America contained Englishmen and Frenchmen, and when there was fighting the flag was the only criterion.' In August, though insisting to the last that John Powers was American, the Chinese handed him over to John E. Ward 'to show commiseration'. (The English prisoner was also handed back.)

News of the Taku disaster took eleven weeks to reach London. After losing a vote of confidence on 10 June 1859 Lord Derby's government had fallen. Lord Palmerston returned to power and was to remain Prime Minister until 1865. Palmerston – now 75 but still full of bounce – was convinced that those batteries at Taku must have been manned by Russians.

His instinct about Russian intrigue in China was sagacious, but the facts this time were against him. The Russians might be looking for ways to manipulate the Manchus, but their arms offer was still being pondered: all evidence goes to show that the Chinese fought so well at Taku without significant foreign aid. To Lord John Russell at the Foreign Office, Palmerston wrote: 'We must in some way or other make the Chinese repent of the outrage ... we might send a military-naval force to attack and occupy Peking.' Though trouble with China had dragged on until middle-class voters were bored by the topic, when news came about this defeat the mood of the moment was vindictive. 'England with France, or England without France if necessary', thundered *The Times*, 'shall teach such a lesson to these perfidious hordes that the name of European will hereafter be a passport of fear, if it cannot be of love, throughout their land.'

Elgin on his return from China, though essentially a non-party man, had been invited to join Lord Palmerston's new government as Postmaster-General. The Tories had been angling for his services, too, and he managed to beat Benjamin Disraeli 553-411 for the Rectorship of Glasgow University. Lord Elgin was popular that year, before the bad news came about Taku.

At the Cabinet session of 17 September, W. E. Gladstone whose private opinion about China happily coincided with his duty, as Chancellor of the Exchequer, to warn against an expensive new war, took the line of criticizing Frederick Bruce's belligerent approach to the Taku Forts. But Bruce's impatience to push on to Peking got staunch support from the senior official at the Foreign Office, Edmund Hammond, who all along had mistrusted Elgin's sympathy with the Chinese, in particular, the way he had let himself be talked out of establishing a British Minister permanently in the Imperial capital.

The danger to the Manchu dynasty of armed foreigners occupying Peking had become part of the conventional wisdom of those British politicians with inner misgivings about the China war. Palmerston was too robust for that sort of hesitancy, even though his own Foreign Minister shared it. He was pretty sure it wouldn't matter: the simple answer, as Palmerston saw it, was to get an army to Peking.

Elgin, while no less uneasy than Gladstone about China, tried to let his brother Frederick down lightly by blaming Admiral Hope. 'My own view is that the Admiral acted like a madman,' he wrote. 'However, there is no chance of blame being thrown on an Admiral.' Lord Elgin went on to warn his Cabinet colleague, Sir Charles Wood: 'If you humiliate the Emperor beyond measure ... you ... imperil the most lucrative trade you have in the world ... The general notion is that if we use the bludgeon freely enough we can do anything in China. I hold the opposite view.' Bruce was instructed by the Foreign Office to send an ultimatum to the Chinese.

The Anglo-French Alliance had suited both Palmerston and Napoleon III, though their fellow-countrymen might think it unnatural. But since its heyday in the Crimea, the alliance had reached its last gasp. From Shanghai on 1 August 1859 a report went to the Chinese Emperor, '... the English and French barbarians are reported to be having troubles themselves at home', though the writer felt obliged to add, 'in matters involving China they always shield one another'.

The trouble was real. Mistrust rose to a crescendo in 1860, when city clerks were inspired by Tennyson's pulsating verse to join up *en masse* as Volunteer Riflemen for fear of a French invasion. For this mistrust there were good enough reasons on both sides. Napoleon III shabbily seized Savoy and the Italian city of Nice, Garibaldi's birthplace, as his price for allowing Italian unity. Could an ally like this be trusted? Others read a sinister portent into the canal the French were cutting across Suez. Nor were the French happy with the British, who had been disobliging about an Italian plot to assassinate the Emperor, organized in London by a refugee of some note called Orsini. As for China, suppose the Protestant British had a secret plan – as well they might – for replacing the Manchus by a subservient Taiping Emperor?

Underlying these exaggerations and absurdities, the Anglo-French conflict just then could be reduced to one simple element. Britain's Royal Navy, for so long dominant on the oceans of the world, had become technically outmoded. Steam and armour-plate made her huge battle-fleet of long-lasting oaken three-deckers obsolete, but the new ironclads were expensive, and the British taxpayer burked paying for them. The French were said to have half a dozen such ironclads in their channel ports, which could knock out all British naval opposition whatever, and land troops at any point they chose along the undefended English coast. (Then why – asked Gladstone coolly – did not the French invade during the Mutiny, when England was stripped of soldiers to send to India? His opposition to war taxation and war scares made Gladstone unpopular, though he was only voicing the second thoughts already apparent among the commercial classes about the profitability, in cash terms, of aggression. The cost of ironclads and of the China war was soon to raise income tax – that immoral tax, which in Gladstone's view put a premium on dishonesty – to the alarming level of 10d in the pound).

The Chinese treatment of the American Commissioner John E. Ward was widely quoted in London by Palmerstonians as showing how Bruce or anyone else would have been humiliated if trying to enter Peking unsupported by an armed force. Ward for his own part had in the end decided to make the detour through Pei-t'ang. Of course, since their victory at Taku the Manchu mood was changing, for the worse; their minds had begun harking back to the good old days of tributary barbarians. Commissioner Ward was kept cooling his heels at Pei-t'ang, for an exemplary three weeks. The journey to Peking was 160 miles. He went part of the way in a 16-oared Chinese sampan. On taking to the road, John E. Ward should have insisted on travelling in the dignity of a sedan chair, as did high-ranking mandarins. But the Chinese

274

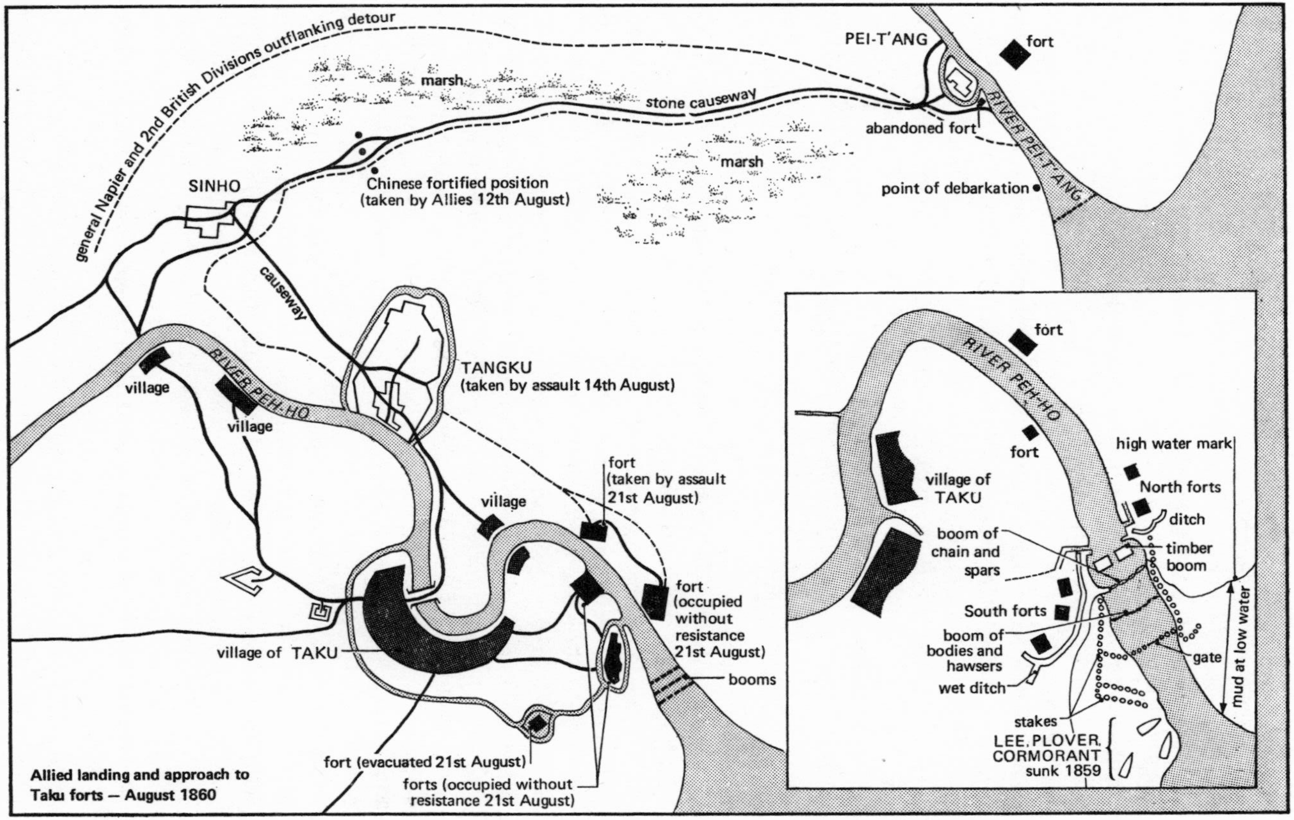
general Napier and 2nd British Divisions outflanking detour
marsh
stone causeway
PEI-T'ANG
fort
RIVER PEI-T'ANG
abandoned fort
marsh
point of debarkation
SINHO
Chinese fortified position
(taken by Allies 12th August)
causeway
TANGKU
(taken by assault 14th August)
village
village
RIVER PEH-HO
village
fort
(taken by assault
21st August)
fort
(occupied
without
resistance
21st August)
booms
village of TAKU
fort (evacuated 21st August)
forts (occupied without
resistance 21st August)
fort
RIVER PEH-HO
fort
village of
TAKU
high water mark
North forts
ditch
timber
boom
boom of
chain and
spars
South forts
boom of
bodies and
hawsers
wet ditch
gate
mud at low water
stakes
LEE, PLOVER,
CORMORANT
sunk 1859

Allied landing and approach to
Taku forts – August 1860

told him that the Russians always travelled by cart. This in fact was how the representatives of subject peoples made their way to the gates of Peking.

The United States Commissioner was put in an unsprung vehicle like a narrow box, pulled by a pair of mules in tandem, trellised over and curtained in front, and floored inside with boards, with no cushion or seat. The road to Peking, good in its day, was constructed of massive granite blocks, five feet long and eighteen inches wide, and like public works elsewhere in disorganized Manchu China the road surface had fallen into neglect. The granite blocks had tilted, and the crevices were filled up with mud. The unsprung cart lurched and jolted so painfully that on the last stretch Commissioner Ward got down and walked. His troubles were not over.

The streets of Peking on 27 July 1859 were lined with thousands, come to see a vanquished enemy arrive in a cart, and make his submission. Had not the Americans fought at Taku, and therefore shared in the defeat? Though well lodged and fed, John E. Ward was not allowed to fly the Stars and Stripes from his legation building, and was prevented from walking the streets freely, or contacting the Russians. A talk with Kuei-liang and Hua Shana about delivering President Buchanan's letter brought up once again the vexed question of the kowtow.

The Chinese were ready to concede that Commissioner Ward, instead of making three successive prostrations, might kneel only once – and knock his head on the floor three times, instead of nine. Ward, a Southern gentleman in speech as in deed, told the Chinese he was 'accustomed to kneel only to God and Woman'. (To which Kuei-liang's reassuring answer had been, 'the Emperor is the same as God'.) John E. Ward offered to enter the Imperial Presence bareheaded, bow low, and retire walking backwards – but he drew the line at bowing low enough to touch the ground with his fingers. This discussion about the kowtow went on for two weeks. American unwillingness to kneel before the Emperor gave rise at one point to a theory that 'foreigners have no knee joints'.

A satisfactory formula was at last worked out. John E. Ward would come in and place himself behind a curtained table so arranged that, from where the Emperor sat on his throne, the American envoy would appear to be kneeling. Court chamberlains at this critical moment would take Ward by the arms, and exclaim, 'Don't kneel! Don't kneel!' (Or possibly – who knows? – might seize their chance to push the Commissioner down to his knees, or even lower.) But this tricky situation never arose. The American cortège with the Presidential letter was ready to set out from Peking to meet the Chinese Emperor amid the breathtaking marvels of the Summer Palace, four miles outside the city walls. But at the last moment, the petulant young Emperor insisted on a full kowtow ceremony. ('His majesty had heard we took part in the recent combat ... He required the kowtow in proof of sincere repentance.') John E. Ward wearily told his staff to take off their uniforms and send away their horses. Next day, he was instructed to leave Peking. Ratifications of the American treaty were formally exchanged, at last, on 15 August 1859, quite unspectacularly, down on the muddy coast, at Pei-t'ang.

Parliament debated the situation created by the Taku defeat in March 1860, after all the essential decisions for pressing on with the war in China had already been taken by the Cabinet. The interchanges this time were exasperated and perfunctory. In the Commons none of the speeches went deep. Except for one eccentric who wanted to 'take possession of Nanking with a force of gunboats ... to keep the internal navigation of the country clear, the silk and tea would come down to us' the soaring perorations that had concealed dreams of conquest were better forgotten. If the Tientsin Treaty could still somehow be ratified, and Britain got decently out of her military embroilment in China, that would be a blessed relief.

Of course, a blast of moral condemnation rose from the radical left, John Bright declaring of 'our transactions with China during the past few years' that 'nothing more vicious can be found in our history; no page of our annals is more full of humiliation because more full of crime'. Another mercantile spokesman asked if 'we were to blow up their forts and bombard their towns and then say, Good people, we are a trading community; we have come here to extend your commerce and ours'. Lord Palmerston trod delicately, admitting of the Treaty: 'Some people think it contains more concessions on the part of the Chinese Government than it was handsome on our part to ask.'

There was sharp criticism in the Lords of the probable cost of the war – where it was admitted that to send an expedition up to Peking could hardly cost less than two and a half millions. Lord Malmesbury, the ex-Foreign Secretary, made it clear that his instructions to Bruce had been sent 'on the supposition that matters would be carried out without any fighting on either side.' He warned that though the derogatory expression 'barbarian' had of late been bandied about, 'the Chinese government is anything but a barbarian government. They are very clever and very well-educated people, and I believe they have very nearly as much knowledge of what is going on as we have ourselves.' Elgin himself pleaded against a formal declaration of war, which would 'carry destruction and devastation among the peoples of China, and ... entail ruin and distress on large bodies of British and other merchants in the China trade'. Here and there in the debate could faintly be heard the accent of morning-after repentance. The Taku defeat had been a shock.

'When our merchants trading with China were under the strict control of the East India Company,' recalled Lord Ellenborough, who had been Governor-General of India in Pottinger's time, 'no wars with China took place.' Speaking of 'the continual succession of wars' since those placid times, Lord Ellenborough – an eloquent defender in his own day of India's opium revenue – exclaimed, 'I know not one of them to which the misconduct of our own people and their own disgraceful avarice has not materially ... contributed.' He regarded the present war with horror, as an unjust war, and went on to declaim, 'It is not, my Lords, lawful to make war for the purpose of making money. To do so is to commit a crime ... It is based on wrong, and wrong will not continually be protected by Providence.' Lord Ellenborough made a veiled reference to a despatch he had received from China when in India, 'giving an account of the sufferings of the Chinese people, in consequence of the prosecution of hostilities, which I durst not publish. I have never generally made known the details of the horrors which came under my notice.' Apparently the facts made public about rape and loot in the first Opium War are only a portion of the truth.

Even before the war issue was debated in the House of Lords, Frederick Bruce did as he was told, and sent an ultimatum to Peking. He demanded an apology for Taku, and the return of the captured ships and guns, a ratification at Peking of the Treaty of Tientsin, and prompt payment of the 1858 indemnity. This ultimatum was rejected by the Chinese in an answer described by Hope Grant, the British army commander, as 'cheeky in the extreme'. On 8 April 1860 war was declared, but in terms which allowed British merchants to continue trading elsewhere in China while military operations were carried on to the north.

Elgin had gone to Paris to consult with Baron Gros, and the

Cabinet then sent him out to China once more, to carry through their policy and clear up a mess only partly of his own making. In politics, Elgin had climbed nearly to the top of the greasy pole – but as he was well aware, if he failed a second time in China, his career would begin a long slide downwards.

France was about to embark on her long programme of systematic conquest between 1861 and 1884 in Indo-China. Therefore, though elsewhere the French might increasingly mistrust the British, in the Far East, by continuing their alliance, the French had more to gain than lose. The Emperor Napoleon III had appointed a General for China, Cousin de Montauban, a cavalryman with experience in Algeria (but he was chagrined to find his authority coupled with that of Baron Gros). When volunteers were called for, a quarter of the entire French army was said to have offered to serve. This hand-picked and high-spirited expeditionary force, numbering 7500, was sent East round the Cape – infantry, thirty guns, but only a handful of Spahi cavalry. By travelling in a P & O steamer via Suez, General de Montauban arrived in China two months before his army. 'A sensible, conciliatory man,' Governor-General Lord Canning had reported as he passed through India, 'but nobody in England seems to know much of him as a soldier.'

General de Montauban – flamboyant, temperamental, talented – owed his promotion to political loyalty, and was aware that his master, the dictatorial Emperor of the French, needed spectacular victories. De Montauban kept one eye cocked all the time for the effect on Paris of his actions in the field. The French had at that time a splendid military reputation, confirmed by their effectiveness at the siege of Sebastopol. The British General, James Hope Grant, was cautioned, however, by the War Office, 'Our object in going to China is to trade . . . An early termination of our Chinese difficulty is therefore most desirable. Our allies probably have different views. They have no great commercial interests at stake . . . Although the two governments are on perfectly friendly terms it is impossible to deny that there exists between the two nations a jealous and uneasy feeling.' Tact would be needed, but luckily tact was one of Hope Grant's virtues.

He had been Lord Saltoun's Brigade-Major during the first Opium War, and in India had commanded the 9th Lancers under Sir Hugh Gough at the bloody encounters of Sobraon and Chillianwallah. During the Mutiny, Hope Grant served at Lucknow. He was a spare, weather-beaten, Bible-reading Scot, good-natured, fair-minded, a man of solid professional ability but so inarticulate

279

that he could sometimes hardly get a coherent sentence together. His young staff officers had to become expert at putting into words what they surmised might be passing through his mind. Hope Grant was a passionate golfer and an expert musician – he reached staff rank, unkind rumour said, because Lord Saltoun, who was musical, needed the services of a cellist. Hope Grant's brother, Frank, was President of the Royal Academy, and, by a coincidence, the Scottish pattern of cousinage made Hope Grant kinsman to Lord Elgin, his eldest brother having married Elgin's sister, Lady Mary Bruce.

Through the fog of Anglo-French misunderstanding, Lord Elgin tried to keep on good terms with Baron Gros, who travelled out with him. Elgin whiled away the trip down the Red Sea with Tennyson's *Idylls of the King*, and the reprinted volume of Russell's despatches to *The Times* which described atrocities in the Indian Mutiny. Off Ceylon the two diplomats survived a shipwreck together, but their friendship was no longer as easy is it had been.

The formal agreement with the French stipulated 10 000 British effectives, but India since the Mutiny was stuffed with idle troops, and over 13 000 turned up at Hong Kong, including a cavalry force of 800 sabres – Dragoons, and two units of Sikh Irregulars. The Sikhs had volunteered. 'Thirty thousand English (fleet and army)', wrote Elgin sarcastically, 'and ten thousand French, ought to be a match' for the Chinese. He thought this force 'utterly disproportionate' and wondered what Parliament would say when the bill was presented. Confronted with a British contingent so much larger than had been agreed in Paris, the French began to feel put in the shade.

'I don't begrudge you a single man or rupee', wrote Canning to Hope Grant, also inquiring cautiously, 'How have you found the behaviour of the native troops, and their officers? Have you any misgivings?' They were all men from the north of India, which had played a role in helping the British put down mutiny in Oudh and Bengal, but on board ship between India and China one Punjabi infantry regiment, still tainted by the Mutiny mood, had objected to their drinking water being served out through a leather pipe.

Troops who were sensitive to the risks of ritual pollution might not necessarily be reliable in an attack on Peking. The peccant Punjabis were sent off to defend Shanghai against the Taiping – thus ingeniously placing potential rebels at loggerheads with actual ones. The sepoys in this campaign, speaking generally,

earned themselves as bad a name as hitherto, treating China
as another Bengal, and civilians as their natural prey, though
some of the Punjabis showed a measure of sympathy with Chinese
Muslims (who were plotting an insurrection of their own against
the Manchu).

A suspicious thought had occurred to someone in London:
what was to stop the French, as they arrived, from planting
themselves on the strategically important headland opposite
Hong Kong harbour – the Kowloon Peninsula? Harry Parkes
was sent off promptly to do a deal with the Viceroy in Canton,
and on 18 March 1860 a breezy stretch of two square miles on
Kowloon, healthier for troops than Hong Kong as well as securing
the British anchorage there, was leased in perpetuity for 500 taels
of silver per annum (or £160).

On this level plain the bearded Sikh horsemen exercised their
chargers. The Sikhs made the ladies' hearts beat faster by their
astonishing prowess at 'tent-pegging' with bamboo-shafted lances,
and by cutting an orange in half with one sweeping blow of the
tulwar when at full gallop. Practice was also made at Kowloon
with an experimental piece of ordnance – the new Armstrong
breech-loading field-gun, a rifled 25-pounder for which China was
to be the proving-ground. The Armstrong was particularly meant
for use against enemy troops massed in the field. The French had
a similar but less up-to-date weapon in the rifled 'Napoleon gun' –
a converted bronze muzzle-loader with studded projectiles,
which in Italy had won for them the battle of Solferino.

In target practice off Kowloon, against floating barrels, the
Armstrong was found to fire as straight and true as a good rifle.
On impact, the shell scattered forty-two pieces of angular metal,
with devastating effect. Though the Armstrong was later found
to be the quickest way of breaking up Chinese cavalry formations,
it also had snags. After every hundred rounds or so, the vertical
ventpiece was apt to fly out, and if, in the heat of battle, the
breech block was not screwed up tight, an Armstrong could back-
fire, to the detriment of nearby artillerymen.

The French had an ingenious new weapon also. They too had
seen the usefulness of the gunboat in warfare up Asiatic rivers –
and had shipped out to China some prefabricated gunboats. The
fifteen component pieces included the machinery, and when
assembled by bolting together – in three watertight compartments
sealed with vulcanized rubber – they had a 75-ton gunboat seventy-
eight feet long, drawing only five feet of water, and armed with a
60-pounder gun.

The troops encamped at Kowloon wore large pith-helmets to protect them from sunstroke. The Chinese found these very funny, and christened their enemy The Hats. Bets were already being offered and taken among Cantonese that this expeditionary force too would be defeated – probably when it tried to pass the Taku Forts. The most spectacular wager – of $50 000 on an Allied defeat – was offered by the Chinese Cotton Guild, stakes to be lodged in the Oriental Bank of Hong Kong. A handful of American businessmen willing to back the Allies proved unable to raise more than $10 000 between them, so the bet collapsed.

A Coolie Corps was once more recruited – the British finding 2500 men at $9 a month, the French 1000. The Corps paraded with stout bamboos at the slope instead of rifles, and were apt on the march to cool their limbs by agitating a fan. Finding men willing to serve was not so easy. The secret societies on Hong Kong, who this time had no private motive for accompanying the Allies into action, had put it about among the Chinese that the Coolie Corps on reaching the north would bear the brunt of the fighting. Recourse was had at last to enlisting Hong Kong's thieves and vagabonds – local crime dropped sharply when the Corps went north. The people of north China soon learned to dread the Coolie Corps more even that the Indians, French or British. ('Lawless and cruel,' admitted Lieut.-Col. Garnet Wolseley, but he added, 'a single coolie was actually of more general value than any three baggage animals; they were easily fed, and when properly treated, most manageable.')

The British usually started any campaign in China by occupying the island of Chou-shan – as a base of supply from which they could command the Yangtze. General de Montauban this time argued for three hours – unsuccessfully – that the exercise was pointless. Two thousand British from the Hong Kong garrison, and about 500 French, including marines, were in the event sent to Chou-shan. By now, the locals knew better than to put up a resistance. On joss-house hill, above the port of Tin-hai, stood two conspicuous poles, one taller than the other. Up the taller pole, the French at once ran the Tricolor. Naval ratings from the British fleet manhandled a ship's spar ashore, so that the Union Jack should fly even higher. The French then sent off to the mainland for a flagpost higher still. This was the present state of what once had been a firm fighting alliance.

The narrow channels between three small islands to the west of Chou-shan had been used of late as a piratical base by a large fleet of junks, commanded by an English seaman, called by the

Chinese Fokie Tom (no doubt from his favourite expletive). A British gunboat, *Bustard*, went in after Fokie Tom and his fleet, through the southern opening between the islands. When the pirates hoisted sail to escape they found their other ways out had been blocked by HMS *Woodcock* and the French gunboat *Alarme*. Fokie Tom and his wife – described as a 'rather good-looking Malay girl' – together with over thirty of his followers, were caught after fighting for their lives. Twenty-six of Fokie Tom's junks were made prize and six burned, but the bulk of his men got away safely to the coast of Chou-shan. A company of the 99th Regiment and some French marines had previously been ordered to block this escape route, but they turned up a couple of hours too late, and complained, of course, that the Navy had started too soon.

Word reached Shanghai on 25 May 1860 that the Taiping had launched a new offensive – timed to coincide with the Anglo-French expedition northward, and intended to take the pressure off Nanking. The city of Soochow, 90 miles distant from Shanghai, had fallen the day before.

The Manchu mayor of Shanghai was an adroit official, reputed to be making at least £40 000 a year in squeeze from the local opium dens. He had cultivated the goodwill of the French and British – as well as sending detailed information about them to Peking. Thanks partly to his shrewd management, the Allies, though planning to attack the Chinese Emperor in the north, proved willing at the same time to defend Shanghai for him against the Christian rebels.

There were 13 000 Chinese Roman Catholics in Soochow. General de Montauban proposed sending 1500 of his men off to protect them, if his British allies would back him with a token force of 400, but the diplomats hardened their hearts against this romantic sideshow. Only a radius of four miles round Shanghai was for the time being to be given protection by the foreigners. Shanghai's brick walls were repaired and the ditch round the city deepened. Royal Marines were posted to command the approaches to the foreign settlement and the Chinese city, while the French held the most exposed of the city's gates. Guns on the walls were so mounted as to be capable of firing grapeshot down the streets of the city, as well as canister at an approaching enemy. The mandarins in Shanghai had reason to fear that as the Taiping

283

army came close, a mass of sympathizers among the poorer classes in the city might rise up and open the gates for them. Baskets filled with the chopped-off heads of 'long-haired' rebel prisoners were hung from the battlements as a deterrent.

Chinese spies who had been told off to observe Lord Elgin and Baron Gros as they left for the north reported that the two diplomats had 'placed their munitions and baggage on board – including bamboo ladders, carts, horses, and dummy barbarians carved out of wood'. Spying worked both ways. Prince Seng sent one of his staff officers, Lieutenant Feng En-fu, to pick up what information he might from the Americans. Feng reported accurately that 'the English and French barbarians intended to seize Pei-t'ang and then make a surprise attack on Taku from the rear'. Some of the 500 guns mounted in the forts at Taku were turned to face inland, as a precaution.

Prince Seng's agent also got from his American informants a close estimate of how many men were being sent north, including '5000 Cantonese rebels [Coolie Corps] and 3000 black barbarians [sepoys]'. Through foreign newspapers, Peking was also able to form a rough-and-ready notion of the growing opposition inside Britain to the cost of the war. ('Their tradesmen form one group, their military men another,' wrote a perspicacious official later that year, 'and the two do not work together. The English barbarians' annual expenditure for hostilities depends entirely on commercial strength.') A few days before this enlightening report reached Peking, Lord Elgin's friend W. E. Gladstone had written him a confidential warning of 'the mixture of indifference and disgust which now marks the public sentiment', reminding Elgin, 'Unless happily you shall have been enabled to get that most miserable business composed before the next session, I think it very likely to be made the subject of some vote which will overthrow the government.'

This time in China, Lord Elgin had much more to worry him. On the London political scene a whispering campaign accused him of being soft with the Chinese and letting the war drag on. His brother had certainly been inept at Taku. All four leaders of the Allied expedition, two Generals and two Admirals were supposed to be on an exactly equal footing – but the French Admiral, soon to be replaced, was disobliging, de Montauban had already voiced strong dissident views of his own, and Hope, promoted to Vice-Admiral and left in command despite his handling of the 1859 Taku attack, was well aware what men thought of him, and stood on his dignity – refusing, for example, to acknowledge the salutes of military men. As well as contending with ill-assorted commanders, and with politicians at home who were pushing him to gain a quick and cheap victory, Lord Elgin had touchy allies with somewhat different war aims. The campaigning season – over a difficult terrain – would be uncomfortably short, from the staggering midsummer heats when the monsoon wind had dropped and transports could safely be towed up the coast, to the freeze-up in November. Those large bets in Canton were a portent. The Chinese had their tails up.

The Allies' seaborne landing would this time take place on a marshy and unwelcoming coast. Prince Seng had the option of deploying his horsemen to pounce on the ships' boats as they brought the troops ashore. But, perhaps misled by guerrilla victories around Canton, Seng appears to have accepted the current view that foreigners were invincible only when under the guns of their warships. The trick, as he saw it, was to lure them inland, on foot. There, his splendid cavalry – numbering about 30 000, of which 6000 were Mongols – would harry the foreign soldiers, as a few years before they had harried the Taiping infantry, until finally the bitter winter came down and the cavalry would have it all their own way. In Seng's plan of campaign there are distant reminiscences of the strategy used by the Russians against Napoleon in 1812. If the Russians were giving Prince Seng the benefit of their strategic advice – and they may have been – they were at the same time helping the French by supplying them with maps of the invasion coast.

The mudflats around the Peh-ho flooded at high tide. After a heavy rainfall, the river overflowed its banks, and spread for miles across country. The cumbersome Allied armies moved north slowly for their landing, and by the time their big fleet of warships and transports was concentrated off the coast, the summer rains were coming down. General de Montauban at first advocated a curious division of responsibility. The French were to make an independent landing, and march up the right bank of the Peh-ho River, while the British put their men ashore further north, and marched up the left bank. De Montauban proposed to land his men twenty-five miles away, march them onwards drawing supplies from his fleet, and then (though he lacked siege artillery) reserve to himself the glory of attacking the southernmost Taku Fort. But his proposed landing place was by now a bog, and the coast a salt marsh with no drinking water, so de Montauban made the best of it, and joined Hope Grant eight miles north of Taku, at Pei-t'ang. Prince Seng's spy had been right about Hope

Grant's plan: to move inland, and take the forts from the rear.

On 31 July a circular storm with whirling clouds of blown sand hit the 213 warships and transports – some of them hired Dutch and American merchantmen – as they took up position in three lines across the bay, southward of Pei-t'ang. By the next day, though rain persisted, the running sea had gone down enough for gunboats to busy themselves towing ashore a procession of ship's boats full of troops, many of them seasick, each man with fifty-six rounds of ammunition and three days' cooked rations, the British wearing their pith-helmets. They had to wade across a wide morass, the mud being so adhesive that one British Brigadier eventually scrambled to firm ground clad in only his shirt. He ordered his men, many of whom also were trouserless, to 'come to attention and shoulder', and they all marched off towards Pei-t'ang, shirt-tails flapping, amazing the French with their sang-froid. Pickets of Chinese cavalry watched the landing from a distance. Rain fell incessantly during the next ten days.

The troops advanced cautiously on the fort defending Pei-t'ang, only to find that the guns pointing over the walls were wooden dummies. The Chinese garrison had gone. (This did not deter the French Colonel, who first entered Pei-t'ang Fort from running up a Tricolor improvised from a white handkerchief knotted to a red-and-blue belt, for which he was mentioned in despatches.)

The retreating Chinese had booby-trapped the courtyard inside the fort. An elderly local inhabitant obligingly pointed out exactly where Prince Seng's soldiers had left their buried mines – gunpowder charges, sparked off by flintlocks yielding to the pressure of marching boots. This old man was soon paid back for his helpfulness, as were most of the other civilian inhabitants of Pei-t'ang.

The troops, after landing seasick in the rain, and marching onward through so much mud, went wild. This old man's two daughters, and many other local women – between forty and fifty of them, according to Harry Parkes's estimate – eluded rape only by poisoning themselves with opium, deliberately strangling one another, or opting for death by drowning – as a rule, in one of the huge waterbutts which stood under the curved and tiled eaves of the houses of the rich. All the other inhabitants fled into the marshland.

General Hope Grant was driven to admit that his Hong Kong coolies were 'for the most part atrocious villians ... the robberies and crimes they committed in the town were fearful'. Many of the

Coolie Corps were opium addicts, and the General was tempted to try the experiment of forbidding them their drug, but this idea proved impractical. As his interpreter pointed out, 'habitual smokers would have pined away, and eventually died'.

The Punjabis also showed a marked aptitude for rape and plunder. Though Hope Grant did his best to deter them, the pernicious example set by coolies and sepoys was unhesitatingly followed by French and English troops – each later on blaming the other for starting soonest and behaving worst: 'ransacking left and right,' according to an eyewitness.

Thirty men were flogged in one day on the orders of the British Provost-Marshal – Captain Con, of the 3rd Buffs – but according to Swinhoe the military interpreter, 'the very provost-sergeants whose very duty it was to suppress looting ... were greater plunderers themselves than most others'. During a week of monotonous downpour, order was slowly and forcibly restored to the two armies.

Pei-t'ang was a small walled town of about 20 000 inhabitants, occupying a patch of hard ground near the right bank of the river – like an island amid the floods. The salt marsh and tidal swamp all around were impassable after rain, but directly across this marsh to the village of Sin-ho – and thence up the left bank of the Peh-ho River all the way to Tientsin – ran a causeway of stone blocks, about nine yards wide and standing clear of the mud.

At 4 a.m. on 3 August a reconnaissance-in-force was sent up this narrow road, 1000 French with three small guns leading the way, under the command of a talented fighting soldier called Collineau. General Collineau had left France for Algeria when a young man of 21, to join the Foreign Legion as a private. He had come home after twenty-five years' absence, a General of Brigade. Collineau had led the Zouaves in the Crimea.

The British infantry accompanying the French on this reconnaissance – 1000 men, including sepoys of the 15th Punjabis – were under Brigadier Sutton. To their left and right were illimitable marsh and swamp; after four miles of trudging up the causeway in wet darkness, they got a glimpse towards dawn of Prince Seng's cavalry, behind small redoubts joined by a crenellated mud wall, holding an entrenched position that crossed and obstructed the stone roadway.

As the doubtful half-light increased, a force of many hundred enemy horsemen showed themselves – Tartar, Chinese and Mongol – and began extending into the marsh right and left, to threaten the column's flanks. This cavalry was armed for the most part with spear and bow-and-arrow, though there were a few muskets

287

and gingalls. They rode wooden saddles and used large iron stir-rups; some wore a pair of squirrel's tails dangling from the cap. Shots were exchanged, but de Montauban and Hope Grant, riding up to see what their men had encountered, were both agreed that since the Allied force included no cavalry, it would be prudent to retire. Mistaking this brief and inconclusive contact for a portent of victory, the Chinese commander sent the usual optimistic report off to Peking. Enemy horsemen that night pushed audaci-ously close to the Allied outposts, brandishing their swords, and striking the grotesque poses that in Chinese military theory were supposed to strike terror into the heart of the foe.

A head-on attack up such a narrow front as the causeway might well have meant a real, not a make-believe, victory for the Chinese. But Hope Grant, in probing north inquisitively across the marshland, had found what he judged to be an adequate second route, outflanking the Chinese entrenchments and just about firm enough underfoot to bear men and horses. On 12 August, before the entire Allied force moved out of Pei-t'ang down the causeway, Hope Grant sent his 800 cavalry and his Second Division under Major-General Sir Robert Napier out of camp first, to take the pathway he had traced across the muddy morass a few hundred yards to the right. Napier's division, making slow work of it, took two hours to advance two miles.

Once they were on their way, the main body of French and British marched more quickly along the stone causeway, headed by three Armstrong guns, which Hope Grant covered against cavalry attack, on each flank and to the rear, by detached com-panies of The Buffs. The moment for testing the new weapon in action was near.

Chinese cavalry, mounted and ready, were extended 2000 yards ahead, in an impassive unbroken line, blocking the way across the marsh. When the gap between the armies had dimin-ished to a mile, the Armstrongs opened up. Their accurate ex-ploding shells tore gap after gap in the Chinese line, the horsemen in the distance closing up and closing up to keep their ranks. The few gingalls which answered the Armstrongs were, of course, outranged.

At last the Chinese cavalry, maintaining its discipline astonish-ingly well under fire, edged off to left and right, as if intending to attack and surround the entire Allied force – including Napier's division, which had been making heavy going of the mud plain out to the Allies' right. The Chinese advanced at the trot. When the nearest British infantry formed hollow square – their tactic to repel cavalry – and the front rank knelt down to fire, some of the approaching Chinese horsemen took heart, in the belief that their barbarian enemy must be trying to kowtow.

The Chinese cavalry got to within 450 yards of the Armstrongs before being checked by a lethal concentration of shells, rockets and rifle fire. 'They bore unflinchingly,' reported General Napier in despatches, 'for a considerable time, such a fire as would have tried any troops in the world.' The Chinese entrenchments were then given a twenty-five-minute bombardment, and as the enemy cavalry reserve emerged from cover, they too were broken up by the three Armstrongs.

A hundred of the foremost Chinese cavalry got near enough to attack, with spears and arrows, one lagging battery of 6-pounders in Napier's division, which had an escort of fifty mounted Sikhs, armed with carbine and pistol as well as lance and tulwar. Though outnumbered, the Sikhs managed to drive off the Chinese attacks, but their horses were too blown from plunging through the mud to pursue. At last, the baffled enemy horsemen streamed away towards Taku.

Active participants in this fight disagree about the size of the Chinese force. Some put their numbers as high as 7000 horsemen, and 5000 is a commonly stated figure. Hope Grant, in his memoirs dictated years after, remembered there having been 4000. Brigadier Sutton – who with General Collineau commanded the reconnaissance, an old cavalry officer, and the man best placed to judge – stated their numbers confidently as under 2000, and perhaps no more than 1500. No doubt the more impressive figures are an indirect tribute to the bold way the Chinese fought. Armed with bows and arrows, spears, and a few matchlocks, they had shown, in Napier's words, 'courageous endurance' against a European force with modern weapons which – if the extreme case be taken – was perhaps ten times their number, and though unaccustomed to modern artillery had stood without flinching the loss by long-range gunfire of several hundred men. Garnet Wolseley admitted that he 'never saw men come on so pluckily'.

From the village of Sin-ho, where the causeway met the Peh-ho River, all the inhabitants had fled, but downstream, connected by a diverging causeway and blocking the way to the forts, stood another small walled town called Tangku; it had served as a cavalry camp. Muzzles of Chinese cannon could be seen protruding from Tangku's crenellated walls, and red banners were being waved defiantly. Above the mud walls peeped a two-storey pagoda, which until lately was Prince Seng's headquarters.

General Hope Grant, who always moved with deliberate and sometimes exasperating Scottish caution, was decidedly of opinion that his mud-stained troops had had enough. General de Montauban, for his part, thought Tangku might be taken at a rush, and off he set down the causeway, leading a force exclusively French, and with some artillery, but not much. He exchanged shots with the forty-five Chinese guns mounted on the walls of Tangku – playing indecisively at 'long bowls' – but in the end was driven back. Once more the French General had let slip a chance for the force under his command to distinguish itself independently.

When the two Generals met, to discuss a plan of attack upon the five Taku forts, this divergence between British and French notions of war came into the open. Hope Grant and de Montauban were supposed to command the entire Allied force on alternate days – a futile arrangement unless they saw eye to eye. Now de Montauban presented Hope Grant with a textbook plan for attacking the forts nearest the sea, with the help of gunboats. But reaching these forts would mean crossing the river, and marching across flooded country with the armies' flank exposed to Chinese cavalry and gunfire.

Hope Grant opposed this plan tooth and nail. He had in Napier a brilliant field officer with training as a Sapper who had made it pretty plain that the uppermost northern, or left bank, Taku Fort (the one nearest to view) had by an error in Chinese military engineering been so placed as to command all the others, with its guns. Hope Grant's plan was simple, and in Montauban's eyes riskily unorthodox. After taking the small walled town of Tangku, just ahead, Hope Grant proposed to attack and possess himself of this one fort, strongly believing that once the other forts downstream came under its guns, they would see the weakness of their position and be obliged to surrender. Seng and his cavalry might escape: this was the price for a quick and simple victory.

Hope Grant was taking a great deal upon himself. The political pressures to reach Peking and get back before winter were already great. A second Taku defeat would knock to smithereens not only his own career but probably the Anglo-French alliance, and very likely bring down the British government. By voicing opposition to de Montauban's plan he was aspersing the brilliant military reputation of the French. But Hope Grant stuck his heels in.

Though de Montauban contested the wisdom of the British plan to the last, when on 20 August 1860 he saw the debate was lost he generously wrote: 'I shall nevertheless send a French land force to work conjointly with our allies ... The object of my observations is, above all, to free myself from military responsibility with reference to my own government.'

For the assault on the 130-yard-square mud fort which Hope Grant had picked upon as particularly vulnerable, Lord Elgin proposed to take a ringside seat, in company with Bowlby, special correspondent of *The Times*, on the roof of the temple inside Tangku, and uncomfortably close to the firing. The French would lend their battery of rifled guns, and about 1000 men, to be led by Collineau. The British planned to put 2500 men into the field under Brigadier Reeves. But what counted in this attack too would be the way guns were handled.

In mud that at times came nearly up to the gun-carriage axles, the British army's heavy pieces – 8-inch mortars and howitzers, and two 32-pounders – were hauled to within 600 yards of the fort. At 800 yards were ranged the field guns, and four 24-pounders. To shift an Armstrong inch by inch through the mud took a team of six horses. The bombardment was to begin at daybreak.

On 21 August 1860, as a first glimmer of light came into the cloudy sky, four French gunboats and four British crossed the bar of the Peh-ho, to fire on the lower south fort, as a diversion. (The army was inclined to feel that the Admiral was not trying quite hard enough.) French and British field guns began at the same time to play on Chinese entrenchments across the Peh-ho River, and dropped shells into another fort within range, so as to keep down the fire that Chinese gunners might otherwise inflict upon the Allies' flank. An answering Chinese fire, from forty-seven guns, began from the fort menaced with attack – but the men and guns of the attacking force had during the hours of darkness been run in so close that most of the Chinese shot flew impotently overhead. The British siege artillery, at close range, hammered heavily at the Chinese embrasures, until one after another their guns were silenced. From the crippled fort, gingall and matchlock fire then took up the tune. 'We were full of admiration', wrote Harry Parkes afterwards, 'for the way the Chinese worked their guns.'

At half past six in the morning the ground for miles around shuddered, as if lifted up and dropped by an earthquake. A deafening explosive roar signalled that an 8-inch shell had been lobbed plump into the Chinese powder-magazine, sending it sky high in a bursting pillar of black smoke. By seven, almost all the Chinese guns inside the fort had fallen silent. The field guns crept up to within 500 yards, so as to cover the advance of the storming party, assembling now only thirty yards from the battered mud walls.

General Collineau led his Frenchmen into the salient near the river. To get his infantry across the protective ditch, coolies who brought up scaling ladders were sent into the water, and made to stand in it up to their necks, with ladders resting on their shoulders, to make a living bridge. Collineau led his men across the ditch, up the wall and into the fort through a large embrasure, a bayonet charge sending the demoralized Chinese away at the run.

Meanwhile, a British 8-inch howitzer had been pushed through the mud to within only fifty yards, and was knocking out a narrow breach through which troops could pass in single file. From inside the fort, Colonel Mann of the Engineers and Major Anson hacked with their swords at the ropes which held the battered drawbridge. It fell, and over went a mass of infantry with fixed bayonet. The British managed to get across two wet ditches, defended by a mass of pointed bamboo stakes – the coolies behaving so well that Hope Grant afterwards gave them an extra month's wages.

There was some hand-to-hand fighting between British and surviving Chinese. One Chinese General had been killed by a shell. The other, a mandarin of the highest military order, fought to the death, refusing to submit. He fell to a shot from the revolver of Captain Prynne of the Royal Marines, who took his adversary's red-buttoned cap with its peacock feather as a souvenir.

Over 1500 defenders fled the fort, leaving 1800 dead. A total of 3600 prisoners eventually gave themselves up to General Collineau, placing their arms on the ground and kneeling in front of him: he at once set them all free. They tore off the badges that distinguished them from civilians, and faded away. The British had lost about 200 killed and wounded, and the French about 100. Six Victoria Crosses were awarded.

Just before 1 p.m. on the same day, an English and a French officer escorted Harry Parkes to parley with two officials sent in under a white flag by Heng Fu, Viceroy of the province. One of the mandarins – called Wang – spoke good English. He had been educated at the American Mission School at Shanghai, and was known to Parkes. He bore a somewhat prevaricating letter from Viceroy Heng, offering to withdraw the booms on the river, and grant the right of transit as far as Tientsin, 'to make peace'. Harry Parkes screwed up this missive, and threw it in Wang's face, telling him loudly that unless all the other forts surrendered within two hours, they too would be taken by storm.

A British eyewitness afterwards remarked unfavourably on Parkes's 'harsh and unnecessarily violent demeanour' towards Wang, who himself protested that such usage 'was not customary among European nations'. He was a mere envoy, and therefore 'ought to be treated with the courtesy common to civilization'. But in the event, Parkes's bullying tone did the trick. Chinese evasiveness was overborne. White flags of surrender soon flew from the unconquered forts, and this was just as well, for not long afterwards a blinding electrical storm began, and rain came down for days, flooding the Peh-ho until river and countryside were all one level of water. The troops were drenched, the siege guns stuck. 'You took the forts,' said the Chinese, as this appalling rain began, 'because the Heavens themselves were against us.'

Tientsin was only a day away by gunboat. On 25 August the cavalry brigade was sent to plod in column along the causeway that followed the north bank of the Peh-ho towards the city, while Elgin and Gros went up in the gunboat *Grenada*. They were on their way to meet Kuei-liang, the elderly mandarin with trembling hands who had negotiated the 1858 treaty. He and the Viceroy of Chihli had been appointed Imperial Commissioners.

After Taku fell, Prince Seng-ko-lin-ch'in and about 100 of his mud-stained followers had been caught sight of in the far distance, jogging north in the pouring rain astride their tough, hairy, fourteen-hands Mongolian ponies. The bulk of Seng's cavalry army was somewhere to the north, and still intact.

Since a Taiping attack on Shanghai was known to be imminent, the 44th Regiment under Brigadier Jephson, and a half battery of French rifled mountain guns were detached from the army and sent hurriedly down the China coast as a reinforcement, together with two companies of French infantry. They arrived too late. The Taiping attack on Shanghai was over.

On 17 August 1860 flames had been seen from Shanghai on the western horizon. Next day, the Taiping army took for their headquarters the Jesuit church and college at Sicawei. (The church was famous for its 'stained-glass windows' ingeniously made of coloured paper, and for its home-made bamboo pipe organ.)

The long-haired rebels next attacked a Manchu fort between

Sicawei and the west gate of Shanghai. The government troops fled at the first onset, and the rebels moved closer to the city. High wooden observation towers inside the walls of Shanghai kept threatening watch on any Taiping sympathizers who might move into the streets, while canister and rifle-fire from the modern weapons of the British, French and sepoy garrison obliged the Taiping soldiers to keep their heads down in Shanghai's suburbs.

On Monday 20 August – with smoke still rising from a fired sugar-factory in the burnt-out French quarter – Taiping flags could be seen advancing to within two hundred yards of the racecourse. They were slowly driven back by an intense crossfire from ordnance mounted on the city wall, and the broadsides of European gunboats in the river. Afterwards, as the Taiping army withdrew, and the dead were counted, the bodies were identified of a number of foreign volunteers, mostly British and American, who had chosen to meet their fate in the ranks of the Taiping.

9 The Burning of the Summer Palace

'Free Trade is Jesus Christ, and Jesus Christ is Free Trade.'
Sir John Bowring

'Take away your opium, and your missionaries, and you will be welcome.'
Prince Kung to Sir Rutherford Alcock, when British Minister at Peking

Lord Elgin was getting the better of his prejudices; Harry Parkes was now, for him, 'one of the most remarkable men I have ever met, for energy, courage and ability combined'. Although in the British chain of command Parkes did not rank high, he was very conspicuous to the Chinese as the British official with whom they most often had to deal. The Cantonese demonstrated this, by offering ing to pay for his head six times more than for the head of a 'barbarian commander'.

Elgin's impressions on this second visit to China had undergone a change. Though he continued to let his private feelings spill over into a journal, this time his conscience was less often wounded. At the back of his mind, Lord Elgin must have been aware of the emerging similarity between his own career and that of his father – who had also reached high ambassadorial rank, only to fall off lamentably, and whose costly passion for the beauty of Greek statuary had made him a public laughing-stock. Elgin is noticeably less sorry, this time out, for the suffering Chinese, and more exasperated by anything whatever from Manchu prevarication to British military obtuseness that by holding him up might cheat him of success.

The extravagance of the campaign also bore painfully on Elgin's thrifty mind – he made a private comment that the war was costing three times as much as it need. In Britain after forty years of peace the figure of the war profiteer was again emerging. Huge profits had for instance been made by fitting out the troops to stand a second Crimean winter. Businessmen – and their

Parliamentary representatives – who paid lip-service to free trade were tempted by the fortunes to be made in war, but resented footing the bill. 'What will the House of Commons say when the bill ... is presented?' Elgin asked his journal on 10 July 1860. 'The expense is enormous.'

On his way up to Tientsin by gunboat once more – with the French marching along the left bank of the Peh-ho, the British on the right – Elgin noted what hard work his army and its train of camp-followers made of moving across country, observing, 'If the people tried to cut off our baggage and refused us supplies, we should find it very difficult to get on.' Prince Seng has been criticized for not devastating the country across which the British had to march – confronting them with scorched earth – but, probably, he could not have bent the local peasants to his will. They might by now know better than to welcome the French and British as liberators, but the popular sentiment, here as elsewhere in China, was covertly or openly anti-Manchu.

On 29 August, in Tientsin, Lord Elgin reminded dignified old Kuei-liang of the ultimatum his brother Frederick had sent the Chinese months earlier. The time had come to pay. Tientsin would be occupied as an army base and a port for trade (thus giving foreigners control over the supply of rice to the capital). The 1858 indemnity of four million taels of silver was to be doubled, with the Taku Forts kept as security until the money was paid. (This increased war indemnity was a windfall for Napoleon III as French merchants at Canton had lost very little, and French war expenses had been proportionately less than British.)

On 6 September the two interpreters, Parkes and Wade, discovered that the credentials of the Imperial Commissioners were defective. (Some thought the scrutiny might well have been made sooner.) Peking had sent them down without giving them power to sign a binding agreement. ('The blockheads', noted Elgin two days later, 'have gone on negotiating with me just long enough to enable Grant to bring all his army up to this point.') Tempting though it was to suppose that these three dummies had been put up, merely to gain time for Prince Seng, the situation inside Peking was too confused for such a devilishly clever plot to have been likely.

But Elgin and Gros had lost a precious week; they decided to apply pressure by moving closer to Peking. They announced their readiness to come to terms with any properly empowered Chinese representatives – but named as venue the walled river-port of T'ungchow, only fifteen miles from Peking itself, and conspicuous for a long way across the broad fields of ripened corn by its twelve-storey, 150-foot-high pagoda.

Should it come to a clash at T'ungchow, the town's 35-foot-high walls might prove too solid for field artillery – and Hope Grant's siege guns were lagging behind somewhere. 'The difficulty of getting our army along', Elgin noted in his journal, 'is incredible; our men are so pampered that they do nothing for themselves.' Napier's Division was left to garrison Tientsin and guard the lines of communication, and the Allied army, much reduced in size, moved implacably north.

The approach of Allied troops to within a day's march of Peking was meant to panic the Manchu Court, and so it did. In long Chinese experience, an alien army moved towards the Imperial capital with one end in view – to overthrow a dynasty grown ineffective and provoking discontent. Prince of Yi, the Emperor's cousin, and Mu Yi, President of the Board of War, gave Elgin and Gros every assurance that they now had proper authority. But let the agreement broached with Kuei-liang be concluded, please, a safe way off, at Tientsin.

Making their presence felt near T'ungchow had been the right move, but Gros and Elgin knew they dare not be too heavy-handed. The Chinese played skilfully on their misgivings: if the Manchu dynasty fell, with what other power in China could France and Britain hope to make enforceable treaties that conceded them so much?

Mu and the Prince of Yi recommended Baron Gros and Lord Elgin to make their way towards Peking not with whole armies, but with a personal escort each of only 1000 men. The Allied plenipotentiaries knew the risk. Were they simply being tricked into leaving behind their terrible guns? Was this a trap – or a reasonable and prudent compromise? Prince Seng-ko-lin-ch'in, deprived by the Emperor of his three-eyed peacock feather for losing the Taku Forts, yet still kept in military command, would be glad no doubt to see his enemies come within striking distance, on foot and in small numbers. But to other high Chinese officials – men dubious that armed resistance could succeed – the risk to the Imperial system was real. The Chinese government was beginning to speak in contradictory voices.

Chinese policy in this emergency lacked a focus because the debauched and sick young Hsien Feng Emperor had totally lost

297

his nerve. Elgin and Gros had been making it clear that they each wanted an interview with the Emperor, face to face and no kowtow nonsense. An argument went on at the Court all through August and September as to whether or not the apprehensive young Emperor should stay in Peking and confront them. Prince Seng advised the young Emperor to 'take a hunting trip to the north', but Prince Seng was a Mongol and might have private ambitions. Some mistrusted the effect on popular morale of the semi-divine Emperor's quitting his capital in a moment of danger; others besought him to stay and fight for his throne.

The fiery twenty-five-year-old Yehonala, the former concubine, now mother of China's heir-presumptive, tried in vain to stiffen the young Emperor's backbone. Officials near the throne became outspoken to the point of contempt. One mandarin observed sardonically, 'Will you cast away the inheritance of your ancestors like a damaged shoe? What would history say of your majesty for a thousand generations to come?'

As the barbarian armies came closer, and argument intensified, the unlucky young man tried to have it both ways. Suppose he left Peking in such a manner that the citizens would think he was going out to fight – but turned around when out of view, and headed for safety? This hapless uncertainty at the very top cramped everyone else's power of decision. At last, late in September, the Emperor bolted for the Imperial hunting lodge, at Jehol, in Tartary, a hundred miles to the north.

Jehol, on the far side of the Great Wall, was yet another eighteenth-century Manchu dream-palace – built in 1780 as a seventieth birthday present for the Ch'ien Lung Emperor in imitation of the Panchen Lama's residence in Tibet. In the autumn of 1793 the Old Emperor had talked affably there with Lord Macartney; sixty-seven years later, the fantasy world of the Manchu Emperors was coming apart.

By 14 September 1860, Parkes and Wade, after a long and persistent argument with the Chinese on procedure, were pretty sure they had come to a clear understanding. The two Allied armies were to halt a little this side of T'ungchow. Lord Elgin and Baron Gros, with escorts of a thousand men apiece, would enter the town, and sign there the convention already established with Kuei-liang. The two Allied plenipotentiaries were then to proceed with their escorts to Peking itself, and exchange ratifications of the long-outstanding Treaty of Tientsin. The Allied armies would wait for them, meanwhile, at a camping ground designated by the Chinese – a place called Chang-chia-wan, three miles short of T'ungchow.

On 17 September Harry Parkes and a few companions who accompanied him on this bright clear day as much from curiosity as from duty, rode forward in a group from the Allied lines before T'ungchow, to settle a few last points of detail. Did the Chinese, for instance, quite understand that Lord Elgin must deliver Queen Victoria's letter into the Emperor's hands in person? The cavalcade that rode with Parkes through yellow cornfields towards the river town with the high pagoda, or were dispersed between T'ungchow and Chang-chia-wan, included Elgin's private secretary, Henry Loch, and Bowlby, correspondent of *The Times*, Captain Brabazon of the Artillery, Colonel Walker, the cavalry's Quarter-Master General, who had arrangements to make about the armies' camp site, with twenty Sikhs and half a dozen Dragoons. Also inside the Chinese lines that morning on similar business were over a dozen representatives of the French, among them Comte d'Escayrac de Lauture, of the scientific mission accompanying the French Army, and Father Duluc, a clever young priest who was General de Montauban's interpreter.

Harry Parkes noticed that today the tone adopted by the Chinese Commissioners was no longer quite so obliging; this might indicate another shift of policy behind the scenes. As if blinded by his own fearlessness where mere Chinese were concerned, Parkes went on exactly as planned, and spent the night of 17 September inside the walls of T'ungchow. Next day, while his party, by now rather spread out, had begun desultorily heading back towards the Allied lines, they could see that overnight Prince Seng had moved up a huge mass of his cavalry, to occupy the very site at Chang-chia-wan which had been set out as a camp for the Allied armies.

If this arbitrary troop movement had been a cunning trap, rather than yet one more indication of the policy disagreements among the Chinese, Prince Seng-ko-lin-ch'in sprang it prematurely, thus losing any chance – if such had been his intention – of ambushing Elgin and Gros. Prince Seng was probably trying in a clumsy way to emphasize that, whatever the Chinese Commissioners might be forced to concede, the two Allied armies were to approach no closer than this to Peking. That same morning Seng gave orders to arrest the parties of French and British who had ventured so nonchalantly inside his lines.

Harry Parkes's first and characteristic reaction had been to go off at once and remonstrate in his fluent Chinese with the Imperial Commissioners about these wholly unauthorized troop movements. Parkes appears to have had no sense whatever of personal risk. He advised Loch to ride back with an escort of two Sikhs, and warn General Hope Grant that enemy cavalry had moved up – but displayed such sang-froid that Henry Loch, having given his message, did not hesitate to ride back through the encroaching enemy to rejoin Parkes. A mandarin offered to take both of them into Prince Seng's presence. Harry Parkes accepted – and Seng at once gave orders for his old antagonist to be made captive, like the rest.

Others were more quickly alert than Parkes to the danger. Colonel Walker, on seeing a French officer manhandled by the Chinese, had ridden to his rescue, but the enemy were too much for him, so Walker decided to cut and run. He managed to gallop his small group of cavalrymen to the safety of Allied lines. But most of the foreigners let themselves be trapped.

Between the two Allied Generals the usual argument broke out. De Montauban wanted an immediate attack; Hope Grant, ever more cautious, was of opinion that any precipitate advance might endanger the prisoners' lives. (In the event, sudden boldness might have saved them.) At last, Wade was sent forward, under a white flag, with a cavalry escort. His orders were to make a reconnaissance of Prince Seng's position, and to warn the mandarin at T'ungchow that, unless all prisoners were sent back unharmed, Peking itself was to suffer attack. As this party of foreign horsemen approached the Chinese cavalry camp their white flag was fired upon, but Wade managed, even so, to get his message through. Though numbering by now only about 3500, the French and British armies moved forward resolutely on Chang-chia-wan – a strongly defended position held by a three-mile-wide mass of Seng's cavalry, totalling perhaps 20 000, who were blocking the way ahead to Peking, and slowly moving outwards on their flanks, to left and right.

Harry Parkes – blue-eyed, fair-haired, quick-witted and nervously intense – found himself in the presence of a burly, short, thick-set Mongol with a red face and a bad complexion – Prince Seng. Parkes's demeanour not being considered respectful enough, he was shoved down to his knees, and his head knocked on the

300

ground in a compulsory kowtow. Harry Parkes as he knelt there in the grip of his captors was obliged also to take the brunt of Prince Seng's accumulated chagrin. 'You have gained two victories to our one,' exclaimed the Mongol General. 'Twice you have dared to take the Peh-ho Forts; why does not that content you? ... I know your name, and that you instigate all the evil that your people commit ... it is time that foreigners should be taught respect.'

As soon as he could get his head up, Harry Parkes began to point out forcibly that he had come to T'ungchow 'by express agreement with the Imperial Commissioners, and solely in the interests of peace'. This made Prince Seng laugh – as if he had a private and sarcastic opinion of the Imperial Commissioners. Parkes was pushed down to his knees once more. 'Write to your people,' Seng ordered him, 'and tell them to stop the attack.' De Montauban and Hope Grant were by now of one mind; from the distance came a beginning growl of gunfire.

'I cannot control or influence military movements in any way,' Parkes told the Mongol Prince frankly. 'I will not deceive Your Highness ...'

The Allied cannon growing more peremptory, Prince Seng was called away to the front. At about 2.30 p.m., Harry Parkes, Henry Loch and a Sikh cavalryman were driven off together towards the Eastern Gate of Peking in the usual deplorable unsprung cart. Parkes was unhappy to observe, as they passed through the gateway at sunset, that he and Loch were being taken to a gaol of the Board of Punishments – places of confinement that in China were universally dreaded.

Other prisoners, British, French and Sikh, taken at T'ungchow that day, were in fact worse off. The ropes binding them had been wetted, and shrinking as they dried began to cut painfully into the flesh of their wrists. A crowd of them were taken to the Summer Palace – as if to placate the timid Emperor by a public exposure and humiliation of his enemies. Some prisoners were left kneeling there for three days in an open courtyard, much of the time without food or water. Their tightly bound hands became hideously swollen, and began to mortify. At last they were divided into four groups, and sent off to different small hill fortresses outside Peking. The less fortunate among them began soon after to succumb from infection and neglect: Bowlby of *The Times* died within four days.

Once inside the gaol of the Board of Punishments, Parkes and Loch were separated, Loch trying in vain to indicate his whereabouts to Parkes by singing the National Anthem. Both were loaded with chains, and Harry Parkes was put in a long cell with about seventy Chinese convicts, all 'reduced by prison filth and prison diet to a shocking state of emaciation'. Parkes was marked down in the nominal roll as 'rebel' – there were five others in the same category, all, like himself, loaded with chains. The less heavily manacled occupants of the cell were thieves and murderers, and they behaved decently to the foreign newcomer: 'instead of following the example set by the authorities and treating me with abuse and ridicule,' said Parkes in his report, 'they were seldom disrespectful, addressed me by my title, and often avoided putting me to inconvenience when it was in their power to do so.'

Under Chinese questioning Parkes seems by his own account to have kept his nerve and displayed the intrepidity one would expect. His first interrogation was at midnight. The mandarins made him kneel before them in chains, and after first pulling him about by the hair and ears, and threatening him with torture, they got ready to note his answers in writing. When the questions began, Parkes managed several times to score.

'Are you Chinese?'

'You can see by my face and hair I'm not.'

'State the name of your head man.'

'Which do you mean – the Ambassador, General or Admiral?'

Parkes's usage of the Chinese equivalents for these high ranks enraged them. Once more they pulled his hair, and employing a more derogatory turn of phrase asked him for the name of 'the head of your soldiers'.

Parkes replied, in English, 'Lieutenant-General Sir James Hope Grant.'

The weird sounds of this exotic name and rank were more than the mandarins could expect to render phonetically, in Chinese. This obliged them to let Parkes give his answers in what terms he chose – a small tactical victory.

Parkes was questioned about the Coolie Corps, and about the range of those dreaded British guns. ('Three miles and upwards.') Ordered to reveal his confederates in Peking, Harry Parkes coolly named the three Imperial Commissioners. Though his answer when asked the population of India was accurate, the figure he gave was larger than they could accept.

On 22 September Harry Parkes was taken away from his good-natured rebel and criminal companions, and locked in a separate cell. Next time a mandarin came in to question him, Parkes was not required to kneel. His knew this alleviation could only mean that the Chinese were reacting to pressure applied by Lord Elgin and Baron Gros. Both plenipotentiaries, while keeping their larger objectives in view were in fact obsessed by the fate of the captives – so many of whom were their intimate acquaintances.

Gros and Elgin now had a task tricky enough to keep their nerves tense and their minds at full stretch. The Allies must use enough pressure to push the Chinese into setting their hostages free, but if this pressure were overdone the prisoners themselves would be the ones to suffer. Already the central Manchu government was incoherent; if it collapsed there would be no one to deal with, and China might fall piecemeal into the hands of rebels. The French and British between them could bring into the field an efficient military force, yet from now on they were inhibited from using it according to the rules of war – to destroy entirely the armed force of the enemy.

Within six weeks, snow would fall, giving Seng's cavalry a better chance against both rebels and invading barbarians. The Allied army, supplied by junks up the Peh-ho, might have to retreat to base once the river froze. The war would then drag on into yet another year – and at a time when in Britain both people and government had already begun making noises indicative of discontent. Even the French, with their long-term plans for getting a foothold in Indo-China, might have second thoughts about fighting another long-drawn-out Crimea, on the far side of the globe.

Baros Gros, a big and patient man, bore the strain impassively, but in Lord Elgin's confident if sometimes haughty demeanour signs of irritation began to break surface. Elgin was sensitively aware that should he waver or misjudge, the prisoners 'would have been lost, because the Chinese, finding they had a lever with which they could move us, would have used their advantage unsparingly'.

Prince Seng's three-mile-wide concentration of cavalry, sprawled across what had been meant for the Allied encampment at Chang-chia-wan, was backed by over seventy guns, some in masked batteries, and his reserves had begun to dig themselves into the sandhills beyond. Seng's position blocked the approach to Peking. The Chinese right, protected by a flanking battery, rested on the walled town of Chang-chia-wan, and the line extended to the bank of the Peh-ho River.

The French – 1000 strong, with some artillery but lacking cavalry – were on the British right. Though numerically small, about 3500, the Allied armies taken together were a disciplined and balanced force of foot, horse and guns, organized to answer to the will of a General who knew how to fight a battle. Seng's cavalry force, though six times larger, was more primitive. Its firepower was based, then as in the Middle Ages, on rapid marksmanship from the saddle with bow and arrow. In the Chinese ranks there were a few firelock muskets, but not many; compared with the Enfield rifle they were period pieces. Battlefield tactics had not changed since the Middle Ages either. Apart from trying to break the enemy's cohesion by a feint retreat, these Asian horsemen had but one simple and vulnerable procedure – to move outwards and around until they could attack an encircled enemy from all sides at once. Their line as it extended could be punctured, and might be outflanked and rolled up. This de Montauban and Hope Grant between them very soon did, in textbook fashion.

The British lent a squadron of their Sikh cavalry to General de Montauban, who could count in his entire army on less than fifty Spahis – horsemen dressed like Arabs and armed with muskets. Allied cavalrymen were heavier, so in all likelihood the impetus of their charge would make the confronting Mongols on their small, hairy ponies give ground. While de Montauban launched his Spahis and Sikhs against the enemy's extreme left flank, the French infantry attacked Chang-chia-wan itself with great *élan*.

The enemy horsemen began to crowd and bunch – Sikhs and Spahis had made a visible dent in their line. They kept up a ragged fire from firelocks and gingalls, but the lethally accurate Armstrongs had been knocking out Chinese gun emplacements, and now began dropping explosive shells on the cavalry formations massed to the enemy's rear. Prince Seng's entrenched reserves were soon in disorder. The 15th Punjabis captured the Chinese flanking battery at the point of the bayonet – and the whole Chinese line began to shift back and turn away from Chang-chia-wan towards the river, as if hinged. King's Dragoon Guards and Sikhs carried their pursuit of the retreating enemy for a couple of miles across a murderous stubble of millet stalks – on purpose cut two feet high as an obstacle to cavalry. 'Down they went like nine-pins as our long-armed "heavies" gave them the point; the weight of horse and man carried everything before it,' exulted the Senior British Chaplain, an eyewitness to the prowess of the Dragoons on their big chargers. The Chinese army was soon in full retreat from Chang-chia-wan. Of the 20 000 men Seng had massed on the battlefield, he lost 1500 killed and wounded, and seventy-four Chinese guns were captured. Allied casualties numbered thirty-five.

On 17 September Lord Elgin had noted in his journal: 'I rode out very early this morning, to see my general before he started, and to give him a hint about the *looting*, which has been very bad here. He disapproves of it as much as I do. . . .' But, on 18 September 1860, in the enthusiasm of victory, the town of Chang-chia-wan was given over to the troops to be plundered, 'as a punishment for enemy treachery'.

'No steps were taken to prevent looting,' noted Robert Swinhoe, 'as the town was a capture in war, and hence lawful booty.' Some of the troops enjoyed smashing things up, others had more of an eye to the main chance. 'A rare old house, with its exquisite carving and hangings, and its rooms filled with curiosities too big to carry away, was completely ransacked,' Swinhoe went on. 'Our people were in this case the destroyers.' Half a million pounds weight of brick tea – Caravan Tea – were found in the town. 'One energetic young officer loaded several carts with tea on his own account, and despatched them to Tientsin.' Old soldiers with uneasy memories of the Crimean winter looked out for the gilded dragon's head which indicated a Chinese pawnshop, and laid their hands eagerly on fur coats.

The most pitiable sufferers in Chang-chia-wan were the Chinese women. One house broken into was full of females, ranging in age from fifty to two. Sticky tins of opium lay on the floor, the air stank of the raw drug and mouths were smeared with it. The womenfolk, rather than be dishonoured, had done their best to commit collective suicide. 'The more conscious of them,' said Swinhoe, 'beating their breasts, condemned the opium for its slow work, crying out, "Let us die; we do not wish to live." ' Whether they wished to live or not, a sympathetic chaplain fetched an army surgeon, and with the help of his stomach pump their lives were restored to all but one of them.

Shaken by this turn in events, Baron Gros wrote to his Foreign Minister in Paris, 'I was heartbroken by the acts of vandalism which I saw committed by our soldiers as well as by those of our allies, each delighted at the chance of heaping upon the other the blame for abominable deeds for which all deserved punishment.' On 21 September the Allied armies advanced from plundered Chang-chia-wan, outflanking T'ungchow. Authority once more imposed its will. When citizens in T'ungchow attacked and killed two of a gang of Canton coolies who were trying to plunder a shop, and gave the others up to the British, the guilty coolies were publicly flogged. Three coolies attempting rape in a field were sentenced by General Hope Grant – the two accomplices got a hundred strokes of the cat apiece, laid on by the Provost-Sergeant, the worst villain was then hanged. But whatever recourse might be made to methods used latterly in India, the damage was done, both to discipline and morale, and Baron Gros had sagaciously put his finger on the nub of it.

British and French troops could always put the blame for bad actions upon each other. To a soldier's mind, this somehow lessened the guilt. Already British and French spokesmen had begun to claim loudly that on a particular scandalous occasion, the other side were the ones to begin, or persist, or exceed, or do worse. The British go on blaming the French, and the French the British, even in memoirs written long after.

Lord Elgin himself – for the time being less alert than his confrère, Baron Gros – fell into the psychological trap of putting the onus on the other fellow. 'The French by their exactions and misconduct', he wrote, in distress of mind at the growing hostility of the local Chinese, at first so friendly, 'have already stirred to resistance the peaceful population ... They are cautious enough when armed enemies, even Chinese, are in question ... but indisputably valorous against defenceless villages and little-footed women'. (The French were saying much the same of the British. '*Quant aux anglais*,' wrote Armand Lucy after the looting of Pei-t'ang, ' ... *ce sont nos maîtres: on ne trouve pas un clou où ils ont passé.*')

For once, Lord Elgin is a prejudiced witness. A comparison of the written evidence from both sides shows that Baron Gros was right: between French and British troops there was nothing much to choose. The British may have been more wilfully destructive, the French more acquisitive. The Sikhs by all accounts behaved worse than either, especially towards women. And all agree in condemning the Coolie Corps, no doubt with good reason – recruited as they were from the criminal underworld of Hong Kong, for so many years a sink of iniquity.

By this time, Harry Parkes was not being at all badly treated. The official who came now to ply him with questions was his old acquaintance Heng Chi, the subordinate Imperial Commissioner, who when Hoppo in Canton two years earlier had by a coincidence been made prisoner by Harry Parkes. The British had treated Heng Chi decently then, and the consideration was now being returned.

Parkes knew that Henry Loch must be somewhere in the same prison. During an interrogation on the afternoon of 26 September he demanded that the two of them be allowed to share a cell, but Heng Chi changed the subject, warning Parkes of the serious view the Council of State was beginning to take of the Allied onslaught: 'By advancing on Peking, they are attacking the Emperor himself.' Heng Chi began opening his mind to Harry Parkes, largely in the hope of somehow using him for conveying hints and threats to Lord Elgin, but partly as if to clarify his own thoughts. Heng's remarks mix serious rumination with the usual devious Manchu bluff, but throw light on his mental uncertainties at this juncture, as one of China's high officials.

On retreating to Jehol, threatened Heng, the Emperor might call on the aid of his allies, the forty-eight Mongol princes – who would gladly lend him hundreds of thousands of their formidable cavalry. (This at least put the Emperor's rapid retreat to Jehol in a favourable light.) As a man who had made a pile of money from Customs receipts when Hoppo, Heng Chi was not to be counted among diehard anti-barbarians. 'Suppose all is lost,' he said glumly, 'the dismemberment of the Empire will follow, and all trade will be at an end.'

The most effective argument being put forward at Court by Prince Seng-ko-lin-ch'in was apparently that no durable peace could ever be made with the Allies: they had found a way of making war pay. They kept coming back for bigger indemnities. Seng was even managing to prove that commercial relations were disadvantageous to China: 'Though the Imperial Treasury might receive four million taels in Customs duty from foreigners annually, this income was almost completely wiped out by the $21 000 000 indemnity of 1842, the 6 000 000 taels claimed in 1858 and the extra indemnity of 10 000 000 taels recently demanded.'

At last, Heng showed his hand, hinting strongly that the man doing his best to bring the fighting to an end was Prince Kung. Gentle, intelligent, more of a diplomat than a soldier, Prince Kung was a twenty-eight-year-old brother of the reigning Emperor, and son-in-law of old Kuei-liang. For the past year he had served on the Colonial Board, which controlled all matters affecting the 'outer barbarians'.

On Prince Kung's behalf, Heng Chi asked Parkes to write to Wade or Elgin, asking for a cease-fire. 'It would have no effect,'

Parkes told Heng candidly, 'on the proceedings of the English Ambassador.' (Prince Kung had in fact crossed the lines four days earlier under a flag of truce, but while their prisoners were still in Chinese hands, Gros and Elgin would have no dealings with him.) Parkes could well imagine Lord Elgin's predicament, and had no intention of making things worse for him by pathetic but irrelevant appeals.

Reminiscing about his own imprisonment at Canton, Heng Chi dropped a hint to Parkes about the great danger he was now in personally. This was true: Yehonala had repeatedly urged the sick Emperor to sign an order for his execution. Parkes was typically austere and forthright about this threat, answering (according to his own account later), 'It is no uncommon thing for the Chinese to deal cruelly with their prisoners, or even to take their lives. But while I should prepare for the worst, I know also that my fate will be determined not by your will but by that of God ... although you would do the Allied force but little injury by killing the few prisoners ... you would by such an act bring down on yourselves a terrible vengeance.'

Embroiled as he was in a Peking faction fight between some losing power and others reaching out to grasp it, Heng Chi was well aware how losers at the last moment are liable to strike out blindly. The only reassurance he could give Harry Parkes, after figuring the risk, was, 'You will be in no danger for the next two or three days.'

Not long after, Parkes and Loch were driven in separate carts to the Kaomio Temple in the north of Peking, and there put in the same room, spacious enough, ten feet by twenty and overlooking a courtyard where soldiers kept watch. They were offered a bath, and from a nearby restaurant an elaborate meal was sent in, of sixteen main and thirty-two subsidiary dishes (alas, they lacked the stomach for it). In the belief that he might derive an advantage for his own side by so doing, Harry Parkes let himself be cajoled by Heng Chi into writing a letter to Lord Elgin which would at least hint distantly at Prince Kung's readiness to become a peacemaker.

Rejecting several emphatic phrases that Heng Chi tried to put in his mouth, Parkes wrote circumspectly: 'The Chinese authorities are now treating Loch and myself well, and we are informed this is done by direction of the Prince of Kung. We are also told that His Highness is a man of decision and great intelligence, and I trust that under these circumstances, hostilities may be temporarily suspended to give opportunity for negotiation.' But Loch, as an additional precaution, scribbled on the letter, using Hindustani words, but as if they were his signature, 'written at the orders of the Chinese government'. The Chinese, as a token of goodwill, had let their two most valuable prisoners send across to the Allied lines for a change of clothes. When the parcel of clean linen came back, Loch and Parkes found embroidered in the corner of a handkerchief a message, using Roman characters but Hindustani words, warning them that an Allied bombardment of Peking was planned to start in three days.

As the two British prisoners were well aware, the moment guns opened fire on the Imperial City, even if the Kaomio Temple itself escaped shelling, their own lives would be forfeit. They played backgammon on a home-made board, and ate sweetmeats, and drank the exquisite China tea sent up to them with the compliments of Prince Kung, and waited.

Prince Seng-ko-lin-ch'in, as well as arguing his opinions at Court, had other duties – not the least important, in Chinese eyes, being to convey the timid but semi-sacred Emperor away from the park of the Summer Palace to his hunting lodge beyond the Great Wall. Not only had the Allies come uncomfortably close to Peking, but there were unnerving rumours that a rebel army was on the march towards the capital.

In the Allied camp, word got about that these rebels were Taiping. The Catholic French once more became suspicious as to what the Protestant and perfidious English might be conspiring. But they were in fact old-fashioned Chinese rebels from Shensi led by a local notability and made angry by the burden of war taxation. In deploying his army, Prince Seng appears to have made up his mind that on balance the Shensi rebels were the greater danger.

On 21 September, the Allied armies, having left Chang-chia-wan two miles behind, took up a position from which they could clearly see Peking. The squared-off, sloping walls of the Chinese capital, forty feet high and sixty thick, with defensive towers at the corners and gateways, looked exceptionally difficult to breach, even with Hope Grant's big guns – which in any event had not yet come up. Villagers in the province, growing hostile, had begun to attack stragglers on the lines of communication. Two Sikhs, carrying despatches, were fired upon as they rode through a village some miles to the rear of Chang-chia-wan, so Colonel Urquhart sent the 8th Punjabis to burn the place to the ground.

This deliberate advance on Peking – which to Gros and Elgin seemed the likeliest way of petrifying the Chinese yet saving the prisoners' lives – brought the French that day into action against Chinese troops at the bridge of Pa-li-chi'ao. General Cousin de Montauban at last got the chance he had been waiting for to distinguish himself against the Chinese at a time and place where no one else would share in the glory.

The stone bridge at Pa-li-chi'ao carried a paved road to Peking over the T'ungchow–Peking canal. The walls and towers of the Chinese capital were distantly conspicuous in the clear autumn air: the canal was Seng's last defensive line. Three thousand French collided there with a much larger force, commanded by General Paou – many of them being Chinese Imperial Guard, distinctive in their black-bordered yellow robes. Later, it began to seem highly probable that General Paou, the Chinese commander, had with him at the bridge as hostages two of the prisoners – the young Chinese-speaking French priest, Abbé Duluc, and Captain Brabazon of the Royal Artillery.

De Montauban's attack on the bridge of Pa-li-chi'ao was high-spirited and irresistible. On the far side of the canal was mounted a battery of Chinese heavy guns, which the French took with a reckless bayonet charge. The Chinese defenders were driven headlong into the canal, some were bayoneted, many drowned. *'L'arme blanche'* had gained yet another victory, but General Paou, mortally wounded and at his last gasp, was said to have ordered the summary execution of his two prisoners. The mortal remains of Père Duluc and Captain Brabazon – presumably thrown into the canal – were never found, though not long after a meticulous search was made through the heap of corpses, different reports of the body-count at Pa-li-chi'ao varying from 500 to 2000. De Montauban lost three dead and seventeen wounded there, and captured twenty-five guns. This brilliant affair read well in the Paris newspapers, and when Napoleon III later ennobled de Montauban, the victorious General chose for his title Comte de Palikao.

Meanwhile, at a wooden bridge over the canal, a mile nearer Peking, the British were gaining an untidier victory. As his cavalry began shoving and crowding the Chinese right flank towards this wooden bridge, Hope Grant mistook a detachment of Tartar cavalry wheeling ahead of him for the French. Not wishing to overrun his allies, he tactfully sidled away. Seeing their enemy turn tail at last, the Tartars charged forward with triumphant yells – to run full-tilt into a British 6-pounder battery, which at

250 yards poured canister, shells filled with musket balls, into their massed ranks.

The blast of canister checked the onrush of the Tartar horsemen, while a charge by Dragoons and wild Sikh irregulars made them turn. Noisily entering the fray, the Armstrongs demonstrated their accuracy by bringing the retreating Chinese cavalry down 'in clumps'.

After inflicting these two defeats, the Allies took and burned the Chinese cavalry camps before Peking, and from the surrounding countryside Chinese peasants came in, to pick up whatever there might be left in the camps after the Allies had pillaged them.

At the roadside beyond the bridge of Pa-li-chi'ao, General de Montauban saw a monument that took his fancy – a large marble tortoise adorned with sculptured dragons and griffins. He very much wanted to ship the tortoise back to France, as a public reminder of his achievement, but it weighed twenty tons.

His failure to hold the Allies along the line of the T'ungchow–Peking canal undermined Prince Seng's political position. He withdrew what was left of his mounted army – defeated but not yet crushed – over the horizon. The supposition was that Seng's men had retired to an entrenched camp somewhere north-west of Peking.

Sikh cavalry sent ahead on a reconnaissance came back to report that between the the Allies and the southernmost walls of the Imperial city there was no more opposition whatever. But necessary reinforcements – Napier's Division, marching up from Tientsin – had not yet arrived, the siege artillery was still awaited, and munitions and supplies, expected up by junk, were running low. Before assaulting the massive walls of Peking – which perhaps could be effectively breached only by springing a mine – the Generals wanted to make sure that Prince Seng was not just round the corner, waiting to pounce.

Despite their succession of easy victories against disproportionate odds, the Allied Generals still had a healthy respect for Seng. They had as yet no clear idea of the way the rebels were dividing Seng's attention, and the squabbling Court handicapping his initiative. The further they moved from base, the more unsettling became the prospect of a counter-attack. Lord Elgin later made this comment on the Generals' indecisiveness: 'I should have preferred crushing the Chinese army ... but as we go to work we might have followed them round the walls of Peking until Doomsday.'

The Russians, however – the only Western power with an establishment inside Peking – could by now clearly identify the winners. They went on currying favour with the Chinese – for example, pleading with the Allies on their behalf not to inflict the crushing weight of the doubled indemnity. But they also made fast friends of the French and British by supplying them with priceless information. 'General Ignatieff was very obliging and friendly', wrote Lord Elgin in his journal on 27 September – they had met the day before. 'He and I entirely agree as to how the Chinese should be fought.'

The Allies had, for instance, no clear idea of exactly where inside Peking their prisoners might be locked away. In any bombardment they would much rather give the prison a miss – and the Russian legation, too. The intelligent and handsome 34-year-old Russian General rejoiced the heart of Hope Grant by giving him a glimpse of a street map the Russians had just made of Peking. Map-making inside the walls of the Chinese capital was of course forbidden, but the Russians had been clever. They discreetly paraded the streets of Peking in a closed cart with a wheel of known diameter, which turned a revolution-counter, and at each street intersection the cart paused for them to take compass bearings.

Peking, formed of two adjacent cities, was roughly an oblong, the longer side running north and south. The old Chinese city was to the south, the more spacious Tartar city to the north. Hope Grant hurriedly sent for Signor Beato, the enterprising Italian freelance photographer who had come upcountry with the expedition. General Ignatieff let Beato take a photograph of his street plan; he also gave some rather slanted information about Peking's defences, which encouraged Hope Grant to enter the northern quarter where streets were wide: cannon are more effective down boulevards. Moreover, Prince Seng and his cavalry were rumoured to be mobilizing somewhere to the north-west of Peking.

At 9 a.m. on 6 October 1860, after waiting for a fortnight under the walls of Peking – the reserve division and the big guns had come up, several days before – Hope Grant and de Montauban at last decided to march their respective armies north-west round the city. They left tents and baggage behind, and carried three days' cooked rations. Their rendezvous was to be the Summer Palace, a few miles outside the city walls.

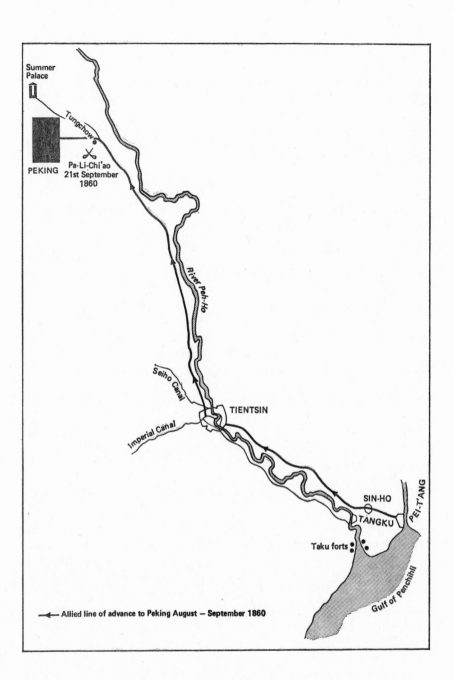

Summer
Palace

Tungchow

PEKING

Pa-Li-Chi'ao
21st September
1860

River Peh-Ho

Seiho Canal

TIENTSIN

Imperial Canal

SIN-HO

TANGKU

PEI-T'ANG

Taku forts

Gulf of Penchihli

Allied line of advance to Peking August — September 1860

The British and French armies on their march around the walls of Peking soon lost each other. So as to attack a Chinese earthwork occupied by a picket of Tartars, Hope Grant diverged to the right. The Tartars retreated towards the city – and Hope Grant found he was no longer in contact with the French, who had meanwhile crossed the rear of his column.

In later life Hope Grant could never be persuaded that the French that morning had not left him in the lurch, and raced away on purpose to be first at the Summer Palace. But a good deal of the British cavalry, though losing contact with Hope Grant and his men, had kept in touch with the French and accompanied them. Both armies at the time were lost, but the British appear to have been slightly more lost.

British cavalry, under Brigadier Pattle, and about 3000 French under General de Montauban, got to the Summer Palace together on the afternoon of 6 October 1860 – the cavalry patrolling the walls to cut off the retreat of those enemy soldiers the French expected to flush out as they stormed the main gate. The palace turned out to be garrisoned not by the Imperial Guard but by a helpless band of 480 Imperial Eunuchs. A couple of them ran towards the French infantry, crying out in high-pitched voices, 'Don't commit sacrilege! Don't come within the sacred precincts!' They were shot down in cold blood. About twenty of the eunuchs, badly armed, attempted to put up some kind of a resistance, but the rest skedaddled.

With his thirteen wives and a large retinue, the Emperor himself had left for Jehol two weeks before, on 21 September. Prince Kung had been staying at the palace until the previous day, but by now was in Peking. Three thousand French troops and the few hundred British cavalry bivouacked for the night outside the palace walls, while a group of officers British and French went inside, guided by a eunuch prisoner, and headed by General de Montauban, who firmly told his entourage that 'he counted on their honour to respect the palace and see it was respected by others, until the English arrived'.

The Summer Palace was a Chinese fairyland – eighty square miles of park across which were dispersed about two hundred astonishing buildings, thirty of them palatial Imperial Residences. The Summer Palace of the Manchus was just such a 'stately pleasure dome' as Coleridge had described in the famous lines written after his opium dream, where:

314

twice five miles of fertile ground
With walls and towers were girdled round:
And there were gardens bright with sinuous rills,
Where blossomed many an incense-bearing tree;
And here were forests ancient as the hills,
Enfolding sunny spots of greenery.

Inside those walls a visionary world had been created for Manchu Emperors to inhabit – the landscape of the Willow Pattern Plate. This vast diversified artificial landscape had once been a flat and boring plain. Earth was dug out to form gentle hills, and water from ornamental canals was fed into these excavations to create lakes, fringed with weeping willows and adorned with water lilies. Across the canals went hump-backed bridges with marble balustrades, their reflections forming by intention a perfect circle in the water. On man-made islands stood brilliantly tiled pagodas. Herds of deer drifted through the trees; goldfish flashed in the water.

The shadow of the dome of pleasure
Floated midway on the waves.

The multitude of buildings included two baroque palaces, roofed with gold, and devised for the Ch'ien Lung Emperor by the Jesuit fathers Castiglione and Benoist, from what they could remember in their exile of the Trianon.

Members of the Imperial family were encouraged to live within these protective walls a life that was dreamlike and remote. Desperate aspects of China's predicament were reflected here in a fantasy form. For example, on the high seas, China might be at the mercy of the fleets of the seaborne barbarians. But on one of his lakes in the palace, her young Emperor had a toy fleet mounted with little brass cannon. There were days when his favourite diversion was to play at naval warfare.

The palace was full of loot.

Here were stored not only ceremonial robes, jewels, jades and the processional treasures of the Court, as well as a huge stock of exquisite baled silk, but an accumulated tribute placed at the Emperor's feet over many years by foreign envoys. Here had been brought together and put in order irreplaceable libraries and collections of splendid paintings. The Summer Palace was the treasure-house of China – such a concentration of visual beauty, artifice and wealth as neither existed nor could once again have been brought into being anywhere else in the world. The people of China had no doubt paid a heavy price, in one way and another, for the beauty of the Summer Palace, but, then, the people of China had created it. The Summer Palace as it stood represented not the Manchu dynasty, but China.

Not surprisingly, the officers French and British, whether level-headed or high-spirited, who clustered near General de Montauban as he stood awestruck in the Emperor's Hall of Audience, or wandered off in groups to the nearby Imperial apartments, began as they glanced around them to feel their fingers itch. Jewelled watches, jade ornaments, pearl necklaces, pencil cases lavishly set with diamonds, lay scattered about like playthings on silk coverlets.

To the victor, the spoils.

The exact sequence of events in this first plundering of the Summer Palace is not a matter about which any one witness has been frank. The French blame the British just as the British blame the French. An attempt is made by officers in both armies to imply that the troops were really to blame, but nobody denies (though none emphasize, and some fail to mention) that officers composed the party which entered the palace at eight on the evening of 6 October 1860, and first began picking and stealing.

Giving evidence before a committee in 1874 (after Victor Hugo among others had condemned powerfully the looting of the palace) General de Montauban in his own defence asserted: 'I had sentries posted, and directed two officers with two companies of marine infantry to protect the palace from depredation and to allow nothing to be moved until the arrival of the English commanders ... thus there would be no pillage.' He also stated categorically: 'Nothing had been touched in the Palace when the English arrived.' (But since the British cavalry unexpectedly accompanied the French army to the palace, this piece of evidence, though verbally accurate, was phrased in a way liable to mislead.)

When General Hope Grant and the bulk of the British army reached the Summer Palace next day – at 2 p.m. on 7 October 1860, a squadron of King's Dragoon Guards having been sent off by Pattle to scour the country and find them – Hope Grant bore witness, 'it was pitiful to see the way in which everything was being robbed', and went on to say (in an account dictated some years later): 'Only one room in the Palace was untouched. General de Montauban informed me he had reserved any valuables it might contain for equal division between the English and French.' According to another witness, what de Montauban in fact said to Hope Grant was, 'See here. I have had a few of the

316

most brilliant things selected, to be divided between the Queen of Great Britain and the Emperor of the French.'

That first evening de Montauban may well have begun with good intentions, but apparently the temptation staring the officers of his party in the face was too much for their powers of self-restraint. After making a reasonable allowance for contradictory accounts and expressions of national prejudice, the course of events was probably something like this. The British cavalry officers were the first to break the spirit of de Montauban's pro-hibition, if not the strict letter, by skylarking – for instance, by firing off their revolvers at mirrors. After that, the French officers felt easier in their minds about pocketing small and portable souvenirs – one of them, for example, picking up a necklace of pearls each as large as a marble 'which he afterwards foolishly disposed of at Hong Kong for £3000'.

Once things had gone this far, the British found it much easier not only to copy the French but also to fasten the blame upon them. These were the cavalry officers Hope Grant later made apology for, as 'gentlemen who, when they found the French making such havoc among the treasures, had thought there could be no harm in appropriating a few things'. Making the best of a bad job, de Montauban had yielded, allowing each officer to 'take one object as a souvenir'.

The first visit was short; by 10 p.m. the lucky officers had left the palace with bulging pockets, and returned to their army's bivouac outside the walls. But the word was out. The troops had been allowed, even encouraged, not long since, to sack a small Chinese town 'as a punishment for enemy treachery'. French private soldiers were paid ten centimes a day, and French, British and Sikhs alike now knew that through the gate was a plunderer's paradise – of which their own officers, so free elsewhere with prohibitions and even floggings, had already sampled the first-fruits.

The two companies of marines which de Montauban had posted as sentries evidently could not hold back a surging mob of would-be looters – indeed Paul Varin, de Montauban's chief apologist, freely admits that the guard itself, officers and men alike, began to pillage. Military discipline collapsed in an orgy of rapacity. Three thousand French troops – with enthusiastic help from their allies – plundered the Summer Palace incessantly for twenty-four hours.

The French army had arrived under the walls of the palace with almost no wheeled transport (one small cart per regiment was the allowance). In the days following, it sent off 300 loaded waggons. 'For nearly two days I was treading on silks, jewels, porcelain, bronzes, sculptures – treasures, in short – worth more than thirty million francs', one young officer wrote to tell his family. 'I think there has been nothing seen like it since the sack of Rome by the barbarians.'

When the British infantry and guns marched up to the palace gates on Sunday 7 October there was no disguising the fact that the French camp was already full of plunder. The French soldiers' tents, said the British Senior Chaplain, were 'a perfect blaze of silk and embroidery'. Coloured bales of priceless silks were strewn everywhere, and private soldiers walked around bejewelled. When the bugle that morning sounded for the British army to parade outside the walls, only about ten men from each company fell in. The British and sepoy rank-and-file were determined on entering the palace as the French had done, and there was no stopping them. 'The General now made no objection to looting ... no pass was required,' wrote Robert Swinhoe, 'the place was open to the ravages of any and all.'

To conciliate Hope Grant, General de Montauban displayed to him the collection of choice objects he had picked out specially for the Emperor Napoleon III and Queen Victoria. The plunder included a pair of identical sceptres in gold and jade – one for each monarch – both formerly in the regalia of their unfortunate Manchu cousin.

Lord Elgin's first sight of this destructive plundering – which must have brought vividly to his mind the boyhood sneers about his father's vandalism in the Parthenon – drew from him a cold and final condemnation: 'I would like a great many things the palace contains, but I am not a thief.' Significantly, the damage being done under his eyes to works of art in the palace was not so distressing to Lord Elgin as the waste – the visible outrage to his lifetime of thrift and carefully calculated self-control. 'Plundering and devastating a place like this is bad enough,' he noted grimly, 'but what is much worse is the waste and breakage. Out of £1 000 000 of property, I daresay £50 000 will not be realized.'

Though less outspoken than Lord Elgin, Baron Gros found the looting equally despicable. But the troops were out of hand. A few others that day shared Elgin's utter disgust. One French army surgeon – a representative of his country at its best – after wandering through scenes of destructive violence for as long as he could bear it, made his gesture. He left the palace holding in one hand his only memento – a leaf plucked from a bush.

Robert Swinhoe, the interpreter who kept a journal throughout the campaign, was present at the collapse of discipline, and the confusion of rank, as the British came to join their French comrades in the work of plunder. 'What they could not carry away', he writes, 'they smashed to atoms. In one room you would see several officers and men of all ranks with their heads and hands brushing and knocking together in the same box, searching and grasping its contents. In another a scramble was going on over a collection of handsome state robes ... others would be amusing themselves by taking "cock" shots at chandeliers ... No one just then cared for gazing tranquilly on works of art; each one was bent on acquiring what was most valuable ... The silk warehouses on the right were burst open, and dozens rushed in over piles of valuable rolls of silk ... though plunderers were conveying them away by cartloads, still the ground was strewed with them ... An officer would be seen struggling under the weight of old jars, furs and embroidered suits ...' What yesterday had been a disciplined instrument for winning battles, extracting cash indemnities and enforcing territorial annexations was today a crazy mob. Temporarily, the disease of acquisitiveness had destroyed both armies.

Authority was re-imposed fairly soon on the French rank-and-file, and without too much difficulty. But the British, normally kept in order by the lash, remained badly out of hand. To bring this orgy of *laissez-faire* under control, an organized market structure had to be imposed from above. 'To make matters more equal for those whose duties prevented them from sharing in the work of spoliation', says Swinhoe, General Hope Grant 'issued orders to call in all the loot acquired by the officers, appealing to their honour as officers and gentlemen to restore faithfully all they had taken. This measure, of course, caused great grumbling.' Gold ingots worth £8000 discovered by Major Anson were also called in.

General Hope Grant appointed prize agents for the army, his highly irregular plan being to auction off the plunder quickly, and divide the proceeds in cash among the men. Since all prizes made in war are the sovereign's property, this unorthodox action put his professional career at risk (but was condoned later by the personal intervention of Queen Victoria).

The auction of plunder took place on 11 October 1860 in the courtyard of the Lama Temple which served as army headquarters, two NCOs acting as auctioneers. The quantity of property was spectacular: 'white and green jade ornaments of all tints, enamel-inlaid jars of antique shape, bronzes, gold and silver figures and statuettes ... immense quantities of rolls of silk ... several of the beautiful Imperial Yellow, a kind prescribed by the Chinese law for the use of his Imperial Majesty alone'.

Each officer who gave up his spoil had the option of buying it back at a price fixed in advance by the prize agents. The public sale went on for three days, and made $32 000, which when added to the value of bullion handed in, amounting to $61 000, gave a total to be divided of $93 000. On 16 October this was shared out, two-thirds going to the men, and one-third to the officers. Each private soldier got $17 (or 72s.) and a field officer about £50. The French authorities let the men keep their plunder, but shared out among them the value of ingots that had been divided between British and French. A French private got about 100 francs.

General Hope Grant's intention in holding this auction was straightforward enough – even commendable. But the economic process afterwards functioned in such a way as to siphon off the more enviable treasures from the troops to the officers – and indeed, though 'numbers of French officers had acquired tolerable fortunes', by and large, from the French army to the British. As M'Ghee, the Senior Chaplain, observed, 'we had Indian allowances, and they had the plunder'.

British officers serving in China received additional pay, and latterly there had been no chance to spend it, so any officers 'who had disposable dollars quickly found means of exchanging them for objects of greater value in the French camp ... You had only to ask the first French soldier you met if he had anything for sale, and he would soon produce gold watches, strings of jewels, jade ornaments or furs.' Though this gave the British an advantage, they were none quite so well placed for amassing works of art as 'one gallant officer, understood to have an unlimited commission from Baron Rothschild'.

Tommy Atkins gave up his loot, and cheerfully took his pocketful of money; most of it soon went on drink. The French soldiers, more abstemious, were 'rolling in dollars' – while their officers accumulated precious objects.

'In either camp', adds Swinhoe, 'nothing was talked of but curiosities purloined from the Summer Palace, and what they were likely to fetch.' At this historic juncture the armies of Queen and Emperor appear to have been thoroughly impregnated with the spirit of Free Trade.

Socially, the British army was no longer what it had been. The pattern of behaviour set by Tory landowners – extravagant rather than acquisitive – had lost authority since their failures in the Crimean War. Many of these young officers were sons of the newly enriched industrial and commercial middle classes, scarcely a generation away from the counting house, and not yet in every case hammered by the new public school foundations into a semblance of gentlemanliness. The French in China were of course continuing their revolutionary-plebeian, Napoleonic tradition of living off the country playing at being noblemen, and looting Rome and Venice to fill the Louvre.

For his own share, General de Montauban had cleverly put on one side the Chinese Empress's jewel casket. On his return to Paris – according to French newspapers of the time – de Montauban offered the Empress Eugénie a necklace of dark grey pearls, valued by an eminent Parisian jeweller at 1 800 000 francs(£72 000), and sought Imperial permission to make a gift of another such necklace – of diamonds, emeralds and large rubies, worth 2 000 000 francs – to the Duchess of Malakoff.

Like the other British Generals, Hope Grant declined his share of auction money, but was presented by his grateful officers with 'one of the handsomest pieces of the booty' – a solid gold ewer, formerly used for pouring rose-water over the Emperor's hands. Hope Grant thought it would come in useful as a claret decanter.

Not all those entering the Summer Palace were quite so grossly self-centred. A Protestant pastor serving as chaplain with the French never lost his professional concern for the moral welfare of the troops: when there was so much else of real value to be picked up he was distressed to find that some of the French should prefer taking the 'boxes fitted with obscene pictures' that they found in the Emperor's bedroom. One British interpreter, when he saw that destruction threatened the Imperial library, managed to get out several waggon loads of books for the benefit of the British Museum. Some plunder was overlooked. Two large lions squatting on pillars near the palace were assumed to be of brass. They were actually solid gold, and, in Garnet Wolseley's words, 'their value would have gone far towards defraying the expenses of the war'.

The 7th of October was the day when the plundering of the Summer Palace by British and French alike reached a maniac crescendo. On the 8th the prisoners held inside Peking were freed. The siege guns had been waiting outside the city since 29 September.

An Imperial courier, riding post-haste from Jehol with an order for the immediate execution of Parkes and Loch, was actually raising dust along the road – and Heng Chi knew it – when he and Prince Kung managed in the nick of time to arrange for the prisoners to be hustled out of Peking.

Two days later, on 10 October, Harry Parkes accompanied Heng Chi to the Summer Palace – or what was left of it. They went there in the hope of finding out what had happened to Weng Fu, the Governor, an old friend of Heng Chi's. Weng was an official known to many Westerners as the man at Canton who in 1842 had tried to build or buy modern warships for the Chinese – only to be reduced, as years went by, to the duty of stage-managing the degenerate young Emperor's mimic naval battles.

Chinese peasants from villages nearby were lurking furtively in the grounds, hoping to pick up what the foreign soldiers might have overlooked. (Later on, since in Chinese eyes the park was sacred, these local men were punished with exemplary severity.) Weng Fu having failed in his duty to protect the palace had most likely drowned himself – and the two of them, Parkes and Heng Chi, discovered his body at last, face downwards in an ornamental lake. Heng Chi sat on the lake shore with his head in his hands as if to block off the sight of all this desolation, and burst into tears.

Gros and Elgin had reached their critical time – five or six weeks before the freeze-up, with munitions running low, and Seng's army still intact. The senseless disorganization caused by the pillaging of the Summer Palace must have touched them both on a sensitive nerve. Luckily the Chinese government had lost the will to fight. The Emperor had fled, his brother, Prince Kung, was ready to capitulate, and Prince Seng-ko-lin-ch'in, in lieu of using his splendid horsemen to harass the Allies' vulnerable lines of communication, was now kept busy by the approach of the Shensi rebels.

There was clearly no time to waste. The day after the first batch of prisoners came back, thirteen guns were placed in position around the An Tung Gate. Trenches were dug and placards posted up, to tell the Chinese of an impending bombardment of Peking. Prince Kung was warned by ultimatum that unless the gate were given up to the Allies as a guarantee of free access, the guns would open fire. This threat involved a risk. Although Parkes, Loch and d'Escayrac, with four French soldiers and a Sikh, had been safe inside the Allied lines for the past twenty-four hours, there were still thirty or more other prisoners, dead or alive, in Chinese hands.

The ultimatum was due to expire at noon. General Napier stood by the battery, watch in hand, as the guns were sponged and run back for loading, when – with less than five minutes to spare – the An Tung Gate creaked open. Peking had yielded.

On 12 October more prisoners were handed over: one French soldier, and eight Sikhs. On 14 October two more Sikhs came in – the last of all to be freed, but so enfeebled that one of them died the same day. The dead British prisoners were buried on a day of black sky and bitter north wind in Peking's Russian cemetery. The French were buried in the old Jesuit cemetery, and the Sikhs took the bodies of their dead comrades, and burned them.

Of thirty-nine men from both armies captured at Chang-chia-wan, only nineteen came back – most of them in a bad state, from having been left kneeling in the courtyard of the Summer Palace, tied up and without food and water. Soon after, Sikh cavalrymen were caught in their quarters, sipping tea and watching with amused pleasure the infliction on two Chinese civilians kidnapped at random of the exact painful treatment – tight bonds, wetted ropes and all – that had been meted out to their dead.

Lord Elgin would appear for the next few days to have brooded no less morbidly than his Sikh cavalrymen over the fate of these prisoners. He managed to convince himself – and, later, others – that some exemplary though bloodless action was needed to intimidate the Chinese, so as to protect from arbitrary cruelty the foreigners from now on living in Peking – they would, of course, include his own brother, Frederick.

Elgin knew very well that the Russians – who had lived in Peking for many decades – had never thought they needed this kind of protection. The succession of well-argued reasons Elgin continued to give for the action he had in mind were presumably his brave try at rationalizing his own horror at the physical pain inflicted by the Chinese on men he knew and liked.

Lord Elgin agreed, first of all, with Baron Gros, that the indemnity should be increased by an extra half a million taels of silver – 300 000 going to the British and 200 000 to the French – partly as a fine on the Chinese for their maltreatment of the prisoners, partly to compensate financially the dependants of those crippled or dead. But would this pinch hard enough?

There was a limit to China's ability to pay, and after listening to Russian arguments Elgin was inclined to think it had been reached. He explained to London that 'it will be necessary to take forty per cent of the gross Customs revenue of China for four years in order to procure payment of the indemnities already claimed'. To this plea, Lord Palmerston's simple comment was, 'I wish Elgin had doubled the indemnity.'

General Ignatieff was also in favour of making a public example of Chinese misdeeds, in a way that would cause them loss of face. He suggested pulling down the dreaded prison of the Board of Punishments, and raising on its site in Peking a monument, with memorial inscriptions in English, French, Mongol, Manchu and Chinese. This monument, intended as a reminder and a warning, should be put under the protection of the foreign diplomatic missions.

For Lord Elgin in his present mood this was not enough either. He made up his mind – and though he talked it over with Hope Grant, the decision appears to have been entirely his own – to burn to the ground what was left of the Summer Palace. Baron Gros was ready to acknowledge that his colleague had been under great strain – become apparent now in the form of acute irritability – but this proposal horrified him: 'a useless sort of vengeance, which alas would not put right any one of the cruel misfortunes we deplore'. The French one and all considered the idea atrocious, in one officer's words, 'destruction for destruction's sake'.

Elgin's later explanations for this extraordinary decision – to his General, to his government, to his wife – begin to bear a laboured air. He reiterates that he wanted the Emperor, not the people of China, to suffer, though it was common knowledge that the young man on whose Imperial pride this act was to have such a minatory effect had already lost his nerve, and bolted. Elgin argues that any other course would have laid a burden on the innocent, though this was hardly true of Ignatieff's proposal for 'loss of face' in the form of a permanent monumental reminder. He certainly won Lord Palmerston over: 'I am heartily glad ... it was absolutely necessary,' said the Prime Minister, when told of the decision to burn the Summer Palace by his Secretary of State for War.

The inward process that was exacerbating Elgin's mind had evidently reached a climax. By giving orders for this excessive act, a sensitive man was hardening his heart – against the quiet but persistent implication that his leniency signalled a lack of nerve, against his mounting irritation with China as an impossible place and an impossible job. Disgusted as he was by the cruelty of war (*'a hateful business. The more one sees of it, the more one detests it'*) Elgin's decision to burn the Summer Palace at least meant that flesh-and-blood injuries done to people he knew intimately would for once be revenged not, as in war, upon other people – on helpless Chinese – but on inanimate objects, on redundant and expensive things. He had suffered all his life from his father's costly obsession with works of art; now works of art would bear the brunt of his revenge.

In a decision that a century later sounds almost insane, there was also a certain element of political cleverness. Elgin's act of vandalism would confuse the minds of well-intentioned men at home, who otherwise were bound to react unfavourably to news of the way British troops had disgraced themselves in the Summer Palace by looting. Elgin was 10 000 miles away from the London newspapers – and Bowlby, *The Times* correspondent, was among the dead. He was well aware that British public opinion in its current bloody-minded mood might easily be made to confound a day of undisciplined plunder, caused by greed, with a deliberate act of 'retribution' for 'Chinese torture'. Elgin might well in the eyes of history be acting atrociously – and he was intelligent enough to know what damage this would be to his fame – but at least he was taking it all upon himself.

Lord Elgin's unilateral decision to burn the Summer Palace marked the end of good feeling between British and French – who had also been wounded in their *amour-propre* by their discovery that most of the Chinese thought the French army were mercenaries, in British employ. The last straw for the French had been when the British contingent arrived 'early' at the gate of Peking so as to be 'first' in a ceremonial march through the city streets which Elgin and Gros had judged appropriate to underline publicly the fact of Allied victory. Baron Gros himself was by nature magnanimous, but into the everyday relations between the Allies this kind of pettiness had entered.

The French in one sense were not sorry to see Elgin act out the part of 'uncontrollably fierce barbarian'. Gros wrote to de Montauban, reminding him that in the eyes both of Europe and of the Chinese people, France, by taking no hand whatever in burning down the Summer Palace, would cut a much better figure. The French knew they had clean hands where opium was concerned, and their treaty had 'legalized' the coolie trade.

French engineers had cleaned out and refurbished the church built in Peking in 1651 by Portuguese Jesuits; they placed a new iron crucifix on top, and the edifice was reconsecrated. The Jesuits themselves had even begun to entertain secret hopes of converting Prince Kung. It was lawful for the first time since the early eighteenth century for Roman Catholic missionaries to travel openly inside China. By December 1860 Père Delamarre, another priest who had served the French army as interpreter, marched triumphantly out of Peking, bearing the Tricolor, and carrying in his pocket legal passports to the twenty-seven French missionaries who had all this time been at work clandestinely in the distant provinces of Kweichow, Yunnan and Szechwan.

On 18 October – sunny, but on the hills along the horizon there was snow – the British First Division under Major-General Sir John Michel marched in good order through the gate of the Summer Palace, and there began systematically to set on fire the two hundred buildings it contained. General Michel himself was not unaffected by his horrid task: when on the point of giving an order to burn down the Ya-tsing Pagoda he was 'struck by its simple beauty, and spared it as a work of art'. The façade of one of the baroque palaces also survived the fire.

In an outhouse the busy soldiers found a pair of brand-new English riding carriages, together with some astronomical instruments, an unused double-barrelled English shotgun, and two howitzers, also new, complete with limbers and ammunition and dated Woolwich 1782. They had been brought to the palace in August 1793 as gifts to the Manchu Emperor from King George III. The wind began blowing chill from the north-west, and for the next two days a pall of thick black smoke from burning palaces and ornamental woodlands drifted ominously over the roofs of Peking.

'The sun shining through the masses of smoke', wrote Swinhoe, who accompanied the First Division, 'gave a sickly hue to every plant and tree and the red flame gleaming on the faces of the troops engaged made them appear like demons glorying in the destruction of what they could not replace ... The Yuen-ming-yuen, or Round and Brilliant Garden, was fast becoming a scene of confusion and desolation, but there was as yet much spoil within its walls.'

The men of the First Division were 'allowed to plunder to their heart's content'. Alas, the more portable loot had long since gone: 'Most of the precious things were so bulky and cumbersome that they were obliged to be destroyed, because nobody could carry them away.' But the lucky 15th Punjabis 'fell in with large quantities of gold ... one officer alone managing to appropriate to himself as much as £9000'.

On 23 October the increased indemnity was paid over in full by the Imperial Treasury. Next day Lord Elgin appeared at the Board of Ceremonies in a green sedan chair, borne by eight porters in scarlet livery, to sign the Treaty. Since Chinese custom decreed that only the Emperor could use eight porters, his style of arrival gave great offence. Elgin was escorted by 400 infantry and 100 cavalry. For fear of treachery – evil rumours having reached him through informants among the Chinese Christians – the processional route was lined with 2000 troops, and Lieutenant-Colonel Wolseley carefully inspected the environs of the Board of Ceremonies for buried mines. A battery of field-guns had been mounted on the wall near the An Tung Gate, and aimed inwards, to open fire on the city in case of need.

With the Summer Palace gone up in flames, personal relations between Lord Elgin and Prince Kung were extremely chilly. The Prince had already lost face by arriving – as good manners decreed – in a sedan chair borne by only six porters. Lord Elgin not only arranged matters so as to keep the Prince waiting for two and a half hours, but on meeting him, according to General Hope Grant, gave him 'a proud, contemptuous look ... which must have made the blood run cold in poor Kung's veins. He was,' adds the General justly, 'a delicate, gentlemanlike-looking man.'

The 28-year-old Prince had dressed for the occasion in a long purple robe of damasked silk embroidered with dragons. His trousers were yellow, his boots were also embroidered, and he wore a jade necklace. During the ceremony of signing, Prince Kung and his party were shocked by the way Elgin nervously shouted at all of them, '*Keep perfectly still!*' when a photograph was being taken by Signor Beato. (The light was bad, and the photograph not a success.) Prince Kung afterwards offered a ceremonial banquet, but Lord Elgin declined. There was always the risk – was there not? – that the food might be poisoned.

Henry Loch, fresh from his imprisonment, was sent off at top speed to London with a copy of the Treaty. News of the Peking prisoners' ordeal was the story of the hour, and Loch on landing at Dover was astonished to find himself a national hero. Royalty were gracious. Prince Albert was concerned – as well he might be – for the stability of the Manchu dynasty, but Queen Victoria was more anxious to hear about the looting of the Summer Palace.

Prince Kung showed up in better spirits at the ceremony on 25 October, with the French. He again wore a jade necklace, but this time sported a hat trimmed with black sable. General Montauban was in full fig, but Baron Gros, having lost his own court uniform in the shipwreck on his way out to China, made an appearance in an ordinary dark suit – with the addition of a braided cap rather like a master mariner's. In a skilfully phrased reference to his own misfortune on the high seas, the Baron managed to commiserate with Prince Kung on the loss of the Summer Palace. After the Treaty was signed, Baron Gros gave the Prince a complete collection of French coins, and framed photographic portraits of Napoleon III and the Empress Eugénie. Refreshments were offered and accepted, and no one was poisoned.

The Roman Catholic Bishop of Peking was formally installed in his diocese, and next day, its job done, the French army withdrew from the city, leaving a battalion to guard the diplomats. The British lingered on until a translation of their own treaty had been posted up in the streets for everyone in Peking to read and bear well in mind. The British got out just in time – their cavalry rode down to Tientsin in a snowstorm, Lord Elgin had to steam his way downriver through floating ice, and seven miles below Tientsin one gunboat, *Slaney*, got herself frozen in.

Of all the Great Powers who managed to get something worth having out of China in 1860 – her year of weakness – the Russians though least forward in the fighting came off best. The treaties by opening up central China to trade and religion gave Russia a long-sought concession – the right to send her ships to the Treaty Ports. The Russians had at last outflanked the Gobi Desert – for so many years China's buffer against encroachment from Siberia. They could surround China henceforth in an embrace friendly or otherwise, by sea as well as by land.

While the French and British armies were busy putting the Summer Palace to the sack, General Ignatieff went out of his way to dissociate Russia from all this vandalism, and took the opportunity to emphasize once more the long tradition of friendship between Russia and China. No doubt in the spirit of this friendship, he persuaded Prince Kung on 14 November 1860 to put his signature to an Additional Treaty of Peking. Prince Kung was just then in no posture to deny any amicable request for frontier rectification. By this treaty the River Ussuri, running parallel to the coast, replaced the River Amur along that stretch of the Russian–Chinese boundary. By making this small alteration on the map, Russia took (and still holds) a tract of China's territory almost as large as Korea, extending southward from the Amur River – the historic frontier – for 72 877 square miles. The Russians, as it turned out, had long had their eye on a sheltered bay facing the

Sea of Japan, very suitable for a new naval base. They built a port there and named it Vladivostok, meaning *Rule the East*.

By 24 January 1861 Prince Kung on mature reflection had decided not to accept the long-standing and generous Russian offer of help against the Taiping: the friendship of the Tsar cost too dear.

Lord Elgin passed the month of December at Shanghai, getting the rest he so badly needed. He read his way through Elizabeth Barrett Browning's *Aurora Leigh* (which like most readers of the time he 'admired greatly'). He went on next to read Trollope's *Doctor Thorne* and Charles Darwin's recent *On the Origin of Species*. Such enterprises as the British had lately been engaged on at Peking were increasingly hard to justify in Christian terms. When the notion of 'the survival of the fittest' as explained by Darwinian popularizers became commonly accepted in years to come, Darwinism was to give a quasi-scientific rather than a quasi-religious justification to this kind of large-scale theft. Elgin found Darwin 'audacious'. He left China on 16 January 1861 – after annexing Kowloon, in accordance with his secret instructions.

Since his General's talented brother was President of the Royal Academy, later in 1861 Lord Elgin not surprisingly found himself Guest of Honour at the Royal Academy Dinner. Landseer sat on his right. Lord Elgin, after dining, produced that evening in his own defence a speech interesting for its insensitiveness, as if indicating that the part of his mind once so tormented by what it met in China must have scarred over.

'I am not so incorrigibly barbarous as to be incapable of feeling the humanizing influences which fall upon us from the noble works of art by which we are surrounded,' Lord Elgin told the long table of well-fed Academicians. 'No one regretted more sincerely than I did the destruction of that collection of summer houses and kiosks, already, and previously to any act of mine, rifled of their contents, which was dignified by the title of Summer Palace of the Chinese Emperor.'

Elgin went on to account for his action by repeating some of the arguments he had used elsewhere, but with an exaggerated emphasis: '... in no other way, except indeed by inflicting on this country and on China the calamity of another year of war, could I mark the sense which I entertained ... of an atrocious crime, which, if it had passed unpunished, would have placed in jeopardy the life of every European in China. I felt the time had come when I must choose between the indulgence of a not unnatural sensibility, and the performance of a painful duty.'

Having thus made clear his own state of mind at the time, Lord Elgin went on, more congenially, to talk to the Academicians about Art.

'I have been repeatedly asked whether, in my opinion, the interests of art are likely to be in any degree promoted by the opening up of China ... I do not think in matters of art we have much to learn from that country ... the most cynical representations of the grotesque have been the principal products of Chinese conceptions of the sublime and beautiful. Nevertheless I am disposed to believe that under this mass of abortions and rubbish there lie some hidden sparks of a divine fire, which the genius of my countrymen may gather and nurse into a flame.'

Later in the same year, Lord Elgin came into his reward, being sent out to replace his friend Lord Canning, in India. During 1864 he died on duty, prematurely, of a seizure.

During the winter of 1860–61 the mere presence of Allied troops encamped at Tientsin deterred armed rebels out of Shensi and Shantung from sweeping upcountry to assault Peking. Prince Seng when sent off with 8000 cavalry and 15 000 militia to crush rebellion in Shantung was so short of artillery that he was reduced to asking the victorious Allies to give him back some of the guns they had captured. But the policy of warlike resistance for so long pressed by this brave, competent and honest if reactionary Mongol General was played out. Seng was reduced to the ranks, and forced to serve for $7½ a day as a private soldier. But perhaps the Chinese had the moral victory.

On 20 December 1860 in the British army's winter camp at Tientsin, pilfering had become so chronic that the Senior Medical Officer was obliged to look around for someone in whose common honesty he could trust. 'It is not safe to entrust property to the care of soldiers', wrote Dr D. F. Rennie, 'so demoralized has the army become by the constant looting ... the Legations at Peking have decided to establish a Chinese agent at Taku.'

In 1864 – by which time the Taiping had been smashed and the Yangtze was opened up – the British enjoyed seven-eighths of all the trade with China. The direct export trade from England to China amounted to £20 260 597 (excluding trade between India and China) and total trade between England, India and China was probably in excess of £100 000 000. Total opium exports from India – most going to China – rose from 58 681 chests in 1859–60 to 105 508 chests in 1879–80. Cotton piece-goods going to China quadrupled, from 113 million yards in 1856 to 448 million yards in 1880. Lord Palmerston, that close student of Adam Smith, had abundantly succeeded in what he set out to do.

In 1869, Alcock negotiated a revised Commercial Convention. Though the Treaty of Tientsin obliged them to submit to 'legalization', the Chinese tried once again to limit their consumption of opium by increasing the duty from thirty to fifty taels per chest. The opium dealers brought pressure to bear on Lord Granville, and the Liberal government of the day refused to ratify. In 1832 opium had provided less than one-eighteenth part of India's revenue, by 1872 it furnished more than one-seventh. In 1870, Sir Wilfred Lawson's motion in the Commons that 'this House condemns the system by which a large portion of the Indian Revenue is raised by opium' was lost by 47 votes to 151. The debate was enlivened by the unexpected sight of William Ewart Gladstone – with thirty years more experience of political reality than when he first denounced it – defending the contribution made by opium to the Indian Revenue.

General Hope Grant was invited at last to Buckingham Palace, and there handed over to Queen Victoria her jade-and-gold sceptre. She also received three huge enamelled bowls, looted from the Emperor of China by Major Probyn, the leader of irregular Sikh Horse, and presented to Her Majesty as a gift from the Army. But this was not all.

A curious breed of small dog had also been encountered at the Summer Palace, and some considerate dog-lover carried the little beasts back home. These lapdogs were brave, intelligent, grotesque, and had been bred to resemble a Chinese heraldic lion. Captain Hart Dunne, of the Wiltshire Regiment, presented one of these 'Pekingese' to Queen Victoria. Aptly named Lootie, it ran yapping happily about the Palace until its death in 1872.

A note on methods
and sources

MONEY VALUES: The Chinese had a currency of copper cash; their silver money was not a coinage, but went by weight and fineness. From the sixteenth century onwards, silver from Mexican mines, coined into dollars, reached Manila in the Acapulco galleon and was traded at Macao for silk. The Chinese accepted Mexican silver dollars in trade, and similar Spanish and American coins later passed into use with them, though not precisely at face value, the Chinese preferring some coinages to others for their weight and fineness, and accepting them at a premium. In this book, for simplicity, such minor differences have been ignored.

Money amounts are assumed here to be interchangeable for the British gold sovereign at a rate of three taels of silver, five dollars and twenty-five francs to the sovereign (though the dollar was usually worth a little more). Between a period when currency was based on gold and silver, and prices were fairly stable, and a time like our own of incessantly inflating paper currency, money comparisons are very difficult to make. Wages give some kind of guide.

A London policeman of the time – an intelligent and literate but unskilled working man, often an old soldier, probably with a family to keep – was thought to have been raised above petty temptation by a wage of a guinea a week. (£1. 1s. 0d.) London dockers twenty years later were compelled to strike to gain a wage rate for casual labour of 6d. an hour. American wage rates were higher. British seamen found it worth their while to jump ship in Texas and work extremely hard in the cattle business for a daily wage of a dollar and their keep.

The cost of living, comparatively, was high at Hong Kong (and higher still at Shanghai, where in 1860 the cost of renting a small house was £400). Able seamen there earned upwards of $25 a month; gunlayers in opium clippers at $45 a month were exceptionally well paid. Between 1840 and 1860 it was taken for granted that a merchant with a small capital and no special aptitude, even though paying high wages to his European subordinates, would normally 'make his pile' in about five years.

Figures given in pounds or dollars to indicate the scope of the China trade or the size of indemnities are therefore in contemporary terms worth very much more than would appear at a glance. For those who from habit make mental comparisons in terms of recent money values, it would seem by and large safe – in 1975 – to multiply sums expressed here in dollars by a factor of seven or eight, and those expressed in pounds sterling perhaps by as much as ten.

CHINESE NAMES: There are many systems of romanizing Chinese names, the more important being associated with one or other of the foreign powers involved in China in the past. Wade-Giles, a familiar current system, is British in origin, Yale, a more modern and accurate system, is American, Latinxua was devised by Russians of the Soviet epoch, some are also very curious – d'Escayrac de Lauture, for instance, invented one for the French which needed a special typeface. All of them, however widely current outside China, seem destined to be replaced in time by Pīnyin, which since 1958 has had the approval of the present Chinese régime.

Wade-Giles is a long-established system for geographical nomenclature, and one on which place-names in *The Times Atlas of the World* are based. But Wade-Giles if followed consistently confronts the reader with Pei-ching for Peking, Nan-ching for Nanking and Kuang-chou for Canton. Conventional names have therefore been given to places which either are likely to be more familiar in an incorrect or arbitrary form – on the precedent of Edimbourg for Edinburgh and Leghorn for Livorno – or which occur in a clearly recognizable form in historical sources. For other place-names, *The Times* usage is followed.

Proper names copied into the text from sources dating from before the time when romanization became systematic – when names were rendered phonetically by guesswork – are no less irregular, but here again, the familiar form has always been preferred to the systematically correct one. Chinese names have been written in a way likeliest for the ordinary reader to identify easily and distinguish at a glance. This is arbitrary, unscholarly and insular, but will bewilder only the specialist. The world needs more bewildered specialists.

SOURCES: Materials for the serious academic history of the Chinese Opium Wars which has not yet been written are abundant. For instance there are over 2000 books and articles, many in Chinese or Russian, on the Taiping Rising alone. To append a scholarly apparatus of references to an essay in popular narrative history, compiled from less than a hundred sources, all secondary, and in only two languages, would be wilfully misleading. Yet the narrative historian writing for the man in the street has valid standards of his own – corresponding to those of the responsible journalist. History is the resurrection of the dead; this book is only a sketch of a possible beginning.

A guide to sources and further reading

(Published in London unless otherwise stated)

Anderson, F., *The Rebel Emperor* (1958): a sympathetic but imaginative narrative account of the Taiping movement.

Anderson, Captain L., *A Cruise in an Opium Clipper* (1935): a Dent clipper off Formosa in the late 1850s.

Bernard, W. D., *Narrative of the Voyages and Services of the Nemesis from 1840–1843:* a classic of gunboat warfare.

Bingham, Commander J. E., *Narrative of the Expedition to China* (1842): emphasizes the naval aspect.

Blake, Clagette, *Charles Elliot, RN* (1959): a modern biography by an American academic.

Bonner-Smith, D. and Lumby, E. W. R., *The Second China War 1856–60* (1955): thoroughly based on Admiralty papers.

Bowring, L. B. Ed., *Autobiographical Recollections of Sir John Bowring* (1877).

Boxer, C. E., *The Dutch Seaborne Empire 1600–1800* (1973).

Checkland, S. G., *The Gladstones* (Cambridge 1971).

Collis, M., *Foreign Mud* (1952): from East India Company days in Canton to the first Opium War, in the light of contemporary memoirs and a resumé of the Jardine, Matheson papers.

Collis, M., *The Great Within* (1941): conflates the contemporary reports of early British embassies to Peking.

Cooke, G. W., *China* (1859): 1857 in Canton as seen by a rather bellicose correspondent of *The Times*.

Costin, W. C., *Great Britain and China (1833–60)* (Oxford 1938): diplomatic history from the British viewpoint, relying on Foreign Office papers.

Dennett, Tyler, *Americans in Eastern Asia* (New York 1941): thoroughly documented from American sources.

Downing, C. Toogood, *The Fan-Qui in China* (1838): life in early Canton days, as seen by an intelligent surgeon.

Eames, J. B., *The English in China* (1909).

Eitel, E. J., *Europe in China: a History of Hong Kong* (1895): prejudiced and slapdash, but gossipy.

Elvin, Mark, *The Pattern of China's Past* (1973): well informed but deterministic economic history.

Endacott, G. O., *A History of Hong Kong* (Oxford 1958).

Escayrac de Lauture, Comte de, *Mémoires sur la Chine* (Paris 1865): head of the scientific mission with the French army, and a prisoner in Peking.

Fox, Grace, *British Admirals and Chinese Pirates 1832–1869* (1940): from Admiralty papers.

Gash, N., *Sir Robert Peel* (1972).

Giles, H. A., *China and the Manchus* (Cambridge 1912).

Giles, H. A., *The Civilization of China* (1919).

Greenberg, M., *British Trade and the Opening of China 1800–1842* (Cambridge 1969): includes a detailed economic account of the opium business in its early days.

Gregory, J. S., *Great Britain and the Taipings* (1969).

Hammond, J. L. and B., *Lord Shaftesbury* (1923).

Hayter, Alethea, *Opium and the Romantic Imagination* (1968): opium in Eng. Lit., and brilliantly done.

Henderson, P., *The Life of Laurence Oliphant* (1956).

Holt, E., *The Opium Wars in China* (1964): a fair-minded popular history from the British point of view.

Hsin-pao, Chang, *Commissioner Lin and the Opium War* (Harvard 1964): balanced, thorough, includes Chinese material.

Hunter, W. C., *The 'Fan Kwae' at Canton* (Shanghai 1911): a young American merchant at Canton in Company days and after.

Hurd, Douglas, *The Arrow War: An Anglo-Chinese Confusion* (1967): a brilliant diplomatic analysis which makes a discerning use of the Elgin Papers.

Jocelyn, Lord, *Six Months with the Chinese Expedition* (1841).

Juillard, L. F., *Souvenirs d'un Voyage en Chine* (Montbeliard n.d.): war experiences of the Protestant chaplain with the French army in 1860.

Kaye, J. W., *A History of the Sepoy War in India 1857–8* (1865–76).

Kennedy, Admiral Sir Wm., *Hurrah for the Life of a Sailor* (1901): experiences as a midshipman at Canton in 1858.

Knollys, H., *Life of Sir Hope Grant*, vol. II (1894): documents and recollections digested by his former ADC.

Krausse, A., *Russia in Asia* (1900): prejudiced against the Russians but well informed.

Lane-Poole, S., *The Life of Sir Harry Parkes* (1894).

Latourette, K. S., *A History of the Christian Missions in China* (1929).

Lattimore, O., *Inner Asian Frontiers of China* (Oxford 1940).

Leavenworth, C. S., *The Arrow War with China* (1901): history for old China Hands.

Lindley, A. F., *Ti-ping Tien-kwoh: the History of the Ti-ping Revolution* (2 vols 1866): romantic adventures of an English gun-runner and mercenary with the Taiping in their last days.

Lubbock, B., *The Opium Clippers* (Glasgow 1933).

M'Ghee, Rev. R. J. L., *How We Got to Pekin* (1862): the campaign as experienced by the senior chaplain.

Mackenzie, A., *The History of the Mathesons* (1900): a work of family piety.

Magnus, P., *Gladstone* (1954).

Martin, W. A. P., *A Cycle of Cathay* (1900): the somewhat hazy recollections of the missionary who interpreted for the Americans during 1859–60.

Meadows, T. T., *The Chinese and Their Rebellions* (1856): contains an early account of the Taiping by an eccentric British official who took their side.

Moges, Marquis de, *Recollections of Baron Gros's Embassy to China and Japan in 1857–8* (1860): by an intelligent and well-informed eyewitness.

Morison, J. L., *The 8th Earl of Elgin* (1928): Elgin as proconsul.

Morse, H. B., *The International Relations of the Chinese Empire 1834–1866* (1910).

Oliphant, L., *Narrative of the Earl of Elgin's Mission to China and Japan* (2 vols 1859): by Elgin's exuberant private secretary.

Ouchterlony, Lieutenant J., *The Chinese War* (1844): an eyewitness account by a young Indian Army officer.

Owen, D. F., *British Opium Policy in China and India* (Yale 1934): tendentious but well documented.

Panikkar, K. M., *Asia and Western Dominance* (1953): well intentioned – from the Asian point of view.

Pelcovits, N. A., *Old China Hands and the Foreign Office* (1948): uses Foreign Office papers to score off the British; occasionally succeeds.

Pratt, Sir J., *China and Britain* (1944).

Price, A. Grenfell, *Western Invasion of the Pacific and its Continents* (Oxford 1963).

Priestley, J. B., *Thomas Love Peacock* (1927).

Redford, A., *Manchester Merchants and Foreign Trade* vol. I 1794–1858, vol. II 1850–1939 (Manchester 1934 and 1956).

Rennie, D. F., *The British Arms in North China and Japan* (1864): the march on Peking seen by the senior Medical Officer.

Rowntree, J., *The Imperial Drug Trade* (1906): the anti-opium campaign and the Royal Commission on Opium analysed.

St. Clair, W., *Lord Elgin and the Marbles* (Oxford 1967).

Scarth, J., *Twelve Years in China* (Edinburgh 1860): memoirs of a Scottish merchant open-minded towards the Chinese.

Scott, J. L., *Narrative of a Recent Imprisonment in China after the Wreck of the Kite* (1841): admirable personal account by a young ship's officer.

Scott, J. M., *The White Poppy: a History of Opium* (1971).

Swinhoe, R., *Narrative of the North China Campaign of 1860* (1861): the journal of an official interpreter.

Swisher, E., *China's Management of the American Barbarians (1841–1861)* (Yale 1951): annotated translations of Chinese foreign policy documents.

Teng, S. Y. *Chang Hsi and the Treaty of Nanking* (Chicago 1944).

Teng, S. Y., *The Taiping Rebellion and the Western Powers* (Oxford 1971): schematic but thoroughly based on Chinese sources.

Turner, F. S., *British Opium Policy and its Results in China* (1876): the case presented by a British anti-opium campaigner.

Varin, P., *Expédition de Chine* (Paris 1862): pro-Montauban, anti-British.

Waldrond, T. Ed., *Letters and Journals of James 8th Earl of Elgin* (1873).

Waley, A., *The Opium War through Chinese Eyes* (1958): uses Commissioner Lin's journal among other Chinese sources.

Wolseley, Lieutenant-Colonel G. J., *Narrative of the War with China 1860* (1862): the best account by a professional soldier.

(Yeh's poem, p. 252, is translated in *The Harvard Journal of Asiatic Studies*, 1941, Vol. 6, p. 37).

Index

Aberdeen, Lord (4th Earl), 140, 158–9
aborigines from Golden River, 144–5
Actaeon, HMS, 220
addiction to opium: in Britain, 28–9,
    75, 110; in China, 28–9, 31, 35–6, 43,
    60, 66–7, 74–7, 82, 113, 146–7, 162–3,
    191, 263, 265; in Coolie Corps, 287;
    life-expectation of addicts in China,
    263; in United States, 177–8
administration of Chinese Empire, 17,
    22; corruption through opium
    addiction, 35, 38, 61, 75
aggressive policy by British, 43–4, 46,
    49–54, 120, 128, 154, 218–19 et seq.
Alarme, 283
Albert, Prince, 232, 327
Alcock, Rutherford, 165, 204, 212, 295,
    331
Algerine, HMS, 69, 115, 121
Algiers bombardment, 52, 63, 91
Aliens Bill, 254
Alligator, HMS, 111, 115
Amerika, 245, 257
Amherst, Lord (2nd Earl): ambassador
    in Peking, 21–3, 54; refusal to
    kowtow, 22–3
Amoy: bombarded by Royal Navy,
    118; Coolie Trade, 176; kept as
    security, 154; massacre when retaken
    from rebels, 199–200; occupied by
    British, 134–6; open to trade, 155;
    Triad take-over, 199
Amur River: and Russian frontier
    dispute, 198–9, 245, 328; Russian
    settlements, 210
Andromache, HMS, 46, 49, 51–4
Ann, 138, 158
Anson, Major, 292, 319
Anstruther, Major Peter, 121–3, 139, 150
Antelope, 173–4
anti-opium campaign: Chinese, 73–93,
    104, 119, 129; Parliamentary, 158–63;
    religious in Britain, 65
area enclosed by China, 20
Armstrong, Commodore, 222–3
Armstrong, Lieutenant, 145

Armstrong field-gun, 281, 304, 311
arrests of brokers, pushers and addicts,
    70, 77
Arrow incident, 213–18, 225–9, 230,
    247; Parliamentary debate, 229–32
Ashley, Lord (later Earl of
    Shaftesbury), 160–2
Astell, J. H., 47, 89
Atlanta, 121
atrocities: Allied armies in China,
    305–6; Coolie Corps, 286–7;
    Imperial troops on rebels, 199–200;
    Indian Mutiny, 243–4; stories from
    China, 235
Auckland, Lord (1st Earl), 67, 95, 98,
    132
auction sales of opium in Bengal, 26, 33
Audacieuse, 240, 244, 248
*Autobiographical Recollections of Sir
    John Bowring*, 206
Avalanche, 247, 259

barbarian threat to China, 18
Barrier Forts: bombarded and
    captured by Americans, 222–3;
    dismantled by British, 218
Basel Missionary Society, 167
Bate, Commander W. T., 220
Beato, Signor, 312, 327
Beddoes, Dr Thomas, 28
Bengal: auction sales of opium, 26,
    33; conquest, 23; cultivation and
    export of opium, 23–4, 26, 33, 39, 73,
    110
Benoist, Father, 315
Bentham, Jeremy, 207
Bentinck, Lord William, 38, 40
Bernard, Lieutenant, 152
Bird & Co., John, 214, 216
bishops' vote in Parliament, 226, 228
Black Swan, 137
Blackwood, Captain P., 49, 51
Blenheim, HMS, 112, 128
Block, Mr, 216
blockades: Canton by Royal Navy, 111,
    113; Pearl River by Chinese, 78–9, 100

339

Index

Blonde, HMS, 112, 118, 134, 153–4
Board of Astronomy, Peking, 59
Board of Ceremonies, Peking, 327
Board of Punishments, Peking, 158, 301, 324
Board of Rites, Peking, 193; suppresses Christianity, 59
Bogue Forts: Battle of the Bogue, 51–3; bombarded by Weddell, 18, 51, 269; destruction, 124–5; guarding Pearl River, 32, 46; reinforced by Teng, 69; strengthened by Lin, 100, 104
Bombay opium trade: sales, 82; stocks, 77; transit, 34, 110
Bonham, Sir George, 168
Bonham, Sir Samuel, 209–10
Bourchier, Captain, 118
Bowlby (*Times* correspondent), 291, 299, 301, 325
Bowring, Sir John: advises against recognition of Taiping, 196; *Arrow* incident, 215–18; attacked in Parliamentary debate, 228–30; Canton entry on pretext, 219–20, 224–5, 232; on Coleridge, 206; communicates privately with Yeh, 244; confidential agent, 207, 227; Consul at Canton, 207–8; Coolie Trade detested, 175–6; deluges Elgin with advice, 241; on Free Trade, 295; Hong Kong governor, 209–10, 232; invites US to make joint demand for diplomatic access to Canton, 222; knighted, 210, 228; naval demonstration on city question, 215; personal understanding with Ministers, 211; radical pacifist and advocate of decimal coinage, 207, 267; rebuked by Malmesbury, 209; replaced by Elgin, 237; ships out Triad sympathizers from Hong Kong, 202; spares Hong Kong bread-poisoners, 234
Bowring, L. B., 208
Brabazon, Captain, 299, 310
Brandywine, 173
bribes to get opium ashore, 66
Bridgman, Elijah, 84
Bright, John, 207, 235, 277
British Army: Amoy captured, 134–5; Bogue Forts destroyed, 124–5, 128; Canton captured, 247–50; Cha-po, Wu-sung and Shanghai occupied, 147–8; Chen-hai and Ningpo taken, 139–40; Chinkiang captured, 150–2; Crimean conflict, 210; defeat at Taku, 270–2; demoralized by looting, 330; expeditionary force sent by Palmerston (1840), 98, 101, 112; flogging, 94; Indian Mutiny, 242–4; looting, 116, 136, 140, 148, 152, 287, 305, 319; Pei-t'ang landing, 285–6; Prince Seng defeated at Chang-chia-wan and Pa-li-chi'ao, 303–5, 310–11; rank and file, 136; repel Chinese

counter-attack on Ningpo, 145–6; social changes, 320–1; Summer Palace destruction, 326; Taku Forts captured, 290–3; Tientsin occupied, 296; Tin-hai taken, 114–17; Tin-hai re-taken, 137; weapons, 242, 281, 288
brothels, 32
Brown, Dr John, 28
Brown Bess musket, 242
Bruce, Frederick, 261, 267, 269, 273–4, 277–8, 284, 296, 323, 329
Bruce, Lady Mary, 280
Bryson, Captain Lesley, 176
Buchanan, President, 245, 276
Buffs, The, 288
Burke, Edmund, 238
Burrell, Major-General George, 115, 117
Bustard, HMS, 283
Byron, Lord, 207, 239

Calcutta, 244, 252
Calcutta, HMS, 249, 256
Caldwell, D. R., 169
calendar, Chinese, 58
Calliope, HMS, 124, 128
Cambridge, 87, 99 (renamed *Chesapeake*), 100, 128–9
Cameronian Regiment, 117
Camoens, Luis Vaz de, 32
canal systems, 20, 310
Canning, Lord ('Clemency', 1st Earl), 237–8, 240, 242–4, 279–80, 330
Canning, George, 207
Canton; access rights, 208–11, 221–2, 247; aggressive policy of British, 43–4, 46; anti-foreign sentiment, 92; blockade by Royal Navy, 111, 113; burning of Factories, 223; captured by Anglo-French, 247–52; comic entry by British, 220–1; Creek Factory, 70–1; designated a trading port, 18–19; destruction of opium by Lin, 84–5; dominated by British, 22, 30; English Factory, 46–7, 50–3; evacuated by British, 86; exercise at, 31; Factories, 71–2, 75, 78–80, 96, 109, 129, 158, 208, 213, 223; free traders, 42; guerrilla harassment, 265–6; looting and demolition of Factories, 129; Petition Gate, 47; ransom of, 126, 130, 154; reign of terror by Yeh Ming-chen on Triad rebels, 200–2; restrictions on Europeans, 30; Seymour's attack, 219; tea transactions, 29–30, 45; threat to Factories by Cantonese, 158; US bombard Barrier Forts, 222–3; urgent necessity of capture, 224, 241
Canton, 169–70
Canton Press, 130
Canton Register, 112
Carnatic, 87–8
Caroline, 167
Castiglione, Father, 315
Catherine the Great, 16
Cawnpore march, 243

340

___2

Cécille, Captain Médée, 150, 155
celibacy of Taipings, 186–7, 191
Chads, Captain H. D., 46
Challenge, HMS, 216
Challoyé, C. A., 125
Chang Ch'ao fa, Brigadier, 115
Chang-chia-wan, 299, 303; looting and vandalism by Allied troops, 305–6; occupied by Anglo-French, 304; Parkes taken prisoner at, 300
Chang Ying-yun, General, 146
Chapdelaine, Father Auguste: execution, 212, 239, 247
Cha-pu capture, 147–8
Charles I, 18
Ch'en Hsieng-liang, 202
Ch'en Ping-chun, 142
Ch'en T'ing-ch'en, 145
Chen-hai: fall of, 139, 142; fiasco of Chinese attempt to re-take, 147
Cheng Tsu-ch'en, 185
Cheong A Lum, 233–4
Chesapeake, see *Cambridge*
Chia Ch'ing, Emperor: end of reign, 35; weakness of rule, 22
Ch'i Lung, 47, 53
Ch'i Shan, Commissioner, 119–21, 123–8; arrest, 127, 129; evasiveness, 124, 128; interviews Captain Elliot, 119, 126; negotiates Treaty of Chuenpi with Elliot, 126–7; readiness to negotiate, 123; succeeds Lin as Commissioner at Canton, 120, 123
Ch'ien Lung, Emperor: audience with Macartney, 15–17, 18, 20, 119, 298; last of the Manchu administrators, 35; reply to George III, 17; retirement, 18, 21–2; Summer Palace, 315
Chin A-lin, 205
Chin A Po, 169–70
Ch'i-ying, 153, 155, 173–4
child labour in Britain, 160
Childe Harold, 239
China Repository, 43–4, 84
Chinese Army, 135–6, 180, 237; opium addiction, 35; recruitment by Lin, 99
Chinese Commercial Guide, A, 141
Chinese Courier, 43
Ching Yih, 22
Chinkiang captured, 150–2
Chinnery, George, 89, 131; brings European painting to China, 40, 58
Chou-shan Island: amphibious disaster by Chinese, 144–5; British base, 138; kept as security, 154; missionary clinic, 116, 141; occupied by British, 113–16, 282; opium centre, 157; returned in exchange for prisoners, 122, 127–8, 130; unfavourable winds and hostile population, 153
Christianity: impregnating British politics, 238; and Indian Mutiny, 242–4; leads to Taiping rebellion, 179–97; spread in China, 57–60;

suppression by Board of Rites, 59, 173
Chu Shih-yun, 151–2
Chu Tsun, 67
Chuenpi: naval action begins war, 103, 124–5; surrender of opium, 80–1, 83; Treaty of, 126–7, which HM Government refuses to ratify, 127
Chusan, 213
Clarendon, Lord (4th Earl), 203–4, 206, 210, 215, 224, 226–7, 229, 235, 246, 254, 262
Clavelin, Père, 187
Cleveland, Captain, 70
Clifton, Captain William, 38
clippers, opium, 38–9, 82, 98, 112, 114, 157, 159, 167, 170, 174
coast trade in opium, 41–2, 45, 65, 73–4, 104, 159
Cobden, Richard, 207, 224, 228–30, 235
Cochrane, Admiral Sir Thomas, 168
Colbert, 204
Coleridge, Samuel Taylor, 28, 206, 314–15
Colledge, Dr T. R., 53–4
Collineau, General, 287, 289, 291–2
Colonel Young, 68
Columbine, HMS, 124, 154, 169–72
Comanjee Hormusjee, 159
Commercial Convention (1869), 331
communications (China–Britain), 92, 233
Con, Captain, 287
Confessions of an English Opium Eater, 94
confiscation of opium by Lin, 80–1
Confucianism, 21, 35, 64, 74, 78, 89, 143, 182–3, 194, 262
Contest, HMS, 176
Conway, HMS, 115, 122
Conyngham, Lennox, 55, 64
Cook, Captain, 20
Coolie Corps, 247, 250, 282, 284, 286–7, 302, 305–6
Coolie Trade, 175–8, 255, 263, 325
Cormorant, 259–60, 270–1
Corn Law agitation, 207
Cornwallis, HMS, 149, 153, 155–6
Coromandel, 216–17, 247, 259
corruption through opium addiction, 35, 38, 181, 263
counter-offensive, Chinese, 142–7
country traders in opium, 26, 31, 40, 41
Coutts, Thomas, 101
Cowasjee, Framjee, 41
Cowley, Lord, 212
Cowper, Lady, 160
Crabbe, George, 29
Crimean War, 199, 210, 225
Cruikshank, George, 235
Cruiser, HMS, 115
Cruizer, HMS, 265
cultivation of opium poppy: in India, 23–4, 26, 33, 39, 73, 110, 157, 263; in Manchuria, 163

Cushing, Caleb, 106–7, 173–4, 212–13
Cushing, J. P., 36
Customs tariffs, 24, 29, 34, 206, 263–4, 307, 324, 331

Dalhousie, Lord (1st Marquess), 242
Danaide, 125
Daniell, 100–1
Dart, 213
Darwin, Charles, 329
Davidson, W., 31
Davis, Sir John Francis, 54, 168, 208, 250
De Bourbelon, 267–9
De Courcy, Comte, 212, 219, 234
De Langrené, Baron, 173
De Lauture, Comte d'Escayrac, 299, 322, 333
De Quincey, 94
decadence and officialdom, 21
degrees offered for purchase, 179
Delamarre, Pierre, 326
Delano, Consul, 107
Delhi atrocities, 243
Denham, Captain, 138
Dent, Lancelot, 53, 77–8, 81, 154, 206, 241, 245
Dent & Co., 37, 53, 62, 69, 78, 87, 89, 154, 165, 191, 213, 255, 264
Derby, Lord, 209, 224, 226–8, 254, 260, 272
destruction of opium at Canton by order of Emperor, 84–5
Disraeli, Benjamin (later 1st Earl of Beaconsfield), 56, 224–5, 231–2, 273
Dobell, Captain, 33
Douglas, Captain James, 87, 99
Douglas, Lieutenant, 121–2
Dove, HMS, 264
Downing, Toogood, 66–7
Dragonne, 246–7, 259
Drinker, Admiral, 201
drug cultures, 27
Druid, HMS, 112–13, 124, 134
Duchala, 269
Duke of Portland, 176
Duluc, Father, 299, 310
Dumaresq, Captain Philip, 173
Dutch East India Company, 30
Dutch Folly anchorage, 213, 219, 221, 247
Dutch spreading of drug habit, 23–4
dysentery: opium as a medicine, 24

Eamont, 213
Earl, Charles, 213–14
East India and China Association, 229
East India Company: Bengal conquest, 23; British imports of opium, 28–9, 75; business with Cohong syndicate, 19; Chinese Customs charges resented, 29; competition with opium, 33–4; dominates at Canton, 30; hostility to missionaries, 57; India monopoly lost (1817), 32–3; monopoly of opium-selling, 23; monopoly of trade with China, 19, 33; monopoly abolished (1833), 42; opium shipments to China, 17, 24, 26, 31; policy of controlled production and high prices, 31, 33; rule ending, 263; staff's life-style, 30; tea trade, 19, 26, 29–30; textile venture loss, 42; treasure at Canton, 53; undercuts price and increases production, 34, 161; washes hands of responsibility for opium trade, 26, 34

Edicts, Imperial: against opium, 25–7, 29, 35–6, 76–8; dissolves War Committee, 266; religious tolerance, 173; unyielding, 237, 251
Edwardes, Colonel, 243
Elgin, Lord (7th Earl), 238, 318
Elgin, Lord (8th Earl): accused of being soft, 284; on Allied generals' indecisiveness, 311; annexes Kowloon, 329; blames French for excesses, 306; on bounty system, 171; in Calcutta during Mutiny, 243–4; capture of Taku Forts, 258–60; career, 238–9, 279; death as Governor-General of India, 330; decision to burn Summer Palace, 324–7; dilemma on opium question, 263; distress at looting of Summer Palace, 318; at fall of Canton, 248–51; goes home, 267; Hong Kong arrival, 240; indemnity for losses at Peking, 323–4; leniency, 241, 250; on looting by troops at Chang-chia-wan, 305; navigates Yangtze to Hankow and Nanking, 264–5; negotiates Treaty of Tientsin, 260–2; obsessed by fate of British captives, 303; paramount representative in China, 233, 237; Peking advance, 296–311; pleads against declaration of war, 278; Postmaster-General, 272–3; refuses truce, 308; Royal Academy address, 329–30; sent back to China to clear up mess, 279–80; state entry into Peking to sign treaty, 327; Swatow landing, 255; Tientsin advance and occupation, 260, 293, 296; touchy allies, 285
Ellenborough, Lord (2nd Baron), 159, 228–9, 278
Elliot, Captain Charles: accepts Canton ransom, 126, 130, 154; action with Napier, 52; adds Hong Kong to Empire, 126; apologetic report on 'Battle of Kowloon', 92–3; asks for assistance from Navy, 67–9; attacks Bogue Forts, 124, 128; authority re-established by Battle of Chuepi, 103–5; bribes officials, 88; British Consul-General to Texas, 131; committed to free-traders' interests, 85; diplomatic instructions from

Elliot, Captain Charles—*cont.*
Palmerston, 97–8; dismissed for his moderation, 130–1; distaste for drug traffic, 63, 71, 105; dodges blockade to run up Union Jack at Canton, 78, 109; early career, 63; fights opium smuggling, 67–73, 77–80, 108; fires on junks to open war, 91; leniency with Chinese, 105–6, 112–13; orders merchants not to trade, 100–2; promises to compensate for destruction of opium, 80, 107; proposes to base trade on Macao, 86; Protector of Slaves in British Guiana, 63–4; protects merchant fleet, 87, 90–1; negotiates return of Ningpo prisoners, 121; Queen Victoria's contempt, 131; responsibility for shipping tea, 64; spares Canton, 130; refuses to yield up murderers, 88–9, 101; succeeds Napier as Chief Superintendent of Trade, 155; Treaty of Chuenpi negotiated, 126–7; tries to regain foothold in Macao, 99
Elliot, Commodore C. G. J. B., 216–17
Elliot, Rear-Admiral Hon. George, 112, 116, 118, 120, 123
Elmslie, 91
embargo on trade, Chinese, 49–50, 80
Emperor's role, 21
Encounter, HMS, 219, 221
Enfield rifle, 232, 242
Erigone, 150, 155
Essentials of Fire Raft Attack, 55
Eugénie, Empress, 321, 328
eunuchs, Imperial, 35, 178, 190, 314
executions, public, 202
Exmouth, Lord, 52
export of opium from India, 23–4, 26, 33, 39, 73, 110, 264, 331
expulsion orders to British, 66, 68, 70
extra-territoriality issue, 106

Fairy, 68
Falcon, 38
Fatshan: cutting-out operation in creek, 240; gun-foundry, 99–100, 223
Favorite, 150
Feng En-fu, Lieutenant, 284
Feng Yun-shan, 183
filibustering, 201
Firedragon Book, The, 143
fire-rafts, Chinese, 53, 55, 104, 118, 129
fire-ships, Chinese, 102–3, 223, 259
Fishbourne, Captain, 200
Fisher, Major, 271
fishermen armed by Lin, 99, 104
Fokie Tom, 283
Fong Ah-ming, 214
Foochow open to trade, 155
Forbes, Robert, 37, 86
Formosa: annexation threat by US, 213; ill-treatment of foreign prisoners, 137–8, 158; opium introduced, 68;

opium as a narcotic, 138; pirates, 200
Fort William, 88
free trade and traders, 42, 43–4, 53, 54–6, 59, 64, 67, 85, 95, 197, 295, 320
French: action at Pa-li-chi'ao bridge, 310; Anglo-French advance on Peking, 296–311; Anglo-French attack Taku Forts, 258–60; Anglo-French failure to force passage past Taku Forts, 268–72; armed alliance with Britain, 239, 273; attack on Triads at Shanghai, 204–5; capture of Canton, 247–52; conquest of Indo-China, 279; Coolie Trade involvement, 255, 263; Crimean War, 210; end of good feeling at British burning of Summer Palace, 325; expeditionary force under de Montauban, 279; friendship with China, 211; looting of Summer Palace, 316–21; misunderstandings with British, 280, 300, 306, 325; new gunboat, 281; non-involvement with opium, 263, 325; Pei-t'ang landings, 285–6; presence in China, 125, 150, 155–6; protest at Chapdelaine's execution, 212; puzzle to Chinese, 236; Sebastopol taken, 210; Taku Forts captured, 289–92; tension with British in Europe, 253–4, 273–4; Tientsin Treaty, 262; and treaty revision, 211–12; Whampoa Treaty, 172–3
Furious, HMS, 247, 255–6, 264, 266
Fury, 170–1
Fusée, 247, 251, 259–60

Gabriel, Dorothy, 167
Galitzin, Prince, 258
Garibaldi, 274
General Election (1857), 235–6
George III: gifts to Manchu Emperor, 326; letter to Ch'ien Lung, 17
Gerbillon, Father, 198
gingalls (Chinese muskets), 248–9, 259
ginseng imports from America, 19–20
Gladstone, Helen, 109–10
Gladstone, John, 109
Gladstone, William Ewart, 109–10, 131, 158, 164, 224–5, 230, 232–3, 237, 273–4, 284, 331
Gobi Desert, 199, 328
God-Worshippers, 180, 183–7
Golden Dragon King, 66
Golden River aborigines, 144–5
Gordon, General, 194
Gough, Major-General Sir Hugh, 117, 129, 132–6, 139–40, 143, 279
Gourlay, Dr, 235
government addiction in China, 35, 38
Governor Findlay, 114
Graham, Sir James, 40, 108, 229, 235
Grand Canal, 113–14, 139, 149, 151, 179, 253
Grant, Captain, 96

Granville, Lord, 331
Great Wall, 20, 192, 298, 309
Gregson, Samuel, 229
Grenada, HMS, 293
Grey, Lord, 49
Gros, Baron, 239–40, 244, 247–8, 253,
    256, 261–2, 278–80, 284, 293, 296–9,
    303, 305–6, 308, 310, 318, 322–5,
    327–8
Guérin, Admiral, 204
gunboat diplomacy: British, 62, 68–70,
    85, 118–21; French, 281
gun-running, 86, 204
Gutzlaff, Rev. Dr Karl, 60–2, 84, 90–1,
    115–16, 140–3, 145, 147, 155, 166–7,
    184, 195, 197, 208
Gutzlaff, Mary, 141

Hai-lin, General, 151–2
Hai-nan Island, 31, 170, 172
Hakkas, 180, 182–4, 186, 188, 191, 197,
    247, 250
Hall, Captain, 100
Hamberg (missionary), 167
Hammond, Edmund, 210–11, 226–7,
    241, 273
Hangchow, 141; build-up of Chinese
    troops, 142
Hankow: Catholics arrested, 172;
    Elgin's arrival, 265; future treaty
    port, 261; Taiping capture, 188;
    Tseng re-takes, 194
Hart Dunne, Captain, 331
Hastings, Warren, opium venture
    (1781), 24, 25, 39
Haughty, HMS, 269
Hay, Captain John C. Dalrymple,
    169–70, 172
Heaven and Earth Society, 180
Hellas, 83
Heng Chi, 306–8, 322
Heng Fu, Viceroy of Chihli, 269, 292–3
Herald, HMS, 154
Herbert, Sidney, 109, 229, 231, 238
Hercules, 82, 95
Hermes, HMS, 200
heroin traffic revived with Japanese
    invasion of China, 162
Hindus, 242–3
Ho Lao-chin, 71
Honan Island: forts occupied, 218
Hong Kong: anchorage for British, 82,
    87, 89, 98, 104; British take-over,
    126, 128, 153; Coolie Trade, 176–7;
    cost of living, 333–4; fever, 166;
    Indian troops, 280; lawlessness, 166,
    168, 234, 245, 306; opium trade, 159,
    165–6, 175–6, 229, 233; piracy, 166,
    168–9, 172; poisoning of bread,
    233–4; rebel organizations, 220;
    reinforcements, British, 133–4;
    Russian arrival, 245–6; sanctuary
    for rebels, 233
Hong merchants: anti-smuggling bond
    required of them, 36, 81; form Cohong

syndicate, 19; granted monopoly of
    trade, 19; managing the barbarians,
    46–8, 54; means of contact between
    foreigners and local authorities, 45;
    nonplussed by arrival of free traders,
    42; lives threatened to make
    foreigners surrender opium, 77–8;
    refuse to trade until opium stopped,
    72; squeezed by Imperial Treasury,
    19, 43; squeezed for ransom money,
    126; threaten to tear down Creek
    Factory, 70; unenthusiastic at first
    offer of opium, 25
Hong Kong Register, 166
Hope, Rear-Admiral James, 268–71,
    273, 284
Hope Grant, Frank, 280
Hope Grant, General James, 278–80,
    285–92, 296–7, 300–2, 304, 306,
    309–10, 312, 314, 316–22, 327, 331
Hoppo (Manchu head of Chinese
    Customs), 18–19, 29, 43, 68–9
Hornet, 201
Houston, Sam, 131
Howick, Lord, 63
Howqua, 72, 76–8, 126, 129, 212,
    221–2, 250
Hsien Feng, Emperor: aided by
    Mongols, 192; anti-foreign, 236;
    debauchee, 178, 203, 236; loses
    nerve, 297–8, 324; mimic naval
    battles, 322; receives US envoy, 277;
    retreat to Jehol, 298, 307, 309, 314;
    and Taiping rebels, 188, 192–3
Hsu Kuang-chin, Viceroy, 171
Hsu Nai-tsi, 65
Hua Shana, 260, 262, 276
Huang, Viceroy, 265–6
Huc, Abbé, 195
Hugo, Victor, 316
Hunan Braves, 193–4, 218
Hung Hsui-Ch'uan, 181–91, 194, 196
Hung Jen-kan, 183
Hunter, W. C., 201
Hunter, William, 72
Huron, 57
Hurst, Consul, 258
Hwangho River changes course, ruins
    peasant farms and wrecks Grand
    Canal, 179
Hyacinth, HMS, 89, 99, 103, 113, 124

I-ching, General, 142–5, 147
Ignatieff, General, 268, 312, 324, 328
I' shan, 127
I-li-pu, 123, 152–3, 155
I-Liang, Viceroy, 120, 158
Imogene, HMS, 49, 51–4
import of opium: by China, annually,
    24, 26, 31, 34, 38, 67, 73; by Britain,
    28–9, 75
income tax, British, 274
indemnities demanded, 154–5, 262,
    296, 307, 323–4, 327
India Gazette, 116

Indian Army, 112–13, 136, 242–4, 253, 280–1, 287, 289, 304, 306, 309, 311
Indian Government revenue from opium, 73, 108, 160, 176, 278, 331
Indian Mutiny, 240–4, 252, 265, 279–80
Indo-China, French conquest, 279
Industrial Revolution, 238
industry in China, 191
Inflexible, HMS, 250, 252
Inglewood, 177
Inglis, Robert, 78
Innes, James, 68–72, 78
intelligence network: British, 140–3, 145, 155, 207, 210–11; Chinese, 143, 284–5; Russian, 199, 246
ironclads, cost of, 274

Jardine, 62
Jardine, David, 116
Jardine, William, 40–1, 43, 46, 48, 49, 54–6, 61, 65–7, 70, 73, 75, 80, 83, 85, 95–8, 105–6, 111–12, 114, 131, 133, 153, 197
Jardine, Matheson & Co., 38, 42, 53, 56, 61, 62, 68–9, 70, 73, 82–3, 87, 96, 98, 130, 159, 165, 233, 255, 263
Jauncey, Captain, 83, 114
Jeanne d'Arc, 204
Jehol, 15, 16–18, 298, 307, 309, 314
Jen-lei-ssu, 223
Jephson, Brigadier, 293
Jesuit missionaries, 58–60, 194, 198, 204–5, 211, 315, 326
John Biggar, 61–2
John Calvin, 176
junks of war, 91–2, 114–15, 118, 218

Kam-sing-moon anchorage, 67
K'an Si, Emperor, 59
Kaomio Temple, Peking, 308–9
Keenan, James, 220
Kennedy, Thomas, 213–15
Keo, General, 137
Keppel, Commodore, 240
Kestrel, HMS, 271
kidnapping: Chinese for Coolie Trade, 175–7; foreigners for hostages, 121–3, 141; see also Shanghaied
King, C. W., 84–5
Kingqua, 201
King's Dragoon Guards, 304, 316
Kite, 121–2, 139, 212
Kowloon: annexation by British, 329; battle of, 90–2; confrontation, 87; leased to British, 281–2
kowtow custom, 16, 21, 22–3, 245, 276–7, 301
Kuan, Admiral, 70, 87, 92, 102–3, 125, 128
Kuei-liang, 260, 276, 293, 296–8, 307
Kung, Prince, 295, 307–8, 314, 322, 326–9
Kyakhta, 267

Lady Hughes, 81
land-surveys by Jesuits, 58
Landseer, Sir Edwin, 329
Larne, HMS, 78, 86, 113, 124
laudanum, 28–9, 110
law, Chinese system, 20–1
Lawson, Sir Wilfred, 331
Lay (interpreter), 261
Layard, 235
Leach, John, 213–14
Ledyard, John, 20
Lee, HMS, 269, 271
legalization of opium, 64–7, 69, 156–8, 211, 245, 263–4, 331
Leibnitz, Gottfried Wilhelm, 15
Le-Ming-tae, 216
Lemon, Colonel, 249
Levant, USN, 222–3
Leven, 259
Liang A-fa, 182–3
Lin Feng-hsiang, General, 193
Lin Li-chu'an, Dr, 203
Lin Tse-hsu, Commissioner: anti-opium campaign, 73–93, 96, 129, 160; appointed High Commissioner at Canton, 74, 181; awareness, 121, 123–4, 236; on British blockade of Canton, 107; buys ship-of-war, 99; death, 186; destroys opium at Canton, 84–5; disgraced, 131, 150; dismissed for excessive zeal, 119–20, 123; Edicts of, 75; encourages new military techniques and armed resistance, 118, 237; establishes refuge for addicts, 113; letter to Queen Victoria, 75–6, 101; prediction on addicts, 66–7; prize-money lists, 113; recruitment policy, 99; stops trade with Britain 'for ever', 104; strengthens Bogue Forts, 100, 104, 136; trading terms, 100–1; tries to sow dissension between British and other foreigners, 106; ultimatum to British ships, 102
Lin Wei-hsi, 88, 90, 101–2, 126
Lintin Island roadstead smugglers' depot, 37–9, 54–5, 67–8, 77, 110, 112
Lo Tang-Kang, 185
Loch, Henry, 299–301, 307–9, 322, 327
Lockhart, Catherine, 141
Lockhart, Dr William, 116, 141
London Missionary Society, 57, 116, 164, 195
looting, 136, 140, 148–9, 152, 250, 305–6, 316–21, 326, 329, 330–1
lorchas, 213
Louisa, 51–2, 55, 90–1
Lowe, Robert, 229
Lu K'un, Viceroy of Canton, 46, 47–8, 49, 50, 53, 54
Lu T'ai-lai, 143
Lucy, Armand, 306

Ma Tzu-nung, 212
Macao: arrival of first iron ship under

Macao—*cont.*
 steam, 118; base for British trade,
  86; British return refused, 99;
  Britons leave, 89; Chinese pressure,
  88–90; European settlements, 30,
  32; free traders arrive, 42; Napier's
  retreat, 54; opium revenue, 99;
  opium shipments, 25, 33–4, 89; silk
  trade, 333; smuggling of opium,
  36, 71; vessels searched, 36
Macartney, Lord (Earl): career, 16;
  Peking mission, 15–21, 35, 66, 119,
  298; refusal to kowtow, 16, 21
Macaulay, Thomas Babington, 63,
  108–10, 229
M'Ghee, Chaplain, 320
McKay, Captain William, 62
McLane, Robert M., 196, 201
Macleane, Captain, 153
Madagascar, 118–19
Madras Artillery, 115, 150
Madras Engineers, 148
Magicienne, 269
magistrates' payment for promotion,
  179
Magniac, Daniel, 37, 56, 60
Maitland, Admiral, F. L., 69–70
Malacca, 25
Malakoff, Duchess of, 321
Malmesbury, Lord, 175, 209, 216,
  227–8, 261, 263, 277–8
Malwa opium, 33–4, 36, 41, 82, 90, 110,
  113, 114, 157, 173
Manchester Chamber of Commerce, 206
Manchester Guardian, 162
Manchu dynasty: atmosphere of
  ignorance, 89; calendar reform, 58;
  campaign against opium, 66, 74;
  Christian religion suppressed, 59;
  Customs policy, 65; decadence and
  decline, 21–2, 27; dissatisfaction with
  rule, 119, 172, 180–9, 199–205, 297;
  domination, 35; Dowager Empress's
  rule, 178; extinction, 162; fortification
  of Peking, 150; French and Russian
  friendship, 211; Jesuit influence, 58–9;
  last great Emperor, 15, 18, 35;
  military reputation, 35; Ming
  capitulation, 152; Mongol horsemen
  called in, 192; panic at approach of
  Allies to Peking, 297–8; punishments,
  66, 81; resist foreign powers by
  armed force, 266; scholarly civil
  service, 35, 178–9; Summer Palace
  destroyed, 324, 326; system, 20–1;
  Tartar military government and
  troops, 35, 124, 135–6, 151–2, 189,
  200; Tientsin Treaty, 267
mandarins and mandarinate: abeyance
  of power, 157; backbone of Chinese
  society, 178–9; bribes to, 42, 62, 114;
  campaign money raised from opium
  tax, 203; duties of, 21; ill-treated by
  barbarians, 148–9; memorials on
  public policy, 236; petition handling,

 47; scholarly civil service, 35
Mangalore, 87–8
Manila opium operation, 82, 86
Mann, Colonel, 292
Marquis, Captain, 72
Marshall, Humphrey, 174, 196, 204
Martineau des Chenetz, Captain, 250, 251
Marx, Karl, 197
 mathematics at the court of Peking,
  58
Matheson, Alexander, 158–9, 197, 229
Matheson, Donald, 116, 131
Matheson, Sir James, 37, 40, 41–2,
  55–6, 69, 78–80, 82–3, 86, 88, 95–6,
  105, 123, 125, 128, 131, 229
Meadows, Thomas, 202
Medhurst, Dr W. H., 57, 195
Medical Missionary Society, 56, 75
medical use of opium, 24, 28
Melville, HMS, 112
memorials on public policy, 236
merchants: income in China of
  Europeans, 334; moral conduct of
  Anglo-Saxons, 60; pressure groups
  in Britain, 97; social inferiors in
  China, 73; see also Hong merchants
Miao tribe, 185
Michel, Major-General Sir John, 326
military prowess of Manchus, 35
military recruitment by Lin, 99
Milner-Gibson, 235, 254
Min River, 142
Minden, HMS, 52
Ming dynasty, 58, 152, 180, 199, 203
Minnesota, USN, 245
Minto, Lord, 52, 63, 132
missionaries, 56–61, 108, 116, 141, 156,
  161, 166–7, 172, 194–6, 198, 204–5,
  211–13, 251, 264
Missions Etrangères, Les, 212
Mitraille, 247, 251, 259
Miu Chia-ku, 144
Modeste, HMS, 114, 118, 124, 128, 134,
  154
Moghul dynasty, 243
money values, 333–4
Mongols: cavalry, 138, 192–3, 266, 285,
  287; Empire, 197; princes, 307;
  reformed calendar, 58
Montauban, General Cousin de, 279,
  282–5, 288, 290–1, 299–301, 304,
  310–12, 314, 316–18, 321, 325,
  327
Moore, Captain, 146
moral obligation code, 21
morphine, 162
Morrison, John Robert, 141, 152
Morrison, Robert, 47, 57, 59
mortar rockets, 143
Moslems, 242–3, 281
Mowqua, 78
Mu Yi, 297
Mukden addicts, 162
Muraviev, Count Nicholas, 199
musket, percussion, 150–1

names, Chinese, 334
Nanking: capital of Taiping rebels,
192–6; Elgin's arrival, 264–5; future
treaty port, 261; indemnity, 154–5;
location, 139; seaborne attack by
Royal Navy, 139, 149–53; slaughter
by Taiping, 189–90, 200; taken by
Taiping, 189–92; Treaty, 153–5, 156,
158, 162, 178–9, 203, 208, 232, 255,
260
Napier, Major-General Sir Robert,
288–90, 297, 311, 323
Napier, Lord (1st Baron), 44–56, 69,
108; aggressive policy fiasco, 44–56
Napoleon III, 232, 239, 273–4, 279,
296, 310, 317–18, 320, 328
Neill, Colonel James, 243
Nemesis, 100, 117–18, 124–5, 129, 134,
152
Nerbudda, 137–8, 158
Nerchinsk, Treaty of, 198
Netherlands Missionary Society, 60
New Zealand annexation, 156
Nicholson, John, 243
Niger, HMS, 202
Nightingale, Florence, 238
Nimrod, HMS, 137, 191, 248, 259
Ningpo: British prisoners, 122–3, 139;
fall of, 139; occupation, 141, 143;
open to trade, 155; ransom, 140;
recapture attempt unsuccessful,
142–7
Noble, Ann, 122, 139
Noble, John, 122
Nye, Gerald, 157
Nye, Gideon, 72

O'Callaghan, Captain, 204
Oliphant, Laurence, 261, 263–5
Olyphant, D. W. C., 56–7
Olyphant & Co., 36, 56, 74, 84
Omega, 167
On the Constitution of Church and State,
238
On the Origin of Species, 329
Opium Question, The, 83
Opium Wars: first (1841–2), 124–55;
second (1857–60), 213–323
Opossum, HMS, 269
Orsini plot, 274
Orwell, 71
Ouchterlony, Lieutenant John, 148,
156
Oudh, King of, 242, 252

Page, Captain, 150
painting, European to China, 40, 58
Pa-li-chi'ao bridge, French action, 310
Palladius, Archimandrite, 257
Palmerston, Lord (3rd Viscount), 48,
65, 69, 92–3, 104, 106, 112, 120, 133,
155, 234; able, but combative, 46;
Aliens Bill leads to his denunciation,
254; appoints Bowring to Canton,
207–8, 217; brought down by Peel,

131; career, 94; concession on Army
flogging, 94; debate on *Arrow* brings
down his government, 224–32;
denounces Ch'i Shan to Chinese PM,
118–19, 128; defeats Peel's censure
motion, 110–11; and free trade, 95,
207, 331; friendship with Lord
Ashley, 160; 'heartily glad' over
burning of Summer Palace, 324;
instinct about Russian intrigue, 272;
instructions to Canton
plenipotentiaries, 45–6, 63, 97–8,
101–3, 132, 153, 208; keeps critics
in the dark, 107–8; life-style, 95;
mistrusted, 94; moves over to
Whigs, 94; out of office, 140, 209;
Parkes impresses, 210–11; pretext
for war, 96–8; on post-war
indemnities, 126; readiness to
shift ground, 94; rebukes Sir George
Robinson, 62; refuses to ratify
Elliot's agreement, 127; returned in
a landslide (1857), 235–6; returned
again (1859), 272; sends army to
Peking, 273; sends Elliot to Canton,
64; sends Napier to Canton, 45;
shares views of William Jardine, 105;
on Tientsin Treaty, 277; vigorous
policy, 55–6, 94; Wellington detests
and rebukes, 49, 108; witticism, 95
Panic Sunday, Calcutta, 243
Paou, General, 310
Parker, Commander Foxhall A., 173
Parker, Dr Peter, 76, 213, 222–3, 234
Parker, Rear-Admiral Sir William,
132–4, 136, 140, 149
Parkes, Harry (Consul at Canton):
arrival in Macao, 141; captures
Viceroy Yeh, 249–50; ceasefire letter
to Elgin, 308–9; confidential
informant to Foreign Office, 210–11;
Consul at Canton, 177, 210; on
coolie atrocities, 286; and Coolie
Trade, 177; deals with lease of Hong
Kong, 281; Elgin relationship, 241,
295; entry into Canton, 211, 215–16,
219–22, 229–30, 232, 240;
exasperation at delays in campaign,
254–5; fearlessness, 299–302; and
Free Trade, 197; interpreter in the
field, 206, 296, 298; prisoner of
Chinese, 300–3, 306–9; protégé of
Pottinger, 141, 153; nervous
irritability, 211; recommends punitive
raids, 266; saved from execution, 322;
seeks apology for *Arrow* incident,
215–18, 224; Taku Forts surrender to
him, 292–3; on Tientsin Treaty, 267;
warns inhabitants to leave Canton,
248
Parliamentary attacks on opium trade,
158–63, 229–30, and on undeclared
war in China, 224–32; debates on
China, 229–32, 236, 254, 277–8
Patna opium, 23, 26, 33, 68

Index

Pattle, Brigadier, 314, 316
Peacock, Thomas Love, 117
Pearl, 90
Pearl River and anchorage, 32, 53, 158, 213, 216–17, 222–4, 247, 251
Peel, Sir Robert: brings down Whigs, 131; budget deficit, 154; cotton fortune, 160; Disraeli's attacks, 225; legalization of opium, 161–2; loses vote of censure motion on war in China, 108–11
Peh-ho River: Allied supply line, 303; Anglo-French advance, 291, 293, 296; blockade suggested, 111; Elgin's advance, 254, 256–60; fortification by Chinese, 119, 138, 258, 268; naval force, Allied, 267–8; Russians refused navigation rights, 245–6
Pei Ch'ing-chiao, 142–4, 146–7
Pei-t'ang: entry port, 268–9, 274; landing of Anglo-French army, 285–6; looting by Allies, 306; ratification of American treaty, 277
Peking: access question, 211, 261, 268–9; Allied advance, 296–311; British and French conventions, 327; burning of Summer Palace, 324–7; indemnity demanded by Allies, 323–4, 327; Jesuit influence at court, 58–9; legalization of opium, debate, 65; looting of Summer Palace, 316–21, 326, 329; Macartney's mission, 15–21, 35, 66, 119; rice supply, 139, 149, 153, 179, 253, 296; Russian convention signed, 328; Russian presence, 198–9, 246, 323; Taiping rebels thrown back, 191–3, 196; Treaty, 327; unease at presence of barbarian traders in China, 42–3; yields to Allies, 323
Pekingese breed, 331
penalties for opium dealers, 77–8, 81, 100
Perboyre, Father, 172
Pereyra, Father, 198
Pestonjee, 128
petition to government by British trading firms, 111
Phlegethon, 134, 170
Phlégéton, 247
Pih-kwei, 251, 255
Pinto, Don Adraio Accacio da Silveira, 90, 99
piracy, Chinese, 22, 37, 166–72, 174, 215, 251, 259, 282–3
Pires, Father, 59
playing off the barbarians, 237
Plover, HMS, 269, 271
police power in old China, 59
population of China, 20, 180
Portsmouth, USN, 222–3
Portuguese: arrival in China, 18; British refused return to Macao, 99; neutrality, 99; piracy, 168; submit to Chinese pressure at Macao, 87–90

Possum, 259
Pottinger, Sir Henry, 131, 133, 136–7, 151–2, 164, 167, 197, 260; browbeats traders, 133–4; and Catholic missionaries, 156; edict against opium smugglers, 158–9; fails to legalize opium, 156–7, 162; hoodwinked about regulation of shipping, 157; impresses by use of pomp, 166; Parkes, his favourite, 141, 153, 210; plenipotentiary at Canton, 130, 132; prevented from sacking Ningpo, 140; proclamation against Imperial Government, 149; rapacity shown by Treaty of Nanking, 153–5; replaced as Governor of Hong Kong, 168; tariff negotiations, 161; threatens renewed warfare, 153, 158
Powers, John, 272
Present Position and Future Prospects of the China Trade, 56
pressure groups in Britain of manufacturers and merchants, 97
price of opium, 25, 26, 31, 33–4, 68, 82–3, 104, 116, 213
prize-money, 113, 136, 140, 152, 170–1, 319–20
Probyn, Major, 331
profiteers, war, 295–6
prohibition: of opium in China, 24–6, 27, 29, 35–9, 67, 73, 76–7, 156–7, 174, 203–4, 263; of smugglers by Elliot, 73
Protestantism, 57, 60, 173, 180, 182, 195–6, 211–12
Prynne, Captain, 292
Pu Chi-t'ung, 86
Punjabis, 280, 287, 309, 326
punishment under Manchu code, 81
Putiatin, Admiral Count, 199, 245–6, 253, 256–7, 261
Pybus, Captain Joseph, 82–3
Pylades, HMS, 118

Queen, 141

ransoms of cities, 126, 130, 140, 148, 152, 154
rebellion in China: peasant revolt during Sung River floods, 75; self-adjusting mechanism, 21; Shantung rebels, 330; Shensi rebels, 309, 322, 330; Triads (Taiping), 179–97, 199–203, 246, 261, 264–5, 283, 293–4, 309
receiving ships for smuggled opium, 37–8, 68, 77, 81–2, 112, 159, 167, 191, 203, 213
Red Rover (first opium clipper), 38
Reed, William B., 174, 245, 262–3
Rees, John, 114
Reeves, Brigadier, 291
Reliance, 72
religion, 57–60, 172–3, 179–97, 238, 242–4

348

Rémi, M., 204
Renard, Major, 243–4
Rennie, Dr D. F., 330
Retribution, HMS, 264
revenue: cotton, 97, 165; opium, 26,
  65, 73, 108, 160, 165, 176, 178, 278,
  331; silk, 165; tea, 29, 34, 108, 165
revival of drug trade with war, 112, 116
Ribout, Lieutenant, 246
Ricci, Father Mateo, 58
rice supply, 139, 149, 153, 179, 253,
  256, 260, 296
Rigault de Genouilly, Admiral, 246,
  249, 257, 259
Riley, HMS, 176
riot at the Factories, Canton, 72
Robert Browne, 176
Roberts, Rev. Issachar Jacox, 183–4,
  196
Robinson, Sir George, 50, 51, 54–5, 62,
  63, 94
Roebuck, John, 225, 229
Roman Catholicism, 57–9, 172, 190,
  194–5, 211–12, 236, 246, 251, 283,
  326, 328
Rosamel, Captain, 125
Rothschild, Baron, 320
Rough and Ready, 201
Rough and Tough, 201
Royal Academy, 329
Royal Commission on Opium, 258
Royal Irish, 147
Royal Navy: Amoy assault, 134–5;
  blue-jackets and marines guard
  opium, 233; Bogue Forts assaults,
  124–5, 128–9; Canton blockaded,
  111–13, 123, 125; Canton bombarded,
  219, 221, 248; Chen-hai attack, 139;
  Chuenpi action begins war, 103;
  force sent to China, 98, 111–12;
  flotilla sails up Yangtze, 264–5;
  gunboat diplomacy, 68, 258–60;
  most mobile and powerful weapon
  of war, 22; Peh-ho River navigated
  by gunboats, 258–60; pirates hunted
  down, 168–72; protecting merchant
  fleet, 99, 102–3; role of world's
  policeman, 63; slave trade campaign,
  174–5; Taku disaster, 269–72;
  technically outmoded, 274; Tin-hai
  bombardment, 115–16; Yangtze
  navigated, 149–50, 154–5, 264–5
Royal Saxon, 102
Russell, Lord John, 225, 272
Russell & Co., 74, 86, 212, 221, 223, 246
Russia: aids Allies with Peking maps,
  312; arms offer to Manchus, 266–7;
  concession grants access to Treaty
  Ports, 328; Crimean War, 199, 210;
  desire for naval base south of Amur
  River, 246; friendship with Chinese,
  211–12, 312, 328–9; frontier disputes
  with China, 198–9; frontier extended
  by Additional Treaty of Peking, 328;
  intrigue in China, 272, 285, 312;

Mongol empire shared with China,
  197; Nerchinsk Treaty ends frontier
  war, 198; offer to put down Taiping
  rebels, 199, 246, 329; opium as
  contraband, 263; presence in Peking,
  198–9, 246, 323; Vladivostok founded,
  329

St Vincent, Admiral Lord, 132
Saltoun, Lord, 279–80
Samarang, 124
Sampson, HMS, 221
San Francisco and Coolie Trade, 176
San Jacinto, USN, 223
Saratoga, USS, 176
Scarth, John, 169, 199, 203, 205, 255
scholars and students, Chinese, 21, 92,
  143–4, 148–9, 181–2
sealskin trade bonanza, 20
Sebastopol taken by French, 210, 279
secret societies, 35, 199, 282
Seng-ko-lin-ch'in, Prince, 192–3, 266–9,
  271–2, 284–7, 289–90, 293, 296–301,
  303–5, 307, 309, 311–12, 322, 330
sepoys, 112–13, 136, 208, 238, 240, 242,
  248, 253, 280–1, 284, 287, 318
Seppings, Sir Robert, 38
serfdom in China, 34, 43
Sesostris, 133
Seymour, Rear-Admiral Sir Michael,
  215–16, 218, 220–1, 223–4, 229, 234,
  240–1, 244, 247–8, 250–4, 256–7, 259,
  268
Shadwell, Captain, 270–1
Shaftesbury, Lord, 227
Shang chu-au Island, 32
Shanghai: annexation demanded in
  Britain, 229; bombarded by French,
  204–5; capture by British, 148;
  cost of living, 333; foreign troops
  defend, 283, 293–4; Imperialists
  reoccupy, 205; open to trade, 155;
  opium trade, 174, 203; threatened
  by Taiping, 283–4, 293–4; trade
  boom, 165; Triads capture, 203
Shanghaied for Coolie Trade, 175
Shannon, HMS, 241
Shantung rebels, 309
Shap Ng Tsai, 169–72
Shektsing guerrilla stronghold
  destroyed, 266
Shensi rebels, 309, 322, 330
Siamese treaty, 210
siege of Canton Factories, 72, 79–80,
  96, 109
Sikh Irregulars, 280–1, 289, 299–301,
  304, 306, 309, 311, 323, 331
silk trade, 164–5, 191, 204
silver: Canton ransom, 126, 130, 154;
  as coinage, 333; Far East trade
  financed by, 73; indemnity for
  losses at Canton and cost of war,
  262, 296; indemnity for losses at
  Peking, 323–4; Nanking ransom,
  154–5, 179; opium payments, 31,

Index

silver—*cont.*
35, 42–3, 64; promotion payments,
179; reserves in Manchu treasury,
66; silk payments, 333; tea
payments, 19, 24, 26, 31, 36
Singapore: anti-British disturbances,
240; shipments of opium, 82, 87, 104
Slaney, HMS, 328
slave trade, 109, 112, 174–8, 255
Small Sword Society, 203–5
Smith, Adam, 95, 197, 331
Smith, Captain H., 89, 102–3
Smith, John Abel, 56, 80, 82, 95–7, 106
smoking techniques, 27
smuggling of opium: bond imposed on
merchants not to smuggle, 81, 85–6,
100–2; British country traders, 31;
clippers used, 38–9; coast trade, 43;
control of smugglers by
Superintendent of Trade, 55; depot
at Lintin Island, 37; footing on
Chou-san, 114, 116, 157; harassment
by Chinese, 36, 39, 67; help from
addicts and bribery, 36, 38; Hong
Kong operations, 159; Imperial edict
against, 76–7; Lin's anti-opium
campaign, 75–85; Macao
organization, 87, 89; Parliamentary
campaign, 160–2; prohibition by
Elliot, 73; receiving ships, 37–8,
68, 77, 81–2, 112, 159, 167, 191, 203,
213; United States identify opium
as contraband, 174; valuable
instrument of British policy, 78;
Warren Hastings' venture
unsuccessful, 25; Whampoa
anchorage for opium ships, 158
Smyrna opium, 33
social sense, Chinese, 21
Society of Divine Justice, uprising of
1813, 22
Soochow falls to Taiping, 283
sources, 335, 337–40
Spahis, 304
Spanish presence, 30, 37
Stanton, Vincent, 121, 123
Staunton, Sir George (father), 16
Staunton, Sir George (son), 16, 17,
18, 22, 23, 161
Stead, Captain, 128
steam navigation, 117–18
steam power, 20, 33
Sterling, Admiral, 202
Stewart, Professor Dugald, 95
Stewart, Captain the Hon. Keith, 220
stocks of opium, 77, 80
Straubenzee, General van, 249, 254–5,
265–6
Sturgis, Mr, 222
Suez Canal, 274
Summer Palace, 16, 17, 23, 58, 277,
301, 312–28, 324–7, 329–31
Sun Yat-sen, Dr, 197
Sunda shipwreck, 76
Sung River floods and peasant revolt, 75

Sutton, Brigadier, 287, 289
Swatow landing, 255
Swinhoe, Robert, 287, 305, 318–19, 326
Sybil, 56
Sylph, 33, 38, 61, 167–8

Tahiti conflict, 156
Ta-hung-a, General, 138
Taiping rebels and rebellion, 179–97,
199–203, 246, 261, 264–5, 283, 293–4,
309, 329–30, 335
T'ai-p'ing T'ien-kuo dynasty
(Heavenly Kingdom of Great Peace),
186, 190–2
Tao Kung, Emperor, 47, 67, 86, 203;
allows magistrates to buy promotion,
179; appoints High Commissioner at
Canton, 74; death, 178; disillusioned
with Lin, 119–20; gifts to
Commissioner Lin, 81–2; grants
toleration to Christianity, 173;
outraged by Treaty of Chuenpi,
126–7; questions habits of
barbarians, 89–90; reform attempt,
35; refuses to legalize opium, 156–7,
161; reproaches himself for Treaty
of Nanking, 178
Taku Forts: Anglo-French attempt to
force passage fails, 268–72; attack on,
256–60; captured by Anglo-French,
290–3; fortifications, 119, 268, 284;
kept as security for indemnity, 296;
Parliamentary debate on defeat,
277–8
T'an, Governor, 256–7
Tangku assault, 289–91
Tartars, 35, 124–5, 134–6, 147, 150–2,
189–90, 200, 287, 310–11, 314
Tattnall, Commodore Josiah, 270–1
taxes by Manchus: land and poll, 34;
on peasants, 43; opium, 203, 264;
war, 309
tea trade and crop, 19, 24, 26, 29–30,
32, 34, 35, 42, 43, 45, 46, 49, 64, 67,
72, 74, 85–6, 90, 99, 104, 127, 129–30,
141, 165, 198, 201, 228, 235, 250,
252–3; stopped in an attempt to
enforce opium ban, 36
Teng T'ing chen, Viceroy, 65–71, 73,
120
Tennyson, Lord, 273, 280
textile trade, 19, 33–4, 42, 56, 97, 160,
161, 164, 206–7, 209, 217, 225, 228,
265, 331
Thistle, 224
Thistle Mountain and the
God-Worshippers, 184, 186–7
Thomas Coutts, 100
Thomas Perkins, 70
Tidder, Thomas, 88
Tientsin: Allied encampment, 330;
Anglo-French advance, 293;
Elgin's advance, 260; occupation by
Allies, 296–7; Treaty of, 260–2,
264–5, 267, 277–8, 299, 331

Tiger Island, 52
Time, 82
Times, The, 160, 165–6, 224–5, 252, 272, 280, 291, 299, 301, 325
Times Atlas of the World, 334
Tin-hai: captured by British, 114–17, 137, 140, 282; opium trade, 157
Toeywhan, 267, 270
torpedoes, floating, 223–4
'torture, Chinese', 200, 325
Towns, Captain, 102
trade, British: deficit (1857), 165; with China following Opium Wars, 331
treasure: flow-back to India, 31; payment for tea, 19, 24, 26
treaty revision, 211–12, 215, 224
Triads secret society, 66, 180, 185–7, 199, 203
Tricault, Commander, 270–1
Ts'ao Cheng, 148–9
Tseng Kuo-fan, 193–4
T'ungchow, 297–301, 305
Tycocktow Fort wrecked, 124–5

undercutting of opium, 33–4
United States: bombard and capture Barrier Forts, 222–3; Civil War, 177–8, 184; Coolie Trade, 175–8; decision not to recognize Taiping, 196; drug addiction, 177–8; envoy reaches Peking overland, 276–7; gun-running, 86; merchants ask for joint naval force, 111; navy irregulars put down Triad rebels, 201; neutrality, 85, 106, 196, 204, 212, 220, 222, 245, 271–2; opium trading, 33, 36, 74, 174, 177–8, 211, 263; refuse to leave Canton, 86; Shanghai trade, 165, 204; shipping tea and silk, 104; threat to annex Formosa, 213; treaty ratified at Peh-tang, 277; Wanghia Treaty, 173–4; Yankee traders, 19–20, 30
Urquhart, Colonel, 309
Ussuri River, 328

values, Chinese scale of, 20
Varin, Paul, 317
Verbiest, Father Ferdinand, 58
Vereenigde Oostindische Compagnie, 23
Victoria, Queen, 75–6, 101, 131, 155, 166, 227, 232, 299, 317–20, 327, 331
Vladivostok founded, 329
Volage, HMS, 89–90, 99, 102–3, 111, 113, 118

Wade (interpreter), 246, 250, 261, 265, 296, 298, 300, 307
Walker, Colonel, 299
Wang, 292–3
Wang Ch'eng-feng, 143
Wang Tao-ch'ung, 250
Wanghia, Treaty of, 173–4
Wanstell, Mary, 61

Ward, John E., 267, 270, 272, 274, 276–7
Warner, Captain, 100–1
Warren, Samuel, 83
Wealth of Nations, 197
Weddell, Captain John: bombards Bogue Forts, 18, 51, 269
Wedgwood, Josiah, 17
Wellesley, HMS, 69, 112, 115, 118
Wellington, Duke of, 49, 54–7, 108, 132; rebukes Palmerston for Napier fiasco
Weng Fu, 322
Whampoa anchorage, 30, 32, 52, 158, 223, 253; action against rebels by irregular US navy, 201; attack on British vessels, 129; British Consulate set up, 266; British ships seized, 36; frigates blockaded at, 53; prohibition on opium smugglers, 72–3; Treaty of, 172–3
White Lily Society: uprising of 1795, 22
white poppy life-cycle, 26–7
Wilberforce, Samuel, 228
Wilberforce, William, 29
Willes, Captain G. O., 269
William IV, 54
Williams, S. Wells, 272
Witt, Chief Mate, 122
Wolseley, Lieut.-Col. Garnet (later 1st Viscount), 282, 289, 321, 327
women's role in China, 190–1
Wong, Admiral, 170
Wood, Sir Charles, 273
Woodcock, HMS, 283
Woosung receiving ships, 203
Wu Chien-chang, 204
Wuchang: execution of missionary, 172; massacre by Taiping Army, 188
Wu-sung capture, 148, 153; French arrival, 150

Xavier, St Francis, 32

Yang-chou ransomed, 152
Yang Fang, 127, 129
Yang, Hsin-Ch'ing, 184, 187–8
Yangtze River: attack by Taiping, 188–9; Elgin navigates, 264–5; opened up to trade, 264, 330; seaborne attack by British Expeditionary Force, 139, 149–53, 155–6; valley made a wilderness by rebellion, 180, 192
Yao Jung, 138
Yarborough, Lord, 38
Yeh Ming-chen (Canton Viceroy): access to Canton discussion, 208–9; archives seized, 250; *Arrow* incident, 214–18; astuteness with foreigners, 206–7; beheading of prisoners, 247; blamed for Hong Kong terrorist act, 233; Blenheim Reach fort captured, 201; bombardment of residence, 218–21, 251; Bowring's

Index

Yeh Ming-chen (Canton Viceroy)—*cont.*
private communication, 244; British
help in breaking rebel blockade,
201–2; captured by Royal Navy, and
Parkes, 250; Chapdelaine case, 212;
disloyalty of followers, 249; exile and
death in Calcutta, 252; fireships ease
out British warships, 223–4;
Palmerston's tirades, 230, 235;
poetry, 252; poisoning of bread in
Hong Kong, 234; prompts Chinese
servants to withdraw labour, 233;
reign of terror in Canton, 200, 251;

snubs William B. Reed, 245; ultimatum
from Baron Gros, 247; war junks
captured, 240
Yehonala, Empress, 178, 193, 298, 308,
321
Yi, Prince of, 297
Yu, Commissioner, 139
Yu-ch'ien, 123
Yu Te-ch'ang, 142
Yuan dynasty, 197
Yuen-hua Academy, Canton (Lin's HQ),
75
Yung-an besieged by Taiping, 187